Precious Enemy

"Strangely, the subject of death and dying is often neglected in contemporary evangelicalism, especially a biblical and systematic theology of death. However, Toby Jennings now fills that gap with this important book on the subject. Not everyone will agree with all of his conclusions but this book should not be ignored. It is a comprehensive and theological treatment of a biblical view of death and more than that, it is about the glorious hope of resurrection found in the work of our triumphant Redeemer. I hope this book receives a wide reading and it leads us to a greater joy and confidence in our triune God in the face of Christ Jesus our Lord."

—**Stephen J. Wellum**, Professor of Christian Theology, The Southern Baptist Theological Seminary; Editor, *Southern Baptist Journal of Theology*

"The topic of death is seldom discussed among biblical and systematic scholars. Many faithful believers live in fear of the unknown as it relates to their own death and the death of their loved ones. The Bible has much more to say on the subject than many think. Toby Jennings provides a full biblical and theological examination of the subject. Jennings highlights the biblical teaching from an evangelical perspective. It is my hope that this book is read by both the scholar and the layperson searching for what the Bible teaches on this difficult issue. While I don't agree with all Jennings' conclusions, the book is an excellent guide for one desiring to understand how God the Father has defeated death in the death and resurrection of his beloved Son."

—**William F. Cook, III**, Professor of New Testament Interpretation, The Southern Baptist Theological Seminary, Louisville, KY

"Contemporary Evangelicalism has few substantial resources when it comes to reflection on what the Scriptures and Christian history have thought and said about death. While the subject of human embodiment has soared in the charts, as it were, of Christian thought, the dissolution of that embodiment has been sorely neglected. Toby Jennings' penetrating study of death helps to fill this significant lacuna. Highly recommended!"

—**Michael A. G. Haykin**, Professor of Church History, The Southern Baptist Theological Seminary

Precious Enemy

A Biblical Portrait of Death

Toby Jennings

◆PICKWICK *Publications* • Eugene, Oregon

PRECIOUS ENEMY
A Biblical Portrait of Death

Copyright © 2017 Toby Jennings. All rights reserved. Except for brief quotations in critical publications or reviews, no part of this book may be reproduced in any manner without prior written permission from the publisher. Write: Permissions, Wipf and Stock Publishers, 199 W. 8th Ave., Suite 3, Eugene, OR 97401.

Pickwick Publications
An Imprint of Wipf and Stock Publishers
199 W. 8th Ave., Suite 3
Eugene, OR 97401

www.wipfandstock.com

PAPERBACK ISBN: 978-1-4982-8067-9
HARDCOVER ISBN: 978-1-4982-8069-3
EBOOK ISBN: 978-1-4982-8068-6

Cataloguing-in-Publication data:

Names: Jennings, Toby.

Title: Precious enemy : a biblical portrait of death / Toby Jennings.

Description: Eugene, OR: Pickwick Publications, 2017 | Includes bibliographical references and index.

Identifiers: ISBN 978-1-4982-8067-9 (paperback) | ISBN 978-1-4982-8069-3 (hardcover) | ISBN 978-1-4982-8068-6 (ebook)

Subjects: LSCH: Death in the Bible. | Death—Biblical teaching.

Classification: BS1199.D34 J3 2017 (print) | BS1199.D34 (ebook)

Manufactured in the U.S.A.

To my precious mother, Helen (Powell) Jennings,
whose death inspired this sentiment:

Losing a loved-one in this nuclear age
Is like dropping a stone into a pond.
The elements retreat only long enough to receive the stone,
But flow again to all but cover any sign
That the stone ever passed this way.
Oh that such a loss were once again
Like the dropping of a stone
Onto a soft, sandy beach
Where the impression would remain
Until the continual, gentle stroke of the tide
Would carry away the stone
And polish the impression like so much fine crystal.

*Precious in the sight of the Lord
is the death of his saints.*

Psalm 116.15

Contents

Preface | ix
Abbreviations | xi

1. **Introduction** | 1
   The Anemic *Memento Mori* of Our Contemporary Setting
   Methodology
   Warrant for This Study
   Summary
   Scope of the Current Work

2. **The Origin of Death** | 36
   Inexorable Law of Nature or Catastrophic Disorder?
   What is Death?
   Conclusion: The Good Providence of God in the Ordinance of Death

3. **Death in the Old Testament** | 72
   Introduction
   Terminology
   The Afterlife in the Old Testament
   The Old Testament and ANE Parallels
   The Relative Value of Human Life in the Old Testament
   Resurrection in the Old Testament
   Life After Death

4. **Death in the New Testament** | 112
   Introduction
   Portrait of the Ethic of Human Life
   The Value of Human Life as Illustrated by Christ's Incarnation
   The Death of the Son of Man
   Anthropological Solidarity: The Church
   Doctrines and Depictions of Death in the New Testament
   The Resurrection

5. **Death and the Church Triumphant** | 140
   A View from the Early Church Militant
   Martyrdom
   We Are Not Our Own

6. **Excursus: The Frowning Providence of Infant Death** | 161
   Hard Sayings about Death
   Framing the Issue
   Augustine on Original Sin and Its Implications for the Destiny of Deceased Infants
   The Consequence of Original Sin/The Meaning of θάνατο᾽
   Argument from Silence
   Imagination Yields to Revelation

7. **The Laud of God for His Ordinance of Death** | 194
   Summary and Concluding Theological Reflections
   Ars Moriendi
   The Beatific Vision

Bibliography | 219
Subject Index | 245
Author Index | 247
Scripture Index | 249

Preface

The phenomenon of death is such a fundamental reality in the universe that notions and commentary concerning it vary from the sober to the comical to the absurd. It remains an enigma to many. Indeed, many consider death a mystery in the full sense of the word. However, only the fool, who—by definition—asserts that life and death are autonomous, is left to grope in enigmatic darkness concerning this mystery. Christianity alone reveals an understanding of this universal reality as the ordained instrument of a good and holy Sovereign. This divine disclosure neglects neither the reality of death's universality or complexity nor the puzzle of so-called problems of evil. The joy and hope of the Christian alone, even in the face of this last enemy, exceeds any multifaceted assault death can deliver. Jesus Christ, the resurrected Lord of Life—and death—confronted and defeated death for the express purpose of assuring *life with him* for his Father's image bearers just as he intended from the beginning.

Why expend so much time, energy, and interest writing about a topic that carries with it such a grave rapport? That question was posed to me several times during the writing of this work. The truth is, I am not sure what precipitated such interest and desire to research and exposit this topic. Nor am I certain what sustains such interest in this particular topic, apart from the revealed truth that the God who created everything out of nothing and orders all of it for his own good and holy purposes—which includes the best interest of the faithful creature he made in his own image—also orders death. If he both ordained it and orders it with the universal impact that he has and does, then it must be a matter worth *his* time, energy, and interest . . . and, therefore, mine, too.

Death, however, is not consuming; rather, life is. That is, the abundant life that my gracious Redeemer has given me is evident to me in more ways than I can count. Fittingly, one of the most significant *blessings* he has furnished for me is the blessing of other lives. The Creator God, who himself is Trinity, knows that being alone is not good (Gen 2.18). He therefore furnished his *magnum opus*, who would bear his own image, with multiplied scores of others of his kind. So many of those image bearers have contributed priceless riches to my own life. For that, I am inexpressibly grateful not only to Yahweh, but also to those individuals—many of whom I will fail to mention in the list that follows.

Because this research concluded my theological education at The Southern Baptist Theological Seminary, I must first express my gratitude to the countless faculty, staff, and fellow students who have touched my life in ways that literally will endure eternity; I look forward to spending it with you all! I am very grateful for the ever-encouraging, gracious, wise exemplars who served as my dissertation supervisory committee, Gregg R. Allison and Michael A. G. Haykin. Committee chair, Stephen J. Wellum, exemplifies a devotion to Jesus Christ and love for his Truth that was arguably the single greatest impact on my theological formation while at Southern. Dr. Wellum's tutelage, brotherhood, and friendship are treasures to me. His stalwart commitment to "rightly dividing the word of truth"—the inscription on the tympanum of Southern Seminary's Norton Hall—is a light to every student who has ever enjoyed the privilege of his instruction, *soli Deo gloria*!

Our Lord has ordained his church as a chief means of conforming us to his image. The two church communities—Five Points Community Church and Ninth and O Baptist Church—that embraced me as a brother and sustained me with indescribable warmth, love, hospitality, and soul care during this season of life will forever be dear to me.

Finally, to my loving family, Tyrone, Curtis, Beverly and Willie, Darryl and Shekini, Danielle, Kelly and Nick (and now Max): "I thank my God in all my remembrance of you" (Phil 1.3). Helen and Eugene Jennings would beam over the mutual love that is *evident* among their children. I, too, am grateful for the gift of life that each of you is to me.

Abbreviations

ACW	Ancient Christian Writers
ANF	*The Ante-Nicene Fathers*
ANE	Ancient Near East
AV	Authorized Version
BAGD	Walter Bauer, William F. Arndt, Felix Wilbur Gingrich, and Frederick William Danker, *A Greek-English Lexicon of the New Testament and Other Early Christian Literature*
BTDB	*Baker Theological Dictionary of the Bible*
BNTC	Black's New Testament Commentary
CD	*Church Dogmatics*
EBC	*Expositor's Bible Commentary*
BECNT	Baker Exegetical Commentary on the New Testament
EDT	*Evangelical Dictionary of Theology*
EQ	*Evangelical Quarterly*
FC	The Fathers of the Church
ICC	International Critical Commentary
IDB	*Interpreter's Dictionary of the Bible*
JETS	*Journal of the Evangelical Theological Society*
JTS	*Journal of Theological Studies*
LW	*Luther's Works*

NAC	New American Commentary
NCBC	New Century Bible Commentary
NCE	*New Catholic Encyclopedia*
NIBC	New International Biblical Commentary
NICNT	New International Commentary on the New Testament
NICOT	New International Commentary on the Old Testament
NIGCT	New International Greek Testament Commentary
NDT	*New Dictionary of Theology*
NDBT	*New Dictionary of Biblical Theology*
NPNF1	Nicene and Post-Nicene Fathers, 1st Series
NPNF2	Nicene and Post-Nicene Fathers, 2nd Series
NovTSup	Supplements to Novum Testamentum
NTS	*New Testament Studies*
OTL	Old Testament Library
PG	Jacques-Paul Migne, *Patrilogia Graeca*
PL	Jacques-Paul Migne, *Patrologia Latina*
PNTC	Pillar New Testament Commentary
SBJ	*Southern Baptist Journal of Theology*
SJT	*Scottish Journal of Theology*
TDNT	*Theological Dictionary of the New Testament*
TNTC	Tyndale New Testament Commentaries
TynBul	*Tyndale Bulletin*
WBC	Word Bible Commentary
WBCS	Westminster Bible Companion Series
WJE	*The Works of Jonathan Edwards*
WJO	*The Works of John Owen*
WJT	*Westminster Journal of Theology*
WSA	*The Works of Saint Augustine*

CHAPTER 1

Introduction

The Anemic *Memento Mori* of Our Contemporary Setting

LIFE. MERELY SPEAKING THIS word stirs emotions and conjures endless vibrant images of fullness and engrossing intricacy. One "walks down memory lane," reminiscing about the riches of life past. One talks of (or disregards) the dignity and the sanctity of life or of sharing one's life with another. Popular magazines and even board games are named in commemoration of life. Fittingly, much ado is made over each new life that enters the world; moreover, each such entrance is celebrated annually. Life is considered so precious that people enter covenants pledging not merely their bodies but their very lives as their most valuable collateral. Indeed, even the constitution of the United States of America rightly acknowledges life as a God given right to all people. No wonder life is so treasured.

The word *death*, on the other hand, does not exactly invite riveting discussion. Rather, because it conjures a host of reflections considered intruding and discomforting, conversation about the topic is awkwardly hurried away. This avoidance is common even in Christian circles, though followers of Jesus Christ have been admonished that their suffering of death may in fact be God's preferred will.[1]

In the modern age (particularly in the west[2]) where the grace of health care and medical advancements have eliminated many diseases and pro-

---

1. See 1 Pet 3:17; 2 Tim 3:12; Matt 10:17–39; Mark 13:9–13; Heb 11:37–40; cf. also Heb 2:9.

2. Consideration of the mindset toward death in every contemporary cultural context and/or world location, though important, would be too voluminous for the present

foundly reduced the mortality rates of bygone history,[3] the prevailing mindset concerning death is significantly different than even four generations ago—never mind that of Christ's newly founded Church Militant. In generations past (particularly the Middle Ages), death was contemplated *coram Deo* much more commonly because mortality rates were so high that virtually no one could escape *having* to think about death. The general expectation today is not that many loved ones—including one's own children—will likely precede one in death. Rather, the expectation is the exact opposite.

So much of the ecology of death and dying[4] has been relegated to sewers and subways of our society (where necessary utilities may be executed without obstructing the comforts and pleasantries of everyday life) that death has become a virtually unnoticed visitor. Many of our predecessors—both biblical and historical—would assert that such a pathos is both subtly and devilishly deceptive and to our own very great detriment. One early British *ars moriendi*,[5] for example, voices its mournful sorrow over such a condition:

---

scope. Therefore, the breadth of death as currently being experienced in regions of the world outside the contemporary West will not be addressed significantly here. At least three facets of the larger extent of death occurring outside the Western world could be considered: the deaths of larger numbers of Christians at the hands of anti-Christian persecutors; the larger number of deaths in developing regions as a result of inaccessibility to medical technologies; and death as a result of ethnic and/or regional clashes. For additional insights into historical and cultural addresses of death and dying, see Ariès, *Hour of Our Death*; Kübler-Ross, *On Death and Dying*; Kübler-Ross, *Living with Death and Dying*.

3. Health care alone cannot be credited with reducing Western mortality rates and subsequently the preponderance of death. Secularism, as well as a more life respecting religious ethic, have virtually eliminated religious persecution as a cause of death in the West (so far), though we are careful not to neglect situations such as the multigenerational clash between Catholics and Protestants in Ireland.

4. Anderson, *Theology, Death and Dying*, 143. Anderson uses the term "ecology" to highlight the "interconnection that exists between the biological function of an organism and its environment." The ecology of human death and dying is a theological concern "because it is fundamentally a human concern and a concern for the dignity of human personhood through the experience of death." More precisely, a human ecology of death and dying means "human life is a co-responsibility that includes the death of one another as part of that mutuality of concern" (148). A proper ecology of death and dying, therefore, should mark a transition from this life to the next characterized by reflection on what it means to be a human being created, both in community and with innate dignity, in the image of and for the purposes of God.

5. Formally translated "art of dying," Charlton T. Lewis and Charles Short suggest that the term may be rendered "science" or "knowledge" of dying; see their article in *A New Latin Dictionary*, s.v. "ars"; see also Reinis, *Reforming the Art of Dying*, 1. The formal title *Ars moriendi*—from the complete title, *Tractatus (or Speculum) artis bene moriendi*—"refers to two related Latin texts dating from about 1415 and 1450 [an

> But it is greatly to be noted, and to be taken heed of, that right seldom (that) any man—yea among religious and devout men—dispose themselves to death betimes as they ought. For every man weeneth himself to live long, and troweth not that he shall die in short time; and doubtless that cometh of the devil's subtle temptation. And often times it is seen openly that many men, through such idle hope and trust, have for-slothed themselves, and have died intestate, or unadvised, or undisposed, suddenly. And therefore every man that hath love and dread of God, and a zeal of (the heal of) man's soul, let him busily induce and warn every of his even christians [sic] that is sick, or in any peril of body or of soul, that principally and first, over all other things, and withouten delays and long tarryings, he diligently provide and ordain for the spiritual remedy and medicine of his soul.[6]

Reflecting on this same dismissiveness of death in our own day, Ray Anderson bemoans, "There is an immensity about death which transcends the biological event of cessation of organic life. The rituals of evasion which surround the contemporary avoidance of death are not because death is considered trivial or incidental, but because we feel an inner sense of bankruptcy before this sacred, and impenetrable immensity."[7] David Stannard agrees that our culture is bankrupt of its capacity to dialogue with death because of the former's loss of a significant sense of transcendent reality. He

original long version composed in 1415 by an anonymous Dominican friar, probably at the request of the Council of Constance (1414–1418, Germany), and a later short version] which offer advice on the protocols and procedures of a good death, explaining how to 'die well' according to Christian precepts of the late Middle Ages." Probably due to the frequency of death in the Middle Ages, as well as the booklet's illustrations, which could be easily explained and memorized, it became enormously popular and was subsequently translated into most West European languages. Some argue that it was the first in a Western literary tradition of such instructional handbooks on death and dying. The genre came to be described generically as *ars moriendi* (thus, in this work the capitalized "*Ars moriendi*" will refer to the specific text, whereas the lower case "*ars moriendi*" will refer to the genre.) Also notable is the fact that this *Ars moriendi* was one of the first texts to be printed with movable type; as a result, it was circulated in nearly 100 editions by 1500, particularly in Germany—the German term for *Ars moriendi* was *Sterbebücher*. See Shinners, "Art of Dying Well," 525–35.

Mary Catherine O'Connor agrees with Shinners that the anonymous 1415 *Ars moriendi* was a later adaptation of an earlier work by theologian and chancellor of the University of Paris, Jean Gerson (1363–1429). Gerson's *ars moriendi* formed the third part of his work *Opus Tripartitum*, presumably written before 1408 and probably circulated at the Council of Constance (1414–1418). The work consisted of a series of instructions in four categories: exhortations, questions, prayers, and observations. See O'Connor, *Art of Dying Well*, 11–17; and Shinners, "Art of Dying Well," 525.

6. Comper, *Book of the Craft of Dying*, 32.
7. Anderson, *Theology, Death and Dying*, 18.

warns that we currently live in a culture "in which virtually every individual can be replaced with such facility that his absence deeply affects at best only his most intimate relations. In a world bereft of ultimate meaning either in life or in death—in which neither the community of the living nor the vision of a mystical but literal afterlife any longer provides solace—modern man, in the face of death, has been forced to choose between the alternatives of outright avoidance or a secularized masquerade."[8] Indeed, our contemporary culture is compelled by this spiritual anemia to treat contemplation of death in very much the same way Israel and her priests regarded the truth proclaimed to them by the prophet Zechariah: "they refused to pay attention and turned a stubborn shoulder and stopped their ears from hearing."[9]

The absence of a proper contemplation of death and dying in our culture has resulted in a further and more insidious sickness; perhaps one may call it "biolatry"—the idolizing of life. Human life is so idolatrously clutched (contrary to both the Bible's depiction of God's righteous and equitable love for human life,[10] and the liberty with which Christ held even his own deity—cf. Phil 2:6) that little or no regard at all is entertained concerning either what comes after this life or the attention divine revelation gives to our end.[11] Many have become mastered by this present life. They have contented themselves with finding sufficient human meaning and purpose merely in the "here and now" such that when death occurs—that is, the robbing of that hallowed contentment—they react as though some grave injustice has been imposed in affront to our humanity. Here lies a most serious flaw with

---

8. Stannard, *Puritan Way of Death*, 194. Stannard pointedly observes, "One of the most deeply disturbing facts of modern life—one that poets and novelists and philosophers and theologians never tire of discussing—is the apparent anonymity and simple unimportance of the individual; except in the most intimate of relationships, few men or women can ever regard themselves or anyone else as truly unique and irreplaceable" (189–90). See also Thielicke, *Death and Life*, 111, where he writes concerning the irreplaceableness of the individual, "The more intimately I am bound to another human being, the more icily and disruptively his death touches me. The well-known psychological effect on me when a close friend dies is but a testimony and reflection of a much more profound reality, namely, the fact that something unique and irreplaceable—or more precisely, something for which there is no substitute—has been destroyed."

9. Zech 7:11; verse 12 tells the grim consequences of such stubbornness. Contemporary culture's dealing with death also looks like the Jews' regard for the truth heralded to them by Jesus concerning his provision of an escape from death (John 8:43–59); or the religious leaders' treatment of Stephen at his declaration of the truth that was before their eyes, which they, too, refused to answer (Acts 7:51–54).

10. For indications of God's equitable discharge of death—even on a mass scale—unimpeded by sentiment, see Gen 6:11–13 with 7:21–23; Exod 11:4–6; 12:29–30, 33; Lev 10:1–3; Num 16:20–21, 32, 44–45, 49; Num 25; Hos 13:4–16; Rev 6:8; 9:15.

11. See Edwards, "Procrastination," 2:237–42; see also Edwards, "Preciousness of Time," 2:233–36.

our view of life and death. Life does not belong to us to *worship* it—for all intents and purposes—as we see fit. In grand scale, no greater ethic seems to be realized than the preservation of (human) life.[12] Just consider how insulting people find the notion of the extermination of the human species.[13] That notion, by the way, is not so insulting to the God who did just that, saving eight souls (Gen 6:23; 7:21–24; 2 Pet 2:5)![14] Rather than idolizing life,

---

12. To the contrary, the glory of the God who created human life—and everything else—is an infinitely higher ethic than preservation of human life (cf. Gen 2:17; 6:5–7; Exod 32:32 [even Moses acknowledges the truth that even his *eternal* life is not as valuable as the glory of God revealed in mercy]; Deut 32:50–51; Josh 7:10–12, 15; Judg 13:22). The anomalous notion of preoccupation with death and dying receives mention in this chapter (cf. the *natuurvolken* in the section below on Bavinck's systematic theology) as well as in the concluding chapter where both martyrdom and the Puritan *contemptu mundi* are treated. Additionally, the notion of the preservation of human life will not consider here the blight of premeditated abortion, which is beyond the scope of this thesis. Suffice it to say here that the very act of abortion disposes of one life to preserve the hallowed contentment of another who, by the very act, evidences idolatry of its own life.

13. That humanity idolizes life is evident by the species' self-aggrandizing revulsion at the notion of its own extermination. We must be careful here, however, to distinguish between the invalid and unjust extermination of the species or of any genocide by a finite creature for any less than justified reasons, on the one hand, and the wholly just extermination of the species that the only wise and holy God executed in the Flood against a rebellious creation worthy of damnation, on the other hand. Such an extermination is not without precedence in the historical accounting of ancient literature. Not only does the Babylonian mythical deity AnuEnlil of *The Epic of Gilgamesh* exterminate the human population because of its annoying noise that disturbs his sleep, only to restart the race with fourteen newly created humans ("The Atrahasis Epic," in Heidel, *The Epic of Gilgamesh*, 113–16), but also, according to the biblical record, Yahweh exterminates the species—save eight souls—and repopulates the earth with that elect eight (2 Pet 2:5). Moreover, Yahweh decimates a nation by putting to death every first born in Egypt—both man and beast—essentially eliminating the future hope and progeny of an entire nation—yeah, even the preeminent world nation at the time. So encompassing was the event that Exod 12:30 underscores, "there was a great cry in Egypt, for there was no home where there was not someone dead." Selah (Exod 11:4–6; 12:29–30, 33). If God (and so-called gods) considers human life of less significance than the manifestation of his own holy will and glory, certainly the creature itself should view human life—God's creation and possession—with the same gravity.

14. Citing Hermann Gunkel, Heidel notes a most poignant and noteworthy distinction between the Babylonian depiction of their gods' genuinely repugnant disposition toward human death and that of the God of the Bible. The biblical account takes very seriously the moral depravity of the prediluvian race of men. In the biblical account of the flood and the extermination of the human species, save eight souls, "no tears are shed, as on Tablet XI:116–25 and 136–37 [of the Gilgamesh epic], over those who perished in the flood; theirs was a just and deserved punishment. In the Hebrew document the ethical motive is so strong that God is portrayed even as regretting the very creation of man; while in the Babylonian, the gods, with the possible exception of Enlil, regret the destruction of man. Although God resolves not to send another flood, he

then, we should consider the reality that we are dust (Ps 103:14; Isa 40:17). The Lord of the cosmos gives and dismisses created human life as he sees fit (Ps 90:3–10). We should, rather, loosely hold our lives—which are not our own anyway, nor are they primarily for our own consumption—with the same dauntless composure that Jesus Christ possessed his deity (though that was indeed his own). That is, he did not consider his deity something to be "clutched" as though it could be taken from him (Phil 2:6). When a life ends—though death *is* an enemy—we ought never, like Job concerning his sufferings,[15] to imagine that some cosmic "violence" has been done.[16]

A healthy *contemptu mundi*[17]—contempt for (this) world—is virtually nonexistent today; the diagnosis is grim. As creatures far removed from the

---

is nowhere represented as *regretting* the diluvial catastrophe." See Hermann Gunkel, *Genesis*, 71, cited in Heidel, *Gilgamesh*, 269; see also *Gilgamesh* (85) for the account of the very ungodlike fear and regret of the gods in destroying humanity, where the gods, "terror-stricken at the deluge," "cowered like dogs (and) crouched in distress" as "they fled (and) ascended to the heaven of Anu."

15. The word חָמָס, *hamas*, "violence" cried by Job in 19:7 may be translated as Job's charge of injustice. (The same word is used in Gen 6:11 of the earth's being filled with "violence" prompting God to deluge it; and in Hab 1:2 in Habakkuk's plea for God's response because "the law is ignored and justice is never upheld.") While God does not, in the end, provide Job with an explanation for his suffering, God does correct Job's misunderstanding of justice (see 38:1–3; 40:1–6; 42:1–6). Further, nothing in the text precludes the statements in 1:2 and 2:10 that "through all this Job did not sin nor did he blame God," from referring to the Scriptures' assessment of Job in regard to his adversities of the immediate context, yet at a point *prior* to his spirited dialogue with his counselors and his 19:7 misstep. Nor do the commendations of Job 42:7 and Jas 5:11 negate such an interpretation; for the commendation of Job in 42:7 comes on the heels of Job's dialogue with God (which is more of God's monologue) in which he acknowledges God's righteousness yet his own finite—and faulty—creatureliness. James' admonition to believers to emulate the endurance of Job commends Job for never renouncing his God despite Job's deeply malformed perception that he held some degree of peer relation to God. Similarly is David commended as "a man after [God's] own heart" (1 Sam 13:14) despite his incorrigible failures, which God had already foreseen when he made such an assessment of one who would acknowledge no God but Yahweh, even in his failures.

16. The true *hamas* is the hubris of a self-absorbed creature who presumes that he is able to order his or his world's course better than a Being who is able spontaneously to generate a universe, sustain its vast and intricate existence moment by moment, and then effortlessly bring that universe to the consummation of his intended purposes without even the most minute detour. The revocation of the grant of life by such a Being should evoke, rather, a response equal to Aaron's at the death of his sons (Lev 10:3) and Job's after he is granted recognition of the true weight of his God's splendor (Job 40:4–5).

17. The term originates first from the title *De Contemptu Mundi*, which was a satirical poem by the monk Bernard of Cluny, ca. 1140. In approximately three thousand verses Bernard excoriates the medieval church for its moral abuses in his day. See Herbermann, *NCE*. At the turn of the thirteenth century, however, Pope Innocent III

Garden where the Author of life walked with the first human beings in the cool of the day (Gen 3:8), we have unconsciously disintegrated (human) life from its sustaining source and tended to idolize it as some mystical apex of all reality, under the power of no one.[18] A balance is needed between a right embrace of the sanctity of life as an invaluable gift from its gracious Giver yet simultaneously its genuine dispensability as nonessential being.[19]

One may get a clearer idea of the gravity of the current cultural milieu by way of analogy. When a malfunctioning human body ceases to produce insulin, proper amounts of that hormone may be reintroduced by artificial yet quite ameliorative means, restoring a proper balance and functioning of

---

penned his more didactic *De Contemptu Mundi*. For several centuries after, Innocent's treatise was regarded as "the seminal statement on the subject of man's relation to the world and the afterlife. . . ." During the following three hundred years Innocent's work was translated and reprinted time and time again—in London, Cologne, Paris, Lyons, Barcelona, and elsewhere—though more often than not under the work's even more revealing subtitle, *Liber de Miseria Humane Conditionis*; see Stannard, *Puritan Way of Death*, 21; and chap. 7 herein.

18. Ancient Greek pre-Socratic philosopher Protagoras similarly boasted, "πάντων χρημάτων μέτρον ἐστὶν ἄνθρωπος, τῶν μὲν ὄντων ὡς ἔστιν, τῶν δὲ οὐκ ὄντων ὡς οὐκ ἔστιν [Man is the measure of all things: of things which are, that they are, and of things which are not, that they are not]." Protagoras' naturalistic implication was that no reality exists apart from what mankind is able to determine is real and/or meaningful. See Plato, "Theaetetus," in *Plato in Twelve Volumes*, §152a. One might argue that this hubris is precisely the sin committed by Adam and Eve in eating from the tree of the knowledge of good and evil (Gen 3:6); they attempted to elevate themselves to the position of Judge of what is good and what is evil—i.e., determiner of reality and meaning (cf. Jas 4:12). This mindset is also depicted in Isa 47:8–11 of the (Babylonian) "sensual one" עֲדִינָה, *awdeen*—one given to pleasures; cf. 2 Tim 3:4), "secure in [his] wickedness," who mimics God, saying, "I am, and there is no one besides me." See v. 12 for God's answer to this haughty biolater.

19. The philosophical notion of *necessary* versus *contingent* being (formerly termed *essential* and *non-essential* being) refers to the distinction between God—as the sole source of all being, and therefore essential for the existence of anything else—and any other thing, which, by nature, is non-essential. In this context, human life (particularly in a post Gen 3:6 world) is doubly dispensable. Indisputably, the human being can be eliminated by virtue of the fact that it is not necessary being. The remainder of the extant created order would not cease to exist upon the elimination of any individual human being or (as sobering as the thought is) upon the elimination of the entire human species, because all other being is not ontologically dependent upon human being for its own existence. Secondly, because of the depravity—i.e., radically corrupted sinfulness—of the human species, the righteous elimination (by the Author of life and death) of any individual or again, of the entire species, is perfectly justifiable (cf. Gen 2:17; 6:5–13; Exod 32:9–10; Num 16:21, 45; 1 Kgs 8:46; 2 Chr 6:36; Ps 8:3–4; 14:3; 53:3; Eccl 7:20; John 3:17–19; Rom 6:23). The grant of life, therefore, may *not* be so valued as it is by contemporary culture. Such a valuing of human life above the value its creator places on it is idolatrous because it supplants the authority of the only true God and Creator/Sustainer of all things.

the body. Similarly, a healthy perspective of human life and death may be achieved by reintroducing a proper *memento mori*[20] into the "body" (i.e., culture) that has ceased[21] to produce on its own the properly functioning balm due to its lack of exposure to the necessary replicating "antibodies" (e.g., a frequency of death similar to that experienced by our predecessors, who consequently sustained a proper and often transformative contemplation of their own end). By properly grasping our mortality—the limitation God has placed on that which is out of bounds[22]—one is given a more clear understanding of the significance of life as a gift from the Supreme Possessor and Ruler of the universe and therefore enabled to live it out deliberately more fully, vibrantly, meaningfully, and as it was designed and intended.[23] We may rightly honor life, yet simultaneously laud the justice and holiness of God in his just execution of any death. This view of life and death is a fitting antidote to the pervasive sin of biolatry.

---

20. The Latin phrase may be translated "Remember you will/must die." The phrase came to represent an art form dating back to ancient Rome. Though varied in presentation, each artistic creation poignantly intended to remind the patron of his own mortality.

21. The same commentary could be made regarding this cultural cessation as Duane Litfin makes regarding a similar cultural necrosis articulated in Weaver, *Ideas Have Consequences*. Litfin regards Weaver's work (which, originally written in 1948, is bit too philosophically foundationalistic for me) as "an intuition of a situation," a situation "'of a world which has lost its center, which desires to believe again in value and obligation' but is not willing to 'face what it must accept' in order to regain that faith." See Litfin, *Conceiving the Christian College*, 164. Similarly here, what has precipitated this book is a sort of "intuition of a situation" in which our culture has failed to engage a "dialogue with death" in order to grasp truthfully the value of life. See also Helm, *Last Things*, 35–36; Carson, *How Long*, 116–20; Anderson, *Theology, Death and Dying*, 116–25.

22. Thielicke, *Death and Life*, 186.

23. The reader may be familiar with the colloquialism, "Keep your friends close, and your enemies closer." If death is an enemy—and it is—then Christians—as those who have been given divine guarantee against any ultimately deleterious effects of death—should come to "know" it so intimately well as to dispel categorically any fear or anxiety of it due to any mystery and/or uncertainty in which it is so often cloaked (at least in our current milieu and, no doubt, by means of the cunning adversary of humanity). Where then is its threat? Where the death of the believer in Jesus Christ is concerned, the one who "had the power of death," who "prowls around like a roaring lion seeking someone to devour" (Heb 2:14; 1 Pet 5:8) is no more than a *paper* lion. The covenant people of the Lord of life and death are vitally empowered to live with appointed abandon for the renown of the creator of humanity who gave them their very existence for *his* purposes, which were never intended to be (nor ultimately can be) thwarted by any fear of death.

Methodology

Not a Biblical Thanatology

Human beings are generally tentative about the unfamiliar and unknown. At the other extreme, we can be quite cavalier about that which is commonplace and routine. A thoughtful balance is achieved by the apostle John as he encourages, "There is no fear in love; but perfect love casts out fear, because fear involves punishment, and the one who fears is not perfected in love" (1 John 4:18). Neither fear nor hubris regarding death is tendered biblically. Rather, love, in accord with the ethic of life both held and revealed by God, saturated with an absence of fear of death as punishment,[24] achieves a properly biblical tension of familiarity with death. Such a disposition so grounds a knowledge of death that this resident enemy is both familiarly understood and viewed as unthreatening as the Savior of the world died to make it so. The consequence of such a transformed pathos is the provision of liberty to release a covetous hold of the present life in exchange for an unimpeded life of conscious glad anticipation that death can bring only gain.[25] To advance such thinking, we must first be mindful of the relation of this present work to the much broader context of what could be considered a whole biblical thanatology.[26]

A comprehensive biblical thanatology would entail a scope far beyond that of a single volume. Some have even suggested that such an undertaking is not possible.[27] In that light, the following will sketch the breadth of such

---

24. Death, never understood as less than the curse of God, must always be grieved by the Christian. At the same time, however, no semblance of punishment can be attributed to the death of a Christian because that penalty has been completely absorbed by Jesus Christ on behalf of the Christian. For further discussion of the nature of death as pertaining to the Christian, see the section in chapter 4 entitled, "Why do Christians die?" Additionally, William Sherlock contemplates regarding this tension, "a man who is delivered from the fears of Death, fears nothing else in excess but God"; see Sherlock, *Practical Discourse*, 111. See also Berkhof, *Systematic Theology*, 670–71.

25. A clear distinction must be made here between the lack of fear of death (exhibited by the likes of Polycarp) and the perverse will to die (exhibited by the likes of suicide terrorists). One is honoring life as the gift of God in proper relation to the infinitely higher ethic of the glory of God; while the other evidences a callous disregard for life—both his own and that of others—to the "glory" of no god who could even be said to have regard for the sanctity of life.

26. The term *thanatology* derives from two Greek words, *thanatos*—death, and *logos*—word or matter, i.e., principle of knowledge, and therefore concerns "the matter of death."

27. Rahner, *Theology of Death*, 18–19.

a work in order to locate the significance of the current more limited work within that much broader context.

Origin of death. Ideas addressed in such an exhaustive undertaking could only begin with a discussion of the biblical writers' development of notions about death and dying as well as the surrounding cultural influences that may have impacted their understanding. Because the Bible claims to be the authoritative revelation of the only true God[28] not merely to the ancient Israelites, but also to all of humanity through the prophetic agency of this elect family of Abraham, a biblical thanatology would also need to begin with an exegesis of the Bible's articulation of the origin of and intention behind the inception of death. That is, contrary to many cultures—both ancient and contemporary—the biblical articulation is that death is not merely a natural constituent of corporeality (or even incorporeality); death's origin is subsequent to the origin of the universe. Consequently, a biblical thanatology would also have to interact with the full breadth of extra-biblical claims to authoritative commentary on death.[29] Alternatively, a biblical grounding of the matter of death would distinguish divinely revealed concepts from those notions that are either merely speculative or purely cultural and/or false religious conjecture.

Theological anthropology. A biblical thanatology would have to outline various views of theological anthropology—that is, the nature and constitution of man in relation to God. If man is to die, and man as a creature is created in the image of something greater, one must understand the relationship between that which can die and the greater, which cannot—if in fact it cannot—and why. What does the Bible mean, for example, when it says that man is created in the image of God? That question alone poses a host of other related questions about the nature not only of man but of

---

28. For fuller treatments of the authority of Scripture, see Henry, *God, Revelation and Authority*, vol. 3; Frame, *Word of God*; Frame, *Knowledge of God*; Bavinck, *Reformed Dogmatics*, vol. 1, *Prolegomena*; Bruce, *Canon of Scripture*; Carson and Woodbridge, *Scripture and Truth*; Carson and Woodbridge, *Hermeneutics, Authority, and Canon*; Horton, *Covenant and Eschatology*; Kline, *Structure of Biblical Authority*; Marshall, *Biblical Inspiration*; Evans and Tov, *Exploring the Origins of the Bible*. For a perspective alternative to the aforementioned theologically conservative scholarship, see also Barth, *Doctrine of the Word of God*, vol. 1, *Church Dogmatics*; Dodd, *Authority of the Bible*; Barr, *Bible in the Modern World*; Barclay, *By What Authority?*

29. For example, Babylonian, Sumerian, Egyptian, Greek, and Roman mythologies; and contemporary false religious writings of Jehovah's Witnesses, Mormons, Scientology, Hinduism, Islam, etc.

God also. For example: Can God, like his image bearer, die?[30] If man, as the image of God, is one person, how is God three persons? Is God male and female? Does God have a body?[31]

Further, because death, on every scheme, radically alters man's constitution, the treatise must engage the multitude of notions of just what that constitution consists. Is man dichotomistic? Trichotomistic? Is he (and God) constitutionally monistic? Dualistic? Because the Scriptures affirm that God is incorporeal (John 4:24; cf. Deut 4:12–18; Ps 115:2–7), and man is created in his image, what of man is incorporeal? What level of importance has the corporeal aspect of man? That is, when the material representation of man reverts to the dust from which it originated, what of man, if anything, continues to exist, and how and in what form (1 Cor 15:35)? If man did not exist as a "living being" until he was embodied (Gen 2:7), when that body is shed, is man still a "living being"?[32] Moreover, must he have a body in order to maintain his designation as the image of God? All of these questions of theological anthropology would need to receive full treatment in a comprehensive biblical thanatology.

State and condition of the dead. The state and condition of the dead must also be considered in any full biblical treatment of the idea of death. If something of man survives the dissolution of his corporeal form—i.e., his body—where and even *when* does that substance go to continue its "life"? Is consciousness afforded it? Or does it exist in some form of unconscious stasis?[33] Or even more unsettling, does it simply disappear from existence entirely only to be reincarnated in either another earthly or a final heavenly

---

30. *Patripassianism*—the doctrine of the experience of suffering by God the Father at the death of Jesus Christ—will be treated in chapter 4 on death in the New Testament.

31. For a thoughtful entertaining of this question, see Augustine, *City of God*, 1082–85; Augustine, *Confessions*, 62–63, 114–15, 126–27, 138–39.

32. Clark, *Interpreting the Resurrection*, 14. Clark is so careful to maintain the status of dead image bearers of God as "living beings" that he defines the state of physical death as "that state of being in which the active forces of life are reduced to their lowest intensity, so crushed and drained away as to be virtually absent. This is the reason why the inhabitants of *Sheol* are not conceived of as strictly non-existent. It is not that faith is groping for some promise of survival. It is simply that the logic of understanding must view the "dead" as "living beings" whose powers have been reduced almost to vanishing point."

33. The term commonly used to refer to such a state is "soul sleep." This idea will be treated in the section on death in the New Testament. (Though the concept is not limited to the dead in the New Testament era only, the illumination afforded by the progressed revelation of the New Testament provides more material to address *psychopannychia*—soul sleep.)

form or "re-membered"[34] from the immaterial substance that is said to constitute it, extant only in the mind of God? Upon undergoing such radical constitutional transformation, on what grounds can one argue that this "person" even maintains identical continuity?[35] If this continuing substance—soul, spirit, life, spiritual body, or whatever one calls it—is incorporeal (as evidenced by the whole material corpse that it leaves behind, lifeless and decadent), then does it exist in some parallel universe or in some unseen dimension or infinitely distant alternative location of our own universe?[36] What is the state of such incorporeal being? That is, *where* can we say is that *place* (if we can even speak of such a state in such terms)?

Considering the temporal mechanics of such a state, *when* can we say is such a *time*? Do the dead enter immediately into the final state upon death[37]—or so it might seem to them (since the passage of time in the afterlife cannot be reckoned assuredly as identical to our own temporality)? Or do these incorporeal substances join the myriads upon myriads of those who have preceded us in death throughout ages past in a state whose timeline concords with our own and where they, as do we, await the consummation of the age (cf. 2 Thess 4:13–17)? As they await, what can be said of their condition? Are they all—righteous and unrighteous—relegated to the same *Sheol* where they exist as some "quasi-bodily entity,"[38] in a "state of being in which the active forces of life are reduced to their lowest intensity, so crushed and drained away as to be virtually absent . . . whose powers have been reduced almost to vanishing point"?[39] Or are the righteous and unrighteous dead alike allotted, respectively, fully conscious and palpable pleasures or torments, either temporarily or finally? All these questions

---

34. Murphy, "Nonreductive Physicalism," in *Whatever Happened to the Soul?*, 128–32; Murphy, *Bodies and Souls*, 121–25; see also Green, *What about the Soul?*

35. For further discussion on the significance of continuity of personal identity, see Evans, *Preserving the Person*; Lints, Horton, and Talbot, *Personal Identity in Theological Perspective*.

36. The existence of distinct beings at infinitely distant alternative locations in an infinite universe (perhaps spatially though not temporally) is not illogical. The concept may be considered, at best, antinomy by the finite mind.

37. Tertullian argued so. The 1439 Council of Florence also appears to concur, stating, "The souls of those who die in actual mortal sin, or only in original sin, immediately descend into Hell." Of course, the Council is not explicit concerning whether it understands the term "Hell" as the final state or merely the place of temporal torment of the unrighteous dead until the final judgment where "death and Hades were thrown into the lake of fire" (Rev 14:20). See Denzinger, *Catholic Dogma*, §693, 220.

38. Cooper, *Body, Soul, and Life Everlasting*, 69.

39. Clark, *Interpreting the Resurrection*, 14.

concerning the state and condition of the dead would receive full treatment in a biblical thanatology.

Relation of the living to the dead. Various theological views of the relation of the living to the dead have waxed and waned over the centuries and have been addressed sometimes even contradictorily within a single tradition.[40] A biblical thanatology would therefore have to engage issues such as any responsibility of the living for the welfare of the dead, as well as the possibility of the dead having any influence over the course of the living; customs of food and drink offerings for the dead; the enigmatic biblical reference to baptism for the dead (1 Cor 15:29); mode of disposal of the body; and death bed and mourning customs and rituals, among other related concerns. Further, because the doctrine of purgatory charges the living with being able to affect the condition and timing of the final state of the dead, this doctrine obviously would occupy significant space in the discussion of the biblical relationship between the living and the dead.[41]

The problem of evil. One of the key questions of the discipline of philosophy is, what is the problem (i.e., with this world, which evidently is not perfect and without troubles)?[42] That question arises chiefly because the reality of

---

40. Rome, for example, has recently stated its opinion dismissing the doctrine of limbo, qualifying, however, that the "ordinary teaching" of this "possible theological hypothesis" "never entered into the dogmatic definitions of the Magisterium." See the 2007 report published by Rome's International Theological Commission, *Hope of Salvation for Infants*.

41. Some ANE funeral and burial practices evidence that food and drink offerings were provided not only at interment but also thereafter, in some instances even as a monthly "mortuary offering." Several possibilities exist for why the offerings were made. Some believed that the dead existing in the underworld would in some way be nourished by the earthly offerings. Others held that deceased family members could either prosper or haunt his survivors and/or progeny. Because provisions from the living was necessary for the welfare of citizens of the underworld, some people believed that one could garner either the favor or disfavor of an ancestor by either providing or neglecting his underworldly need of sustenance. Moreover, failure to bury the dead prevented admission to and rest in the underworld; denial of either food and drink offerings and/or burial compelled the undead to roam the earthly realm disturbing the living and being reduced to finding what sustenance he could from the garbage thrown out into the street. Still others sacrificed food or drink offerings to the gods of the underworld in solicitation of the favorable disposition of the gods toward their deceased loved ones. See Heidel, *Gilgamesh*, 152–57, 165.

42. Five key questions in philosophical pursuit are Who am I? Where did I come from? Where am I going? What is the problem? What is the solution? For further discussion regarding worldview formation, see Nash, *Life's Ultimate Questions*, 13–19; Nash, *Faith and Reason*, 21–34; Sire, *Universe Next Door*, 20–23. In the former text, Nash introduces the study of philosophy with a section on worldview framing in which

death and decadence in the universe seems to indicate precisely that a problem does exist. For this reason, some might argue that a biblical thanatology would have to include as prolegomena a discussion of the problem of evil.[43] That discussion would obviously largely entail reflections on thanatology.

In addressing the problem, the secular philosopher is compelled to presume that the normal state of the universe ought to be inherently without problem. The Christian philosopher, however, may admit to the discussion the authoritative revelation that all was made originally, indeed, "very good"—i.e., without even the semblance of a problem (Gen 1:31). Without arbitrarily insisting that certain paradigms be ruled inadmissible, the Christian approaches the question with the full integrity of examining all of the available data in order to present a most tenable answer, which some argue is the *only* tenable answer.[44] The problem of evil, then—and of death—and its incursion upon the universe, as well as its relation to God, can be addressed viably from the perspective of divine revelation.[45]

Pastoral counsel. A final concern that should be included in any biblical thanatology is sage and compassionate yet honest shepherding from those

---

he poses many basic questions that shape one's worldview. In the latter he suggests that "A well-rounded worldview includes what a person believes on at least five major topics: God, reality, knowledge, morality, and humankind" (*Faith and Reason*, 30). Sire lists seven basic questions essential to the formation of a worldview.

43. For helpful discussions of the problem(s) of evil, see Feinberg, *Many Faces of Evil*; Feinberg, *No One Like Him*, 777–96; Frame, *Doctrine of God*, 160–68; Erickson, *Christian Theology*, 436–56.

44. Schaeffer, "He Is There," 336–37. Admitting the host of rationally available interpretations of reality, Schaeffer muses, "The strength of the Christian system—the acid test of it—is that everything fits under the apex of the existing, infinite-personal God, and it is the only system in the world where this is true. No other system has an apex under which everything fits. That is why I am a Christian and no longer an agnostic. In all the other systems something 'sticks-out,' something cannot be included; and it has to be mutilated or ignored. But without losing his own integrity, the Christian can see everything fitting into one place beneath the Christian apex of the existence of the infinite-personal God who is there." Further, of the genesis and ordering of the universe necessarily by the infinite-personal God, and of man's constitution as both finite and personal, Schaeffer heralds, "It is not that this is the best answer to existence; it is the only answer. That is why we may hold our Christianity with intellectual integrity. The only answer for what exists is that He, the infinite-personal God, really is there" (ibid., 287–88).

45. For spirited and edifying discussions on warranted belief in the divine and revelation thereof, see Morris, *God and the Philosophers*; Plantinga, *God and Other Minds*; Plantinga, *God, Freedom, and Evil*; Plantinga, *Warrant and Proper Function*; Plantinga, *Warranted Christian Belief*; Plantinga and Wotersdorff, *Faith and Rationality*; Woltersdorff, *Reason Within the Bounds of Religion*; Schaeffer, *Francis A. Schaeffer Trilogy*; Frame, *Knowledge of God*.

who are both charged by Jesus Christ and genuinely concerned to "keep watch over the souls" (Heb 13:17) of those who are candidates for transition from this life to the next. Concerning the grace and responsibility of the church to nurture its members and bear witness to the world in the art of dying, Gregg Allison counsels,

> One final stage in the application of salvation also intersects with the church's missional endeavor. Though glorification—the reception of resurrection bodies at the return of Christ—is still in the future, at the death of its faithful members, the church announces the hope of their ultimate resurrection at their funerals (or memorial celebrations). While it grieves at the loss of its loved ones, the church also preaches the blessed hope of the Lord's return and the resurrection of all Christ followers that will accompany this future event. Death, though very real and deeply sensed at funerals, is not the last word, and the missional church verbally carries its deceased members beyond the grave to their ultimate, glorious destiny still to come. Funerals, standing as a strong counter-cultural witness against the surrounding culture of death and hopelessness, are an important element of the missional church.[46]

Spiritual leaders of the church of Jesus Christ, faithfully serving by means of Word and Spirit, equip the saints to war valiantly, fearlessly. They preach and instruct candidates for death concerning the unassailable sovereignty of the God who calls them to trust him completely, so that in every valley of the shadow of death, they may be prepared to resound joyously, "Blessed be the name of the Lord!" Such pastoral counsel will encourage regular, godward contemplation of one's death as invaluably instructive for how one is called to live godwardly in this present age (Titus 2:12).[47] That counsel will also admonish how one may die well to the glory of Christ his God, as well as entrust the keeping of the souls of his loved ones to the discriminating infinite wisdom of a good and faithful Creator in doing what is right (Gen 18:25; 1 Pet 4:19; cf. Ps 119:68). Only the believer in Jesus Christ, so nurtured by the church, can confidently and biblically affirm

---

46. Allison, *Sojourners and Strangers*, unpublished draft.

47. Godly living in the present age ought not to be understood merely in regard to personal sanctification. The Psalmist prayed, "So teach us to number our days that we may present to you a heart of wisdom" (Ps 90:12). The ninth resolution of Jonathan Edwards reads, "Resolved, to think much on all occasions of my own dying, and of the common circumstances which attend death"; Jonathan Edwards, "Resolutions," in *WJE*, 1.lxii. Gregory the Great admonished, "He will greatly rouse himself to doing good works who always bears in mind his end"; Shinners, "Art of Dying Well," 525.

that he has died already and that his life is hidden with Christ in God (Col 3:3). Consequently, the fact that death no longer has a sting can be wholly embraced by the believer in Christ in order to sustain and propel him daily in a life of faith. He is made confident that his life cannot be terminated at death because it is hidden irremovably in God with Christ who ever lives to make intercession for him (Heb 7:25). From the infinite resources of the ever living object of our faith that is Christ, the believer is sustained uninterrupted throughout this present life, through death, and into the new age. Only Spirit-filled members of the church of Jesus Christ can so instruct and nurture candidates for death in this universal and ultimately insuppressible reality. No proper biblical thanatology could be without this epilogue.

Shape and Thesis of the Current Work

Biblical authority. Many have convincingly argued that postmodernity has taught us at least that a modernist version of foundationalist epistemology cannot be sustained. Philosophical postmodernism's "chastening"[48] of modernism's classical foundationalism has exposed the fallacy that complete objectivity is attainable on the stage of human reason alone. That is, finite human reason/observation alone cannot draw universal significance from finite historical events.[49] Even Augustine acknowledged long ago that, "since we are too weak to discover truth by reason alone and for this reason need the authority of sacred books, I began to believe that you [God] would never have invested the Bible with such conspicuous authority in every land unless you had intended it to be the means by which we should look for you and believe in you."[50] Indeed, no "God's eye" perspective of knowledge—i.e.,

---

48. The term "chastened foundationalism" seems to have been coined by Clark, "Narrative Theology and Apologetics," 512. For further discussion on the demise of classical foundationalism and options for its replacement, see also Carson, *Gagging of God*; Carson, *Becoming Conversant*; Vanhoozer, *Is There Meaning in This Text?*; Wolterstorff, *Reason within the Bounds of Religion*; Wood, *Epistemology*; Erickson, Helseth, Taylor, *Reclaiming the Center*; Plantinga, *Warranted Christian Belief*; Plantinga and Wolterstorff, *Faith and Rationality*; Bonjour, *In Defense of Pure Reason*; Thiel, *Nonfoundationalism*; Kirk, "Confusion of Epistemology," 131–56.

49. Lessing, "Über den Beweis des Geistes und der Kraft," in *Gotthold Ephraim Lessings sämtlichen Schriften*, vol. 13, 4:11–8:20. German Enlightenment philosopher Lessing famously characterized this gap between the "accidental truths of history" and the "necessary truths of reason" as an "ugly great ditch" (*der garstige breite Graben*) that could not be forded. Divine revelation, however—which Lessing disavowed—may legitimately ground the finite historical crucifixion of Jesus Christ as universally significant.

50. Augustine, *Confessions*, 117.

pure objectivity—can be grasped apart from the omniscient God's volitional disclosure of it. Thus, a "fabric of theology"[51] for the playing-out of the "drama of doctrine"[52] where God speaks and acts such that finite creatures can have certain knowledge can only be achieved with a high view of the authority of Scripture and an interpretive framework grounded by the Bible's own categories (e.g., themes such as creation, fall, redemption, consummation). Affirming, then, Carl F. H. Henry's assertion of "divine revelation as the basic epistemological axiom,"[53] what follows will presume the authority of the biblical Scriptures' commentary on all things thanatology and, accordingly, that death is a righteous imposition by the Creator God upon his rebellious created order[54] at some time subsequent to its originally very good genesis.

Thesis of the current work. Rather than addressing the multitudinous questions comprised in a whole biblical thanatology, the more specific import of this work is to evince that a biblical portrait of death limits both the value and ethic of human life in contradiction to the pervasive yet allusive sin of biolatry. The value of human life is not infinite. It is bounded by both the finitude of its creation and the reality and breadth of death as the cherubim with flaming sword—as it were—appointed specifically to delimit that value.[55] The Bible articulates that the value and principle of human life are dwarfed in comparison to the infinitely greater ethic of the glory of the God who created human life as arguably chief among many means for the very

51. Lints, *Fabric of Theology*.
52. Vanhoozer, *Drama of Doctrine*.
53. Henry, *God, Revelation and Authority*, 1:225.
54. Adam alone, out of all of the countless trillions of creatures, bears both the image of the Creator of all things and the responsibility for all those things, being created in solidarity with those things (cf. Gen 3:19). For that reason, all creation is cursed with Adam. On the notion of Adam's worship leadership of the created order, see Due, *Created for Worship*, 7, 141. Concerning the application of death to nonhuman creation, see Feinberg, *No One Like Him*, 622–23, 779; Feinberg, *Many Faces of Evil*, 23, 194; Thielicke, *Death and Life*, 150–53, 207–10.
55. Cf. Gen 3:22–24. So that man would not "take also from the tree of life, and eat, and live forever," God "stationed the cherubim and the flaming sword which turned every direction to guard the way to the tree of life." The "sword" always in Scripture, either explicitly or implicitly and by the determination of God and/or man, represents judgment (for a sampling see Gen 34:26; Exod 5:3; 22:22–24; Num 14:43; Deut 28:20–22; Josh 6:21; 8:24–27; Judg 7:13–14; 1 Sam 22:19; 2 Sam 12:10; 1 Chr 21:7–13; esp. 1 Chr 21:27–30; Esth 9:5; Pss 22:20; 78:56–62; Isa 1:18–20; Jer 15:3; Ezek 5:12; 32:2–11; Rom 13:4; Rev 2:16; 19:21). The judgment of God concerning his treasonous and now gravely disfigured image bearers was that they were no longer qualified to retain and steward his gracious, self-emanating gift of life. The "flaming sword" of death is the only vehicle in creation that prevents access to life.

purpose of displaying his own splendor. The creature ought to be readily disposed, then, to bless the Creator, who both gives and takes away (life) in exhibition of his own glory. To facilitate this thesis, some but not all of the same issues necessary in a full biblical thanatology will indeed be undertaken here yet with an eye toward the thesis rather than with a more general thanatological locus.

Warrant for This Study

The above outline of a biblical thanatology helps to illustrate the need for the address of the current derivative topic. To the best of my knowledge, no such work as a full biblical thanatology appears in print anywhere—even though, as admitted, this work does not undertake that task—nor does any publication that treats death as a halt for biolatry. Works that treat broadly some facet of death as the core concern are almost as rare. Three treatises approach a thanatology (though certainly not purely biblical). First is Alan Segal's *Life After Death: A History of the Afterlife in Western Religion*.[56] Segal examines historical developments and teachings about the afterlife from the world's three monotheistic religions—Judaism, Christianity, and Islam—in order to determine how each seeks to understand the ultimate meaning of life on earth. Second, Phillipe Ariès' *The Hour of Our Death* charts cultural and historical developments of Western death and funerary rituals from the medieval period through the twentieth century, subjectively attempting to obtain "an unconscious expression of the sensibility of the age."[57] Finally,

---

56. Segal, *Life After Death*.

57. Ariès, *Hour of Our Death*, xvii. An alternately published version of Ariès' work bears the subtitle *A Landmark History of Western Man's Changing Attitudes Toward Death—and Life—Over the Last One Thousand Years* (New York: Oxford University Press, 1991). Ariès, a historian, is not concerned with the biblical theological import of the traditions he surveys. Rather, his (perhaps elitist) concern is to evidence an ever changing nature of attitudes toward death, changes imperceptible to the non-historian. Ariès candidly discloses, "The historian of death cannot read with the same glasses as the historian of religion. He must not regard [clerical] documents as what they were in the minds of their authors: lessons in spirituality or morality. He must look behind the ecclesiastical language and discover the background of common ideas that was taken for granted and that made the lesson intelligible to the audience—a background that was common to literate clerics and to the people, and that therefore expressed itself in a naïve style" (xvii). Even more revealing concerning his reason for surfacing such changes, Ariès continues, "The ideas that Christians have entertained about death and immortality have varied over the ages. How significant are these variations? They will seem minor to the philosophical theologian or to the simple and pious believer, each of whom tends to simplify his faith and reduce it to fundamentals. To the historian, however, they will seem highly significant, for he will recognize them as the outward

Elisabeth Kübler-Ross' 1969 *On Death and Dying* offered a seminal statement on the psychology of mourning death that today still shapes numerous disciplines' perspectives on dying, though clearly not written from a theological viewpoint.[58] Kübler-Ross intimates one motivation for her study: "If all of us would make an all-out effort to contemplate our own death, to deal with the anxieties surrounding the concept of our death, and to help others familiarize themselves with these thoughts, perhaps there could be less destructiveness around us."[59] The tactic of familiarity with the enemy death that Kübler-Ross employs clearly yields a conclusion distinct from the goal of the same defense tendered from a theological perspective.

Such a pulling back of the curtain of public discussion regarding death and dying, however, did prompt publication of a collective work that same year. *The Dying Patient* "contained a bibliography of 340 titles published after 1955, all in English, on the subject of dying, as distinct from funerals, cemeteries, or mourning."[60] Certainly fruitful study may be derived from all the above mentioned works; however, none of them appears to have as its chief end engaging a biblical portrait of death as the delimiter of the value of human life in light of its idolization.

Systematic Theologies

Personal eschatology, the locus of systematic theology that addresses end of life issues, is typically included at the end of dogmatics or systematic theologies. To what degree, then, do these texts engage death as it pertains to the

---

signs of changes, all the more profound because unnoticed, in the idea that people in general, not just Christians, have had of their destiny" (95–96). Ariès' logic suggests that if mankind's understanding of humanity's "destiny" is ever evolving, then its fundamental understanding of answers to any of life's ultimate questions is equally fluid, regardless of which Authority one asserts.

58. Kübler-Ross, *On Death and Dying*. Helmut Thielicke insightfully remarks regarding Kübler-Ross' work (referring to its German title, *Interviews mit Sterbenden* [Interviews with the dying], so titled due to the 500 interviews conducted by Kübler-Ross for her study), that such works still do not contradict "the fact that the reality guarded by this taboo [of death] may sometimes be very interesting to us, and that there are authors of both books and movies who enter its sphere and without breaking the seal enunciate the questions that it poses." This profound insight gives us a picture of just how cunning is the enemy death; it may even be closely examined by disciplinary paradigms that still fail to yield its true significance as ordained by its Master. See Thielicke, *Living with Death*, 30.

59. Kübler-Ross, *On Death and Dying*, 27.

60. Ariès, *Hour of Our Death*, 589. See also Feifel, *Meaning of Death*.

ethic and value of human life? The following will survey several reputable representative dogmatics to determine the answer to that question.

Charles Hodge. In volume 2 of his three-volume *Systematic Theology* Charles Hodge extensively treats theological anthropology, including discussions on the genesis, unity, and constitution of man both as originally created and after the Fall. He affirms that "death is the penal consequence" of Adam's and Eve's rebellion; they were not created mortal, as the Pelagians avow.[61] In the course of a paragraph, Hodge equates sin with mortality and every consequent form of evil, contrasts the blessedness of life with the misery of death (physical and spiritual), and notes the redemption from death that Christ provides.

In volume 3, in his section on eschatology, Hodge addresses the state of the soul after death. Here he affirms that the notion of a future embodied life is taught in both testaments. Further, God's progressive revelation in the New Testament substantiates an intermediate state between death and a general resurrection. There the deceased experience either blissful glory or miserable torment, consciously yet temporarily, until the return of Christ for final judgment. Hodge rejects "Romish doctrines" of purgatory and limbo. Beyond these things Hodge appears to regard any further understanding of the nature of death as common knowledge, very much the same way Hermann Schultz—whom Hodges quotes affirmatively—grants that "all the books of the Old Testament assume that men are in some way or other to live after death. . . . It is not taught, but assumed as self-evident truth, immanent in the consciousness of the people."[62]

Louis Berkhof. In his nearly eight hundred-page *Systematic Theology* Louis Berkhof occupies less than two pages in the section on hamartiology to delineate that death, as a consequence and punishment of sin, is comprised of physical, spiritual, and eternal components. Physical death is not natural, but a part of the penalty of sin. It is the dissolution of body and soul. Spiritual death entails the pollution of sin and separation from the living God because of sin. Eternal death means complete separation from God, yet simultaneous incursion of the full wrath of God.[63] In his

---

61. Hodge, *Systematic Theology*, 2:115–20; cf. 248–49.

62. Ibid., 3:719; for Hodge's full treatment of life after death including resurrection, see 713–89. See also Schultz, *Die Voraussetzungen der christlichen Lehre*, 207.

63. Berkhof, *Systematic Theology*, 226, 259–60. Berkhof does not flesh out what he means by the terminology "separation from God." One must assume that he refers more precisely to separation from any grace of God for the experiencing of the *presence* of holy God in unrelenting wrath.

section on general eschatology Berkhof devotes about twenty-five pages to individual or personal eschatology in which he addresses physical death, immortality of the soul, and the intermediate condition (including purgatory and psychopannychia) as part of the discussion regarding all those who have died prior to the parousia, both believer and unbeliever. Here he notes that "It is quite impossible to say exactly what death is," but we do know that it "means a break in the natural relations of life."[64]

Millard Erickson. In his *Christian Theology* Millard Erickson essentially follows Berkhof regarding thanatology as evidenced by his frequent citation or direct quotation of Berkhof as well as his echoing Berkhof's dissection of death into physical, spiritual, and eternal components. Like Berkhof, Erickson also addresses death in terms of individual eschatology in a section that follows cosmic eschatology. He also discusses virtually all the same foci found in Berkhof. He affirms, too, that death, as a direct consequence of Adam's sin, is not natural. Adam and Eve were constituted with contingent immortality rather than inherent immortality. That is, similar to Augustine's distinction between being "mortal" versus "subject to death," Adam would have lived forever had he not sinned.[65]

---

64. Ibid., 668, cf. 668–94.

65. Erickson, *Christian Theology*, 452, 628–30, 1172–90. While not intending disrespect for Erickson's contribution, note must be made here of a lack of linguistic and/or conceptual precision in his treatment of thanatology. First, Erickson repeats, no fewer than six times, Berkhof's notion of eternal death as *separation from the presence of God*, but also like Berkhof, he does not flesh-out the meaning of such phraseology or the implications of such imprecise wording. Upon a single usage of the wording (as in Berkhof) one may assume the common understanding of "separation from the *gracious* presence of God"; but failure to explicate the wording given six self-provided opportunities could perhaps be emended in a subsequent edition. Second, Erickson suggests that "God himself sees death as an evil and *a frustration of his original plan*"; yet in the same paragraph, and without explaining the apparent contradiction or how God's purposes may be "frustrated," Erickson writes that God himself is the one who sent death—this frustration of his own plan (1177; emphasis added). Third, Erickson seems to equivocate over whether heaven is a place. Amid a discussion concerning the nature of the bodily resurrected saints' eternal communion with a God who is spirit, Erickson writes, "It would seem that heaven is a state, a spiritual condition, rather than a place" (1239). Fourth, Erickson's treatment of paedosoterism evidences less than precise conceptual care. He roundly argues, on the one hand, that "all begin life with both the corrupted nature and the guilt that are the consequences of sin" (654), yet on the other hand, and without either substantial theological reflection or careful scriptural exegesis, that "Although they [infants] have made no conscious choice of Christ's work (or Adam's sin for that matter), the spiritual effects of the curse are negated in their case" (655–56). When Erickson states that his reasoning "does not rest upon merely a sentimental impulse" (654), his treatment of the subject here provides no substantial evidence to support that assertion. This issue of paedosoterism will be addressed in

One deviation Erickson makes from Berkhof (though he fails to substantiate either his criticism of Berkhof or his own opposing view) concerns the answer to the question, why do Christians die? Berkhof hypothesized that God uses death as one of many means of sanctification and proving of believers' faith.[66] Erickson asserts that Berkhof's "effort . . . appears to be a somewhat strained explanation." He continues, "A better approach is simply to consider death one of the conditions of humanity as now constituted; in this respect, death is like birth."[67] Implications of Berkhof's suggestion as well as a rejoinder to Erickson will be presented in chapter 4 of this work where the question will be treated in more detail.

Robert Reymond. Like Berkhof, Robert Reymond, in a section on anthropology and seven effects of the Fall in his *A New Systematic Theology of the Christian Faith*, mentions death as a result of Adam's first transgression.[68] After a passing mention of death as the state from which many will be glorified,[69] Reymond's next discussion of death comes in the section on general eschatology. He gives no special attention to personal eschatology as does Berkhof. Any mentions of the end of the individual are subsumed in the state of the group. About five pages are devoted to the intermediate and future states of the deceased.[70] Apart from the important discussion on the redemptive purposes of Christ's death,[71] as well as a lengthy section on the debate between eternal punishment versus annihilationism,[72] Reymond gives no further attention to thanatology. In none of his discussions is the origin, nature, or weight of death given significant attention. Reymond, like many of his contemporaries, appears to assume his readers' concurrence with him that the nature and significance of death need be given no further attention than understanding that it is the cessation of life as we know it in exchange for either the "sheer rapture" of heaven or the "sheer horror" of hell.[73]

more detail in chap. 6 of this work.

66. Berkhof, *Systematic Theology*, 670–71. So also, Grudem, *Systematic Theology*, 810–12.

67. Erickson, *Christian Theology*, 1179.

68. Reymond, *New Systematic Theology*, 449.

69. Ibid., 795. Reymond includes here a footnote regarding the origin and development of the Catholic doctrine of purgatory.

70. Ibid., 1017–22.

71. Ibid., 627–69.

72. Ibid., 1068–85.

73. Ibid., 1068. In deference to Reymond and others, however, one must consider the task and space limitations of a systematic theology, despite "creative license" to take various excurses.

Wayne Grudem. Wayne Grudem's nearly thirteen-hundred-page *Systematic Theology* contains fifteen pages of thoughtful commentary on death and the intermediate state, primarily addressing the experience of believers. In addition to proposing an answer to why Christians die, Grudem treats the intermediate state, including soul sleep and purgatory, and Christ's ultimate defeat of the last enemy. Of the systematic theologies surveyed, only Grudem gives particular attention to the ethic of human life in contrast to the higher ethic of obedience and faithfulness to God.[74] Citing passages like Acts 20:24; 21:13; 25:11; and Rev 2:10–11, Grudem contends (for three paragraphs) that "[o]ur obedience to God is more important than preserving our own lives." He concludes, "Even in times where there is little persecution and little likelihood of martyrdom, it would be good for us to fix this truth in our minds once for all, for if we are willing to give up even our lives for faithfulness to God, we shall find it much easier to give up everything else for the sake of Christ as well."[75]

Herman Bavinck. Herman Bavinck[76] most edifyingly engages a conversation on the nature of man in volume two of his significant *Reformed Dogmatics* (originally published 1895–1901). In typical reformed theological fashion, he affirms death as a consequence of Adam's sin and that death is communicated to all humanity because of humanity's unity with Adam as its federal head. Contrary to the assertion of Rome, death would not have been the natural terminus of man apart from God's granting him at creation a *donum superadditum* ("superadded gift") that rendered him "engraced or pleasing to God,"[77] though "before the fall, our first parents did not yet enjoy the eternal heavenly Sabbath; the state of integrity was not the state of glory."[78] That is, as Augustine had noted adroitly, a very important distinction exists between "the ability not to sin (*posse non peccare*) and not to die (*posse non mori*), which Adam possessed, and the inability to sin (*non posse peccare*) and the inability to die (*non posse mori*), gifts that were to be bestowed along with the glorification of the first man in case of obedience and now granted to the elect out of grace."[79]

---

74. Other notable systematic theologies were reviewed but articulate nothing distinct from the views mentioned here.

75. Grudem, *Systematic Theology*, 813; see also Sherlock, *Practical Discourse*, 111.

76. Bavinck's analysis is located out of chronological order here, last in this survey of systematic theologies, due to his more comprehensive address of the nature of death than all of the others, which better illuminates the weight of death for the topic at hand.

77. Bavinck, *Reformed Dogmatics*, 2:539–40.

78. Ibid., 563.

79. Ibid., 560, 566. See also Augustine, *City of God*, 22:30; Augustine, *Literal*

Bavinck's dialogue with death occurs next in volume 3 entitled *Sin and Salvation in Christ* where he spends about three pages under the heading "Death" in his chapter on the punishment of sin.[80] Here he delineates that, according to Gen 2:17 and 3:19, the full execution of the penalty against sin is not merely physical death; for there is a sense in which death was in fact immediate upon transgression. Also, contrary to the Pelagians, Socinians, Rationalists, and many theologians of Bavinck's day, death is not to be viewed as natural.[81] "In the perishability of life, we see the manifestation of the judgment of God (Pss 90:7–12)."[82]

Bavinck briefly surveys a few peoples (e.g., "people of nature [*natuurvolken*]," [sic] romantics, stoics, etc.) who, although they "recognize in death an unnatural power and flee from it as long as they can," nonetheless accept death without fear because of their (faulty) belief that "death of humans is a logical and natural consequence of their existence." Bavinck then concludes the section by arguing against the assertion of science on its own terms. If matter and energy are immortal (viz. the first law of thermodynamics), and the individual human composition is biologically renewed every seven years, "Why then is the physical organism that is composed of such materials and forces and cells mortal?" Why indeed do cells decay? Moreover, why does death occur more often not as a result of "the decline of one's vital powers"—i.e., old age (particularly in Bavinck's day[83])—but as a result of illness or accident of some sort? Bavinck concludes—as must the scientist—that "Death is a mystery in the full sense of the word."[84]

Later in volume 3, in separate sections on Christ's humiliation and exaltation, Bavinck again discusses death. The latter section may be

---

Meaning of Genesis, 3:2; 6:25; Augustine, *Admonition and Grace*; Augustine, *Enchiridion*, 104–07; Augustine, *Against Julian*, 5:58; 6:5.

80. Bavinck, *Reformed Dogmatics*, 3:182–84.

81. In a footnote Bavinck lists the following: F. Schleiermacher, *Christian Faith* §59; R. A. Lipsius, §414. A. Ritschl, *Christian Doctrine of Justification and Reconciliation*, III, 345ff.; J. Kaftan, *Dogmatik*, §29; Smend, *Lehrbuch der alttestamentlichen Relgionsgeschichte* [sic], 504; Marti, *Geschichte der israelitischen Religion*, 193; Clemen, *Sünde*, I, 233ff.; Köberle, *Sünde und Gnade im religiösen*, 54; Matthes, "De Inrichting van den Eeredienst bij Jerobeam, I Kon. 12:26–33," 239–54; Beth, "Über Ursache und Zweck des Todes," 285–304, and 335–48 demonstrates that science has not up to this point been able to explain the riddle of death but considers death to be natural to all earthly creatures and subordinates all exegesis of Scripture to this point of view. See Bavinck, *Sin and Salvation in Christ*, 183 n. 45.

82. Bavinck, *Sin and Salvation in Christ*, 184.

83. For details of European and New England mortality rates of the eighteenth and nineteenth centuries, see Stannard, *Puritan Way of Death*, 55–56, 101–2, 152, 176.

84. Bavinck, *Sin and Salvation in Christ*, 184–85.

summarized as Bavinck's discussion of Christ's victory over death as the avenue to resurrected life for himself and the renewed humanity now sanctified for covenant relationship with God through federal union with the last—i.e., consummate—Adam.[85] The former section, undoubtedly and fittingly, includes Bavinck's most enriching and poignant statements about the nature of death found in any of the four volumes. Here death is noted as the culmination of Christ's humiliation. In this section, which skillfully refutes what the Reformed consider errant interpretations (even by a significant number of church fathers) of the *descendit ad inferna* clause of the Apostles' Creed, Bavinck seizes this perfect opportunity to define the nature of death as tasted by Christ. The nuances and pathos of death articulated by Bavinck warrant quoting him at length here.

> [T]he Roman Catholic doctrine of satisfaction was totally concentrated on Christ's physical suffering and death, and no need was felt for a suffering by Christ in his rational soul, for his dying a spiritual death, for his undergoing unspeakable distress and hellish torments in the work of salvation. But Scripture speaks of Christ's "soul-suffering" in language that is much too strong (Matt. 26:37–38; 27:46; Mark 14:33–34; 15:34; Luke 22:44; John 12:27; Heb. 5:7–8) for it to be restricted to his sensitive soul [i.e., the *sensing*, in contrast to merely the *rational* facet of Christ's soul]. Many Catholics, accordingly, acknowledge that Christ's rational soul was nevertheless in some indirect fashion—through resistance, management, or sympathy—involved in his suffering. And all the Reformed without exception opposed the opinion of Catholics, confessing that Christ bore the wrath of God and tasted the spiritual death of his abandonment also in his soul, although there was no room there for the most horrid element in the punishment, for self-accusation, remorse, or despair. But all this does not in any way alter the other fact that the state of death in which Christ entered when he died was as essentially a part of his humiliation as his spiritual suffering on the cross. In both together he completed his perfect obedience. He drank the cup of suffering to the last drop and tasted death in all its bitterness in order to completely deliver us from the fear of death and death itself. Thus he destroyed him who had the power of death and by a single offering perfected for all time those who are sanctified (Heb 10:14).[86]

---

85. Ibid., 418.
86. Ibid., 417.

Certainly the consummate death that Christ tasted ὑπὲρ παντὸς (Heb 2:9) left *nothing* unatoned that the Father intended to reconcile.[87]

Bavinck's final discussion of death comes in the final volume of his *Dogmatics* entitled *Holy Spirit, Church, and New Creation*.[88] Over the course of several chapters Bavinck provides not a full thanatology, but material germane to how "The Spirit Makes All Things New"—the title of the section on eschatology. Here Bavinck discusses the state and condition of the dead from the event of death through to the resurrection. He unpacks notions such as immortality, provisional versus consummate terminus after death, the location of the dead, including development of a local division between the righteous and unrighteous dead, purgatory, psychopannychism, implications of the communion of the saints (*ecclesia triumphans, patiens*, and *militans*), resurrection of the body, judgment, and the Beatific Vision.

While Bavinck commendably gives great care to the topic of death as it impinges upon other systematic theological loci, the fact remains that his intent is never to address the nature of death as an ordinance and instrument under the direction of the sovereign God to delimit the value and ethic of human life against the sin of biolatry.

Treatises on Life and Death

Helmut Thielicke. Several texts do provide a theological treatment of death in attempt to re-familiarize our contemporary culture with conceptions of the subject that have become so distant to us. Among them are Helmut Thielicke's originally anonymously published *Death and Life* and the revised version *Living with Death*.[89] In these works Thielicke contemplates deeply

---

87. The death that Christ experienced had to be equal in every degree to the death that any human being could possibly experience in order to render redemption efficacious as well as make true the statement that Christ tasted death ὑπὲρ παντὸς. Gregory of Nazianzus argued similarly regarding the incarnation of the divine Son, "The unassumed is the unhealed, but what is united with God is also being saved." See Gregory of Nazianzus, "Letter 101," in *On God and Christ*, 158. Aloys Grillmeier translates the same phrase, "That which is not taken is not healed, but whatever is united to God is saved"; see Grillmeier, *Christ in Christian Tradition*, 1:321; cf. 115, 321, 351.

88. Bavinck, *Reformed Dogmatics*, 4:589–730.

89. Thielicke, *Living with Death*, ix. As Thielicke (1908–1986) discloses in the preface of the revised work, the original work was composed during "the horrors of aerial bombardment and the dictatorship" of war torn Germany. Because Thielicke "was forbidden to travel, speak, or write at the time," due to scrutiny of his activity with the Confessing Church, the work could not be published in Germany. So, a manuscript was smuggled to Switzerland, where it was anonymously published by Oikumene (Geneva) and used in theological instruction courses for German prisoners of war around the

the personal character of death,[90] arguing that at the heart of personhood is relations, among which the relation to God is paramount. Both physical and spiritual death, in different senses respectively, impact the human being's relation to God. Thielicke concludes that meaningful human life transcends mere *bios*; it is *zoe*—life with God.[91]

Karl Rahner. Karl Rahner's *On the Theology of Death* treats the Catholic Church's doctrine of death in detail, though it is not a full biblical thanatology; Rahner himself says such a task is an impossibility.[92] Because he has constrained his work to Catholic dogma, Rahner admits that his method "does not permit a systematic presentation of the theory"; and further that "an attempt to begin with a full, systematic theology of death would lead, unavoidably, to a neglect of the explicit doctrine of the Church in favour of private theological *theoremata*"[93]—a hesitation that does not so constrain fellow Jesuit theologian Michael Simpson. In his own treatise (summarized below), Simpson, after quoting Rahner here, avers, "I believe that it is only by opening personal theological investigations to the discussion and criticism of others that there can be a development in real theological understanding for the deepening of one's faith."[94] Nevertheless, Rahner thoughtfully[95] treats

---

world. The "completely rewritten" version derives from Thielicke's lectures to all the faculties at the University of Hamburg, where Thielicke founded and served as dean and professor of the theology school. The revised version retains the pathos of his own brushes with death experienced during the war as well as "dark periods of sickness," likely as a result of ongoing complications from thyroid surgery.

90. By "personal nature/character of death" Thielicke refers to the weighted reality of death as it impacts the *personal* individual in contrast to the generic *im*personal notion, "it is people that die, not I myself" (Thielicke, *Living with Death*, 23, 125), or Kübler-Ross's "It was the other guy, not me, I made it" (Kübler-Ross, *On Death and Dying*, 27). Further, "we cannot isolate [death] again as a biological phenomenon but have to understand it in terms of the history between our I and God's Thou in which it stands" (Thielicke, 127). Citing Luke 12:16–34, Thielicke defines the human person in terms of the question, "What is left of you and your being when you are subjected to the subtraction of death?" (Thielicke, 16; cf. 84–84, 120).

91. Thielicke, *Living with Death*, 153.

92. Though Rahner comments not from within a Protestant evangelical framework, his contribution provides keen insights concerning Roman Catholic notions of thanatology, as well as a nuanced view of the question of Adam and Eve's mortality at their creation (a view that will be addressed in chap. 2). He also treats the issue of martyrdom—integral to thanatology—where Protestant systematic theologies do not.

93. Rahner, *Theology of Death*, 18–19.

94. Simpson, *Death and Eternal Life*, 10.

95. Rahner's treatment of this doctrine is a thoughtful but ultimately unconvincing response to the Protestant understanding of death in its entirety as introduced by Adam's sin.

Rome's consideration of death as a natural phenomenon, the physical and spiritual facets of death, the import of the unity of the Christian's death with Christ's, then concludes with an important epilogue on martyrdom—the consummate dying that is "the act of freedom," a testimony to the lifelong dying of the Christian witness.[96]

Michael Simpson. With "considerable originality" Michael Simpson peers into life after death in his attempt to understand the apostle Paul's affirmation that "no eye has seen nor ear heard, nor the heart of man conceived the destiny God has prepared for those who love him" (1 Cor 2:9). *The Theology of Death and Eternal Life*[97] begins with a historical survey of both Catholic and Protestant eschatological thought within the church. As mentioned above, Simpson moves beyond Rahner's Catholic dogma, but fails to treat his subject with Rahner's rigor. Like Rahner, however, Simpson does not attempt a full biblical thanatology. Rather, he investigates biblical teachings concerning negative and positive aspects of death, the transformation that occurs at the resurrection, judgment, and an eternal afterlife that qualitatively transcends the current spatio-temporal realm with distinct implications for both believer and unbeliever.

Ray Anderson. Ray Anderson's *Theology, Death and Dying* has already been mentioned.[98] While more of an *ars moriendi* (as opposed to a biblical thanatology) Anderson very insightfully directs our thinking about death and dying in accord with the biblical articulation of the dignity of human personhood in the experience of death. That is, the experience of death is infinitely more than the termination of biological functions. Attendants of death—whether the dying, himself, or mourners—must not neglect the multifaceted theological significance of what is occurring at (human) death. Numerous implications apply, not the least of which include the single most significant transition of an image bearer of God,[99] the execution of God's Gen 2:17 promise, the solidarity of members of the human race with one another (not to mention with the created order) as their finitude is irresistibly exhibited, and the inescapable provocation to contemplate transcendent meaning beyond our parochial immanence.

---

96. Rahner, *Theology of Death*, 92–93, 104–5; cf. 89–127.
97. Simpson, *Death and Eternal Life*.
98. Anderson, *Theology, Death and Dying*.
99. Of course, one may argue that the single most significant transition a human being may make is the transition from death to life that occurs when one is born again by faith in Jesus Christ—that transition determining the final outcome of the transition of death. However, in terms of the reconstitution of human nature that takes place at death—body and soul—and that nature's cosmic reorientation, no other event can compare.

Paul Helm. Also notable is the chapter in Paul Helm's *The Last Things: Death, Judgment, Heaven, Hell* entitled "Death and Dying."[100] In his treatment of personal eschatology, Helm contributes to the dialogue with death for our contemporary setting by instructing on matters such as the assurance of God's meticulous providence over death, the unnaturalness of death, and the hope and faith the Christian may have in the actual experiencing of death as well as the promised resurrection to follow.

Derivative Works

Numerous other works address some of the derivative issues mentioned above such as Old Testament[101] and New Testament studies of death and/or the state of the dead in the afterlife,[102] godly living in light of the brevity of life, dying well,[103] theological anthropology, and eschatology.[104]

---

100. Helm, *Last Things*.

101. Cribb, "Speaking on the Brink of Sheol." Cribb performs a form critical analysis of nine Old Testament death accounts in order to assert that "a definable and distinct genre of death story" exists in the Old Testament from which we may glean theological significance. Apart from a survey of similarities between Israelite and ANE death traditions, Cribb's study does not share direction with the current work. Jarvis Williams also submitted a doctoral dissertation to The Southern Baptist Theological Seminary in which he exegetes several key Old Testament and Maccabean texts on voluntary death for the benefit of another. Williams argues "how martyr traditions informed Paul's theology of atonement and why their influence on his theology of atonement does not undermine the soteriological value of Jesus' death for the nations." So, neither does Williams' thesis focus on death in light of a biblical portrait of the value and ethic of human life, as endeavored here. See Williams, "Maccabean Martyr Traditions in Paul's Theology of Atonement."

102. Küng, *Eternal Life?*

103. Several *ars moriendi* still exist in print—though no longer in circulation. Examples of scholarly *ars moriendi* are Reinis, *Reforming the Art of Dying*; Kiernan, *Last Rites*. A host of popular level variations on *ars moriendi* (e.g., in the genre of hospice or "dignity in dying" movements or pastoral care) are in current publication; but because they intend the more specific focus of consoling either the bereaved or the dying, their purpose is not to treat a biblical theological import of the nature of death. For examples of evangelical works on consoling the bereaved or dying see Lewis, *Grief Observed*; Moll, *Art of Dying*; Duncan, *Fear Not*.

104. For discussions of theological anthropology, see Hoekema, *Created in God's Image*; Prokes, *Toward a Theology of the Body*; Pannenberg, *Anthropology in Theological Perspective*; Cooper, *Body, Soul, and Life Everlasting*; Robinson, *The Body*; Shults, *Reforming Theological Anthropology*; Green, *What about the Soul?*; Jeeves, *From Cells to Souls*; Murphy, "Nonreductive Physicalism"; Flew, *New Approach to Psychical Research*. For discussions of eschatology, see Bultmann, *History and Eschatology*; Ratzinger, *Eschatology*; Balthasar, "Eschatology."

Summary

Certainly other works treat any number of related concerns. None of the works surveyed for this study, however, appear to center their interests on death as the indispensable scalpel in the hand of a master surgeon performing a life-giving operation. Indeed, none of them casts death as the fragrant antidote to the sin of biolatry, nor appears to recognize that such a sin even exists. On these grounds the current work appears to be warranted.

Scope of the Current Work

Ask any commanding general for key counsel in tactical warfare and he will likely advise, "Know your enemy." The apostle Paul—a Holy Spirit gifted spiritual war general—counseled likewise concerning our intelligence of the strategies of "him who had the power of death, that is, the devil" (Heb 2:14).[105] The apostle admonished vigilance "so that no advantage would be taken of us by Satan, for *we are not ignorant of his schemes*" (2 Cor 2:11, emphasis added). One of the most instructive ways to be a student of one's enemy is to grasp the import of that enemy's origins. For that reason this work will share with a biblical thanatology the initial priority of debriefing intelligence about the origin of death.

At root of much of our culture's antipathy toward death is not a lack of professed knowledge regarding death's introduction into our world as much as it is an unfamiliarity with its holy origin. The more any culture secularizes, the more distant it becomes from that which is transcendent. Unfortunately, that same distancing distances culture from concern about and answers to ultimate questions—questions (and answers) that transcend any culture's parochial circumstance. Only that which transcends the immanent can comment on the parochial with any ultimate meaning. The better acquainted we are with the holy, righteous, and good purposes for the inception of death, the more unintimidated we will be to dialogue with this enemy, having vanquished the "inner sense of bankruptcy before this sacred, and impenetrable immensity."[106] Chapter 2, therefore, will begin the discussion with an examination of the origin of death.

Because divine revelation is the basic epistemological axiom, the Old and New Testaments of the Bible will serve respectively as the intelligence

---

105. The apostle Paul is not being insinuated as the author of the letter to the Hebrews. The Hebrews reference here intends no more than to show that the enemy against which the apostle warns is one and the same as him who had the power of death.

106. Anderson, *Theology, Death and Dying*, 18.

base for the next two chapters' discussion of the enemy, death. The Old Testament provides revelation of God's interaction with humanity including his covenant relations with certain of them. The foundations of death, then, as revealed to and understood by these covenant members of humanity, will serve as infinitely reliable intelligence. In fact, one of the chief purposes of God's disclosure to these initial covenant families is so that through them the remainder of the human family also might have access to God's sole provision of rescue from the death that he himself instituted universally, millennia before many of those to be rescued even existed.[107]

These Old Testament covenant families firmly held the notion of the relationship between life as the favor of God and death as the disfavor and curse of God. Understanding why they held this view is foundational for understanding the Old Testament's portrait of death. This portrait is also a necessary precursor to the biblical storyline of redemption. Although the Old Testament uses language such as "the way of all the earth" (Josh 23:14; 1 Kgs 2:2) to describe it, death is never dismissed merely as some innocuous facet of the natural cycle of all life in the universe to be accepted—no questions asked. Death is not natural; it is not the way things are supposed to be.[108] Death is indeed an enemy. To be sure, however, the biblical tension is that it is an institution equally ordained with good intentions by the created order's holy God—good intentions, by the way, that both *are* good (Ps 119:68) and *will* consummate in ultimate good (Isa 45:10)—incomparably to many derelict creaturely good intentions.

Regarding the notion of an afterlife, many have asserted that the Old Testament is predominantly silent and that the concern of the Israelite, rather, is the blessedness of this knowable life. Some have gone even too far in suggesting that no concept at all of life after death can be ascertained therefore from the Old Testament Scriptures.[109] This latter proposal will be proven insubstantial. One thing we can affirm is that Old Testament Israel strongly hoped in her God that whatever came after this life would entail the blessedness of communion with her covenant Lord for the faithful as well as

---

107. See Gen 12:3 (cf. Gen 18:18–19) and 10:32, where the same word מִשְׁפָּחָה, *mishpachah*, "families" is used respectively both of the "families" that God promised to rescue from death through Abraham's offspring, and of the progeny of Noah—i.e., all the "families" of humanity. See also 1 Cor 10:11–14, where a recapitulation of the covenant families' overindulgences in the present life, and the consequences that followed, closes with the admonition to all those who would learn from their mistakes to "flee from idolatry [perhaps even read *biolatry*]."

108. See Plantinga, *Not the Way It's Supposed to Be*.

109. Gaster, *IDB*, 787A. Contra this assertion, see Wright, *Resurrection of the Son of God*, 103–206; Tromp, *Primitive Conceptions*, 4, cf. 196.

his punishment for the guilty—i.e., those who rejected him as Lord.[110] Here in this covenantal promise of eternal communion with God is the groundwork laid for what the church would later come to describe as the Beatific Vision of God.

Anticipation of that vision is advanced in the progressed revelation[111] of God found in the New Testament. Chapter 4, then, will undertake the task of examining the New Testament's far more detailed—though still not exhaustive—revelation about death. Here is where, because of the Messiah's advent to disclose to us the Father as well as the mysteries of his will undisclosed to date by the provisional revelation of himself in the Old Testament, intelligence on the enemy death is made much more readily available to us. In fact, disclosed to us in the New Testament is the full demise of death, having been vanquished utterly by Jesus Christ—God the Son incarnate.[112]

---

110. The Book of the Law along with the Ten Commandments constitute Israel as a nation (cf. Deut 31:26). Exodus 20 and Deut 5 ground Israel's covenant relationship with her God. Foundational in Israel's understanding of God's relationship with humanity is that he is the Sovereign Judge, "who keeps lovingkindness for thousands, who forgives iniquity, transgression and sin; yet he will by no means leave the guilty unpunished, visiting the iniquity of fathers on the children and on the grandchildren to the third and fourth generations" (Exod 34:7; Num 14:18). The parallel passages Exod 20:5 and Deut 5:9 qualify the blessing with the words "to those who love me and keep my commandments"—concerning the faithful and favored; and the curse with the words "of those who hate me [elliptically, "and disregard my commandments"]"—concerning the faithless and guilty. Because Israel equated death as punishment for "iniquity, transgression and sin," yet God's covenant promised forgiveness of this guilt, Israel would have had to have some notion of God's remission of that punishment after death if God's promise of communion with the forgiven was to hold.

111. As Heb 1:1 notes, God's Old Testament revelation was πολυμερῶς, *little by little*, or *on many occasions*, and πολυτρόπως, *in many ways*. See Nestle, *Novum Testamentum Graece*, 146–47; Bauer, BAGD, s. v. "πολυμερως" and "πολυτρόπως"; Koester, *Hebrews*, 177. In addition to the diverse qualities of divine wisdom, these terms speak of the progressive nature of God's self-disclosure as well as the capacity for both judgment and blessing in such revelation. The progressive nature of God's self-disclosure under the old covenant indicates that "God had provided something better for us [new covenant citizens of God's kingdom], so that apart from us they [old covenant citizens of God's kingdom] would not be made perfect" (Heb 11:40); that is, the consummate self-disclosure of God in the old age would not occur until the institution of the prophesied new covenant (see Isa 59:21; Jer 31:31–34; Ezek 16:60–63; 36:22–38; 37:24–28). So, not only is *illumination* regarding death (and other biblical teachings) more clear in the New Testament than in the Old Testament, but also God's *revelation* of himself and his plan has progressed.

112. Heb 2:14–15 asserts the very point that with the advent of Jesus Christ, the proclamation of "D-Day" is made and freedom is won for the families of humanity. The text reads, "Therefore, since the children share in flesh and blood, he himself likewise also partook of the same, that through death he might render powerless him who had the power of death, that is, the devil, and might free those who through fear of death

Death itself has been given a lethal injection such that all the families of the earth may be rescued from its otherwise insurmountable threat. The holy and gracious God, who justly instituted death against humanity in the first place, also simultaneously ordained escape from his wrath of death for any who would simply believe that he has done so. Intelligence gathered from the New Testament revelation, therefore, has the capacity to equip the families of humanity with weaponry against death that renders this enemy not only impotent, but even gain for those whose "earnest expectation and hope" (Phil 1:18–21) is in the truth declared by this intelligence. Moreover, warlike engagement of this truth is no mere impact on the individual. The family of humanity thusly in covenant relationship with Almighty God armed with this *memento mori* and *contemptu mundi* can, without covetous concern for self, transform this world—as it has done in ages past—by emanating God's splendor throughout his dominion.[113] Such armament is necessary for engaging the subject matter of the subsequent chapters.

Having surveyed biblical truths about death,[114] chapter 5 will provide an exhibition of the lauding of God in his ordinance of death by the valiant martyrs of the early Church Militant, who by their faithful witness ascended the Golden Stair to become the Church Triumphant. The apostle Paul's admonition concerning at least one rationale for the divinely appointed recording of the history of God's providential superintendence of the revelatory events among his covenant people Israel could also well apply here to the accounts of the passion of members of Christ's body in the church's infancy. Paul affirms that "these things happened to them as an example, and they were written for our instruction, upon whom the ends of the ages have come" (1 Cor 10:6, 11). That is, not only is contemplation of one's own end instructive for living in the present, but also eminently instructive is reflection on and following the examples of those who avowedly affirmed the ordinance of God above the value of their own lives and whose faithful witness to Truth has been attested with their own blood.

Death is an enemy. As such, it makes war relentlessly, indiscriminately. To be sure, death is no sentient enemy, despite the reasoned personification

---

were subject to slavery all their lives." See also Col 2:12–15.

113. Cf. Acts 17:6 where the accusation is made of Paul, Silas, and the early Church Militant that they "have turned the world upside down," ESV, AV; and Col 1:6 where of this gospel is said "in all the world also it is constantly bearing fruit and increasing"; and Hab 2:14 and Isa 11:9 where the proclamation is made that "the earth will be filled with the knowledge of the glory of the LORD as the waters cover the sea."

114. Regarding purported "truth" in titular form, see MacArthur, *Safe*. The subtitle is certainly debatable, considering the contents of the little book assuredly written with good intentions. A rejoinder to the thesis of this book is included here in chapter 6.

of death in Scripture[115] and so here. The providence of death occurs nowhere beyond the divine appointment of the sovereign God of the Bible. At this juncture of God's sovereignty and the reality of unanticipated death—both physical and spiritual—one encounters some of divine revelation's most difficult sayings. Because of this dilemma, and because death "never says, 'Enough'" (Prov 30:16), and because the import of Christ's having "tasted death for everyone" (Heb 2:9) at least partially entails the defeat of every facet of death that could bring injury in any ultimate sense for the believer, one cannot, one must not avoid grappling with these very difficult truths of divine revelation. Chapter 6, then, will first briefly encourage biblical reflection on some of life's most tragic deaths. It will then take up the most difficult topic of infant death and perspectives on the eternal state of those dying in infancy or in some otherwise cognitively incompetent state. Obviously, no biblical thanatology should avoid this necessary conversation. Neither should any work, such as the current one, whose aim, again, is to admonish joyful embrace of a biblical portrait of the ethic of human life and death in relation to the infinitely greater ethic of the glory of the God who lords life and death in accord with his own infinitely good purposes.

The concluding chapter will propose that we understand death and God's instrumental use of it not as cause for contempt of ill-ordered circumstances, but as cause for the laud of God for his good and holy ordinance of death. In exercising such a disposition, which exalts God truthfully in all of his divine perfections—not merely those that placate anthropocentric sensibilities—and consistently humbles the creature to recognize both his creaturely finitude and his just due apart from the grace of the just Judge, is one means that God himself has provided for his refashioning *magnum opus* to mortify the cardinal sin of biolatry.

A proper perspective of the prospect of death ought also to lead every person to consider the poignant question posed by Francis Schaeffer, "How then shall we live?" If any meaning whatsoever is to be ascribed to a life lived under the sun, the steward of that life must seriously consider his own significance and end (Ps 90:10–12). Judgment based on how that steward has invested the gift given him will surely follow his promised end. Death, then, serves well as a megaphone[116] to call the living to attention concerning

---

115. Job 26:6; 28:22; Ps 49:14; Prov 30:16; Jer 9:21; Hos 13:14/1 Cor 15:55; Hab 2:5; Rev 6:8; cf. Job 18:13; Pss 18:4–5; 23:4; Prov 27:20; Isa 14:9; 28:18; 38:18.

116. Lewis, *Problem of Pain*, 93; see also Thielicke, *Living with Death*, 125. Thielicke writes, "In other words, a personal relation means that I must not complain against God when death comes. God is telling me something by it. In my death he is reacting to me. There is a message in it. I see God's hand and word aimed at me."

Further, Sherlock reflects on death as a divine governor. "Since the fall of man,

what they do with the life they now possess (John 9:4; Gal 2:20; 1 Tim 4:16). William Sherlock agrees.

> If it be certain that we must die, this should teach us frequently to think of Death, to keep it always in our eye and view. For, why should we cast off the thoughts of that which will certainly come, especially when it was so necessary to the good government of our lives, to remember that we must die? . . . and no man will practice [the wisdom that contemplation of one's mortality engenders], who does not often remember that he must die: but he that lives under a constant sense of Death, has a perpetual antidote against the follies and vanities of this world, and a perpetual spur to virtue.[117]

Theological implications of our view of death will also be considered. Our full confidence in the sovereignty of God should govern our every disposition and thought concerning death. If God is the Lord of life and death, then our worship of him ought to be reflected in our dialogue with death. Our ministry to the dying and/or bereaved ought to reflect an ecology of death and dying commensurate with the biblical revelation of the value of human life—no *less* valuable than biblically articulated, nor certainly any *more* valuable than biblically articulated.

---

mortality and Death is necessary to the good government of the world: nothing else can give check to some men's wickedness; but either the fear of Death, or the execution of it; some men are so outrageously wicked, that nothing can put a stop to them, and prevent that mischief they do in this world, but to cut them off: this is the reason of capital punishments among men, to remove those out of the world, who will be a plague Old Testament mankind while they live in it. For this reason God destroyed the whole race of mankind by a deluge of water, excepting Noah and his family, because they were incurably wicked." See Sherlock, *Practical Discourse*, 94–95.

117. Sherlock, *Practical Discourse*, 105.

CHAPTER 2

The Origin of Death

FROM THE BEGINNING OF creation, God intended an exhibition of his splendor in that creation.[1] His *magnum opus* is a creature made in his own image—man. After creating a host of other forms of life and being, the divine Trinity counseled,[2] "Let us make man in our image" (Gen 1:26).

> Then the Lord God formed man of dust from the ground, and breathed into his nostrils the breath of life; and man became a living being. (Gen 2:7)

Thus appeared for the first time as a "living being" (*nephesh*) man, God's premier creation—the only one in all of creation, in fact, that would reflect the radiance of God's multifaceted splendor and be an "icon" *in* creation of the essence of the living God (Heb 1:3).[3]

Amid the diversity of God's creation, humanity alone was fashioned as the image-bearer of the Creator. Because the One who fashioned human life in his own image has life in himself, so also was man to have life (John 5:21–27). The life of Adam, as the only creature made in the image of the

---

1. Cf. Gen 1:3 with 1 John 1:5; Isa 11:9; Hab 2:14.

2. The Trinity is implied by the Gen 1:26 phrase, "Let us make man in our image." If the "us/our" here refers to the godhead only, this reference is the Bible's first Trinitarian reference. Alternative arguments suggest the first person plural may refer to God and his heavenly court. The most significant objection to this assertion, however, is that the Bible nowhere suggests that man is made in the image of or by angels. For further discussion, see Calvin, *Commentary on Genesis*; Aalders, *Genesis*; Leupold, *Exposition of Genesis*, 182; Hoekema, *Created in God's Image*, 12–13.

3. For more on the notion of Jesus' incarnation as the "character" or "icon" of the Creator in creation, cf. Heb 10:1; Wis 7:26; 1 Cor 11:7; John 6:27; see also Moffat, *Critical and Exegetical Commentary on the Epistle to the Hebrews*, 9; Attridge, *Hebrews*, 41–48; Ellingworth, *Epistle to the Hebrews*, 96–100; Guthrie, *Letter to the Hebrews*, 65–67; France, *Hebrews*, 13:37–39.

Creator, was to reflect not merely physical animation, but a *quality* of life distinct from other living creatures and unique to the Giver of life himself.

> It is not a transitory life, and is therefore not to be conceived on the basis of the reality that is limited by death. As original life from God it is a primal datum, which is not derivable from any other given fact and does not allow of any immanent grounding.[4]

If death were the end of Adam, then, this quality of life would cease to be a reality in God's *magnum opus*, thereby nullifying God's intended purpose not only for the creation of man, but for all of creation (Rom 8:19–23). Provision for the continuation of "life" for Adam, therefore, must figure into God's original intention.

Life is a grant of God; its termination is an overturning of the proper order of God's original very good creation. That "life" is continued in some sense beyond death, then, is paramount not only in relation to immortality but also to resurrection.

> The idea of life comes to its fulfillment in the *notion of immortality*. . . . The idea of immortality expresses itself . . . in the picture of a continuing life of the soul [*nephesh*]. . . . The idea of life comes to expression . . . also in the picture of a material resurrection from the grave in the sense of a reconstituting of corporeality at the end of time.[5]

This "reconstituting of corporeality at the end of time" echoes both the original creation of man at the beginning and his inauguration into the renewed creation at his rebirth (i.e., when one is born again by faith allegiance with Jesus Christ, the consummate human). All of these events point toward the fulfillment of the purpose of the living God to exhibit his glory in creation by granting to his *magnum opus* that which he possesses in himself—namely, life. The intrinsic value of human life, then, because of its capacity to mirror uniquely the splendor of creation's Creator, is obviously vast and immeasurable.[6] Death, equally obviously, is a clear enemy of that

---

4. Kunneth, *Theology of the Resurrection*, 74. See also Pelikan, *Shape of Death*, 35, where Pelikan agrees, "Death acquires an inordinate importance if it is claimed that the total existence of a man is suddenly and irrevocably terminated when he dies."

5. Ibid., 34–35.

6. "Immeasurable" is not synonymous with "infinite." This distinction will receive fuller treatment in the next chapter.

end. Accordingly, death serves as the perfect foil to mark both the immeasurable value of human life and at the same time the relatively limited value of it.

Inexorable Law of Nature or Catastrophic Disorder?

Imagining the universe absent the reality of death (and the second law of thermodynamics) is such a challenge that some have argued that death is simply a natural constituent of the created order (cf. 2 Pet 3:4 in regard to the early reality of Peter's having to confront such an errant mindset). Lloyd Bailey, for example, has argued that "Death . . . was not an irrational intruding enemy but part of an ordered, controlled harmonious creation. Biological life and death are not separate phenomena, as if the latter intruded to thwart the Creator's design. They are bound together as part of a singular divine will for his creatures."[7] Phenomenologically, this proposition seems quite sensible. From what authority, however, does Bailey derive such a notion? Does he exegete some revealed message from this "Creator"? Or has he received a direct communiqué of the Creator's "divine will" affirming the assertion? No, Bailey has not consulted the divine will of the Creator;

---

7. Bailey, *Biblical Perspectives on Death*, 58. See also Meilaender, *Neither Beast Nor God*, 100, where Meilaender writes, "But frailty and decline are part of being human; in all of us the fires of metabolism eventually die down." In private conversation with Meilaender, following a lecture entitled *Death and Dying* that he delivered at The Southern Baptist Theological Seminary on Tuesday, September 13, 2011, he elaborated to me that he believes such decline—necessarily linked with aging, according to Meilaender—is a constituent part of the pre-fall created order.

Karl Rahner also, contra Augustine, Aquinas, Anselm, and John Calvin, presents Rome's argument that death was to be the natural end of Adam regardless of whether or not he transgressed (see below); see Rahner, *Theology of Death*, 92–93; and Schwally, *Das Leben nach dem Tode*, 83. See Erickson, *Christian Theology*, 1177, for a somewhat conflicted articulation that death thwarts the plan of God. For opposing arguments, see Augustine, *City of God*, 510–13; Anselm, *Cur Deus Homo?* 1:9; 2:2, cited in *A Scholastic Miscellany*, 122–23, 147; Aquinas, *Summa Theologica*, 1:97:2; Calvin, *Institutes*, 2:1.6.

Theodore of Mopsuestia also had denied against Augustine (and/or Jerome) that the sin of Adam was the origin of death. He averred, "Adam was to die in every hypothesis, whether he sinned or did not sin. His sin injured himself only and not the human race." See Swete, "Theodorus of Mopsuestia," 4:938, 942; see also McLeod, *Theodore of Mopsuestia*, 86–94.

As an example of the contemporary cultural normalcy of such a concept, Steve Jobs, late CEO of Apple, in a commencement speech delivered at Stanford University in 2005, said, "Death is very likely the single best invention of life. It is life's change agent. It clears out the old to make way for the new. . . . Your time is limited, so don't waste it living someone else's life." Jobs' comments, while contextually admonishing, remain, at best, desensitizing of the reality of death as both an enemy and a divine judgment. See Jobs, "Commencement Address."

for God's self-disclosure in biblical Scripture attests no such thing. Apart from divine revelation, neither Bailey nor the remainder of mankind would have any hope of truthfully understanding the enigma that is death. All that could be contemplated about why life must end are the often very erudite hypotheses, like Bailey's, that have been proffered as truth. Of course, no certain truth can be asserted about what death is except by the author of life and death himself (Deut 32:39; 29:29). Because "divine revelation [is] the basic epistemological axiom," as premised in chapter 1, we must inquire of biblical Scripture for certainty concerning this enigma. The key biblical texts that provide insight regarding the inception of death are Gen 2:17; 3:17–19, 22–24; and Rom 5:12–20; 6:23.

From man's first breath, he was given a clarion indication that the splendor of his Creator's sovereign will is of greater value than his own life. Among the first responsibilities given by the Creator to the newly formed Adam was the liberty to eat from any vegetation in the Garden to sustain his life, but the prohibition, upon penalty of death, of indulging the fruit of a single particular tree (Gen 2:16–17). The command is succinct and without any elaboration of what *death* would entail. Keep in mind that Adam had never yet had any experience with the phenomenon.[8] Because the inspired text does not specify, we may only speculate one (or a combination) of at least three things concerning Adam's cognition of the seriousness of the proposed penalty: (1) Adam knew what death was from some earlier disclosure by God, (2) God elaborated to Adam on this occasion the significance (either partial or in full) of the penalty, but the author of Genesis does not include the elaboration in the inspired text, or (3) Adam knew only that he was given an explicit directive from his perfectly trustworthy and good Creator Sustainer and that would suffice for Adam's childlike faithful obedience; no consequence could add or subtract anything from the seriousness of disobeying the revealed will of his worthily adored Sovereign. Whatever Adam's understanding, the proverbial gauntlet had been laid down; *death* would be the recompense of man's distrust of his Creator Sustainer.

The first inspired elaboration of what death would involve is found, literally, in the very next chapter of the human saga. Here we have the first two biblical usages of the word אָרוּר, "*cursed*."[9] The word carries the significance

---

8. This argument assumes a model in which death and decay are intrinsically linked with the Fall and, therefore, had not yet entered the created order.

9. Gen 3:14, 17. The word is used later in Genesis toward Cain (4:11) and Canaan (9:25) to indicate their state of being under the wrath of God. Fascinatingly, John seems to portray in the eschaton a particular reversal of God's curse of death. Rev 22:3, which heralds the end of the curse, follows immediately on the heels of Rev 22:2, which heralds readmission to the perennially healing Tree of Life present throughout the

of the hot displeasure of the flawlessly holy God coupled with an evacuation of his favor in exchange for his equally flawlessly just wrath.[10] The concept is always levied in contrast to blessing, both of which are construed in the context of covenantal relations and ultimately under the sovereign determination of God alone.[11] Up to this point in Scripture, the creation had been "blessed."[12] Now it is cursed. This contrast, clearly linking life with the blessing and death with the curse, is probably most evident in Joshua's ultimatum to Israel in Deut 30:19–20 to partake of the tree of life where Adam faltered.

> I call heaven and earth to witness against you today, that I have set before you life and death, the blessing and the curse. So choose life in order that you may live, you and your descendants, by loving the Lord your God, by obeying His voice, and by holding fast to Him; for this is your life and the length of your days, that you may live in the land which the Lord swore to your fathers, to Abraham, Isaac, and Jacob, to give them.

God's premier curse is the direct and immediate consequence of Adam's disobedience (Gen 3:17).[13] Fittingly, the serpent is cursed first for its leading role in the desecration of God's image. Ironically, however, death does not come to the serpent as a result of its own rebellion against the divine order. Rather, as sole image bearer of God and vice regent of his creation, upon Adam alone falls the responsibility for contracting death on

---

Garden—now a *hagiopolis*, a "Holy City" (Rev 21:10).

10. Further, see the section below entitled "The Reason for Death."

11. Ferguson, "Curse, Accursed," 139. Of God's singular authority over blessing or cursing, Ferguson writes, "The curse is totally under Yahweh's control. It is his power, not magical forces, which brings about the curse. His sovereign decision alone decides who merits being cursed (1 Kgs 8:31–32). He cannot be forced into action by proper wording or ritual. Thus a curse could not be used capriciously as a weapon against one's personal enemies." See also Evans, "Blessing/curse," 397–401. Evans assures rightly, "Although bad things can and do happen to those who belong to the kingdom, those who are part of God's people cannot be under the curse; rather they are blessed" (401).

12. See Gen 1:22, 28; 2:3; 5:2. Interestingly, the first two articulations of God's "blessing" are coupled with the result of being fruitful and multiplying and filling the earth. Blessedness, then, seems to be intrinsically linked with proliferation of life throughout the creation. Death, decay, and decline prior to the Fall would have indicated some contradiction to the blessed state; yet we have no inspired indication that anything in creation evidenced that any such curse had yet been rendered. For an argument for "backward causation," suggesting that death was a retroactive curse proleptically introduced into the created order in anticipation of Adam's rebellion, see Dembski, *End of Christianity*, 124–57.

13. The serpent, too, is cursed as a direct consequence of its disobedience to God's divine order; however, (1) it alone is cursed as a result of its action, and (2) death is not entailed in the serpent's cursing.

behalf of the entire created order.[14] Thus, Adam next is cursed. Here, for the first time in the inspired record (and possibly also to Adam), death is given a fuller definition. First, death involves God's cursing of the ground (i.e., the creation) from which Adam was formed as the whole creation's life-blood, as it were, as the distinct being created as the representation of the Creator of all things. Rather than a pristine, harmonious, mutually supportive, and completely transparent universal order, death now radically perverts God's originally "very good" creation with disharmony, toil, subterfuge, and injury. The "ground" that was designed and created for fruitfulness, multiplication, and proliferation of *life* now exhibits signs of its undergoing "decreation"—decay, decline, degeneration—death. Beauty has been turned to ashes. Second, at the end of Adam's now toilsome earthly days, death would consume him such that he would "return to the ground, because from it you were taken; for you are dust, and to dust you shall return" (Gen 3:19). Apart from any later revelation of postmortem existence or articulation of spiritual (rather than merely physical) death, this disclosure would appear to mark the end of both man and his bearing of the image of God—a grave consequence indeed; in fact, precisely the consequence the serpent had contrived.

God's "very good" creation is manifestly no longer that. An intruder has now spoiled the *natural* order. That this intruder, death, is neither an autonomous and unguided natural constituent of the cycle of life nor the inevitable product of routine concession to common grace is indicated by the fact that God himself intentionally both prevented *and prevents* access to life (Gen 3:22, 24). This restriction of access to life *is* death.[15]

The inception of death articulated by the Old Testament is linked to all humanity in the New Testament chiefly in Rom 5:12–21.

---

14. Cf. Gen 1:26–28; Rom 8:19–23. One might think this assertion far too great an assessment to rest on the shoulders of only *one* of countless trillions of creatures in the universe. Remember, however, that Adam *alone*, out of all of those countless trillions of creatures, bears both the image of that Creator of all things and the responsibility for all those things, being created in solidarity with those things (cf. Gen 3:19). On the notion of Adam's worship leadership of the created order, see Due, *Created for Worship*, 7, 141. Concerning the application of death to nonhuman creation, see Feinberg, *No One Like Him*, 622–23, 779; Feinberg, *Many Faces of Evil*, 23, 194; Thielicke, *Death and Life*, 150–53, 207–10.

15. Isa 66:24; Mark 9:43–48; 2 Thess 1:9; and Rev 14:9–11; 20:11–15 all seem to indicate that destruction via death will be forever the final state of all those not *in* Christ—the God who possesses life in himself (John 5:26). So, *death* is not merely the prevention of access to physical life, but prevention of access to the God who *is* life (John 14:6; 1 John 5:11–13, 20; cf. Deut 30:19–20; 32:46–47; Prov 4:13). See also n. 41 below. For further articulation of "What is Death," see the section below thus entitled.

> Therefore, just as through one man sin entered into the world, and death through sin, and so death spread to all men, because all sinned—for until the Law sin was in the world, but sin is not imputed when there is no law. Nevertheless death reigned from Adam until Moses, even over those who had not sinned in the likeness of the offense of Adam, who is a type of Him who was to come.
>
> But the free gift is not like the transgression. For if by the transgression of the one the many died, much more did the grace of God and the gift by the grace of the one Man, Jesus Christ, abound to the many. The gift is not like *that which came* through the one who sinned; for on the one hand the judgment *arose* from one *transgression* resulting in condemnation, but on the other hand the free gift *arose* from many transgressions resulting in justification. For if by the transgression of the one, death reigned through the one, much more those who receive the abundance of grace and of the gift of righteousness will reign in life through the One, Jesus Christ.
>
> So then as through one transgression there resulted condemnation to all men, even so through one act of righteousness there resulted justification of life to all men. For as through the one man's disobedience the many were made sinners, even so through the obedience of the One the many will be made righteous. The Law came in so that the transgression would increase; but where sin increased, grace abounded all the more, so that, as sin reigned in death, even so grace would reign through righteousness to eternal life through Jesus Christ our Lord.

Here Adam's contracting the condemnation of death through his own disobedience is shown to be a universal contagion by virtue of the human race's solidarity with its *prototokos*—the pattern or germination of its kind.[16] The inspired apostle contends that death reigns over the entire human population, indeed, even over those who, by virtue of their not being *personally* humanity's *prototokos*, *could* not condemn all humanity to death with the race's initial and all-contaminating sin. Death does not come to us merely as the consequence of our own personal sins; it is our due by virtue of our

---

16. The Greek term πρωτότοκος is used in Col 1:15, 18 of Christ as the "firstborn" from the dead—i.e., the firstborn of the new creation restored from the curse of de-creation—death (cf. Rom 8:29; Heb 11:28; 12:23; Rev 1:5). Like Adam (in Rom 5) is humanity's loadstone prior to the advent of Christ, so Christ is the life-restoring loadstone for all humanity in solidarity with him by grace through faith (cf. 1 Cor 15:45). See Bauer, BAGD, s.v. "πρωτότοκος." For more on the notion of human solidarity, see also Augustine, *City of God* 13; Augustine, *On Sin*, 1:1–11, cited in Murray, *Imputation of Adam's Sin*, 30 n. 41–43.

metaphysical nature reckoned in Adam.[17] The apostle thus weighs humanity's station in regard to life and death with the encompassing affirmation, "For the wages of sin is death, but the free gift of God is eternal life in Christ Jesus our Lord" (Rom 6:23).

Variations of Contingent Immortality

Pelagius. In the fourth century, on the basis that mankind was constituted by God with an ability to please God by faith unaided by saving grace (that is, "salvation," *per se*, was unnecessary; for no wrath, from which to be saved, even exists for such a one), Pelagius contended that man's original constitution was naturally decadent; that is, Adam and Eve would have died even if they had not rebelled against God's command. Eternal life would have been granted the first humans upon successful completion of a probationary period of exercising the meritorious faith with which they were originally constituted.[18] Pelagius' disciple Caelestius propounded the teaching, hav-

---

17. For an insightful treatment of the debate between representative and realist anthropologies, which fairly analyzes key questions and the respective exponents' arguments, see Murray, *Imputation of Adam's Sin*. Murray removes the ambiguity and obfuscation of the debate asserting, "Hence the crux of the question is not whether the representative view discounts seminal union or natural headship or community of nature in that unity which exists between Adam and posterity but simply and solely whether the necessary *plus* which both views posit is to be interpreted in terms of an entity [i.e., numerically identical human nature] which existed in its totality in Adam and is individualized in the members of the race or in terms of a representation which was established by divine ordination. It is on that restricted question that the debate must turn. Other questions undoubtedly emerge in connection with this restricted question but, relatively, they are subordinate and peripheral. Confusion can be avoided only if the real crux is appreciated and debated on the basis of the pertinent data. . . . [The questions of hereditary depravity and realist versus representative anthropology] are not identical and to fail to distinguish them leads only to confusion and to misapprehension of the *status quaestionis*" (27, 32). For further discussion, see chap. 3, "Anthropological Solidarity: Israel," and chap. 4, "Anthropological Solidarity: The Church."

While endorsing neither representative nor realist anthropology, Tom Schreiner contends, "One cannot separate the representative and constitutive roles of Adam and of Christ in these verses [Rom 5:15–19]. Those who are in Adam and those who are in Christ actually become sinners and righteous, respectively. . . . This is powerful evidence that righteousness in Paul, although forensic, cannot be confined in every instance to forensic categories." See Schreiner, *Romans*, 288.

18. Pelagius's teaching that Adam's initial sin entailed no transmission of any consequence to Adam's progeny is a different (heretical) concern than that of death as originate from sin. For Pelagius, then, the original constitution of man is identical to all of Adam's progeny—i.e., in a state of no guilt. Of necessity then, Pelagius has to disassociate sin and death because, as is evident, all people die, whether or not they have sinned like Adam. That assertion is precisely antithetical to the statement and reasoning *for*

ing agreed with Theodore of Mopsuestia that "Adam was to die in every hypothesis, whether he sinned or did not sin. His sin injured himself only and not the human race."[19]

Pelagius' apt foil, Augustine, was more than up to the task of confronting this "novel" teaching. Augustine addressed the error with a campaign of such theological acumen and clarity of thought that would amass such a corpus of theological instruction on the doctrine of original sin—as well as on baptism and other doctrines such as predestination—that the opinion of the church concerning these things would not be notably moved for the next millennium. Against the Pelagians, Augustine argued that the entire human race has "contracted original sin from him *who is the pattern of what was to come* (Rom 5:14). For in him the pattern of condemnation was established for his posterity yet to come who would come into being from his lineage. Thus, from the one man all are born destined for condemnation, from which only the grace of Christ sets them free."[20] By this "pattern of condemnation" Augustine refers to the righteous judgment of both natural and spiritual death contracted by mankind as a direct result of Adam and Eve's seminal transgression. Truly, Augustine held no such notion that the

---

the association of sin and death presented by the inspired apostle Paul in Rom 5:14, "Nevertheless death reigned from Adam until Moses, even over those who had not sinned in the likeness of the offense of Adam, who is a type of Him who was to come."

This probationary concept did not originate with Pelagius. "Theophilus was exemplary of the second-century fathers, holding that the Garden of Eden was probationary." So writes David Smith in his *With Willful Intent*, 44. Theophilus (d. 181) taught that humanity possessed a kind of indeterminate constitution, capable of either mortality or immortality. Had Adam exercised his free will in consistent obedience, he would have achieved immortality. His disobedience, however, incurred mortality for him and his posterity. Theophilus also taught, however, that Adam's disobedience brought sin and mortality to humanity, but not seminal guilt. See Kelly, *Early Christian Doctrines*, 168, cited in Smith, *With Willful Intent*, 20–21.

Also in need of consideration in the question of Adam's original condition is the condition of Jesus' human nature and the degree of its parallelism to Adam's. Was Jesus' human nature confirmed in perpetual obedience—by virtue of the nature's *person* possessing also deity—in a way that Adam's nature was not—his *person* being solely creature? Would Jesus have eventually died (had he not been murdered)? His resurrection evidenced the impossibility of death's power to hold him—i.e., his constituent immortality (Acts 2:24).

For further discussion of the nature of the life-sustaining capacity of the Tree of Life and the concept of a probationary period for Adam and Eve, see Hodge, *Systematic Theology*, 2:116; Heidel, *Gilgamesh*, 143; John of Damascus, "An Exact Exposition," 9:29, cited in Horton, *Christian Faith*, 414n10; Turretin, *Institutes*, 1:473–77.

19. Swete, "Theodorus of Mopsuestia," 4:942; cf. 938; see also McLeod, *Theodore of Mopsuestia*, 86–94.

20. Augustine, *Punishment and Forgiveness*, 1:13, 41. Augustine refers to Christian baptism in affirming, "only the grace of Christ sets them free."

God of Truth, whom Augustine considered "above all things, to wish for nothing else, to think of nothing else, to love nothing else,"[21] would have cursed Adam with death apart from a just cause for such a penalty.

Karl Rahner. Karl Rahner, writing as a Catholic, asserts that Adam and Eve would have "died" even if they had not transgressed God's command.[22] The nuances of language used to articulate this view may characterize it better as temporary mortality; for it, too, teaches that original human being was not created immortal—that is, in the form in which it would exist for eternity. "It is not legitimate, however, to infer from this proposition of faith [i.e., that before sin man was not subject to death] that the first man in Paradise, had he not sinned, would have lived on endlessly in this life."[23] In order to obtain a nature capable of existing for eternity, mankind, as originally created, must undergo a supernatural transformation, a "death without dying . . . without suffering any violent dissolution of his actual bodily constitution through a power from without."[24] The "mortal" Adam, upon progression to full maturity of life, would have arrived at a state of metamorphosis into his final and consummate form.

For Rahner, "death" is both natural and unnatural. It is natural from the standpoint that all humanity is constituted as flesh and blood, which the apostle Paul instructs "cannot inherit the kingdom of God; nor does the perishable inherit the imperishable" (1 Cor 15:50). Rahner articulates Rome's distinguishing between what is perishable and what is imperishable in regard to human constitution and death.

> Catholic theology still holds, as against the Protestant reformers and the Jansenists, on sound theological grounds, that death is also a natural event; or, to state it more cautiously, that the death which we actually do experience has also a natural essence. The decisive theological reason, omitting many others, is that death shall not only be a consequence, and expression, and a punishment for sin, but also . . . a dying with Christ, the participation

---

21. Augustine *On Order* 2:20:52; 119, 121; see also Brown, *Augustine of Hippo*, 103.

22. Rahner, *Theology of Death*, 40–63, 92–93, 104–5; cf. 89–127. One should note that Rahner is not the *ex cathedra* spokesperson of Rome. See also Ratzinger, *Catechism*, 284–88, who, although possibly in agreement with Rahner's nuanced understanding of the nature of death, articulates, "Death was therefore contrary to the plans of God the Creator and entered the world as a consequence of sin. 'Bodily death, from which man would have been immune had he not sinned' is thus 'the last enemy' of man left to be conquered" (285); Ratzinger, *Eschatology*, 92–99.

23. Rahner, *Theology of Death*, 42.

24. Ibid.

> in and appropriation of his redemptive death. Since death is also to be the very opposite of sin, and since it cannot be both the consequence of sin and dying with Christ at the same time ... then death must have a proper, natural essence, which contains the potentiality of dying in both directions [i.e., in Adam unto damnation or in Christ unto salvation] and which is finally reduced to one or the other of these possibilities by the attitude with which man, as a person, sustains this natural essence.[25]

The natural essence of death, then, is that all persons will "die;" that is, all will be transformed for eternity, as purposed from the beginning, only now for perpetual communion either with God's grace or his wrath. Though one sense of death, to be sure, "is something that ought not to be,"[26] because its process was introduced by the sin of Adam, "it is never *merely* a natural process, though it must also be a natural element, for it could not otherwise be an event of salvation or damnation and yet remain one in all men."[27]

Conditional immortality is not a view exclusive to either Pelagianism or Roman Catholicism. Many Protestants, too, both have held and hold this understanding of the nature of man as originally constituted in the image of God. For example, Old Testament scholar and Orientalist, Friedrich Schwally argued from Gen 3:19 that the cause of death is the original decadent composition of the human body. (Of course, this premise must apply also to all material creation.) Therefore, Adam and Eve would eventually have to eat of the tree of life in order to escape the *natural* inevitability of death.[28]

Millard Erickson. Millard Erickson contends "physical death was not an original part of the human condition. But death was always there as a threat should the human sin."[29] Death is an unnatural, foreign, and hostile enemy to God's original design. Adam and Eve possessed the ability to live forever; but they also possessed the ability *not* to live forever if they forfeited the

---

25. Ibid., 44.
26. Ibid., 46.
27. Ibid. An assessment of this view will follow below.
28. Schwally, *Das Leben nach dem Tod*, 83. Many argue that Adam and Eve never partook of the Tree of Life because that would have transformed their extant life—a contingent immortality—into an absolute immortality. This view of the benefit of eating from the Tree of Life seems more static, however, than the biblical articulation of dynamic ongoing communion with the living God of life—i.e., continually partaking of and being sustained by the fruit of him who alone *is* life. More on this notion will follow below. See also Heidel, *Gilgamesh*, 143.
29. Erickson, *Christian Theology*, 1176–77.

privilege of life. They were, as Augustine put it, *posse non peccare et posse non mori*. Thus, they were created with "contingent immortality."[30] Erickson also contends that Adam and Eve did not partake of the tree of life while in the Garden, but would have been granted access to the tree upon successful completion of a probationary period of obedience.

Death as a Direct Consequence of Sin

Charles Hodge. Agreeing with Augustine, and citing both the apostle Paul and Martin Luther, Charles Hodge argues from Scripture against Pelagius' notion that man was created mortal.[31]

> It is expressly stated in Scripture that death is the wages of sin. In the threatening, "In the day that thou eatest thereof thou shalt surely die," it is plainly implied that if he did not eat he should not die. It is clear therefore from the Scriptures that death is the penal consequence of sin, and would not have been inflicted, had not our first parents transgressed.... According to one view adopted by man of the fathers, Adam was to pass his probation in the earthly paradise, and if obedient, was to be translated to the heavenly paradise, of which the earthly was the type. According to Luther, the effect of the fruit of the tree of life of which our first parents would have been permitted to eat had they not sinned, would have been to preserve their bodies in perpetual youth. According to others, the body of Adam and the bodies of his posterity, had he maintained his integrity, would have undergone a change analogous to that which, the Apostle teaches us, awaits those who shall be alive at the second coming of Christ. They shall not die, but they all shall be changed; the corruptible shall put on incorruption, and the mortal shall put on immortality. Two things are certain, first, that if Adam had not sinned he would not have died; and secondly, that if the Apostle, when he says we have borne the image of the earthly, means that our present bodies are like the body of Adam as originally constituted, then his body no less than ours, required to be changed to fit it for immortality.[32]

---

30. Ibid., 1177.
31. See also Rahner, *Theology of Death*, 40–63.
32. Hodge, *Anthropology*, 116.

Hodge is convinced of the biblical link between sin and death. He is also convinced, however, of the remaining necessity of some form of transfiguration prior to mankind's entrance into eternity.

Herman Bavinck. Contrary to the Pelagians, Socinians, and Rationalists, as well as many theologians of Herman Bavinck's day, Bavinck objects that death is never to be viewed as either natural or necessary.[33] Though the full penalty against sin is not enacted immediately upon Adam's transgression, Bavinck asserts, neither is (physical) death itself the consummation of God's punishment of sin. "Only after the judgment of the last day does it strike the guilty with all its severity."[34] The timing of the execution of death notwithstanding, Bavinck acknowledges the clear biblical teaching of "the bond between sin and death."[35]

Author's Assessment

Temporary mortality. Rahner provides a certainly thoughtful analysis. At least two concerns are problematic, however. First, Rahner provides a broader definition of death than is commonly articulated by either the Christian community at large (or the general public, for that matter) or Scripture. For example, Helmut Thielicke's articulation of his understanding of death suggests that, on multiple levels, nothing about it is natural. His thoughts on the subject appear more consonant with the Christian community at large and represent a contrast to Rahner's understanding; so, they are worth quoting at length here.

> In biblical thought human death is simply unnatural. At no time and in no place is it the expression of any sort of normality of nature, as if it signified the necessary ebb in the rhythm of life.

---

33. In a footnote Bavinck writes of those who apparently exegete from their observance of the phenomenon of death rather than from divine revelation, "F. Schleiermacher, *Christian Faith* §59; R. A. Lipsius, §414. A. Ritschl, *Christian Doctrine of Justification and Reconciliation*, III, 345ff.; J. Kaftan, *Dogmatik*, §29; Smend, *Lehrbuch der alttestamentlichen Relgionsgeschichte* [sic], 504; Marti, *Geschichte der israelitischen Religion*, 193; Clemen, *Sünde*, I, 233ff.; Köberle, *Sünde und Gnade im religiösen*, 54; Matthes, 'De Inrichting van den Eeredienst bij Jerobeam, I Kon. 12:26–33,' 239–54; Beth, "Über Ursache und Zweck des Todes," 285–304, and 335–48 demonstrates that science has not up to this point been able to explain the riddle of death but considers death to be natural to all earthly creatures and subordinates all exegesis of Scripture to this point of view." See Bavinck, *Sin and Salvation in Christ*, 183 n. 45, 159.

34. Bavinck, *Sin and Salvation in Christ*, 160.

35. Ibid., 159, 183–84.

> Death is rather the expression of a catastrophe which runs on a collision course with man's original destination or, in other words, directly opposite to his intrinsic nature. . . . Thus it becomes clear even here that death always indicates divorce from God and thereby an ultimate disorder. Death and separation from God go together. Death is un-nature; death ought not be (Deut 30:15-16; Eph 2:1; Rom 7:10, 13; John 5:24; Jas 1:15). To this extent death is the enemy. . . . Death really is unnatural. Death ought not to be. But insofar as it nevertheless is, it constitutes only the symptom of a much deeper unnaturalness, namely, that we have torn ourselves loose from God, that we are no longer in the Father's house (Luke 15:11 ff.), and that we have thus alienated ourselves from our intrinsic nature of being God's children. . . . Death is unnatural since it most assuredly conflicts with man's original destiny to be near God; for wherever God is, there life reigns, not death.[36]

In no uncertain terms, Thielicke rejects any notion of death as a natural phenomenon, however one seeks to frame the argument. The mortality of Adam and Eve is established only with the Fall; it cannot be substantiated as the essentially natural state of the creature in anticipation of his transition to eternity, as Rahner suggests.

Of course the Bible articulates that all who die will die either in league with the first Adam—unto eternal condemnation—or with the last Adam—unto eternal life; there are no exceptions. God's inspired revelation, however, never conjoins *union with Christ* and *death* in any sense of penal consequence of Adam's disobedience. Union with Christ frees sons of Adam from the curse of the law of sin and death (Rom 8:2). "Dying with Christ" is always understood biblically as a putting to death of death—that is, putting off the "decreative," death perpetuating, rebellious, sinful, fallen human will and nature in exchange for joyful submission to the law and life of God, a state achievable only in and by the one new man, Christ Jesus.[37] So, to say that all are destined for "death" either unto salvation or damnation is not strictly accurate. The biblical voice concerning death is always cursedness.

---

36. Thielicke, *Death and Life*, 105, 108, 113-14. In Thielicke's own words, "In working out the personal character of human death . . . we find ourselves in essential agreement with the basic thoughts of Luther concerning this problem" (150). Thielicke, therefore, notes Luther's assessment of the unnaturalness of death: "Man's death is in itself truly an infinite and eternal wrath. The reason is that man is a being created for this purpose: to live forever in obedience to the Word and to be like God. He was not created for death. In his case death was ordained as a punishment of sin." See Luther, *LW*, vol. 13, 94, cited in Thielicke, *Death and Life*, 153 n. 8.

37. Cf. for example, Rom 6:1-11; Eph 2:4-6; Col 3:1-4.

The light of God's salvation involves no darkness at all. The biblical voice concerning salvation is always glorification, not "death." One cannot experience salvation in "death" in the strictest sense. Using the terminology in the way Rahner (and Rome) does, therefore, as erudite as is the rhetoric, is more confusing than helpful.

Secondly, the erudition of Rahner's argumentation betrays, perhaps, his commitment to the authority of Catholic dogma rather than to the authoritative epistemological axiom of divine revelation. Neither his definition of death nor his association of it with any "natural essence" can be substantiated by any biblical texts or any biblical framework of creation, fall, and redemption. The repeated biblical antithesis of life and death, blessing and curse, is simply too forthright to abide such a statement of the thesis as Rahner's.

Contingent immortality. A model of contingent immortality is not entirely without merit; for no creature possesses inherent life. Life must be both sourced and sustained by something other than the creature. However, the implication of a view in which Adam and Eve were to be granted access to the fruit of the tree of life upon graduation—as it were—is that, although the tree was indigenous to the garden and not forbidden, Adam and Eve never partook of its fruit.[38] This assertion rings highly implausible; for, indeed, eating from the tree of life was granted freely from the beginning by God himself (Gen 2:9)! Only fruit from the tree of the knowledge of good and evil was forbidden (Gen 2:16–17). Upon Adam and Eve's transgression, God recognized that had man *continued* to "stretch out his hand and take also from the tree of life, and eat" (Gen 3:22), he would have lived forever in an ever more corrupting and self-injuring state. Thus, God banished them

---

38. Such a notion seems even to contradict Moses and Paul as they write, "You shall not muzzle the ox while he is threshing" (Deut 25:4; 1 Cor 9:9; cf. 1 Tim 5:18). To be sure, the apostle interprets Moses' statement as referring to God's concern that the gospel laborer earn his bread by his ministry; but the principle that is insisted is that the one who cultivates a garden ought not to be prevented from access to the fruit of that which he cultivates—unless explicitly prohibited, as in the case of the tree of the knowledge of good and evil (Gen 2:17). Adam's responsibility from the very beginning of his creation was in fact to cultivate the Garden (Gen 2:5, 15). To suggest that he was prevented from access to its fruit contradicts Moses' inspired principle as interpreted by another inspired author, Paul.

from any *further* access to the tree of life.[39] Herein is evidenced the *grace* of God in death, by the way.[40]

An interpretation, on the other hand, that suggests Adam and Eve did eat regularly from the tree of life as the very means of sustaining the life that was given them at their creation is consonant with the New Testament's teaching that the renewed person's life is sustained by virtue of his uninterrupted union with Christ, who *is* the life.[41] Credence is given to this

39. The Hebrew (and English) verbal and grammatical construct of Gen 3:22 does not indicate, as probationary period proponents presume, that Adam's "stretch[ing] out his hand [to] take also from the tree of life, and eat" would have been a first occurrence. The language and context are amenable to the premise that Adam and Eve already had been eating regularly from the tree's fruit.

40. Irenaeus *Against Heresies* 23:6. Irenaeus agrees, "Wherefore also He [God] drove him [man] out of Paradise, and removed him far from the tree of life, not because He envied him the tree of life, as some venture to assert, but because He pitied him, [and did not desire] that he should continue a sinner for ever, nor that the sin which surrounded him should be immortal, and evil interminable and irremediable. But He set a bound to his [state of] sin, by interposing death, and thus causing sin to cease, putting an end to it by the dissolution of the flesh, which should take place in the earth, so that man, ceasing at length to live in sin, and dying to it, might live to God." See also Pelikan, *Shape of Death*, 25–26, 106–7.

41. John 6:53; 5:21; 11:25; 14:6; 1 John 5:11, 13, 20; cf. Rom 8:9. John of Damascus seems to support such a view. He writes, "The tree of life, on the other hand, was a tree having the energy that is the cause of life, or to be eaten only by those who deserve to live and are not subject to death." See also n. 9 above; John of Damascus, "Exact Exposition," 29, cited in Horton, *Christian Faith*, 414n10; and Turretin, *Institutes*, 1:473–77.

Further, the tree of life in the Garden of Eden seems somehow representative of the presence of God himself (see Gen 3:8; Deut 8:3 with 32:47 and John 5:26; 6:26–58; Ps 27:1b, 8; see also Prov 3:18; 11:30; 18:12; and 15:14 where the phrase "tree of life" is used metaphorically as a source of vitality). God's eternal purpose has been to dwell in the midst of his creatures/people (Gen 3:8; Jer 24:7; 31:33; Ezek 37:27; Zech 2:10–11; 2 Cor 6:16; Heb 8:10; Rev 21:3). Adam and Eve possessed life so long as they partook of God's means, the tree of life (Gen 2:9, 16). When they rebelled by eating from the forbidden tree (Gen 3:6), they were expelled from both the Garden and access to the tree of life; moreover, as an act of mercy and grace, an angel with a flaming sword was appointed "to guard the way to the tree of life" so that Adam and Eve would not be enabled to continue immortally in their sinful, corrupted, and God-forsaking state (Gen 3:22–24). The nearness of their God was now no longer there good (Ps 73:28); it was their death (Gen 2:17; 3:7–8, 17–19; Exod 33:3, 5; Isa 59:2). God is immutable in his purpose; he still purposes to dwell in the midst of his people. Life *will* belong to Adam—i.e., man, God's image bearer—the One without sin (Matt 23:22; 1 Cor 8:3; 2 Cor 5:21; John 1:12; Col 2:10; Rev 2:7; 22:2, 14). The one who is *in Christ* possesses life (Rom 8:9; 1 John 2:25; 5:11–13). As long as that one remains in God, he will possess life (John 6:51, 58; 17:12; Phil 1:6; 1 John 2:17, 24). Only those who are *in Christ* (Rom 8:32; 8:9; Eph 2:6; Col 2:10; 1 John 2:22–25) will be beneficiaries of the Beatific Vision where they will be made partaker of God's own divine nature. This transformation will grant them the "unimaginable heightening" of their being by possessing God's own nature as the means of their life, thus making it and them eternal; see Augustine, *City of God*, 361,

interpretation by the Old Testament when one considers equation of Christ with Wisdom in the book of Proverbs in conjunction, too, with the book's own correlation of wisdom and the tree of life (Prov 3:18; 11:30).[42] Yet more support is added to the argument when one considers John's vision in Revelation 22:2 of the eschatological tree of life, where fruit from this tree—as indigenous among the land of John's vision as the original tree was בְּתוֹךְ, *in the midst of* or *among*, Adam and Eve's Garden (Gen 2:9; 3:3), appearing "on either side of the river"—produces "twelve [kinds of] fruit, yielding its fruit every month, and the leaves of the tree are ει' θεραπείαν τω"ν εςθνω"ν"—a phrase which may be interpreted legitimately as "for the life preserving health of the peoples." The tree of life in Genesis, then, whose fruit sustained the lives of Adam and Eve, anticipates not only the New Testament's life-giving Son of God,[43] but also the life sustaining Ancient of Days of John's

---

444, 499–500, 567, 939, 1022, 1082–89; and chap. 7 herein.

42. Augustine makes just such a correlation: "Man, then, had food in the other trees, but in the tree of life there was a sacrament. And what did it signify except wisdom, of which it was said, *She is a tree of life to those who lay hold of her*, just as it was said of Christ that He is a Rock pouring forth water to all who thirst for Him?" Augustine continues even more definitively, "Thus Wisdom, namely Christ Himself, is the tree of life in the spiritual paradise to which He sent the thief from the cross. But a tree of life which would signify Wisdom was also created in the earthly paradise. . . . It was possible, however, that through a tree, that is, through a corporeal creature used as a sacrament, Wisdom could be signified in the earthly Paradise. . . . the tree of life both existed as a real material tree and at the same time symbolized Wisdom." See Augustine, *Literal Meaning of Genesis*, 42, 38–41. For other studies on the equation of Christ and Wisdom in the book of Proverbs, see O'Donnell, *Beginning and End of Wisdom*.

43. Adam and Eve's lives arguably were sustained by provision from the tree of life (Gen 2:9, 16; 3:22–24; see also nn. 38–39, 41–42 above). When they were justly restricted from access to that provision, they necessarily experienced the only alternative—death; so did all of their posterity (Rom 5:12, 14, 18), even when God supplied them with provisional manna—"bread from heaven for you," "which your fathers did not know" (John 6:49; cf. Exod 16:4, 35; Deut 8:3, 16).

Because partaking of the Lord's Supper is entails "eating the flesh of the Son of Man and drinking His blood"—without which no one could possess life (John 6:53; Matt 26:26–29 and pars.; 1 Cor 11:24–25)—and because the Son "has life in himself" (John 5:21, 26), and because "the tree of life which is in the paradise of God" and yields provision "for the healing of the nations" (Rev 22:2) typifies the life-giving Son (Rev 2:7; 1 Cor 15:45), partaking of the Lord's Supper by faith appears to signify the provision of *life* for New Testament image bearers of God in the same way that partaking of fruit from the tree of life in the Garden of Eden sustained *life* for Adam and Eve. Death results to anyone who does not partake of this fruit of the tree of life—i.e., Christ, who *is* the life (John 1:4; 6:51; 11:25; 14:6; Col 3:4; 1 John 1:2; 5:12; cf. Lev 17:11), even the bread of life (John 6:35, 48–51). The significance that this notion gives to the ordinance of the Lord's Supper should not go unnoticed. If one does not partake of the Supper in faith, one is necessarily consigned to death (John 6:53–58). If one neglects partaking of the Supper, one not only disdains God's gift of *life* from Himself (John 5:26), but one

eschatological Apocalypse; He is, after all, the inherently living Alpha and Omega.

Further, a view that asserts that death (whether understood in the common sense or in Rahner's sense) would have occurred regardless of rebellion cannot do exegetical justice to the assertions of either Rom 5:16 that "death [entered the world] *through* sin," or verse 18 that "through one transgression there *resulted* condemnation to all men" (emphasis added); for death certainly cannot be reckoned as anything less than condemnation of God's originally very good creation.[44] Contrary to the argument of Rahner, Rome, and Pelagius, therefore, death was not to be the natural terminus of Adam had he not sinned prior to his successful completion of a probationary period. As Augustine firmly avows, "We must therefore admit that the first human beings were created under this condition, that they would not have experienced any kind of death, if they had not sinned."[45] Rather, at worst, an unspeakably glorious beatification that evades any semblance of death awaited Adam. This same beatification (albeit now, *through* death—the "Golden Stair"[46]) does await all those who by faith are in solidarity with the last Adam—the "life-giving spirit" (1 Cor 15:45) and consummate human—Jesus Christ.[47] The death promised in Gen 2:17 to Adam the Lesser and all his progeny upon his initial all-contaminating transgression no longer has any sting for any offspring of Adam the Conqueror.

What is Death?

Asking the question "What *is* death?" can precipitate either an ontological or adjectival reply.[48] The catastrophic inception and nature of death has

---

also will not "live forever" (John 6:58) just as Adam and Eve were intended to do by partaking of God's provision of and for life.

44. Again, this argument assumes a model for the age of the earth in which death and decay are intrinsically linked with the Fall and, therefore, had not yet entered the created order.

45. Augustine, *City of God*, 512.

46. See Stannard, *Puritan Way*, 152, 176.

47. Augustine, *City of God*, 361, 444, 499–500, 567, 939, 1022, 1082–89. Augustine revels that the Beatific Vision—the consummate imparting of life—for believers in Christ will be an eternal and ever-increasing bliss of immediate knowledge of God. See chap. 7 for further discussion.

48. Commenting on the assessments of an empirical paradigm, Herman Bavinck retorts that agnostic scientists must acknowledge that "Death is a mystery in the full sense of the word." See Bavinck, *Sin and Salvation in Christ*, 184. To be sure, empirical science can provide no rationale for how matter and energy, which purportedly are immortal (viz. the first law of thermodynamics), and the individual human composition,

been treated above. We may conclude that death ontologically is the God ordained penal consequence of Adam's rebellion, the unnatural "decreation" of God's original "very good" creation. Death would never have entered the created order apart from the faithless disobedience of God's crowned creation, image bearer, universal worship leader, and vice regent—man.

In addition to the nature of death, we must also familiarize ourselves with the *character* of death as delineated by Scripture. More often than not, because we view death as evil—and in important senses, rightly so—we also unconsciously reckon that death cannot be associated with God in any salutary way. We therefore tend to default to a view of death as commendable in no sense whatsoever. We say easily and rightly that God is not the author of *evil* (Ps 119:68; Isa 6:3; Hab 1:13; 1 John 1:5); but we cannot say with equal justification that God is not the author—i.e., originating Sovereign—of *death* (Gen 2:17; 3:22-24; 6:5-13; Exod 32:9-10, 39; Num 16:21, 45; Isa 45:5-7; Rom 6:23).[49] We must bifurcate in this way, then, the evil of

---

which is biologically renewed every seven years, can still result in a mortal product. The ontological reply to the question "What is death?" can be provided sensibly only on an ideological (i.e., theological and/or philosophical) paradigm because no understanding of such a phenomenon can be derived apart from the basic epistemological axiom of divine revelation, which can be neither substantiated nor falsified on an empirical model. The discussion herein, therefore, is proffered from a properly compatible theological and philosophical framework.

Various theologies posit differing understandings of exactly what death is. The process conception of death, for example, views the "perpetual perishing" of all temporal actual entities from subjective immediacy into immortal objectivity as the "ultimate evil." See Whitehead, *Process and Reality*, 517, cited in Feinberg, *No One Like Him*, 168, 170. A more traditional understanding of death is in view in this essay, one in which "death is the absence or withdrawal of breath and the life force that makes movement, metabolism, and interrelation with others possible," yet "more than the cessation of all physiological processes. . . . By divine command (Ps 90:3), the body returns to dust and the spirit goes back to God who gave it (Gen 2:7; Eccles. 12:7)." See Ferguson, *BTDB*, s.v. "Death, Mortality." See also Jeffery, *Pierced for Our Transgressions*, 118-24.

49. Of God's decree of evil, Don Carson writes, "A sovereign and omniscient God who knows that, if he permits such and such an evil to occur it will surely occur, and then goes ahead and grants the permission, is surely decreeing the evil. But the language of permission is retained because it is part of the biblical pattern of insisting that God stands behind good and evil asymmetrically. . . . He can never be credited with evil; he is always to be credited with the good." Carson further challenges theologians to allow the inspired authors' language to retain its boldness concerning these things: "Some theologians are shocked by and express bitter reproach against other theologians who speak of God 'causing' evil in any sense. At one level, they are to be applauded: everywhere the Bible maintains the unfailing goodness of God. On the other hand, if you again scan the texts cited in this chapter [numerous texts are listed exemplifying a compatibilistic doctrine, among which are Gen 50:19-20; Lev 20:7-8; 1 Kgs 8:46ff.; 11:11-13, 29-39; 12:1-15; Isa 10:5ff.; John 6:37-38; Phil 2:12-13; Acts 4:23-31], it must be admitted that the biblical writers are rather bolder in their usage of language

death as instigated by the murderer Satan, from the good holiness of death as instituted by the Sovereign of both life and death—God (Deut 32:29; Isa 45:5–7).[50] Failure to make this distinction inevitably presents quandary. Adjectivally, then, death is either good—yes, *good*[51]—or evil, depending on the context from which it is discussed.

Given the alternative option of living forever in an ever decomposing yet never finally consuming state (Isa 66:24; Mark 9:44, 46, 48), death was most certainly a good grace that God extended to man, not merely for the sake of sustaining the integrity of God's own holy glory, but also for man's welfare—with both temporal and eternal implications. As Wayne Grudem rightly insists, "Our obedience to God is more important than preserving our own lives."[52] In this sense, death is a good and preferable thing when contrasted with disobedience to the God who sustains life for his purposes rather than for those of any other. Superseding Grudem's voice on this matter and weighing the gravity of eternal death is the voice of Christ himself:

---

than the timid theologians! . . . The problem looks neater when, say, God is not behind evil in any sense." Carson, *How Long*, 224–25.

50. Satan "was a murderer from the beginning" (John 8:44). Though death was infinitely wisely constructed and ordained by God for his ultimately good and glorious purposes, Satan plays his duly ordained roll in instigating death. Deceived and deceiving as his unholy nature constrains him to be, Satan regards death not as the glorious display of the integrity and holiness of God that it is. Rather, he regards it as a means that he can use craftily as violence against God and any of his designated image bearers.

Regarding the double agency of Satan's evil acts as ordained by a good God, actions performed compatibilistically by two agents—God and the creature—may be considered, without logical contradiction, both good *and* evil. John Calvin comments regarding Satan's activity, "Therefore, whatever men or Satan himself may instigate, God nevertheless holds the key, so that he turns their efforts to carry out his judgments." Calvin elaborates, "Satan is properly said, therefore, to act in the reprobate over whom he exercises his reign, that is, the reign of wickedness. God is also said to act in His own manner, in that Satan himself, since he is the instrument of God's wrath, bends himself hither and thither at His beck and command to execute His just judgments. I pass over here the universal activity of God whereby all creatures, as they are sustained, thus derive the energy to do anything at all. I am speaking only of that special action which appears in every particular deed. Therefore we see no inconsistency in assigning the same deed to God, Satan, and man; but the distinction in purpose and manner causes God's righteousness to shine forth blameless there, while the wickedness of Satan and of man betrays itself by its own disgrace." See Calvin, *Institutes*, 1:230, 311.

51. Ware, *God's Greater Glory*, 120. Ware remarks on the good nature of the sovereign God who ordains all things that come to pass as One from whom *only* good can come. Carson also affirms that "from God's perspective these things [death, famine, pillage, natural disasters, etc.], insofar as they exact penalty and restore justice, must be assessed as good"; Carson, *How Long*, 45.

52. Grudem, *Systematic Theology*, 813.

> I say to you, my friends, do not be afraid of those who kill the body and after that have no more that they can do. But I will warn you whom to fear: fear the One who, after he has killed, has authority to cast into hell; yes, I tell you, fear him! (Luke 12:4-5)

One of Christ's implications here is that although human life is indeed immeasurably valuable, it is evidently not the highest value when compared with the infinitely higher ethic of obedience for the sake of the glory of God. On this reckoning of death in contrast with a life of disinterest in God's will, death is viewed as good.[53]

The Reason for Death

Isaiah 40:15-17 assesses the relative value of human life.[54]

> Behold, the nations are like a drop from a bucket, and are regarded as a speck of dust on the scales; behold, He lifts up the islands like fine dust. Even Lebanon is not enough to burn, nor its beasts enough for a burnt offering. All the nations are as nothing before Him, they are regarded by Him as less than nothing and meaningless.

Contextually, Isaiah is painting a picture of the universe's Sovereign who has graciously elected to redeem unworthy Israel. Contrasting the haughty vaunts of man's wisdom and power against God's omnipotence, Isaiah lays bear the utter futility of comparing the finite with the infinite. Because human life is merely one of many means of displaying the splendor of God, in comparison to that splendor, human life is "meaningless." Death has muted man's brandishing of his sword as the definitive demarcation of his finite value. As long as man faithfully acknowledges the reality of his own creaturely finitude and his utter dependence upon the Source of his life,[55] he will do well and live (cf. Gen 4:6-7; Hab 2:4; Rom 1:17). When that faith is vacated, the grant of life is necessarily forfeited and the glory of God persists. As Karl Barth notes, "My turning from God is followed by God's

---

53. See also n. 57 below where Martin Luther reflects on the "very great good" death of the righteous and the "very evil death of the wicked."

54. Oswalt, *Book of Isaiah*, 60-62; Goldingay, *Isaiah*, 225-27; Motyer, *Prophecy of Isaiah*, 303-04; Childs, *Isaiah*, 303-05; Brueggemann, *Isaiah 40-66*, 22-25; Smith, *Isaiah 40-66*, 82; Whybray, *Isaiah 40-66*, 26.

55. Gen 3:4-6 (cf. Rom 1:18-23) depicts Adam and Eve's succumbing to the serpent's tempting lie to transcend their creatureliness and "be like God"—a failure with which the tempter was already quite familiar (Isa 14:12-15).

annihilating turning from me. When it is resisted His love works itself out as death-dealing wrath."[56] Death, then, is no bullying retaliation of an almighty power against an infinitely weaker opponent. It is the perfectly reasonable and expected order where Life reigns; Adam knew so (Gen 2:17).

Divine revelation also articulates not merely the fact of death but also the reason for death. Accordingly, Thielicke explains that only death[57] can sufficiently evidence the gravity of the decreative disorder between holy God and unholy man.[58] Not only does death attest to the quantitative distinction between the Creator God's infinitude and creature man's finitude, but it also clearly indicates the qualitative distinction at the point of guilt and wrath.

> The issue is finally not one of quantitative disparity between two entities, but one of qualitative breakdown between two persons. What is involved here is not the different sizes of two parties, but a juridical verdict. Death therefore is visible representation not of the disparity between the two, but of the judgment. It hovers, so to speak, right over the point of fracture in the fellowship between God and man.[59]

The creature has volitionally disregarded the covenant relationship for which his Creator originally designed him. No consequence short of death could reconcile such a cosmic rift between God's holiness and the sinner.[60]

---

56. Barth, *CD*, 3, §59, *Creation*, 253.

57. Death here does not refer merely to the cessation of man's biological functions and the separation of body from soul. The full corpus of the biblical articulation of death is in view. Luther elaborates on the Bible's meaning of death: "There is a double death, namely, the natural or, better, temporal one and the eternal one. Temporal death is the separation of body and soul. But this death is a symbol and a parable; it is, in comparison with eternal death (which is spiritual), like a picture of death painted on a wall. This is why Scripture very frequently calls it sleep, rest, or slumber.... Also eternal death is twofold. One is a very great good. It is the death of sin and the death of death, by which the soul is freed and separated from sin and the body from corruption, and the soul is united by grace and glory with the living God.... Thus sin dies, and also the sinner when he is justified, for sin does not ever return, as the apostle says here: 'Christ dies no more,' etc. (Rom 6:9).... The other death is eternal and a very great evil. It is the death of the damned. Here it is not sin and the sinner that die, while man is saved, but it is man that dies while sin lives and remains forever. This is the 'very evil death of the wicked' (Ps 34:21)." See Luther, *Lectures on Romans*, vol. 15, 179–80, cited in Thielicke, *Death and Life*, 151n6.

58. Thielicke, *Death and Life*, 131–32.

59. Ibid., 140.

60. One is expected immediately to equate this statement with the death of the infinitely valuable life of the only begotten Son of God, which singularly can mend such a rift.

Every death, therefore, is an expression of the uncompromisingly holy nature of God.[61] The God-breathed words of the prophet Habakkuk proclaim of God, "*Your* eyes are too pure to approve evil, and you cannot look on wickedness *with favor*" (1:13). In rebellious Adam all humanity is reckoned unholy, wicked, and worthy of God's damnation. The "Judge of all the earth," who must judge in impeccable accord with his holy nature (Gen 18:25), cannot dismiss irreconciled human sinfulness—either essence or action—without impugning his own holy character. Such an impugning could never be reality, however; for no paradox could withstand the existence of a holy God who is not. Death *must* be in a rebellious world where Life reigns, at least until the last enemy—indeed, the reason for the last enemy—is abolished (1 Cor 15:25–28). For such a gracious volitional exhibition of his righteous splendor by means of death—for his own pleasure as well as for the benefit of his creature—God is to be lauded.

The Ineluctability of Death

Despite *The New York Times*' announcement that Elisabeth Kübler-Ross had "declared war on the denial of death in America"[62]—although Kübler-Ross

---

61. Motyer, *NDBT*, s.v. "Judgment." Defining justice in light of God's holiness, Motyer writes, "Since 'judgment' is 'setting everything to rights' [God] is seen as a God of order and perfection; this is part of what the Bible calls 'the beauty of (his) holiness' (*cf.* 1 Chr. 16:29; 2 Chr. 20:21; Pss. 29:2; 96:9; 110:3; *etc.*). In all its aspects judgment is an out-shining of the divine holiness (Ps. 50:1–6). Thus Isaiah 5:16 links the key words together. 'The Lord of hosts is exalted in judgment and God the Holy One displays his holiness in righteousness.' When 'judgment' (*mispat*) and 'righteousness' (*sedaqa*) are paired like this (*cf.* Gen. 18:19; 2 Sam 8:15; Pss. 33:5; 89:14; 99:4; Is. 1:21; 5:7; *etc.*) 'righteousness' refers to principles and 'judgment' to practice. So, for example, in Isaiah 32:1 'righteousness' belongs to the king and 'judgment' to the princes; the throne embodies righteous principle and the executive arm practices just government. So it is also with the heavenly throne and its occupant (Isa 5:16): he is in himself, holiness; in his rule he embodies righteous principles and displays his holiness in acts of 'judgment' whereby he puts everything to rights. Since, however, judgment is an application of holiness it involves punishment as well as reward, condemnation as well as approbation." See also Edwards, "Justice of God," 1:669–70; Frame, *Doctrine of God*, 446–68; and Carson, *How Long*, 110–16. For discussions of death in the nonhuman animal world, see Luther, *LW* 13, 107; cf. 106; Feinberg, *No One Like Him*, 622–23, 779; Feinberg, *Many Faces of Evil*, 23, 194; and Thielicke, *Death and Life*, 150–53, 207–10.

62. While no such exact quotation can be found in a query of *The New York Times* quotations, the back cover of Kübler-Ross' 1999 *Tunnel and the Light* attributes the quotation to the *Times*. In 2004, however, the online *The New York Times Magazine* pondered of Kübler-Ross, "Did she simply become drunk on death—burned out or so outraged by it that it was now death itself, and not its denial, on which she had declared war?" See Rosen, "The Final Stage."

herself affirmed in her 1991 book *On Life after Death* that her "real job" was "to tell people that death does not exist"[63]—unfortunately, much sophistry concerning the personal character of death is propagated by popular literature on death, dying, and the afterlife.[64] What makes many of these works a detriment to the discussion rather than a helpful contribution is that they engage the topic or even *fact* of death while at the same time either completely ignoring or missing the *why*—the teleology—of death. The charade is, as Helmut Thielicke puts it, an attempt to override death's personal finality "with intensive clamor and concentrated self-anesthesia."[65] Such unwitting toying with the topic only adds to the confusion and malaise that perpetuates both an idolizing of this present life and a blindness to the weighty biblical significance of death as the boundary ordained by a holy God against a finite creature whose unholy hubris continues to rebel against that boundary, grasping, rather, for equality with God. In fact, many of these very works inevitably disregard divine revelation, identically mimicking, therefore, Adam and Eve's grasp for equality with God.

In such a world where Life reigns yet rebellion exists, death should come as no more of a surprise to those who disregard divine revelation (Rom 1:18–20) than should topographical rearrangement as a result of the

---

63. Kübler-Ross, *Life after Death*, 34, quoted in Rosen, "Final Stage." "Death Does Not Exist" is also the title of the second chapter of *On Life after Death*.

64. See, for example, Piper, *90 Minutes in Heaven*; Wiese, *23 Minutes in Hell*; Burpo, *Heaven Is for Real*; and the less farcical though still theologically untenable Kübler-Ross, *Tunnel and the Light*.

65. Thielicke, *Death and Life*, 132. Joseph Ratzinger, writing prior to his papal ascension as Benedict XVI, also recognizes the tendency of our modern culture to anesthetize itself concerning death. He analyzes, "The growing phenomenon I have in mind is in fact a third attitude which Pieper, once again, has aptly called the 'materialistic trivialisation of death.' On television, death is presented as a thrilling spectacle tailor-made for alleviating the general boredom of life. In the last analysis, of course, the covert aim of this reduction of death to the status of an object is just the same as with the bourgeois taboo on the subject. Death is to be deprived of its character as a place where the metaphysical breaks through. Death is rendered banal, so as to quell the unsettling question which arises from it." See Ratzinger, *Eschatology*, 70.

John Hick comments on the same cultural phenomenon: "There is however a form in which we are all today extremely familiar with the phenomenon of death—indeed, familiar almost to the point of boredom—namely on the television screen. Children as well as adults see men being shot and otherwise deprived of life very frequently on films and TV. It was reported from a meeting of the American Academy of Pediatrics in 1971 that by the time a child in the United States is fourteen years old he can be expected to have seen, on average, 18,000 people killed on television! *This does not however constitute a facing of our mortality, but is on the contrary another defence against it, another device for not facing it.* For those 18,000 deaths on the screen simply trivialize death and make it unreal to the viewer" (emphasis added). See Hick, *Death and Eternal Life*, 86–87.

shifting of tectonic plates. That is, the reality of moral law ought not to be doubted any more than the reality of laws of physics—both of which have been designed and decreed by the same Creator and Sustainer of the one as well as the other. The fool has affirmed in his heart the latter and not the former.

Realities such as death and so-called natural disaster, while not part and parcel of the original "very good" created order, are now inescapable constituents of a fallen order—one that has postured itself intentionally in opposition to the designed mores of its Creator. Because such tragedy is embedded in the current order, the question is often asked, "How could a good God allow evil and suffering?" In light of God's gracious self-disclosure, which again is inevitably disregarded by one who asks such a question, one might responsibly retort, "How could a holy God not?"

So-called "gratuitous evil"[66] and tragic death in our world precipitates a pathos among the creature that attempts to refuse any responsibility on his part and dismiss any notion that any such judgment could be fitting. This escapism that almost fictionalizes death arises out of mankind's aversion to contemplating the personal character of death and his deserving of such judgment; that is, the very reality that the unique and irreplaceable individual "I" will one day succumb to the horror and absence of death. Alfred Hoche captures well the pathos of such denial.

> It is a curious drama that man, who knows the supreme and inescapable law about the cessation of every life all around him and of every life that has ever been lived, still finds it personally oppressive to yield to that law. The notion strikes him as unbearable that this fantastic subjective world that he carries within himself, and that exists in this particular shape but once in time, should simply be wiped out. It is unbearable simply to collapse at the side of the road while the others travel on, conversing as though nothing had happened. . . . The vividness of this feeling . . . makes mockery of all logic.[67]

---

66. In the conversation of the problem(s) of evil, the phrase "gratuitous evil" is sometimes used to describe evils in the created order that are considered excessive. However, one may argue legitimately that no such thing as "gratuitous evil" exists, at least not so far as any creature can judge. Certainly no finite creature—and that includes everything in existence except God—possesses the capacity to determine just how much wrath from an infinitely holy Sovereign can be equitable penalty against a creation in rebellious confederation with its premier. For a thoughtful treatment of the problem(s) of evil, see Feinberg, *Many Faces of Evil*; Carson, *How Long*, 17.

67. Hoche, *Jahresringe*, cited in Thielicke, *Death and Life*, 16 n. 11. See also Anderson, *Theology, Death and Dying*, 3, 11–12; and Tolstoy, *Death of Ivan Ilych*, 43–44. Contemplating his own death apart from divine revelation, Ivan Ilych queries, "It cannot be

Despite all attempts to evade the weighty verities of death, despite popular, even entertaining treatments of the subject, death and its seriousness remain inescapable. Death will not be abolished until its abolition is accompanied by this current fallen order.

Ineluctability notwithstanding, death remains an enemy of nature, a universal curse, and is always to be regarded so.

> While coming death is obvious, and thus is something which is natural and expected, it is also unnatural. For death brings our life, which is a gift of God, to an end. Just as a person might have to smash his car window in order to get inside, to do something violent and destructive in order to achieve some end, so death has come, inflicted deliberately by the hand of God, but inflicted for wise and holy ends. Death may be natural, and necessary, yet it does not represent the true fulfilment of mankind. It is not inevitable, part of a biological process that could not be otherwise. It is a judgment.[68]

> The curse of God is not something that is merely spiritual, affecting the soul's relation to God but nothing else; rather it has affected the whole of the animate creation, and has resulted in changed physical processes. So that the divine judgment, recorded in Genesis, "Cursed is the ground for thy sake . . . thorns also and thistles shall it bring forth to thee . . . unto dust shalt thou return" (3:17–19), is equivalent in power and kind to the first creative words "Let there be . . ." It is a curse of the deepest and most extensive kind.[69]

The voice that decreed by divine fiat creation *ex nihilo* and sustains that creation by the word of his power is the same voice that decreed its decreation in exhibition of his holy dominion over any rebellion by and perversion of that creation. To be sure, the punishment does suit the crime; however, death—and all its accoutrements—remains an unwelcome necessity in a created order that has failed to worship in truth its holy Creator.[70]

---

that I ought to die. That would be too terrible. . . . It's impossible! But here it is. How is this? How is one to understand it?" Tolstoy also pictures Pyotr Ivanovich's escapist coping with death by generalizing it "as though death were an event that was proper only to Ivan Ilych and alien to himself"; see Thielicke, *Living with Death*, 11.

68. Helm, *Last Things*, 34.

69. Ibid., 38–39.

70. That the entrance of death is unwelcome especially by Christ, the Creator of life, is indicated by his expression of indignation toward it at the resurrection of Lazarus. The verb used in John 11:33, 38 to describe Jesus' contempt toward death is ἐϲμβριμάδμαι (*embrimaomai*). According to John Stott, the term is used of the snorting of horses,

The Utility of Death

Megaphone to the living. Carefully balanced on the other hand, however, a proper perspective of the prospect of death—a healthy *memento mori*—ought rightly to lead every person to consider the poignant question posed by Francis Schaeffer, "How should we then live?"[71] If any meaning whatsoever is to be ascribed to a life lived under the sun, the steward of that life must seriously consider his own significance and end (Ps 90:10–12). Judgment based on how a steward has invested the gift given him will surely follow his promised end. Death, then, serves well as a megaphone[72] to call the living to attention concerning what they do with the life they now possess.[73]

> If it be certain that we must die, this should teach us frequently to think of Death, to keep it always in our eye and view. For, why should we cast off the thoughts of that which will certainly come, especially when it was so necessary to the good government of our lives, to remember that we must die? . . . and no man will practice [the wisdom that contemplation of one's mortality engenders], who does not often remember that he must die: but he that lives under a constant sense of Death, has a perpetual antidote against the follies and vanities of this world, and a perpetual spur to virtue.[74]

---

and was transferred to the strong human emotions of displeasure and indignation. See Stott, *Cross of Christ*, 68n4; see also Jeffery, *Pierced for Our Transgressions*, 121–22; and Carson, *How Long*, 266, chap. 7 n. 2.

71. Schaeffer, *How Should We Then Live?* See also 2 Peter 3:11–12.

72. Lewis, *Problem of Pain*, 93; see also Thielicke, *Living with Death*, 125. Thielicke writes, "In other words, a personal relation means that I must not complain against God when death comes. God is telling me something by it. In my death he is reacting to me. There is a message in it. I see God's hand and word aimed at me."

73. See John 9:4; Gal 2:20; 1 Tim 4:16. The *Dance of Death* appeared in art and literature in the late 13th century for the same purpose. The *Dance* originated in the form of a poem, which was the subject of a carving on the façade of the Church of the Innocents in Paris, commissioned by Jean, Duc de Berry. The poem, "Le Dit des trois morts et des trois vifs" [The dance of the three dead and the three living], tells of three young men of considerable social station who, while on a hunting excursion, encounter three corpses in various stages of decomposition. In the dialogue that ensues, the living contemplate mortification while the dead admonish the living to improve their ways in light of the brevity of their own condition. The hunting motif illustrates the nature of death as the ultimate hunter of all men. The theme of the *Dance* captures the universal nature of the need to contemplate one's death. Paul Binski writes, "The living, regardless of their temporal or spiritual station in life as popes, emperors or kings down to the very humblest, even children, are compelled by dancing cadavers to cavort with them as a *memento mori*." See Binski, *Medieval Death*, 153–54; cf. Boase, *Death in the Middle Ages*, 104.

74. Sherlock, *Practical Discourse*, 105.

A healthy *memento mori* further asserts,

> To expect Death every day, is like expecting thieves every night [Matt 24:42–44; 1 Thess 5:2]; which does not disturb our rest, but only makes us lock and bar our doors, and provide for our own defence. Thus to expect Death, is not to live under the perpetual fears of dying, but to live as a wise man would do, who knows, not that he *must*, but that he *may* die to-day.[75]

A morbid and debilitating preoccupation with one's own death is not in view here, one "which would put an end not only to all innocent mirth, but to all the necessary business of the world."[76] Rather, William Sherlock admonishes the living, much like Moses and Peter and John before him,[77] to a sober sensibility that each person will inevitably come to his own end where he will meet the Judge of all the earth and give an account for all his "deeds in the body, according to what he has done, whether good or bad" (2 Cor 5:10). Such sobriety will free the wise man from fear of death because when it arrives he will be prepared to meet it favorably; for "a man who is delivered from the fears of Death, fears nothing else in excess but God."[78]

The fact that death followed by divine judgment ineluctably will seize each of us (2 Cor 5:10; Heb 9:27) should provoke the wise man to live in such a way that what awaits him after death will not be despair, lamentation, and wrath in infinitely greater magnitude than he has experienced on his worst earthly day. Rather, he should pursue what will tend to both his greatest joy and his Maker's greatest glory in the hereafter.[79] As James puts it, he should "so speak and so act as those who are to be judged by the law of liberty" (Jas 2:12).

Divine governor. Part of God's judgment upon humanity at the Flood was to decrease the human lifespan.[80] Death, then, appears to have been insti-

---

75. Sherlock, *Practical Discourse*, 194. Further, Helm writes, "An emphasis upon such aspects of the biblical teaching [about death; e.g., living daily in light of the very real potential of one's own sudden entrance into eternity] will be thought by many to be macabre, but only by those who have been inoculated by modern culture into postponing the thought of one's death. Yet such an attitude is not a distinctively twentieth-century one but is characteristic of anyone who is preoccupied with this life to the virtual exclusion of what may follow." Helm, *Last Things*, 40.

76. Sherlock, *Practical Discourse*, 107.

77. See Ps 90:12; 2 Pet 3:11–12; 1 John 3:1–3.

78. Sherlock, *Practical Discourse*, 111; cf. Luke 12:4–5.

79. Piper, *God's Passion for His Glory*, 34–39; see also Flavel, *Mystery of Providence*, 188–90.

80. Gen 6:3 may be interpreted as God's decree to decrease mankind's lifespan

tuted by God in part as a deterrent to the advance of sin's ingenuity. If sinful mankind were permitted to live for hundreds of years, or even for millennia, he might well become as crafty at his vile rebellion against his Maker as is another of God's fallen[81] creatures—Satan—who *has* existed for millennia now. Man bears the image of the Maker, however—a privilege not granted to the serpent. Satan has not been so graced[82] with death (yet!) as a boundary to his villainy.

Sherlock elaborates on death as a divine governor.

> Since the fall of man, mortality and Death is necessary to the good government of the world: nothing else can give check to some men's wickedness; but either the fear of Death, or the execution of it; some men are so outrageously wicked, that nothing can put a stop to them, and prevent that mischief they do in this world, but to cut them off: this is the reason of capital punishments among men, to remove those out of the world, who will be a plague to mankind while they live in it. For this reason God destroyed the whole race of mankind by a deluge of water, excepting Noah and his family, because they were incurably wicked.[83]

Death illustrates the sustained and unassailable dominion of the sovereign Lord over every created being—corporeal and incorporeal—even over "rulers . . . powers . . . the world forces of this darkness, [and] the spiritual forces of wickedness in the heavenly places" (Eph 6:12).

Sign of the seriousness of sin. The biblical storyline maintains an intrinsic link between sin and death throughout its narrative for the express purpose

---

generally to 120 years from the hundreds of years that people lived prior to the Flood (see Gen 5:5, 8, 11, 14, 17, 20, 27, 31; 9:29; but Gen 11:32; 23:1; 25:7). An alternative interpretation of this passage suggests that God determined that the delay from the decree until the Flood would be 120 years. See *ESV Study Bible*, 61, text note on 6:3; see also Calvin, *Commentary on Genesis*; Aalders, *Genesis*; Leupold, *Exposition of Genesis*.

81. Satan's "fallenness" is veridical in as much as Isa 14:12 refers to Satan's fall and Rev 12:9 definitively refers to the fall of Satan and his angels to the earth. Concerning the origin of his evil, the Scriptures provide no information. By the time he engages Adam and Eve, however, this incorporeal yet created being had become "more crafty than any beast of the field which the LORD God had made" (Gen 3:1).

82. Death is a grace even to those who will incur damnation, for it curtails, in some sense, the "storing up of wrath" (Rom 2:5; cf. 1:22–32) by which they will experience "eternal destruction, away from the presence of the Lord and from the glory of his power" (2 Thess 1:9).

83. Sherlock, *Practical Discourse*, 94–95.

of signifying the seriousness of sin.[84] The covenant people of God—both old and new covenants—must be reminded perpetually of the seriousness of sin. Death is that constant reminder, as a permanent statute throughout our generations. The Old Testament Levitical sacrificial system served as this perpetual reminder for the former covenant people. For New Testament covenant people of God, the Lord's Supper is the Law's parallel reminder of the seriousness of sin, "for as often as [we] eat this bread and drink the cup, [we] proclaim *the Lord's death* until he comes" (Luke 22:19; 1 Cor 11:23–26; emphasis added). In light of the seriousness and just consequence of sin, this remembrance of God's grace to humanity that grants a stay of our own eternal execution should evoke awe striking gratitude and worship as often as we "proclaim the Lord's [vicarious and sacrificial] death." In this way is the Eucharist biblically observed in light of the seriousness of sin and death.

Freedom from sin. Even though death is an unwelcome intrusion into the created order, because it remains under the dominion of God (Deut 32:39; 2 Kgs 5:7; Rev 1:18), there are facets of it that not only God but also we may deem valuable. Although God "takes no pleasure in the death of the wicked" (Ezek 18:23; 33:11), and there is a sense in which he has "no pleasure in the death of anyone who dies" (Ezek 18:32), he declares "precious in the sight of the Lord is the death of his saints" (Ps 116:15). That is, for the one who consummates his judgment of death *in Christ*, not only is a crown of righteousness and life laid-up for him (2 Tim 4:8; Jas 1:12; Rev 2:10), but also a mutually joyous reconciliation with his God (John 17:20–24; Luke 15:20–24; Zeph 3:17) where pleasures forevermore await him (Ps 16:11). Additionally, for the one who delights in bearing the image of God, not only does the transition of death conclude the pains and evils of this life (Job 14:1–3; Eccl 4:1–3; Isa 57:1–2), but it also makes an end of sins and vices as the saint's sanctification is consummated in glorification (Phil 3:21). In this freeing regard to "fairest death," Martin Luther affectionately consoles:

---

84. No one in Israel's community would have been unfamiliar with the perpetual sights, sounds, and smells of death in the daily slaughtering of animals—each one explicitly because of the people's sin. Much like Israel was reminded daily that the shedding of blood is supremely necessary to make it possible for the holy God to dwell in the midst of an unclean people without the infinitely glorious radiance of his very holy presence consuming them (Exod 33:3, 20; Num 16:21, 45; Heb 12:29; John 18:6 [See the excellent discussions regarding the chief end of God as dwelling in the midst of his people in McKelvey, *NDBT*, s.v. "Temple."]), so the occurrence of death is a daily reminder to all God's image bearers of not only the seriousness of sin, but also the brevity and finitude of their earthy existence. How should we then live is underscored (see Pss 39:4; 90:12; Jas 2:12; 2 Pet 3:10–14; 1 John 3:2–3). For further discussion, see the section below entitled, "Why Do Christians Die?"

> The other blessing of death is this, that it not only concludes the pains and evils of this life, but (which is more excellent) makes an end of sins and vices. And this renders death far more desirable to believing souls . . . than the former blessing. . . . This alone, did we but know it, should make death most desirable. But if it does not, it is a sign that we neither feel nor hate our sin as we should. For this our life is so full of perils—sin, like a serpent, besetting us on every side—and it is impossible for us to live without sinning; but fairest death delivers us from these perils, and cuts our sin clean away from us.[85]

Oh glorious redemptive day![86]

Conclusion: The Good Providence of God in the Ordinance of Death

Ruminating the questions "What is death?" and "Why death?" inevitably leads to contemplation of the providence[87] of death; that is, how may one understand the ordering of death? Death does not simply "happen"—any more or less than any other transpiration in the created order—as though its occurrence is nothing more than an unguided coincidence with the natural order of things. As we have seen, death is the *lex talionis* for an infinitely heinous offense against an infinitely holy God. Death is not accidental; it is meticulously[88]—rather than generally—providentially ordered by the God of the Bible in accord with his holy purposes.

---

85. Luther, "Fourteen of Consolation," 42:150, cited in Kerr, *Compend of Luther's Theology*, 241. In the paragraph prior, Luther compares Israel's life-giving gaze at Moses' brazen serpent with our faithful contemplation of the death of Christ. He observes, "Death, then, to believers is already dead, and hath nothing terrible behind its grinning mask. Like unto a slain serpent, it hath indeed its former terrifying appearance, but it is only the appearance; in truth it is a dead evil, and harmless enough. Nay, as God commanded Moses to lift up a serpent of brass, at sight of which the living serpents perished, even so our death dies in the believing contemplation of the death of Christ, and now hath but the outward appearance of death. With such fine similitudes the mercy of God prefigures to us, in our infirmity, this truth, that though death should not be taken away, He yet has reduced its power to a mere shadow. For this reason it is called in the Scriptures a 'sleep' rather than death."

86. Eccl 7:1b; Rom 7:24–25.

87. The AV, the NASB, and the ASV translate the Greek term προνοίας (*pronoias*) as "providence" in Acts 24:2. The NIV translates the Hebrew term פְּקֻדָּה (*pequddah*) as "providence" in Job 10:12. No other commonly used modern English translations use the term. "Care," "visitation," and "foresight" are alternative English renderings.

88. God providentially orders both good and evil according to his own ends (Job 2:10). Just how God preserves and governs his creation is broadly understood in one of

John Calvin grounds God's providential ordering of the universe—*contra* unguided "happenings"—in his having created it.

> ... having found him Creator of all, forthwith to conclude he is also everlasting Governor and Preserver—not only in that he drives the celestial frame as well as its several parts by a universal motion but also in that he sustains, nourishes, and cares for, everything he has made, even to the least sparrow ... we must know that God's providence, as it is taught in Scripture, is opposed to fortune and fortuitous happenings.[89]

Because death is included in God's disposing of action within the created order, no sufficient ground exists to conclude that the entrance or occurrence of death must operate outside of God's "infallible foreknowledge, and the free and immutable counsel of His own will, to the praise of the glory of His wisdom, power, justice, goodness, and mercy," and in accord with "His own holy ends."[90]

---

two ways: general sovereignty and specific sovereignty. General sovereignty maintains that, "God has sovereignly established a type of world in which God sets up general structures or an overall framework for meaning and allows the creatures significant input into exactly how things turn out.... General sovereignty allows for things to happen that are not part of God's plan for our lives; it allows for pointless evil." See Sanders, *God Who Risks*, 225–26.

On the other hand, specific sovereignty is sometimes called meticulous providence because of its claim that God has foreordained and exhaustively controls all things in order to accomplish his ends. The present contention is that the specific sovereignty view best interprets the scriptural evidence (see for example, Gen 50:20; Deut 32:39; 1 Sam 2:6–8; 2 Kgs 5:7; Job 42:2; Pss 50:10; 115:3; 135:5–7; Prov 16:4, 9, 33; 21:1; Isa 10:15; 29:16; 64:8; 46:9b–10; Lam 3:37–38; Dan 4:32–35; Jonah 1:4; Matt 8:23–26; Rom 8:28; 9:15–21; Acts 2:23; 4:27–28; 17:28; Eph 1:11; Phil 2:13; Jas 4:15; 1 Pet 1:20). Bruce Ware also rather candidly contends that the Lord meticulously reigns over all. He writes, "None of God's creation, heavenly or earthly, can challenge, disrupt, thwart, or frustrate his comprehensive will. We his creatures are, in this sense, 'accounted as nothing [Dan 4:35],' and we had best bring to an end the arrogance and presumption of thinking otherwise [A footnote here notes Dan 4:37—Nebuchadnezzar's humbling acknowledgment of God's absolute reign.]. God is glorious, in part, because he reigns over all." Ware cites as "spectrum texts" (biblical texts that affirm that God is in complete control of "both ends of the spectrum" and everything in between), Exod 4:11; Deut 32:39; 1 Sam 2:6–7; 2 Kgs 5:7; Ps 75:6–7; Isa 45:5–7; and Lam 3:37–38. See Ware, *God's Lesser Glory*, 150. For a thorough discussion of the distinction between general sovereignty and compatibilistic specific sovereignty, see Feinberg, *No One Like Him*, 642–743.

89. Calvin, *Institutes*, 1:197–98.

90. Hodge, *Popular Lectures*, 39, cited in Cottrell, *What the Bible Says*, 27 n. 61. Hodge eloquently adds, "God is in the atom just as really and effectually as in the planet. He is in the unobserved sighing of the wind in the wilderness as in the earthquake which overthrows a city full of living men, and his infinite wisdom and power are as

God ordains all things that come to pass, "having been predestined according to His purpose who works all things after the counsel of His will" (Eph 1:11). We may affirm, therefore, that particular appointments of death are meticulously ordered by God. At the same time, however, we need not assert that God has determined how long every person shall live by an absolute and unconditional decree.[91] That is, often God providentially ordains the length of days of individuals in accord with their compatibilistically free[92] compliance with God's natural and moral ordinances.[93] Other occasions of death, to be sure, are sovereignly determined by the divine mind in accord with his secret will[94] (which, by the way, does not discord with his revealed will). Even particular incidents of death, then, are appointed by God.[95]

> No man can go out of this world, no more than he can come into it, but by a special Providence; no man can destroy himself, but by God's leave; no disease can kill, but when God pleases; no mortal accident can befal [sic] us, but by God's appointment; who is therefore said to deliver the man into the hand of his neighbour, who is killed by an evil accident, Deut. xix. 4, 5.[96]

---

much concerned in the one event as in the other."

91. Sherlock ponders, "Now when I say the time of our Death is uncertain, I need not tell you, that I mean only it is uncertain to us; that no man knows when he shall die, for God certainly knows when we shall die, because he knows all things; and therefore with respect to the fore-knowledge of God, the time of our death is certain"; Sherlock, *Practical Discourse*, 117.

92. For a treatment of compatibilistic free agency of the creature, see Feinberg, *No One Like Him*, 677–734.

93. Carson, *How Long*, 114.

94. Cf. Deut 29:29a. For a nuanced view of the will(s) of God, see Piper, "Are There Two Wills in God."

95. See Gen 2:17; Deut 32:39; 2 Sam 2:6; 28:19; Ps 139:16; John 12:4; 21:18–19; Heb 9:27. Job 14:1–5, for example, articulates not that particular individuals' deaths are predetermined, but that man's lifespan is determinately finite (cf. Acts 17:26). The parable of the rich fool in Luke 12:20 is more indicative of God's decreeing the particularity of one's departure from this world. God's meticulous providence over death is seen abundantly in Scripture in how both individuals and populations come to meet death. The modes of *providing* death are various: immediate action on God's part, disaster or plague, illness, or action mediated through another creature—either intentionally or inadvertently. The biblical record amply attests to these accounts; see for example, by immediate action of God: Gen 3:22–24; 5:5; by disaster or plague: Gen 6–7; 19:24–25; Exod 11–12; 2 Kgs 19 (esp. vv. 32–37); Job 1:12–22; Num 11; 16:20–35, 44–50; by illness: 1 Sam 25:37–38; 2 Kgs 4:8–37; 2 Chr 18–23; by mediated action: Gen 4:3–11; Deut 7:2, 16 with Josh 11:20, Deut 2:24–37, and Isa 10:5–7; 1 Kgs 22:34–35; 2 Kgs 2:23–24.

96. Sherlock, *Practical Discourse*, 180–81.

William Sherlock here rightly affirms Yahweh as Lord of both life and death. In the eyes of the Sovereign of the universe, no such thing exists as "accidental" death or even someone's "determining his or her own death" by suicide apart from God's providential ordinance.

God-ordained Entrance of Death

When God created the cosmos, the earth and all that is in it, including man—his *magnum opus*, he declared it "very good" (Gen 1:31). The darkness of evil and death was nowhere seen in God's completed work. Before the foundation of the world, however, God intended to manifest his glory not only as Creator but also as Redeemer (Eph 1:4; 3:8–11; 1 Pet 1:20). How could God manifest himself as redeemer of that which had no need of redeeming? Enter: death.

When God charged Adam that he would die in the day that he rejected God's gracious provision and Lordship (Gen 2:17), that Adam would do precisely as forbidden was not unexpected by God. Moreover, it was ordained by God. How then can God not be morally accountable for the evil of the Fall? God can be causally responsible for his decree yet not morally accountable for the creature's action because the agent who acts freely in accord with his desire is culpable for a given action, not the one who decrees the sufficient circumstances.[97]

---

97. The temptation of Adam and Eve by the evil one and their failure into sin and consequent death may certainly be considered evil. The entrance of death, however, as ordained by God—from whose nature only that which is good may come (see Ware, *God's Greater Glory*, 120)—may be considered both good and evil. John Calvin offers constructive insight concerning what has been termed *double agency*. Actions performed compatibilistically by two agents—e.g., God and the creature—may be considered, without logical contradiction, both good *and* evil. Calvin asserts, "Therefore, whatever men or Satan himself may instigate, God nevertheless holds the key, so that he turns their efforts to carry out his judgments" (*Institutes*, 1:230). Because of God's omniscient, omnipotent dominion over every creature—including Satan—creaturely ill-motivated and evil actions are simultaneously *provided* by God in accord with his good and holy purposes without impugning his holy character. See for example, Isa 10:5–7, 13–19; John 6:64–65, 70–71; 19:10–11; 11:49–52.

For further discussion of God's preceptive/revealed will and his decretive/secret will viz. Deut 29:29 and primary and secondary agency, see Feinberg, *No One Like Him*, 694–701. Feinberg argues, "Though some think the decree causes the deeds to occur, we have already shown that this is not so, because the decree is not an agent nor does it exercise causal powers.... While God decrees the circumstances in which we let ourselves become tempted and fall into sin, he neither tempts us nor enables or empowers us to do evil, nor does the decree. We do these acts in concert with our desires, and hence do them freely (in the compatibilistic sense), and what one does freely is something for which one is culpable." See also Frame, *Doctrine of God*, 174–82.

The intrusion of death into the created order,[98] then, comes as a corruption of God's originally very good creation; it is nonetheless providentially ordained. It was ordained as God's righteous judgment against a rebellious creation in hope of redemption of that creation (Rom 8:20–21). Death, then, is a cursed deviation—albeit ordained—from God's natural blessed order. This *provision* also entails the aforementioned grace extended to Adam and all his progeny against the alternative option of living forever in an ever more corrupting and decomposing yet never finally consuming state. Both this extension of grace and the display of the integrity of God's holy character in not acquitting the guilty exhibit the good providence of God in his ordinance of death.

Concurrence with This Good Providence of God

As creatures created in the image of and granted free agency by our Creator, we can choose prayerfully whether or not we will do any number of things (Jas 4:15); but we cannot choose not to die. Death, as the righteous judgment of God upon the disobedient creature, is inevitable. The inevitability of death ought not, however, to dissuade us from boldly engaging the God-provided means of prolonging life. Life remains a gift from God; as the classic Christmas carol *Joy to the World* heralds, "He comes to make his blessings flow far as the curse is found." Prolonging life in honor of the God who gave it is completely in accord not only with God's provision for stemming the curse, but also with God's admonition (Deut 4:40; Eph 6:2–3; Ps 91; Prov 3:1–2, 8, 16–18). Such righteous provision and admonition contributes to making God's blessings flow far as the curse is found.

Death Is Not Final

In some senses death certainly can be viewed as conclusive. Viewing life only from a temporal perspective, the Preacher charged, "Whatever your hand finds to do, do it with all your might; for there is no activity or planning or knowledge or wisdom in Sheol where you are going" (Eccl 9:10; cf. 1 Cor 15:32). Death terminates all hopes of any further earthly endeavors—educational or career goals, marriage plans, childbearing and rearing,

---

98. Jeffery, *Pierced for Our Transgressions*, 121–22. Concerning the application of death to nonhuman creation, see Luther, *LW* 13:107; Feinberg, *No One Like Him*, 622–24, 779; Feinberg, *Many Faces of Evil*, 23, 194.; Thielicke, *Death and Life*, 150–53, 207–10.

ministry plans, book deals, retirement, budding friendships, and anything else under the sun for which one could hope. In this sense, sadly, death is final.

True, God ordained death, yet he did not conclude his story of humanity's encounter with death without the hope of resurrection. Physical death, therefore, is not ultimately final—either for the Christian or the unbeliever. Woefully, for the unbeliever, annihilation is not the culmination of death;[99] rather, what awaits the one who tramples under foot the only life giving Son of God, insulting the Spirit of grace, is "a terrifying expectation of judgment and the fury of a fire which will consume the adversaries" (Heb 10:27–29; see also Matt 13:49–50; 25:41). For the Christian, however, just as the penalty for sin has been both remitted and vanquished by the perfect Christ, such that "it was impossible for death to hold him" (Acts 2:24), so death will not be able to hold any of those who are *in Christ*. Holy God ordained death because of sin. The same sovereign God also ordained life through Jesus Christ the Lord.[100]

---

99. Helm, *Last Things*, 115–19; Morgan and Peterson, *Hell under Fire*; Peterson, *Hell on Trial*. Edwards, "Concerning the Endless Punishment," 2:515–25.

100. Jeffery, *Pierced for Our Transgressions*, 171–73.

CHAPTER 3

Death in the Old Testament

Introduction

THE ORIGIN OF DEATH being established, we may now turn to what the Old Testament has to say about the nature of death—as sparse as that may be—considering that the afterlife and the underworld were not a particular concern of the Old Testament writers.[1] In its discussion of death, however, the Old Testament weaves a few key concepts: God's relationship with humanity, particularly his covenant people; the contrast of alsoran death with principal life; the paramount ethic of the glory of God; and the relative value of finite human life under the sun. Several terms are used by ancient Israel (as well as her Semitic neighbors) to designate the state, location, inhabitants, and/or condition of the dead. Because the intent of language is to communicate meaning, and the definition of terms is crucial for a common understanding of that meaning in regard to our topic, we will begin by examining the language of the Old Testament's dialogue with death.

Terminology

The language used in the Old Testament in reference to death stands in contradiction to those who argue that the Old Testament has "no formal doctrine concerning the destination and fate of the dead; all that it says

---

1. Johnston, *Shades of Sheol*, 85.

on the subject belongs to the domain of popular lore."[2] Numerous thanatological terms are used with both dogmatic assertion and varying nuances of meaning.

Shĕ'ôl

The Hebrew term שְׁאוֹל, *Shĕ'ôl* is "generally translated with 'the realm of the dead.' It denotes the subterranean spirit world, the grave, the state or condition of death, and the brink of death, or the like."[3] Used sixty-five times in the Old Testament, the AV translates the term *Shĕ'ôl* variously as *grave* (thirty-one times), *hell* (thirty-one times), or *pit* (three times).[4] The NASB retains the word *Sheol* all sixty-five times. The ESV retains the word sixty-three times, seemingly arbitrarily translating it *pit* in Job 33:18 and *grave* in Song of Solomon 8:6 with a text note indicating the original as *Sheol*. The Old Testament sometimes characterizes this realm of the dead as a physical location "under" or "in the innermost parts of the earth," i.e., the netherworld. Several passages indicate this localizing of the underworld.[5]

Though debated whether *Shĕ'ôl* is typically used to describe the place of all of the departed—both godly and ungodly (see below)—the synonym אֲבַדּוֹן, *'abaddôn* is usually used to refer to the place of destruction.[6] Two

---

2. Gaster, *IDB*, 787A. Tromp finds insubstantial such assertions as Gaster's, arguing that the concept of an afterlife "was hardly as marginal in Israelite thought as is often supposed"; see Tromp, *Primitive Conceptions*, 4, cf. 196.

3. Heidel, *Gilgamesh*, 173–77. In n. 134 Heidel writes, "The fact that the common Old Testament designation for the grave is קֶבֶר is no proof at all that *Shĕ'ôl* cannot have the same meaning. קֶבֶר is the general word for 'grave' while *Shĕ'ôl* is used primarily in poetry, occurring only eight times in prose, out of a total of sixty-five passages." As a reference to the *underworld* see: Num 16:30–33; Deut 32:22; Job 11:8; 26:6; Pss 49:16; 139:8; Prov 15:11, 24; Isa 7:11; 14:13–15; 57:9; Amos 9:2. As a reference to the *grave* see: Job 24:19–20; Ps 141:7; Isa 14:11 (cf. Job 21:26); Ezek 32:6–27; also Gen 42:38; 1 Kgs 2:5–9; Pss 30:4; 86:13; 89:49; Prov 23:13–14 with 19:18 and 29:1; Jonah 2:3 (=2:2 in English); see also Gen 37:35; 42:38; 1 Sam 2:6; Job 7:9; 17:16; 21:13; 24:19; 33:18; Pss 16:10; 30:3; 55:15; 139:8; Prov 5:5; Isa 14:9, 11, 15; Hos 13:14. See also Johnston, *Shades*, 73–75; Martin-Achard, *From Death to Life*, 36–37; Pryor, "Eschatological Expectations," 49–50; Tromp, *Primitive Conceptions*, 21–23.

4. Hoekema, *Bible and the Future*, 95–96.

5. Heidel, *Gilgamesh*, 178; Johnston, *Shades of Sheol*, 108–9 (Num 16:30, 33; Deut 32:22; Ps 139:8; Isa 14:13–15; Amos 9:2 and Job 26:5; cf. Prov 15:24).

6. Heidel, *Gilgamesh*, 177; Johnston, *Shades of Sheol*, 85 (Job 26:6; 28:22; Ps 88:12; Prov 15:11; 27:20).

other synonyms for *Shĕôl*, usually translated "pit," are שַׁחַת, *shahath*[7] and בֹּר, *bôr*, and can refer to either the grave or the netherworld.[8]

Without question, biblical references or inferences to this realm of the dead depict individuals in a state of conscious existence, rather than either unconscious existence or annihilation.[9] The Israelite did not, however, view this alternative state of consciousness as merely that. Life was understood as the gift of God for his image bearers; death is always mentioned in terms ultimately unfavorable to life.[10] In Eccl 19:5, Qohelet mourns, "For the living know they will die; but the dead do not know anything, nor have they any longer a reward, for their memory is forgotten." Of this realm of the forgotten Joseph Ratzinger notes that it is "a kind of un-life among the shades . . . banished into a noncommunication zone where life is destroyed precisely because relationship is impossible . . . simultaneously being and nonbeing, somehow still existence and yet no longer life."[11] He continues that man's failed attempt to divinize himself—i.e., the Fall—resulted in his relegation to a "Sheol-existence, a being in nothingness, a shadow-life on the fringe of real living."[12] Of Jewish ambivalence toward leaving the body at death, Elwell and Keefer write, respectively, of the apostle Paul that he "does not look forward to being bodiless,"[13] nor does he "relish the unnatural state of death."[14]

---

7. Heidel, *Gilgamesh*, 177; Johnston, *Shades of Sheol*, 84, 85; Martin-Achard, *From Death to Life*, 38 (Job 33:18–30; Ps 30:10; 55:24 Isa 38:17; 51:14; Ezek 28:8).

8. Heidel, *Gilgamesh*, 177; Johnston, *Shades of Sheol*, 83–85; Martin-Achard, *From Death to Life*, 38 (Pss 28:1; 30:4; 88:5; Isa 14:15–19; 38:18; Lam 3:55; Prov 28:17).

9. See, for example, 1 Sam 28:11–19 with 1 Chr 10:13; Matt 22:31–32/Mark 12:25–27/Luke 20:34–38 (in reference to Exod 3:6, 16); Matt 27:50–53; Luke 23:43; Phil 1:23; 1 Thess 5:10; Rev 6:9–11; cf. Isa 14:9–20; Luke 16:19–31; Heb 12:22–23. Further, the prohibition of necromancy in Lev 20:27 and Deut 18:11 would be superfluous if the people perceived no such thing possible. See also the headings below entitled "*Rĕphā'îm*" and "*Nephesh*."

10. Qohelet does not contradict this assertion when, in Eccl 4:2–3 or in 7:1b. In his intentionally specific focus, Qohelet is contrasting, here, not the *nature* of life and death, but the toils and snares of life in a fallen world in isolation from the sustaining grace of God in contrast to the avoidance of those particular troubles that is the lot of the dead. We must be careful, however, not to assume that Qohelet is here suggesting that this temporal life is all there is, or that he is denying an ultimate and eternal consequential judgment of the dead (cf. Eccl 11:9; 12:7, 14). Again, he is merely contrasting phenomenologically the immediacy of this present life with the alternative. Job 3; 10:1 and 14:13 similarly bemoan this (specific) contrast (cf. Isa 26:19–20).

11. Ratzinger, *Eschatology*, 80–81.

12. Ibid., 156.

13. Elwell, *BTDB*, s.v. "Intermediate State."

14. Keefer, *BTDB*, s.v. "Paradise."

Israel did not deny that God somehow ruled over whatever took place in *Sheol*—though her understanding of the economy of *Shĕ'ôl* was vastly distinct from that of her Babylonian and Egyptian contemporaries whose underworld hosted a pantheon of chthonic[15] deities. The Old Testament *Shĕ'ôl* is both created and ruled by Israel's singular sovereign God. He is neither chief among many gods, viz., henotheism; nor has he delegated to other *'elohîm* (see below) rule of elect segments of his created order. Israel often referred to this God as "the living God";[16] but he is not merely a deity who is personified *life*, akin to other ANE deities. He is the sovereign Lord of life and death who both created life and gives and rescinds it at his pleasure.[17] *Shĕ'ôl*, then, as a temporal creation, much like its inhabitants, is completely under his dominion; both admission to and dismissal from this "place" are at the discretion of "the living God."[18]

Philip Johnston summarizes of *Shĕ'ôl*, "So it is a term of personal engagement. Whatever the origin of the term, there is no hint of Sheol being a deity. Descriptive details are very sparse, but suggest a somnolent, gloomy existence without meaningful activity or social distinction. There is certainly no elaborate journey through the gates or stages of the underworld, in Mesopotamian or Egyptian style. So [for ancient Israel] there was no great concern with the ongoing fate of the dead."[19]

The fate of all? As mentioned above, whether or not only the unrighteous dead go to *Shĕ'ôl* is debated. To be sure, the usage of the term is predominantly in relation to the ungodly; yet because the judgment of the dead in

---

15. From the Greek χθονιος, *chthonios*: "in, under, or beneath the earth," from χθων: "earth," the term refers to the realm of the underworld.

16. Deut 26; Josh 3:10; Pss 42:2; 84:2; 2 Kgs 19:4, 16; 1 Sam 17:26, 36; Jer 10:10; Hos 2:1; etc. See Martin-Achard, *From Death to Life*, 12.

17. Deut 32:22, 39; Job 26:6; Ps 139:7–8; Prov 15:11; Amos 9:2.

18. Both Tromp and Kaufmann perhaps go too far in their limitation of the relationship between the omnipresent, omnipotent God and Sheol. Kaufmann suggests, "To be sure, JHWH rules Sheol, yet there is no relation between him and the dead." In the same vein, though Tromp affirms that "Yahweh is Lord and Master of Sheol," he also asserts, "Sheol is Sheol because the living God is not there," arguing that David's assertion in Psalm 139 is not to be taken literally, but only hyperbolically in terms of its "vivacity and expressivity." Contrarily, however, the omnipresent living God who "fills all" (Eph 1:21–23; 4:9–10) and whose power is exercised in some sense throughout the entirety of the created order (Heb 1:3) cannot be characterized as either absent from or bereft of any kind of relation to any place in that created order. Frankly, Hell is Hell *precisely because of* the holy God's wrathful *presence* against all that is unholy. See Tromp, *Primitive Conceptions*, 199–200; and Kaufmann, *Religion of Israel*, 314, cited in Tromp.

19. Johnston, *Shades of Sheol*, 85.

Shĕʾōl is not mentioned in the Old Testament,[20] those represented as righteous also descend to *Shĕʾōl*.[21] Alexander Heidel does not think so, however. Convinced that "Neither Psalm 49 . . . nor any other passage in the Old Testament teaches an intermediate state or sojourn (*status medius* or *intermedius*) for the righteous after death,"[22] Heidel argues that the Old Testament does not depict the souls of all the deceased as descending to *Shĕʾōl*. He suggests that both Psalms 49 and 73 indicate a distinct destination for the righteous/faithful than the unrighteous/unfaithful upon death.[23] He even demands that "Ps 73:26 says *explicitly* that even *after death* God will be the 'portion' of the righteous 'forever.'"[24]

Heidel's interpretation here is too static, however. Apparently leaving no category distinction between temporal and ultimate end of the righteous dead, he conflates the two. The psalmists appear rather to be referring only to their ultimate end—which better fits the contexts. Their immediate adjournment, then, remains *Shĕʾōl*, and their consummate end is the blessedness of communion with God—which Heidel assumes is the only import of the texts. Johnston also argues convincingly *contra* Heidel.

> [Heidel's argument] ignores the prophetic pictures of Sheol's inhabitants speaking (Isa 14:10; Ezek 32:21). It posits different meanings of Sheol within the same passage (Isa 14:11–15). It assumes identity between the specific term "Sheol" and the more general term "death." And it arbitrarily determines the meaning of Sheol by theological assessment of the associated individual, which results in the contradiction that the pious go to Sheol (when it means the grave) but not to Sheol (when it means the underworld).[25]

The argument that only the unrighteous adjourn to *Shĕʾōl* is therefore unconvincing. The Old Testament witness regards *Shĕʾōl* as the temporary state of all the dead.[26] Not until the intertestamental period do we begin to

---

20. Pryor notes, "The nearest thing to eternal punishment in the prophets is an obscure statement in Isa. 66:24. 'And they shall go forth and look on the dead bodies of the men that have rebelled against me; for their worm shall not die, their fire shall not be quenched, and they shall be an abhorrence to all flesh'"; see Pryor, "Eschatological Expectations," 53.

21. For example, see Gen 37:35; Isa 38:10; Job 17:13–16; Ps 88:4.

22. Heidel, *Gilgamesh*, 186 n. 168.

23. Ibid., 184–91.

24. Ibid., 190 (emphasis added).

25. Johnston, *Shades of Sheol*, 74.

26. See Ps 89:48; Eccl 9:7–10. As Pedersen puts it, "Sheol is the entirety into which all graves are merged"; see Pedersen, *Israel*, 462, cited in Tromp, *Primitive Conceptions*, 10, 133.

see a more clear understanding of distinct locations for the righteous and unrighteous dead.[27]

Rĕphā'îm

The language of the Old Testament definitively describes conscious existence beyond death—albeit a far less desirable state than earthly life—not simply of dream images or figments of one's imagination, but of persons. The Hebrew term רְפָאִים, rĕphā'îm (shades) is used of these persons—both righteous and unrighteous. The form rāphè (weak) implies that the dead have been deprived of physical strength by death. These rĕphā'îm are described variously as a "shadowy, insubstantial existence,"[28] "quasi-bodily entity,"[29] or "state of being in which the active forces of life are reduced to their lowest intensity, so crushed and drained away as to be virtually absent . . . whose powers have been reduced almost to vanishing point"[30] The Old Testament uses the term sparsely in reference to the dead (only eight times in four poetic books of the OT).[31] This rarity, however, is not due either to the semantic limitation of the term or the variety of other terms used in reference to the dead, but to the equal rarity of the Old Testament's concern for the state of deceased persons.

---

27. Wright, Resurrection, 86, 140. The term Hades is the usual Septuagint translation of Sheol. Having undergone semantic revision during the intertestamental period, where the netherworld comes to be understood as being divided into two regions, Hades came to be used typically of the realm of only the unrighteous dead (cf. Luke 16:19–31), rather than all of the deceased as Sheol signified. Joseph Ratzinger traces the development of the notion of distinct locations of the dead back to the 150 BC Ethiopian recension of the book of Enoch, twenty-second chapter. Rather than the nondescript Sheol of Israel's earlier prophets, the author articulates a more detailed "space" where the unjust await final judgment in darkness, yet the just "dwell in light, being assembled around a life-giving spring of water." Further tracing the development, Ratzinger cites the Fourth Book of Ezra, ca. AD 100. Here not only do the righteous enter eternal blessedness, but the unjust enter immediately into final torment. Rabbinic Judaism also held a view of entrance into the final state immediately upon death, one path leading to Gehenna, the place of damnation, the other leading to paradise or Abraham's bosom—terminologies present also in New Testament Christianity. Such notions of separate conscious existence also inhere in the Qumran Essene community. See Ratzinger, Eschatology, 120–25.

28. Johnston, Shades of Sheol, 128; Martin-Achard, From Death to Life, 34–36.

29. Cooper, Body, Soul, and Life Everlasting, 69.

30. Clark, Interpreting the Resurrection, 14.

31. Job 26:5; Ps 88:10; Prov 2:18; 9:18; Isa 14:9; 26:14, 19; implicit in Prov 21:16. See also Johnston, Shades of Sheol, 128–42.

The term is also used of a particular Canaanite people group, possibly Philistine ancestors. Context, however, always distinguishes the ethnic *Rĕphā'îm* from the deceased; when used of the deceased, the term is always used in conjunction with the notion of *Shĕ'ôl*, the dead, or death.[32]

Isaiah 26:14, 19 is a significant passage in which the term is used. The passage both alludes to the conscious existence of those in some form of temporal intermediate state and affirms their future bodily resurrection—a topic that will receive fuller treatment below.

> The dead (*mētîm*) will not live, the departed spirits (*rĕphā'îm*)
> will not rise;
> Therefore you have punished and destroyed them,
> And you have wiped out all remembrance of them.
>
> Your dead (*mētîm*) will live;
> Their corpses will rise.
> You who lie in the dust, awake and shout for joy,
> For your dew *is as* the dew of the dawn,
> And the earth will give birth to the departed spirits (*rĕphā'îm*).

Inquiring of the continuity of personal identity in bodily resurrection, John W. Cooper notes of the term's usage in this passage,

> Highly significant for our inquiry is the fact that the term for the deceased both in v. 14b and v. 19d is *rephaim*, the word used in Isaiah 14 and throughout the Old Testament to designate the dwellers in Sheol. So here we have an unequivocal link between the future bodily resurrection and the inhabitants of the underworld realm of the dead. On the great day of the Lord, the *rephaim* will be reunited with their bodies, reconstituted from the dust, and they will live as the Lord's people again.[33]

The *rĕphā'îm* here are still not beyond the reach of God's sovereign dominion. Even their end will be determined by God. The term used in this context confirms not only the personal reality of the inhabitants of *Shĕ'ôl*, but also Israel's confidence in some form or another of a posthumous resurrection.

In addition to *rĕphā'îm*, the term אֱלֹהִים, *'elohîm* is also used of inhabitants of *Shĕ'ôl*. This Hebrew word is typically used for "God" or "gods," but

---

32. The first occurrence of the reference to the Canaanite Rephaim is in Genesis 14:50; see also Deut 2:11, 20; 3:13; Josh 12:4; 2 Sam 5:18. See also Johnston, *Shades of Sheol*, 128, 130–34.

33. Cooper, *Body, Soul, and Life Everlasting*, 64.

may also refer to other supernatural beings such as angels or spirits.[34] Notably, in 1 Sam 28:13 the apparition of Samuel—a human being—is called *'elohîm*.

Nephesh

Another significant term used in the Old Testament to indicate persons' post-mortem conscious state of existence is נֶפֶשׁ, *nephesh*. It does not necessarily refer only to the eternal part of a person commonly understood as a *soul*; the concept is closer to selfhood or life-force. It is that which is given man at creation, but then returns to God at his death. It connotes "that which is vital in man in the broadest sense."[35] The term is used in the Old Testament of one's breath (though perhaps by synecdoche), one's appetite, or a person.

Nephesh is used in Gen 35:18 of Rachel's departing "soul." That is, that which distinguished Rachel as Rachel departed from the land of the living; the text does not indicate that her "soul" ceased to exist. The more likely implication is that her conscious existence returned, in some sense, to the Lord who gave it (Eccl 12:7). Elijah also uses the term in 1 Kgs 17:21 praying for God to restore the "life" of the son of the widow of Zarephath. Both of these instances refer not merely to a last *breath*, but to "their personal being—a substantial, separable soul or self."[36] One may not, however, categorically exclude from the term's significance any reference to the body; for alternatively, in Hag 2:13 the same term is translated "corpse."

בְּתַחְתִּיּוֹת הָאָרֶץ, "Depths of the Earth"

This phrase, translated variously as "innermost parts of the earth" or "depths of the earth," sometimes seems to refer to the grave or the place of the dead—as in Pss 63:9 and 71:20; however, upon closer inspection, it need not at all refer to physical death or the location of the dead. Rather, the psalmist may be using the phrase to refer to vicissitudes unfathomable by the finite human mind.[37] In the New Testament, Matthew uses a near identical phrase, "the heart of the earth," to describe the state of Christ's death in compari-

---

34. Johnston, *Shades of Sheol*, 142–49; Martin-Achard, *From Death to Life*, 33–34; Pss 8:5; 82:1, 6.

35. Von Rad, *Old Testament Theology*, 153.

36. Cooper, *Body, Soul, and Life Everlasting*, 61; see also Pryor, "Eschatological Expectations," 50.

37. For usage of the phrase where death is clearly not indicated, see Pss 95:4; 139:15.

son to the state of being of Jonah when he was experiencing the corrective discipline of God.[38] Paul also uses a variation of the phrase in Eph 4:8–10. Quoting Ps 68:18, Paul explains that in order for Christ to have *ascended*, he must first have "*descended* into the lower parts of the earth." Paul's parallel contrast here seems to refer not to a "descent into hell"—as many (including the framers of the "*descendit ad inferna*" clause of the Apostle's Creed) interpret 1 Pet 2:18–19 to suggest—but to the incarnation of the second person of the Trinity—Christ's *descending* from the infinitely "higher" realm of heaven to the lower, temporal, and corporeal realm of earth.[39]

The phrase as used in the Old Testament, then, may be interpreted validly as referring either to the physical location of the dead or merely the adverse condition of the soul.[40]

The Afterlife in the Old Testament

The promise that the covenant God of the living[41] made to Abraham in Gen 15:15 for a long life (shown fulfilled [in relative terms] in Gen 25:8) is still but a concession. As argued in the previous chapter, eternal life was the human schema before the Fall.[42] The life of Adam, as the only creature made in the image of the Creator, was to reflect not merely physical animation,

---

38. Matt 12:40; Jonah 1:17. One may argue that Matthew intends to relay not merely the location of Christ in the grave, but—similarly to the psalmist's articulation of the experiential state of the soul under adversity—the "agony of death" (Acts 2:24) as he "tasted death for every man" (Heb 2:9). For more on the agony of death as experienced by Christ's rational soul, see Bavinck, *Sin and Salvation in Christ*, 417; and Calvin, *Institutes*, 1:513–15.

39. Some who have interpreted 1 Pet 3:18–20 to refer alternatively to Christ's netherworld mission include: Irenaeus, Cyril of Alexandria, John Calvin, Friedrich Spitta, Francis Beare, Bo Reicke, Ernest Best, C. E. B. Cranfield. For a survey of the early church tradition of Jesus' descent into hell, as well as opinions contrary to a netherworld interpretation, see Elliott, *1 Peter*, 706–10; Schreiner, *1, 2 Peter, Jude*, 183–89; Dalton, *Christ's Proclamation to the Spirits*, 124–34; Kistemaker, *James, Epistles of John, Peter, and Jude*, 139–40.

40. Cf. for example, Christ's allusion in Matt 26:38 and Mark 14:34, "My soul is deeply grieved, even to the point of death."

41. Matt 22:32; Mark 12:27; Luke 20:38 with Exod 3:6.

42. For the argument that man, though mortal, would have continued in life eternally had he not fallen, see Bavinck, *Sin and Salvation in Christ*, 183; Berkhof, *Systematic Theology*, 668; Erickson, *Christian Theology*, 1172–90; Hodge, *Anthropology*, 92–93, 115–20; cf. 248–49; Reymond, *New Systematic Theology*, 449; Horton, *Christian Faith*, 387; Helm, *Last Things*; Thielicke, *Death and Life*, 113; Ratzinger, *Eschatology*, 80. For the argument that man would have died naturally even if he had not fallen, viz. Plato and Pelagius, see Rahner, *Theology of Death*, 89–147.

but a *quality* of life distinct from other creatures and unique to the Giver of life himself.

> It is not a transitory life, and is therefore not to be conceived on the basis of the reality that is limited by death. As original life from God it is a primal datum, which is not derivable from any other given fact and does not allow of any immanent grounding. The primal life of the resurrection of Jesus means the genuine life to which all other life bears a secondary relation.[43]

If death were the end of Adam, then, this quality of life would cease to be a reality in God's *magnum opus*, thereby nullifying God's intended purpose not only for the creation of man, but for all of creation (Rom 8:19–23). Provision for the continuation of life for Adam must, therefore, figure into God's original intention.

The death of both the righteous and the unrighteous, then, was viewed by the descendants of Abraham—those to whom were entrusted the oracles of God, which we now consider (Rom 3:1–2)—as a display of the disfavor of God. Life—long life—evidenced the favor of the living God. This ethos of life that permeated ancient Israelite culture because of her notions of her covenant relationship with her God consistently whispers a conviction that her God's blessing of life, merely as it exists under the sun, does not contain the full extent of the blessing. Though death, as the just curse and disfavor of God, appeared to terminate any semblance of his blessing, that such a terminus could be the end of the story for a people in covenant relationship with the Creator God of the living was unconscionable.

Life as Blessing, Death as Curse

The Old Testament does not provide great detail about the state of the deceased. Its primary concern is that the life given by the God of the living[44] be lived in fidelity to the covenant relations established by that God with the members of the human family that he has chosen for such relationship (cf. Isa 38:18–19).[45] The life that "now is" sufficed and was embraced by the

---

43. Kunneth, *Theology of the Resurrection*, 74.

44. Because the Old Testament does not express much interest in the state of the deceased is insufficient reason to assume God has nothing to do with the dead. As discussed above, the fact that God is the God of the living does not negate his sovereignty over Sheol or the dead (see Deut 32:39; Isa 45:5–7; Acts 10:42; 2 Tim 4:1).

45. In view here is God's discriminating love in sovereignly electing Abraham and his family to be his (Old Testament) covenant people from among the numerous possibilities of human families (see Gen 12:3b; 22:18 with Acts 3:25; Exod 19:5–6 with 1

Israelites as the favor of God. Rejection of the covenant was met with the consequent curse of being cut off from God's people, including all the rights and privileges pertaining thereto. Thus, death, as consummate evidence of that cutting off, was equated always with the privation of the favor of God and the negation of (all that is) life.[46] Because the Old Testament writers conceived of life as the blessing of God and death as the absence of that blessedness, this cutting off from the presence of God's grace may be characterized as consummate absence—absence from the privileges of vocation and procreation, from God's good creation in nature, from communion with the posterity of Israel, from all the blessings of life, "no longer having a share in all that is done under the sun" (Eccl 9:6). In this vein did Qohelet write in Ecclesiastes 9:5, "For the living know they will die; but the dead do not know anything, nor have they any longer a reward, for their memory is forgotten." Robert Martin-Achard similarly bemoans, "Death is essentially absence, separation, disappearance; the dead man is the absent *par excellence*, the vanished man."[47] One may certainly understand how, for the Israelite, this "disappearance" from all that vested his very being aptly communicated the curse of God.

Pet 2:9; Deut 7:3–14; Amos 3:2; Rom 3:1–2). Much more can be said in regard to both non-Jewish proselytes who were grafted into the Abrahamic covenant and the doctrine of God's sovereign election to salvation by faith. The implications of the Abrahamic covenant as God's initiation of a new faith humanity—comprised of all of the families of Adam (and Noah)—with which he would establish covenantal relations for eternity are riddled throughout the Abrahamic saga—both Old Testament and New Testament. For treatment of the nuances of God's discriminating election to covenant relationship, see Carson, *Difficult Doctrine*; Horton, *Covenant and Eschatology*; Horton, *Covenant and Salvation*.

46. See Tromp, *Primitive Conceptions*, 10, 44, 111, 122, 127–28, esp. 129–30, 154. Prov 7:27 and 9:18 summarize the disfavor of God and departure to Sheol upon the one who departs from the gracious covenant.

47. Martin-Achard, *From Death to Life*, 42. Additionally, Johnston iterates that many of Israel's Psalms portray life as the only avenue of communion with God. The chastening "gaze" of the LORD may result in death where the psalmist departs and "[is] no more" (Ps 39:13). There in *Shĕôl*, one can no longer praise Yahweh (Pss 6:5; 115:17); communion with the living God appears to be cut off there. See Johnston, *Shades of Sheol*, 200–01.

Divorce—as it were—from the living God[48] was often punishable by (immediate) physical death,[49] but always signified spiritual death[50]—the state of being without hope of any ultimate good, either in this age or any age yet to come—as a direct consequence of being an enemy of the gracious God of the living, who alone is able to provide good and redeem from the mastery of death. Life is the reward and gracious gift to the righteous (i.e., those in faithful covenant relationship with Yahweh); but death is the retribution for wickedness.[51]

The Aaronic Benediction as Instructive of Israel's Understanding of Life as Blessing and Death as Curse

The righteous receive more than the blessedness of life merely in this present age.[52] God has provided for them a blessedness in the future—beyond

---

48. Here is rationale for taking the institution of earthly marriage much more seriously. Just as earthly marriage is a metaphor of the life-giving covenant relationship between Christ and his bride (i.e., God [the Son] and his covenant people), and earthly adultery is a metaphor of spiritual infidelity (i.e., idolatry; cf. Jer 3:1–9; Jas 4:4; Mal 2:10–16), so earthly divorce, just as graphically, pictures departure from God's covenant, the ultimate consequence being the curse of death—the antithesis of all that God desires for his good creation.

49. Immediate death was the mandated penalty for capital offenses: Exod 21:12–14; Lev 24:17–21; Num 35:16–21, 22–28, 30–31; Deut 19:4–6, 11–13; as well as some non-capital offenses: Exod 21:15–17; 22:18–19; 31:14–15; 35:2; Lev 20:2–5, 10, 13, 15, 27; 24:14–23; Num 15:32–36; Deut 13:1–18; 17:2–7; 22:20–24; 24:7. See Johnston, *Shades of Sheol*, 42–43.

50. Gen 17:14 first iterates severance from the covenant and therefore spiritual union with the God of the covenant. The Old Testament discloses a litany of other violations of the covenant that are punishable by such spiritual severance. See also Matt 12:31–32; Eph 2:12. Further, citing Gen 17:14 of God's warning that the uncircumcised will be "cut off from his people," Augustine argues against the text's assertion of mere temporal death as punishment for the sin. He adjures, "For, pray tell me, what evil has an infant committed of his own will, that for the negligence of another in not circumcising him, he himself must be condemned, and with so severe a condemnation, that the soul must be cut off from his people? It was not of any temporal death that this fear was inflicted, since of righteous persons, when they died, it used rather to be said, 'And he was gathered unto his people;' or, 'He was gathered to his fathers:' for no attempt to separate a man from his people is long formidable to him, when his own people is itself the people of God." See Augustine, *Grace of Christ and On Original Sin*, 2:35, in *WSA*, I/23, 452.

51. Cf. Prov 9:11, 18; 10:17, 24–25, 27; 11:19.

52. Pryor presents a helpful discussion regarding the development of Israel's eschatology, juxtaposing the blessedness (or cursedness) of the present age with the age to come. Pryor suggests that, rather than adopting her views of the termination of the present age and the initiation of a new age from the agriculturally influenced

death—that transcends even the lifting-up of his countenance upon them for *shalom* in the present life. The Israelites acknowledged at least an undeveloped notion that that blessedness would include a bodily resurrection (Dan 12:2; Isa 26:19).[53] The Old Testament understanding of a bodily resurrection will be addressed with more detail below. For now, however, the question at hand is what is the ancient Israelite understanding of death in relation to life in this present world?[54]

From Israel's founding as a nation (Exodus 20), at the core of their covenant relationship with the God who formed them was the revelation of the blessings of God's presence[55] for obedient faith that evidenced love for him, in contrast with the curse of his disfavor and "cutting off" from his gracious presence in consequence for faithless rebellion that evidenced hatred for him (Exod 20:5–6; Deut 5:9; 7:9–10). The promise of God to bless his faithful people as well as Israel's reciprocal confidence that God would provide them fullness of life are communicated in the priestly benediction with which God inaugurated his new kingdom of priests. When the nation was newly constituted, God gave Moses a charge to command Aaron and the Levitical priests to bless God's covenant people with the formulaic blessing

---

cyclical paradigms of her ANE neighbors (*contra* Robinson, *Prophecy and the Prophets*, 197–98; Cerny, *Day of Yahweh*, 32–41; and Charles, *Eschatology*, 51), "The source of Israelite eschatology lay in her concept of her God as the God of all history. To the prophets of Israel, all history is God's history. 'To this extent we are justified in saying that Israel's unique conception of God as the God of history is the root of eschatology'" (Mowinckel, *He That Cometh*, 153). Pryor convincingly concludes, "Israel's faith in her God as the God of history and as a perfectly just God led to the development of an eschatology. If God is a God of righteousness, then right *must* triumph. If not in the present, then in the future, the will of God will be done"; see Pryor, "Eschatological Expectations," 34, 36.

53. Elwell, *Baker Theological Dictionary*, 375, 676–79. Wright, *Resurrection*, 99–128. Ps 16:10–11 also seems to provide at least a vague hope of life beyond the grave for God's holy one. The psalmist—writing what the apostle Peter interprets as a messianic prophecy (Acts 2:24–31)—anticipates a "path of life" at the right hand of God where there are "pleasures for evermore." Though no alternative destination as definitive as *Shĕʾōl* is named, the psalmist clearly has in mind some eternal communion with God beyond death. For a similar message, see Pss 49 and 73. See also Johnston, *Shades of Sheol*, 200–07.

54. For a fuller treatment of the significance of life for the Old Testament Israelite, see Martin-Achard, *From Death to Life*, 3–15.

55. In Exod 33:14–16 Moses acknowledges that not merely God's temporal gifts, but his very presence is the nation's good and how, by that presence, they "may be distinguished from all the other people who are upon the face of the earth." See also Ps 73:23–28 where Asaph sings, "But God is the strength of my heart and my portion forever" and "But as for me, the nearness of my God is my good"; and Gen 17:8 where God promises to his new covenant humanity, viz. Abraham, that "I will be their God" (cf. 2 Cor 6:16); as well as the consummation of that promise in Rev 21:3.

found in Num 6:24-26. Aaron and his progeny—Israel's priests—were to "put [God's] name upon the people" via this pronouncement and then God would bless them accordingly (v. 27). The literary structure of synonymous parallelism in this Aaronic benediction is helpful for gleaning insight into the ancient Israelite understanding of the significance of life and death.

> The Lord bless you, and keep you;
> The Lord make his face shine on you,
> > And be gracious to you;
> The Lord lift up his countenance on you,
> > And give you peace.

Because synonymous parallelism reiterates the same idea in different ways with each strophe further informing the meaning of the others, one can better grasp from this passage the Hebrew understanding of the state of blessedness. First of all, the context of the benediction is between God and his covenant people. (Note the usage of the second person singular in each strophe; however, with a context that assumes a collective singular.[56]) The Israelite hearer, then, would include himself in the invocation and blessing as a member of the unitary covenant community, not merely as an individual in solitary relationship with the Lord—Yahweh.[57] This communal understanding is integral, too, to Israel's notion of death as curse.

The blessing of God meant the prosperity of life for the righteous (Deut 30:15a); not merely economic prosperity, but fruitfulness in one's every endeavor as he images God, whether in vocation or procreation (Ps 1). Part and parcel of the value of this blessing was being in community with the people of God (Gen 12:2; Deut 28:1-14; 30:5-9, 20; Ps 1:1, 5). Isolation from the covenant community—of which death is the ultimate picture—is

---

56. The collective singular is marked by the plural phrase "sons of Israel" and the third person plural "them" in v. 23. Further, in personal correspondence (31 May 2011), Russell Fuller notes, "The singulars are probably used . . . because it may refer [to] an individual or the collective (the group). This occurs frequently in the Bible, as for example, in Deut 7. In verses 1-3, the singular 'you' is used, but in verse 4 the plural is used, 'the anger of the Lord will be hot against you.' The other 'yous' in verse 4 are singular. The verbs of verse five are plural (you), but in verse 6 pronouns are singular again, 'For you are a holy people.' The pronouns in verse 7-8a are plural, but 8b-11 switch to singular. Verse 12 is back to plural. And this goes on and on. So does the context demand in Numbers 6:24-26 assume a collective singular? Yes, I think so, but I think the blessing could be applied to a singular (individual) when necessary, but in this context a collect[ive] singular is probably in view."

57. The mention of the personal name of the Lord three times as the surety of the blessing reinforces the injunction in v. 27. See text note at Num 6:24-26 in the NIV; Barker, *New International Study Bible*, 199.

always portrayed as a cursed thing and never considered a good thing by the Old Testament.[58] The blessedness of life in isolation from the community, then, is inconceivable to the Israelite mind. The Israelite's identity was so intimately connected with his communion with God's people that the prosperity of life meant nothing to him, as an individual, if the favor of God did not perpetuate to his posterity and his nation (i.e., the covenant family). This notion of communal blessedness is seen in the farewell speeches of both Jacob and Moses (Genesis 48; Deuteronomy 33).[59] The notion of blessedness, then, goes far beyond the state of mere individual, temporal, circumstantial happiness.[60] To the Israelite, blessedness meant to be in the favor of the God of the covenant and all that that entails.

Secondly, the parallelism of the terms "bless you," "make his face shine on you," and "lift up his countenance on you" is in apposition to the terms "keep you," "be gracious to you," and "give you peace." Both the parallels and the appositions inform the meaning of the blessing. To be blessed by Yahweh, then, means to have his "face shine on you (collective singular)." To have one's "face shine on you" meant to be "faced" or "looked on" pleasingly and favorably and to receive benevolence in accord with that pleasure and favor. Adam and Eve were so "faced" by God's presence when he would commune with them in the Garden in the cool of the day, prior to their being compelled by their own guilt to hide themselves from God's face when they recognized their own forfeiture of the high privilege of being *coram Deo*—before God's face (Gen 3:8). God similarly caused his face to shine on Noah. That is, "Noah found favor in the eyes of God" such that his life was spared when God exterminated the entire human species except Noah and his family (Gen 6:8). Moses also was so countenanced by God, who "used to speak to Moses face to face, just as a man speaks to his friend" (Exod 33:11; Deut 34:10), such that Moses' own face reflected the light of God (just as, by the way, ever-sanctifying Christians do now by looking into the face of Jesus Christ [2 Cor 3:7–18]; and will in eternity [1 Cor 13:12]). To "lift up one's countenance on you" meant much of the same favorable turning of one's face toward you with good will (cf. Luke 2:14).

---

58. Cf. Gen 2:18; Num 5:3; 12:15; Isa 5:8. Lev 13 paints a picture of the leper who is to be isolated from the community, "outside the camp." The leper is an Old Testament picture of the cursed sinner cut off from the blessings of God's covenant people.

59. Martin-Achard, *From Death to Life*, 24.

60. In light of the Hebrew conception of blessedness and cursedness, one may see why the concept of blessedness is very ineffectively communicated by Bible translations that render the Old Testament Hebrew term בָּרַךְ, *barach* or the New Testament Greek term μακάριος, *makarios* merely as "happy."

The apposition of blessing involves God's "keeping," that is, "guarding" or "protecting" his covenant people with an unassailable security. When God shines his face upon a people, they receive and are sustained by his grace—the lavishing upon them of provisions and benefits that they have no capacity to obtain for themselves, nor of which they are worthy (Ps 104:27–30; Exod 34:9; Deut 7:6–10). The lifting up of God's countenance upon a people is linked to his securing them in a state of *shalom*—peace. This idea of *shalom* is inimitably more than the mere absence of war; it is a whole state of being where all of life—as itself the blessing—is both right and well.[61] This state of *shalom* can come only from the *presence* of Yahweh—the living God who himself gives life as the blessing and death as the curse (Gen 1:27–28; 2:17; Deut 30:19; 32:39; Isa 45:5–7).

The Israelites had a whole context, then, from which to understand God's granting of life—even long life—as his blessing, and the termination of that life as his disfavor and curse. A significant part of that context was their understanding of Yahweh as the God of the living. Accordingly, Israel's attention was not given to speculative realities of what happened after death but to the revealed Yahweh-reflecting blessing—life;[62] God's curse, needless to say, was neither much desired nor ruminated.

The Old Testament and ANE Parallels

Like any people of any time, ancient Israel was not isolated from impact by the cultures around her. Also like any people, however, Israel both possessed many of her own internally developed cultural distinctives and, as an independent culture, made determinations of what alternative cultural

---

61. Cf. Ps 133:3b. Horatio Spafford's hymn "It is Well with My Soul" well expresses the heart of the one who is experiencing God's shalom. Spafford penned the hymn after several traumatic events in his own life, including the 1871 death of his own son (another later born son would die in infancy; only two later born daughters would survive), the great Chicago Fire of the same year, and the 1873 deaths of his four daughters who died tragically when their ship from New York to France, the SS Ville du Havre, sank twelve minutes after providentially colliding with another ship, the Scottish Loch Earn. Spafford was to have accompanied his family, but was delayed by zoning business due to the Chicago Fire. On his journey to Europe to meet his grieving wife, Spafford penned the hymn as his ship passed near the spot where his daughters died. The opening lines reflect Spafford's thoughts as he mourned his daughters' deaths: "When peace like a river, attendeth my way, When sorrows like sea billows roll; Whatever my lot, Thou hast taught me to say, It is well, it is well, with my soul." See Phillips, *Well with My Soul*.

62. Pss 56:13; 133:3b.

distinctives it would and would not assimilate into its own. Such cultural intercourse has led some ANE (Ancient Near East) scholarship to assert that, rather than originating as divinely ordered statutes, many of Israel's beliefs and practices were adopted from preexistent ANE cultures and that Israel (as well as early Christianity) is "deeply indebted" to these other ANE cultures for many of its own tenets.[63] Such a presumption, however, is ill advised as a foregone conclusion.

63. For example, considering the etymology of the notion of resurrection, Egyptologist Erik Hornung comments on the Egyptian Christian practice of mummifying corpses (also an Osirian funerary practice) until it was discontinued when Islam entered the region. Hornung equates Jesus' crucifixion with Osirian traditions. He concludes that while Christianity rejected the paganism of its neighboring cultures, early Christianity remained "deeply indebted" to Ancient Egyptian cult. See Hornung, *Secret Lore of Egypt*, 73–75.

Egyptologist E. A. Wallis Budge also suggests a possible equation of Christianity and Osirian cult. He writes, "The Egyptians of every period in which they are known to us believed that Osiris was of divine origin, that he suffered death and mutilation at the hands of the powers of evil, that after a great struggle with these powers he rose again, that he became henceforth the king of the underworld and judge of the dead, and that because he had conquered death the righteous also might conquer death. . . In Osiris the Christian Egyptians found the prototype of Christ, and in the pictures and statues of Isis suckling her son Horus, they perceived the prototypes of the Virgin Mary and her child." See Budge, *Egyptian Religion*, 61–107.

Marvin Mayer attempts to reconcile the cultural distinctives by noting that some scholars categorize the notion of dying and resurrecting deities in the mystery religions as mythical, while the death and resurrection of Christ is unique in its historicity. The agrarian (and Osirian) concept of the dying and rising of crops by season is said merely to arrive at its consummation in the Christian story. See Mayer, *Ancient Mysteries*, 254. See also Robinson, *Prophecy and the Prophets in Ancient Israel*, 197–98; Cerny, *Day of*, 32–41; and Charles, *Eschatology*, 51.

Several biblical scholars convincingly argue for the uniqueness of Israelite notions of the afterlife. New Testament scholar Bruce M. Metzger notes that in one account of the Osirian myth, Osiris dies on the 17th of the month of Athyr and revives on the 19th— similarly to Christ's rising from the dead on the third day. Metzger rightly observes that Osiris' underworld revivification can hardly be compared with Christ's bodily resurrection. Metzger, *Chapters in the History*, 19. David Macleod likewise observes, "Perhaps the only pagan god for whom there is a resurrection is the Egyptian Osiris. Close examination of this story shows that it is very different from Christ's resurrection. Osiris did not rise; he ruled in the abode of the dead. As biblical scholar, Roland de Vaux, wrote, 'What is meant of Osiris being "raised to life?" Simply that, thanks to the ministrations of Isis, he is able to lead a life beyond the tomb which is an almost perfect replica of earthly existence. But he will never again come among the living and will reign only over the dead. This revived god is in reality a "mummy" god.' . . . No, the mummified Osiris was hardly an inspiration for the resurrected Christ. . . . As Yamauchi observes, 'Ordinary men aspired to identification with Osiris as one who had triumphed over death. But it is a mistake to equate the Egyptian view of the afterlife with the biblical doctrine of resurrection. To achieve immortality the Egyptian had to meet three conditions: First, his body had to be preserved by mummification. Second, nourishment was provided

Analysis from The Epic of Gilgamesh

The Epic of Gilgamesh[64] is one of the most significant literary works of ancient Mesopotamia. Not only does the saga include variations of a creation account, but it also depicts a global flood, including a Noah-type figure, Utnapishtim. From this saga, the modern world has gleaned many insights into the ancient world's notions of death and the afterlife. Concerning the epic Alexander Heidel effuses, "The Gilgamesh Epic, the longest and most beautiful Babylonian poem yet discovered in the mounds of the Tigro-Euphrates region, ranks among the great literary masterpieces of mankind. It is one of the principal heroic tales of antiquity and may well be called the Odyssey of the Babylonians." Of the nature of the epic and its commentary on death Heidel muses, "The Gilgamesh Epic is a meditation on death, in the form of a tragedy. To consider the matter in logical arrangement, the epic is concerned, first of all, with the bitter truth that death is inevitable. All men must die; 'For when the gods created mankind, they allotted death to mankind, but immortal life they retained in their keeping.' The gods assemble and pass on life and death. And from their decrees there is no escape." The account comes to us from twelve large tablets dating to the seventh century BC discovered in the mid-nineteenth century "among the ruins of the temple library of the god Nabu (the biblical Nebo) and the palace library of the Assyrian king Ashurbanipal (668–ca. 633 BC), both of which were located in Nineveh, the later capital of the Assyrian empire." Numerous other parallel tablets and fragments have come since to contribute, sometimes contradictorily, to the epic.[65] Because of the unparalleled significance and relevance of the Gilgamesh epic to the topic at hand, as well as the comprehensive nature of Heidel's analysis, Heidel will serve as the primary resource here for comparison and contrast of Israelite and other ANE notions of the afterlife.

---

by the actual offering of daily bread and beer. Third, magical spells were interred with him. His body did not rise from the dead; rather elements of his personality—his Ba and Ka—continued to hover over his body." MacLeod, "Resurrection of Jesus Christ," 169. Further, Wedderburn argues that the Ancient Egyptian concept of resurrection excludes the "very negative features" of the Judaeo-Christian tradition, considering that the Ancient Egyptians conceived of the afterlife as entry into the glorious (chthonic) kingdom of Osiris. Wedderburn, *Baptism and Resurrection*, 199.

64. Readers will grasp the significance of the epic in relation to the present topic by reading the epic itself as well as Heidel's *The Epic of Gilgamesh and Old Testament Parallels*.

65. Heidel, *Gilgamesh*, 1–3; 10–11, 70.

Comparison and Contrast

Though many similarities exist between Israelite and other ANE cultures' notions of the afterlife, the distinctions usually make all the difference in the world. For example, in Israelite thinking, *Elohim* could not be subject to death; whereas for many of Israel's ancient neighbors, deities could die. Babylonian and Assyrian accountings provide no insight into the origin of death. The phenomenon appears as a reality, however, even among the realm of the proverbially immortal gods prior to the creation of man. While these deities could not die a "natural" death, they could have their lives taken through acts of violence, usually perpetuated by other gods.[66] Israel, on the other hand, subscribed to no such pantheon of deities;[67] Yahweh alone was sole God of the entire created order. Moreover, he was also *the living God* who, having no beginning or end, could not succumb either to other so-called deities or death.

Unlike the biblical account (Gen 2:17; 3:19; 5:5; Rom 5:12–14; 6:23), on the Mesopotamian scheme, death is not limited to the created order as the penal consequence of the chief creature's faithless rebellion against a singular gracious Sovereign. No, death—as an already extant and inexorable law of nature—was a constituent element of man's constitution allotted him by the gods at his creation. "For when the gods created mankind, they allotted death to mankind, but life they retained in their keeping."[68] There was no need for any justification for subjecting mankind to death; "according to the main Babylonian creation story, man was formed with the blood of wicked Kingu and therefore was evil from the very beginning of his existence."[69]

Regarding the condition of the dead, the Mesopotamian portrait involves eternal service to the gods in an underworld;[70] partaking of the

---

66. For example, "Apsu and Mummu were killed by Ea; Ti'amat lost her life in combat with Marduk; Kingu and the Lamga deities were slaughtered for the purpose of creating mankind; Ereshkigal's husband Gugalanna met with a violent death; youthful Tammuz in some way lost his life through Ishtar's fault; and Ishtar descended to the underworld alive but was deprived of life in the dark and gloomy hollow." Heidel, *Gilgamesh*, 137–38.

67. Historical *descriptions* of departure from the *prescriptive* religion of Israel, in obeisance to idols such as Molech, Ashtoreth, Milcom, Chemosh, etc. (see Lev 20:2; 1 Kgs 11:7, 33; 2 Kgs 23:10, 13), are insufficient as evidence of polytheism as fundamental to the Israelite cult. Rather, such historical and/or anthropological discoveries merely evidence that Israel, like all sons of Adam, was prone to pervert the revealed truth of God.

68. Tablet X, col. iii, ll. 1–5. Heidel, *Gilgamesh*, 70, 138; see also 143.

69. Heidel, *Gilgamesh*, 70, 138. See also *Enuma Elish*, Tablet VI.

70. The Anunnaki are the administrators of justice in the underworld. See obverse, 32, reverse, 31–33. Heidel, "Ishtar's Decent to the Underworld," 122, 126.

nature of the gods; and silent, undisturbed, gloomy darkness. The Hebrew model, on the other hand, depicts persons either resting or sleeping (Job 3:11–13, 17–18; 13:4; 14:12; 17:16; Ps 76:6–7; Jer 51:39; Dan 12:2, 13; Prov 21:16; Isa 57:1–2); in silence (Pss 6:6; 30:10; 94:17; 115:17; Isa 38:18); or in a place of destruction (Job 26:6; 28:22); or the land of forgetfulness (Ps 88:13; Eccl 9:5–6; Job 14:21).[71]

On the ancient Babylonian scheme death also did not signify the absolute end of one's existence, but merely a transition to the underworld where the disembodied spirit would make its silent, dark, and gloomy abode for eternity.[72] Though the deities live in either "high heaven" or the "underworld,"[73] no indication is given that they experienced any degree of blessedness or cursedness or greater or lesser divine power as a direct result of their respective abodes—though a hierarchy of deities exists, Anu being the father of the gods and head of the pantheon. Only realms of dominion and environmental conditions of these spirit abodes are indicated. The underworld—the destination of all mankind upon death: "high priest and acolyte," peasant and king, even Etana (king of Kish who was carried to heaven by an eagle)—is an eternal realm of gloomy darkness where all mankind will continue to serve the deities of the underworld.[74] The unfortunate picture of the afterlife in the Gilgamesh tragedy is a dismal, sad, and dark eternal existence in a "land of no return," to "the house whose occupants are bereft of light, where dust is their food and clay their sustenance,"[75] to

---

71. Heidel, *Gilgamesh*, 193.

72. Tablet XII, 11–13, esp. 23. Heidel, *Gilgamesh*, 95ff. Gilgamesh's instructions to Enki upon his descent into the underworld to retrieve the former's "pukku" and "mikku" seem to indicate the somber and morbid silence of the underworld. Gilgamesh instructs, "Do not be clothed with clean raiment, or they [i.e., the dead] will cry out against thee as if thou wert a stranger; . . . Do not hurl a spear in the underworld, or they . . . will surround thee; . . . Do not make a sound in the underworld; or the wailing of the underworld will seize thee" (ll. 14–28. Heidel, *Gilgamesh*, 95–96; see also 193).

73. Fragment I, Obverse, 8, 35. Heidel, "Nergal and Ereshkigal," 129. See also Tablet VI, 81. Heidel, *Gilgamesh*, 52.

74. Tablet VII, col. vi, 33–54. Heidel, *Gilgamesh*, 60–61. Obverse, 32–36, "Ishtar's Descent to the Underworld," in Heidel, *Gilgamesh*, 122–23. Additionally, the epic notes, concerning the gods' dependence on human service, "a rather repugnant parallel" (Heidel, 256) to the Genesis 8:21–22 account of Noah's sacrifice to the Lord after the flood. When Utnapishtim is enabled to leave his ark, he "poured out a libation on the peak of the mountain. . . . The gods smelled the sweet savor. The gods gathered like flies over the sacrificer [sic]." See Tablet XI, 156–61. Heidel, *Gilgamesh*, 87. Further, see Tablet XI, 113–14; Heidel, 85 for the account of the "terror-stricken" gods "cowering like dogs" and fleeing to "the heaven of Anu" at the tumult of the flood catastrophe.

75. Tablet VII, col. iv, 36–37. Heidel, *Gilgamesh*, 60; Obverse, 7–8; 63, Heidel, "Ishtar's Decent to the Underworld," 121, 124.

the place where Enkidu—temporarily released from the underworld via a wind-like spirit by permission of the gods "that he may declare the ways of the underworld"—can say to Gilgamesh of his body only that "Vermin are devouring it as though it were an old garment. . . . [and it] is full of dust."[76]

Funerary Practices

Food and drink offerings for the dead. Some ANE funeral and burial practices evidence that food and drink offerings were provided not only at interment but also thereafter, in some instances even as a monthly "mortuary offering."[77] Several possibilities exist for why the offerings were made. Some believed that the dead existing in the underworld would in some way be nourished by the earthly offerings. Others held that deceased family members could either prosper or haunt his survivors and/or progeny. Because provisions from the living was necessary for the welfare of citizens of the underworld, some people believed that one could garner either the favor or disfavor of an ancestor by either providing or neglecting his underworldly need of sustenance. Moreover, failure to bury the dead prevented admission to and rest in the underworld; denial of either food and drink offerings and/or burial compelled the undead to roam the earthly realm disturbing the living and being reduced to finding what sustenance he could from the garbage thrown out into the street. Still others sacrificed food or drink offerings to the gods of the underworld in solicitation of the favorable disposition of the gods toward their deceased loved ones.[78]

Social status. One's earthly social status was understood to follow him into the underworld. So, in addition to food, drink, and other material substances being buried along with the deceased, often buried along with deceased royalty was his or her servants. These servants may have yielded their lives

---

76. Tablet XII, 81, 93–96. According to Tablet XII, 104–49, however, the outlook is somewhat more favorable; nevertheless, the closest thing to heaven remains man's earthly life. Heidel, *Gilgamesh*, 12, 99–101.

77. Heidel notes a communique of King Ammiditana of the First Babylonian Dynasty. Ammiditana writes to one of his officials, "Thus (says) Ammiditana: 'Milk and butter are needed for the mortuary offerings of the month of Ab. As soon as thou seest this my tablet, let a man of thy command take thirty cows and one (pi) of butter and let him come to Babylon. Until the mortuary offerings are completed, let him supply the milk. Let him not delay, (but) let him come quickly!'" Heidel, *Gilgamesh*, 151–52.

78. Heidel, *Gilgamesh*, 152–57, 165.

voluntarily so as to continue their own underworldly welfare at the hand of their master or mistress.[79]

Disposal of the body. Similar to their Mesopotamian neighbors, interment was the prevailing method of disposal of the body for the Hebrews also. Their motivation for burial, however, appears to be significantly different. Heidel distinguishes, "Although there is no Old Testament proof that burial was considered essential to the comfort of the departed or to the safety of the survivors, as was the case in Babylonia, Assyria, and other countries, it was nevertheless regarded as a deed of kindness to bury the dead (2 Sam 2:5), while it was a disgrace to be left unburied (1 Kgs 14:11–13; 16:4; 21:24; Jer 16:4; 25:33; Ps 79:3; Eccl 6:3) or to be exhumed (Isa 14:19; Jer 8:1–2)."[80] One might also argue that burial aided in maintaining both ceremonial cleanness and environmental prophylaxis.[81]

Personification of Chthonic Deities:
Not an Israelite Trait

Another key distinction between Israel's notions of the netherworld in contrast to her ancient neighbors concerns the personification of natural phenomena as deities. Citing Christopher Barth, Nicholas Tromp argues, "One might say that, in Israel, there was an evolution from a mythological conception of Death to the belief in the Enemy: Satan, the Devil. This phenomenon suggests that the image of Death remained that of a personal power throughout Israel's history."[82] Tromp draws from several conceptions and terminologies employed by Israel's ANE neighbors to equate Israel's own understanding of death and the netherworld.[83] One might argue con-

---

79. Ibid., 160.

80. Ibid., 166.

81. Cf. Num 5:2; 19:11, 13; Deut 21:23; Hag 2:13.

82. Tromp, *Primitive Conceptions*, 100; cf. 99–107, 160–61; see also Barth, *Einführung in die Psalmen*, 57, 59.

83. Tromp's farfetched equations even interpret Job's (literal) reference to his mother's womb, in Job 1:21, with the earth or the netherworld. Further attempting to substantiate this line of thinking, Tromp argues unreservedly from Ps 139:13, 15, "Here there cannot be the slightest doubt about the equation of the mother's womb and the depths of the nether world. So there appears to be a proper logic in this way of thinking. Indeed man can be said to return to the nether world, for he came from there"; see Tromp, *Primitive Conceptions*, 122–23. Rachel Hallote makes similar unwarranted equations of Israel's and her ANE neighbors' personification of death; see Hallote, *Death, Burial, and Afterlife*, 112–14; cf. 102–22.

trary to Tromp, however, that because some concrete or abstract reality is personified does not necessitate its being a "personal power." That presumption ignores the very intent of the literary device of personification in the first place—to portray something that is known *not* to be a person as personal for the purpose of identification, either emotionally or intellectually. Certainly Israel's confidence in the personal and singular dominion of "the living God" over not only the false gods of Egypt (Exod 10:1–2, 16–17; 20:3; Isa 19), but also over life and death (Deut 32:39) precluded any notion of a personal "Death" in any sort of contest with Yahweh. Assertions like Tromp's here are therefore unsubstantiated and unwarranted.

Similarities Do Not an Etymology Make.

Although similarities certainly exist between Israelite conceptions of the afterlife and other ANE cultures, those similarities need not constitute either a shared origin or a common significance.[84] Heidel lists five significant distinctions between Mesopotamian and Hebrew eschatological beliefs that establish the independence of Israelite cult from her ANE neighbors.

1. In Mesopotamia man was created mortal with death as the natural result of his constitution. In Israel man was created with never ending life and succumbed to unnatural death as a result of his sin.

2. The Mesopotamian underworld had its own pantheon of deities. The Old Testament depicts one Sovereign God of life and death.

3. The Mesopotamian underworld was the final destination of all men without distinction. In the text of the Old Testament (Heidel argues) "there is not one line which *proves* that at least in the early days of Hebrew history the souls or spirits of all men were believed to go to the nether world; but there are passages which clearly and unmistakably hold out to the righteous the hope of a future life of bliss and happiness in heaven."[85]

---

84. For the notion that Israel's ANE neighbors significantly impacted development of her own ideas see Day, "Development of Belief," 231–58; and Day, "Resurrection Imagery," 125–33.

85. Heidel, *Gilgamesh*, 222–23. While I disagree with Heidel that *Shĕōl* is the destination of only unrighteous Old Testament figures, one may correctly assert—*contra* Mesopotamian eschatology—that *Shĕōl* or the underworld is not the *final* destination of any figure, Old or New Testament; the righteous will ascend to heaven to be with Christ, while the unrighteous will descend to the lake of fire where they will incur the eternal and just wrath of the holy God whose grace they have rejected.

4. In Mesopotamia the dead and living were interdependent. The Old Testament delineates a clear distinction between the realm of the living and the realm of the dead, such that the dead have no knowledge of what occurs on earth, no disembodied spirit can affect the living, either for better or for worse, nor can the living in any way alter the lot of the departed soul.[86]

5. "Even the latest Babylonian and Assyrian records reveal nothing of a resurrection of the flesh, a doctrine so clearly set forth in Daniel and Isaiah. A deity descending to the underworld may be released from the realm of darkness, but the dead among men are condemned to an eternal sojourn in the great below, cut off from all hope of entering the body again and of rising from the grave."[87]

Heidel rightly concludes, then:

> These differences set the eschatology of the Mesopotamians and that of the Hebrews as far apart as the east is from the west. It is therefore quite obvious that the eschatology of the Old Testament did not develop from that of the Babylonians and Assyrians. What similarities do exist can be attributed either to common observations (such as the inevitability of death and the impossibility of breaking the shackles of the grave and of returning to the mundane life) or to a common heritage (such as the belief in the continued existence of the spirit after death, or the idea of a judgment of some kind).[88]

Citing Hermann Gunkel, Heidel further notes a most poignant and noteworthy distinction between the Babylonian depiction of the gods' genuinely repugnant disposition toward human death and that of the God of the Bible. The biblical account takes very seriously the moral depravity of the prediluvian race of men (which mirrored the often equally immoral behavior of virtually the entire host of ancient pantheons). In the biblical account of the flood and the extermination of the human species[89]—save eight

---

86. Some have argued that the righteous dead may be granted knowledge of earthly events by Christ in accord with the Father's redemptive purposes. This divine granting of special privilege could also account for Samuel's ability to interact with Saul (1 Sam 28). See for example, Augustine, *City of God*, 943–44; cf. lii.

87. Heidel, *Gilgamesh*, 222–23.

88. Ibid., 223.

89. From a human perspective the Noahic flood of Genesis 6–7 must be the most catastrophic event in history. Some estimates place the earth's population at well over three billion at the time of the flood. Based on conservative population growth calculation models, founder of the Institute for Creation Research Henry Morris asserts,

souls—"no tears are shed, as on Tablet XI:116–25 and 136–37, over those who perished in the flood; theirs was a just and deserved punishment. In the Hebrew document the ethical motive is so strong that God is portrayed even as regretting the very creation of man; while in the Babylonian, the gods, with the possible exception of Enlil, regret the destruction of man. Although God resolves not to send another flood, he is nowhere represented as *regretting* the diluvial catastrophe."[90] This stellar display of holiness—exceeded only in the death of the Son of God—is precisely the disposition of God over which every creature in creation should exult on account of the justice of God in exhibiting that holiness, even in his ordinance of death. Indeed, contrary to self-preserving, self-indulgent pity,[91] God is to be lauded for his holy ordinance of the death of that which is unholy.

The Relative Value of Human Life in the Old Testament

The God of the Bible evidently places immeasurable value on human life as indicated by his decree that the one who willfully destroys one life (or even an animal that causes the death of a human) forfeits his own life (Gen 9:5–6). This high value of human life is derived directly from the value of the life that God himself possesses (John 5:21, 26); human beings are, after all, created in God's own image and after his likeness (Gen 1:26). While the life

---

"Multiplication was probably more rapid than assumed in this calculation, especially in the earliest centuries of the antediluvian epoch. For example, if the average family size were eight, instead of six, and the length of a generation ninety-three years, instead of one hundred, the population at the time of Adam's death, 930 years after his creation, would already have been 2,800,000. At these rates, the population at the time of the Deluge would have been 137 billion! Even if we use rates appropriate in the present world ($x = I$ and $c = 1:5$), over three billion people could easily have been on the earth at the time of Noah." See Morris, *Biblical Basis for Modern Science*, appendix 6.

Not unlike our present world, at the time of the flood, life flourished and the perpetuity of the race was assumed fact (Luke 17:26–27). Yet in the sight of humanity's Creator, it was a vile and infinitely God-dishonoring existence (Gen 6:5). The wholly just and premeditated decision of humanity's Creator was to terminate the fatally diseased "experiment." As Bruce Ware soberly notes, "The *whole world*, save a few people and animals, was deliberately killed by God in this action," much like a homeowner disposes of an untoward colony of ants. Is such a portrait a crassly characterized catastrophe? Or a perfectly praiseworthy act of a holy Sovereign (cf. Job 9:12; Eccl 8:4; Isa 45:9; Rom 9:20–22)? See Ware, *God's Lesser Glory*, 150.

90. Gunkel, *Genesis*, 71, cited in Heidel, *Gilgamesh*, 269; see also 85 for the account of the fear and regret of the gods in destroying humanity, where the gods, "terror-stricken at the deluge," "cowered like dogs (and) crouched in distress" as "they fled (and) ascended to the heaven of Anu."

91. For examples of the complete absence of pity in the decree of death see Deut 7:16; 13:6–11; Isa 9:14–17; Ezek 8:18; 9:5–6.

that God possesses is indeed of limitless value because he is the universe's only infinite being, the life that human beings (or any other creature, for that matter) possess cannot attain to infinite value because of the creature's inherent finitude. The immeasurable value of human life, therefore, remains relative, as evidenced clearly by the entrance of death into the created order.[92] Human life, then, is neither (absolutely) necessary nor must it be sustained despite any challenges to the contrary.[93] Human life is not an end in itself. The purpose of human life is to reflect to the created order a host of realities about the God who created it (Eph 3:10). It is of such value to God that he will eventually put an end to death (1 Cor 15:26). More, as revealed in the New Testament, he added to his own divine nature a human nature, which will subsist in the own person of the Son for eternity (Phil 2:5–11). In every instance of death in the Old Testament, the living God evinces his ascription of the value of life.

92. The God of the living had established before the creation of the world that honor of his sovereignty over the universe would be more valuable than the life he created in his own image (cf. Ps 119:89–91). Upon the creature's rebellion against that fiat, Gen 3:22–24 records that God, so that man would not "take also from the tree of life, and eat, and live forever, . . . stationed the cherubim and the flaming sword which turned every direction to guard the way to the tree of life." This "flaming sword" of death, prohibiting access to life, is God's divinely ordained and publicly executed delimiter of the value of human life. For such a display of his own honor, consistency, trustworthiness, integrity, promise, impartiality, justice, holiness, and a host of his other perfections, he is to be lauded by the entirety of his created order, and no creature should deign to say to him, "What are you doing?!" (Job 9:12; Eccl 8:4; Isa 45:9; Rom 9:19–21).

93. Ethical arguments for the preservation of human life abound; yet "teleological suspensions of the ethical" are rarely, if ever, considered. How many a commoner considers absolute duty to God (as divinely revealed by God—not some internal, subjective, personal dereliction of truth) of greater value than the ethic of preserving human life? Søren Kierkegaard suggests that such a suspension is precisely what propelled Abraham, the father of all the faithful (Rom 4:11–12, 16), as he anxiously wrestled with dispensing with the ethical norms of both his own day and his own conscience in order to submit to an infinitely higher divine purpose. Recognizing his own creaturely finitude, Kierkegaard accurately assesses that love for God is infinitely more significant than one's own temporal contentment. "Temporality, finitude is what it all turns on. I am able by my own strength to renounce everything, and then find peace and repose in the pain; I can put up with everything even if that demon, more horrifying than the skull and bones that put terror into men's hearts—even if madness itself were to hold up the fool's costume before my eyes and I could tell from its look that it was I who was to put it on; I can still save my soul so long as it is more important for me that my love for God should triumph in me than my worldly happiness." Kierkegaard, *Fear and Trembling*, 78.

Anthropological Solidarity: The Community of Israel

Several accounts in the Old Testament record the deaths of many as a result of the transgression of a few or even one. Several observations may be made concerning this apparent ethical dilemma. Of one thing we can be certain: whether one meets death in isolation from or as a direct consequence of association with the specific transgression of others, justice has not been annulled; for Gen 2:17 and Rom 3:23, 5:12–19, and 6:23 are true. That is, death is the just penalty for *every* sinner—i.e., every offspring of Adam. *When* that death occurs is ultimately of no consequence to justice (Eccl 8:11).

Secondly, the Old Testament portrays a most intimate communion between the members of the covenant community, significantly due to the unitary covenant relationship that the diverse but unitary chosen people had with their universal covenant God.[94] In such compact relationship and covenantal communion, the actions of the one more than influence and affect the whole; they are integral to the whole. For example, in Deut 5:9–10, Yahweh discloses to his covenant people that he is a God "visiting the iniquity of the fathers on the children, and on the third and the fourth generations of those who hate me, but showing loving kindness to thousands, to those who love me and keep my commandments." God's "visiting"—i.e., judgment—falls not upon individuals only, but upon the "generations of those who hate me"—i.e., all those who are complicit in disregard for the holy covenant. That God's lovingkindness is equally zealous, however, is indicated by his "checking" of the plague that had already taken the lives of 24,000 Israelites when Phinehas, the son of Eleazar the priest, the son of Aaron, motivated by zeal for God's glory—rather than the self-absorbed and complacent disregard for God's holy command that characterized Phinehas' nation—"made atonement for the sons of Israel" by putting to death the two flagrantly disobedient violators of the covenant. For his faithful act of valuing God's glory above human life, God established his "covenant of peace" not only with Phinehas, but also with "his descendants after him" (Numbers 25).[95]

---

94. The elect singular nation of Israel is comprised of a multiplicity of diverse individual image bearers of God; nevertheless, the nation is *one* nation in *unitary*—that is, indivisible—covenant relation to Yahweh. God's covenant is not primarily with independent individuals, but with Abraham's "seed"—i.e., a faith community consisting of a body of individuals.

95. A similar corporate judgment is found in Joshua 7 where Israel is again presented as a collective singular representative body of God. Though Achan, the son of Carmi, is individually guilty for having "committed a disgraceful thing in Israel" (v. 15), the inspired record says that "the *sons of Israel* acted unfaithfully" (v. 1, emphasis added) and "*Israel* has sinned, and *they* have also transgressed my covenant which I

Thirdly, these accounts may be an indication of some degree of corporate and/or metaphysical solidarity of the group.[96] Because Adam and Eve not only individually, but also *together* reflect the image of God, so Israel, as the new faith humanity seeded by Abraham, in some regard constitutes a diverse yet unitary whole. Diverse instances of death, then—whether individual or *en masse*—represent a unitary judgment against violation of the law of God. Thus, no death—however or whenever it occurs—may result in charging God with injustice.

Depictions of Death in the Old Testament

The accounts of deaths in the Old Testament—whether individual or *en masse*—provide a framework for discerning the relative value of human life in juxtaposition to the infinitely higher value of the multifaceted glory of the living God.[97] To be sure, many ancient peoples—even some within Israel—demonstrated their belief that life was of less value than a placated god. Seldom, however, do we find individuals sacrificing *their own* lives for the sake of a deity; instead, the life of *another* is sacrificed—often one's own offspring.[98] While the practice of child sacrifice does demonstrate a relative

---

commanded *them*" (v. 11, emphasis added). Further, God would not remove his judgment until the people consecrated themselves and "removed the things under the ban from [their] midst" (v. 13). Herein lies a significant commentary on the responsibility of the (covenant) community to steward the morality to which its individual members subscribe.

96. See chaps. 2, 4, and 5 for discussions related to the principle of humanity's metaphysical solidarity.

97. Defining justice in light of God's holiness, J. Alec Motyer writes, "Since 'judgment' is 'setting everything to rights' [God] is seen as a God of order and perfection; this is part of what the Bible calls 'the beauty of (his) holiness' (cf. 1 Chr 16:29; 2 Chr 20:21; Pss 29:2; 96:9; 110:3; etc.). In all its aspects judgment is an out-shining of the divine holiness (Ps 50:1–6). Thus Isa 5:16 links the key words together. 'The Lord of hosts is exalted in judgment and God the Holy One displays his holiness in righteousness.' When 'judgment' (*mispat*) and 'righteousness' (*sedaqa*) are paired like this (cf. Gen 18:19; 2 Sam 8:15; Pss 33:5; 89:14; 99:4; Isa 1:21; 5:7; etc.) 'righteousness' refers to principles and 'judgment' to practice. So, for example, in Isaiah 32:1 'righteousness' belongs to the king and 'judgment' to the princes; the throne embodies righteous principle and the executive arm practices just government. So it is also with the heavenly throne and its occupant (Is. 5:16): he is in himself, holiness; in his rule he embodies righteous principles and displays his holiness in acts of 'judgment' whereby he puts everything to rights. Since, however, judgment is an application of holiness it involves punishment as well as reward, condemnation as well as approbation." See Motyer, *NDBT*, s.v. "Judgment." See also Frame, *Doctrine of God*, 446–68; and Edwards, "Justice of God in the Damnation of Sinners," 1:669–70; Carson, *How Long*, 110–16.

98. See 2 Kgs 16:3; 17:17; 2 Chr 33:6; Ps 106:37–38; Ezek 16:20–21.

(de)valuing of human life, because of its perversion of God's ethic of human life, this reprehensible and God-cursed practice[99] exhibits biolatry in a most heinous form by destroying the life of another to preserve the contentment of one's own life.

The value of human life is communicated early in the biblical account of humanity. The living God is omnibenevolent, giving life to all (Deut 32:39; 2 Kgs 5:7; Neh 9:6; Acts 17:25); yet his good creation has staged an insurrection (Eccl 7:29). God does not, however, out of hot-tempered vindictiveness, employ death or suffering as retaliation against an infinitely weaker enemy. Death is simply and rightly the just punitive consequence of departure from the gracious provision of the omnibenevolent God. His ordaining and execution of his promise of death (Gen 2:17) as the consequence of rebellion portrays both his intention and power to meticulously order his will in earth as it is in heaven where "all things are subjected to Him . . . so that God may be all in all" (1 Cor 15:28). Life and death are shown over and over again in the Old Testament to be instruments of a sovereign God employed at his discretion for good and glorious purposes.

Forty-two youths. A most striking account of a divine death sentence is found in 2 Kings 2:23–24. Forty-two youth are mauled to death by two female bears. The very brief account—detailed entirely in only two verses—provides a clear indication, too, that this was no unfortunate accident. Rather, it was the direct result not only of the children being sinners—i.e., offspring of fallen Adam—worthy of capital punishment, but also as a direct consequence of their being cursed *in the name of the Lord* for dishonoring the revelation of God by taunting the Lord's prophet Elisha. The moral of the story: the honor of the God who graciously gives life is of more value than that life itself—even the life of children.

A young only son. In 2 Kings 4:8–37, the same prophet is providentially led to extend the blessing of the Lord to a prominent, faithful, and generous, yet childless woman from Shunam. A year after Elisha promises the woman a son, the Lord brings it to pass precisely as predicted. When the child was older, however, one day while working in the field with his father, the child apparently suffers a sun stroke. He is carried to his mother's lap whereupon he dies at noon. What case can be made that the boy's death resulted from anything more than the natural effect of over exhaustion in the heat of the day? First, a convincing case may be made that God exercises meticulous

---

99. See Lev 18:21; 20:2–5; Deut 18:10; Jer 32:35; Ezek 16:21; 20:31; 23:37.

control over weather.¹⁰⁰ So, the conditions conducive to the lad's head malady—whether weather related or not—were brought about at just that time by God's ordinance. Second, the text indicates that God was executing a plan that he chose not to disclose to the involved parties, including Elisha (4:27). Third, a case could be made that the biblical accounts of resurrections—which, needless to say, must be preceded by death—are revelatory of God's redemptive power and purposes (see the very similar account in 1 Kgs 17:17–24 involving Elijah and a widow at Zarephath; also John 11:4, 25–27, 41–42).¹⁰¹ In light of the outcome (4:37; cf. 1 Kgs 17:24), the account of this Shunammite woman and her son can well be interpreted as such. Here, God's meticulous ordinance and execution of and resurrection from death clearly display his supreme power over the curse of death. Human life and death, then, are shown to be instruments used by God for his greater—and sometimes undisclosed—purposes; life is not the ultimate value.

Eli's sons. Not only is God zealous about his covenant people, but those who bear the responsibility of the priesthood are held to an even higher standard, and are thus less exempt from judgment. Because Eli's sons were priests who "did not know the Lord," and because of their base and overtly God-dishonoring behavior, God *desired* to put them to death (1 Sam 2:12–17, 22–25; 3:13–14).¹⁰² First Samuel 4:11 records Hophni's and Phinehas' deaths during a siege by the Philistines. Moreover, the culmination of Eli's negligence in fathering both his own sons and Israel as her priest, led on the same occasion to the glory of God departing Israel (1 Sam 3:11–14; 4:21–22).

Aaron's sons. Before even one generation had passed of those whom God had miraculously, gloriously delivered from Egyptian bondage, the very leaders that God appointed as his mediators—Aaron's sons Nadab and Abihu—had to be put to death by God for their public disdain of God's holiness (Lev 10:1–3). When Moses informed their father, he also solemnly charged Aaron that both he and his sons knew full well what the Lord had required. So, rather than grieving God's divine sentence, "Aaron, therefore, kept silent" (v. 3), acknowledging that the holy glory of the Lord who had both created them and delivered them from Egyptian "death" was of greater value than the lives of his own two sons. Indeed, the passage appears to

---

100. See Exod 14:21; Num 11:31; 1 Kgs 17:1; 18:1, 41–45 with Jas 5:17–18; Job 1:12, 16, 19–20; Jonah 1:4; Mark 4:37–41; Acts 27:14–44.

101. Frame, *Doctrine of God*, 283–84.

102. For an excellent discussion on the different senses of God's desire, see Piper, "Are There Two Wills in God," 117–19.

indicate that the holy glory of God is so much more valuable than human life that Aaron was under injunction not to grieve the just execution of his own unholy offspring.

Korah. Numbers 16:20–35, and 44–50 presents the account of God's sovereign appointment of the deaths of rebellious Korah, his family and associates, and later, thousands of those who stood with him against God's delegate, Moses. The climax of the account as articulated by Moses evidences the irrefutable immediate action of God to exalt his glory in opposition to recipients of his grant of life who exhibited their ingratitude toward the Giver. Clearly, their lives were of less value than God's order.

> If these men die the death of all men or if they suffer the fate of all men, then the Lord has not sent me. But if the Lord brings about an entirely new thing and the ground opens its mouth and swallows them up with all that is theirs, and they descend alive into Sheol, then you will understand that these men have spurned the Lord. As he finished speaking all these words, the ground that was under them split open; and the earth opened its mouth and swallowed them up, and their households, and all the men who belonged to Korah with their possessions. So they and all that belonged to them went down alive to Sheol; and the earth closed over them, and they perished from the midst of the assembly. (Num 16:29–33)

Beside the plague that God used to chasten (to death) the rebellious supporters of Korah (Num 16:44–50), God used another plague to chasten the Israelites at Shittim where "the people began to play the harlot with the daughters of Moab." When Phinehas—about whom the Lord testified was "jealous with my jealousy"[103]—executed the unfaithful Israelite Zimri and his Midianite lover, Cozbi, "the plague on the sons of Israel was checked," but not before God had already judged and put to death 24,000 Israelites (Num 25:1–9).

Providentially hardened hearts. Because "the earth is the Lord's and all it contains, the world and those who dwell in it" (Ps 24:1), the Lord determined to depose the Canaanites, who occupied the land that its owner (i.e., God) had determined to give to his own covenant people, not as a token of their greatness, but as an indication of his absolute authority to do what he will with what belongs to him (Deut 7:6–10).[104]

---

103. For a biblical definition of God's jealousy, see Frame, *Doctrine of God*, 458–59.
104. Barker, "Conquest and the Ethical Question of War," in *NASB*, 271. Of Israel's

The Canaanites, whose iniquity had reached capacity, were placed under God's ban—the devotion to God of all that is his to dispense with as he sees fit (Gen 15:16; cf. Exod 23:23-33; Deut 7:1-2, 16, 26). God employed his covenant people Israel as the means of judgment against the vilely rebellious Canaanites.[105] Under the leadership of Joshua, Israel was to carry-out God's direct command to "utterly destroy" and "consume all the peoples whom the Lord your God will deliver to you; your eye shall not pity them" (Deut 7:2, 16). How was this plan against Canaan providentially guaranteed? Joshua 11:20 informs us.

> For it was of the Lord to harden their hearts, to meet Israel in battle in order that he might utterly destroy them, that they might receive no mercy, but that he might destroy them, just as the Lord had commanded Moses.

Pharaoh and Egypt. The dramatic account in Exodus 11-12 of the decimation of the Egyptian nation[106] breathtakingly illustrates God's deliberate and immediate power to take and spare life to accomplish his purposes of judgment and redemption.

> ... and all the firstborn in the land of Egypt shall die, from the firstborn of the Pharaoh who sits on his throne, even to the

---

Canaanite conquests, Barker writes, "Joshua is the story of the kingdom of God breaking into the world of nations at a time when national and political entities were viewed as the creation of the gods and living proofs of their power. Thus the Lord's triumph over the Canaanites testified to the world that the God of Israel is the one true and living God, whose claim on the world is absolute. It was also a warning to the nations that the irresistible advance of the kingdom of God would ultimately disinherit all those who opposed it, giving place in the earth only to those who acknowledge and serve the Lord. At once an act of redemption and of judgment, it gave notice of the outcome of history and anticipated the eschatological destiny of mankind and the creation."

105. Barker, *NASB*, 25, text note on Gen 15:16. "Just how sinful many Canaanite religious practices were is now known from archaeological artifacts and from their own epic literature, discovered at Ras Shamra (ancient Ugarit) on the north Syrian coast beginning in 1929. Their 'worship' was polytheistic and included child sacrifice, idolatry, religious prostitution and divination."

106. Honeycutt, *Exodus*, 347. Honeycutt writes, "The death of the firstborn was of unusual significance, not only because of the extent of the disaster but because the firstborn symbolically stood for the entire offspring." In light of the significance in the ancient world of the firstborn—those who represented the progeny of an entire nation, the intent of God to decimate the Egyptian nation in the birthing of his own nation cannot be easily dismissed. Additionally, this final plague was a decisive blow against Egyptian theology: at midnight, the time when the Egyptian sun god Re was said to overcome the darkness, God would take the life of the firstborn of Pharaoh—who was considered son of the sun god Re. See also Enns, *Exodus*, 245; and Stuart, *Exodus*, 265-66.

> firstborn of the slave girl who is behind the millstones; all the firstborn of the cattle as well (Exod 11:5).

> For I will go through the land of Egypt on that night, and will strike down all the firstborn in the land of Egypt, both man and beast; and against all the gods of Egypt I will execute judgments—I am the Lord (Exod 12:12).

> Now it came about at midnight that the Lord struck all the firstborn in the land of Egypt, from the firstborn of Pharaoh who sat on his throne to the firstborn of the captive who was in the dungeon, and all the firstborn of cattle. Pharaoh arose in the night, he and all his servants and all the Egyptians, and there was a great cry in Egypt, for there was no home where there was not someone dead (Exod 12:29–30).

As with the Canaanites, "it was of the Lord to harden [Pharaoh and the Egyptians'] hearts" for the execution of his just genocide.[107]

Greedy Israelites. Though God elected Israel as his covenant people, they were not exempt from God's judgment by death. Numbers 11 records God's anger being aroused by Israel's God-dishonoring disposition and behavior. First, for complaining (in much the same disloyal way they had as recorded in Exod 15:22–27; 16; and 17:1–7), the Lord's anger was kindled, and a fire broke-out[108] and consumed some of those on the outskirts of the camp. Next, after God had graciously provided sustenance for them in the wilderness, "while the meat was still between their teeth, before it was chewed, the anger of the Lord was kindled against the people, and the Lord struck the people with a very severe plague." Why? Simply because they "had been greedy" (Num 11:31–34). Here again is the character of God shown to be more valuable than even masses of human life.

Israelite elders. God's judgment is heightened when it concerns his own covenant people; for he is a jealous God.[109] When his people played the harlot with the daughters of Moab, God commanded Moses to "Take all the

---

107. For the Bible's characterization of Pharaoh hardening his own heart, see Exod 7:13, 22; 8:15, 19, 32; 9:7, 12, 34–35; 1 Sam 6:6. For wording that indicates that God providentially hardened Pharaoh's heart, see Exod 10:1, 20, 27; 11:10; 14:8; cf. Rom 9:17.

108. Barker, *NIV*, 206, text note on Num 11:1. This phrase sometimes refers to fire ignited by lightning (as probably in 1 Kgs 18:38; see also Job 1:16).

109. See Exod 20:4–6; 34:14; Num 25:11; Deut 4:24; 5:8–10; Josh 24:19; 2 Cor 11:2; 1 Pet 4:17; and Frame, *Doctrine of God*, 458–59.

leaders of the people and execute them in broad daylight before the LORD, so that the fierce anger of the Lord may turn away from Israel" (Num 25:4). A more direct command of capital punishment cannot be given. Further, because the Midianites with whom Israel played the harlot had turned the Israelites hearts away from God, he commanded Moses to "be hostile to the Midianites and strike them" (v. 18). In the same way, God's later command of the execution without pity of the apostate Israelites of Samaria would extend even to pregnant women (Hos 13:16).

Apostate Israelites. Ezekiel 9 records the acrimony of God's anger with his rebellious covenant people. Here again God commands the deaths of those among his people who profaned his name. Verses 6–10 reflect the resoluteness with which God had determined to judge his people. In "utterly slaying" the disobedient, God is not as concerned about the people's vain formalism as they are. God's anger burns so hot against his rebellious covenant people that he even commands, "Defile the temple and the courts with the slain" (vv. 6–7; cf. Matt 12:6; 23:16–22). So hot is God's wrath that Ezekiel pleads, "Alas, Lord God! Are you destroying the whole remnant of Israel by pouring out your wrath on Jerusalem?" (v. 8). God retorts with the forehead of flint that he charged Ezekiel to have in confronting rebellious Israel (3:8–9), "But as for me, my eye will have no pity nor will I spare, but I will bring their conduct upon their heads" (9:10).

These few poignant accounts represent only a sampling of exhibitions of the justice of God in his ordinance and execution of death. Truthfully, there is not one instance of death in the Old Testament for which one cannot attribute glory to God for the exhibition of his righteous splendor. To be sure, death remains a cursed deviation from God's very good natural order (Gen 1:31). One must never, however, release the tension of its also being completely rightly ordained.[110] From this perspective not only may one—even *must* one—praise this action of God, but one may also even understand death as, in at least some sense, good.

Resurrection in the Old Testament

With all of its toil, grief, and disappointment, exactly what about corporeal existence did Israel clutch so much that the notion of a return to bodily existence for eternity was not simply repugnant to them? As detailed above,

---

110. The thrice-holy God, out of his good nature, has sovereign and just power over both blessing and cursing (Deut 11:26–28; 30:19; 32:4, 34–35; 39–41; Job 2:10; Isa 45:6–7; Ezek 18:4).

for the Israelite, life is constituent of the blessing of God, while death evidences divine disfavor. Because mankind was created to reflect the image of his Creator in a body, bodiless existence could not fully be considered life, and thus, neither the blessing of God. Although no formal doctrine of resurrected life is developed in the Old Testament, embodied life was nevertheless preferable to any form of nondescript "absence" as *rĕphā'îm*. Hope in the eternal living God evoked anticipation of some form of living eschatologically—the blessing of life forever (Ps 133:3)—in a way that even death could not conquer.[111] Israel's anticipation of the blessing of life was one that would entail not the disappointments of this age but eternal shalom with the living God. Living, after all, was the original design for mankind at his constitution in God's image (Gen 2:7).

Here we have a clear indication of the synchronous nature of theological doctrines. Israel's understanding of the revealed God (revelation, inspiration) as both "the living God" and the God of the living (theology proper), as well as her understanding of the nature of human life (anthropology) as originated by that same God in his own image (creation, cosmogony), inevitably prompted some concept of an embodied afterlife (eschatology).[112] Concurrently, Israel's understanding of Yahweh as the God of history (theism) who is both just and righteous excludes an eschaton in which justice is unreconciled (theodicy).

To be sure, eschatology was not significantly referenced in Israel's early history. Neale Pryor provides insight concerning why. Israel had been anticipating national security and prominence under a glorious Davidic king in her early context. When, upon defeat and exile and dispersion and governance by other nations/peoples, and ever increasing disappointment that such a glorious dominion might occur, "the men of God more and more began to point the people toward an eschatology—a time in the future when her dreams would be realized, when God would punish the aggressor and vindicate his people."[113] Further, Pryor rightly notes (as does 1 Pet 1:10–12) that the answers to the people's questions that the inspired prophets rendered were not their own contrived resolutions and prognos-

---

111. Cf. Pss 16:8–11; 49:15; Song 8:6; Acts 2:24–36; Hos 13:14. Additionally, the references to "awaking" and "afterward" in Pss 17:15b, 73:24b, and 139:18b, as well as Job's declaration in 19:25–27 may be construed as referring to resurrected life. Both Johnston and Ratzinger take Psalm 16 not only as a Messianic prophecy, but also to apply to all the faithful. Peter's assessment of this Psalm's reference to Christ does not preclude its simultaneous reference to all the "holy ones," i.e., the faithful/redeemed; see Johnston, *Shades of Sheol*, 201–02; Ratzinger, *Eschatology*, 87–88.

112. For a fuller treatment of the premise of an anticipated embodied afterlife, see Martin-Achard, *From Death to Life*, 206–22.

113. Pryor, "Eschatological Expectations," 36, 51–52.

tications in attempt "to explain a seemingly inexplicable predicament;" they were the answers that God provided both to his covenant people and, by extension, through Israel—as his prophetic voice (Rom 3:1–2)—to all of his image bearers for all time.[114] "To this extent," asserts Sigmund Mowinckel, "we are justified in saying that Israel's unique conception of God as the God of history is the root of eschatology."[115] That eschatology included a notion of bodily resurrection that would not receive more clarity—on the progressive revelation timeline—until the intertestamental period and the New Testament era.[116]

One of the clearest indications of Israel's awareness of some form of eschatological bodily resurrection is found in Dan 12:1–2.[117] Contextually, Daniel is prophesying to captive Israel of her eschatological destiny with her God. A *prima facie* reading of the text indicates that "everyone who is found written in the book[118] will be rescued. Many of those who sleep in the dust of the ground [a clear reference to Gen 3:19, of which Daniel would have been keenly aware] will awake, these to everlasting life . . . ." Daniel does not contemplate, here, a bodily resurrection because of some temporal and self-interested sense of justice (*contra* Gatch[119]), but because, under the

---

114. Ibid., 37–38; cf. 32–59.

115. Mowinckel, *He That Cometh*, 153, cited in Pryor, "Eschatological Expectations," 34.

116. See Martin-Achard, *From Death to Life*, 185–90.

117. C. D. Elledge writes that the passage "provides our earliest definitive literary evidence for resurrection in the Old Testament"; see Elledge, "Resurrection of the Dead," 25. John Collins avers that there is "virtually unanimous agreement among modern scholars that Daniel is referring to the actual resurrection of individuals from the dead"; see Collins, *Daniel*, 391–92, cited in Wright, *Resurrection*, 109n107. See also Ratzinger, *Eschatology*, 90.

118. Arguably the Book of Remembrance—of "those who fear Yahweh and who esteem his name"—referenced in Malachi 3:16 and/or the Book of Life—of the righteous who overcame humanity's enemy by faith in the blood of the Lamb and "did not love their life even when faced with death!" (Rev 12:11)—referenced in Ps 69:28, Phil 4:3, and Rev 3:5; 13:8; 17:8; 20:12; 20:15; 21:27. Interestingly, this Book of Life is referenced most often in the Bible in the eschatological Apocalypse of John; perhaps because life has always been the intended end of God's image bearer.

119. Gatch, *Death*, 41. Interpreting what he thinks "the writer of Daniel" means by this "radically new" view, Gatch presumes, "Daniel does not, it must be noted, base this hope of a postmortem life upon some notion of the nature of man but upon his faith that, in the divine economy, wisdom and virtue must be rewarded. And he can only conceive of this life as a corporate one within a restored and transformed Israel." Gatch seems to restrict interpretation of the meaning of death and of Israel's eschatology to the community, to the exclusion of implications for the individual. He writes, "because the predominant concern was with the People and its historical destiny, the question of the significance of death for the individual rarely arose and was essentially

inspiration of the Holy Spirit, he is confident not in a god of the dead, but in the blessing of life forever secured for his covenant people by the God of the living.[120] In fact, earlier in the same prophecy, Daniel grounds this confidence to "be strong and do exploits" (Dan 11:32 AV) precisely in knowledge of the living God.[121]

A second passage from which one may assert Old Testament Israel's notion of a bodily resurrection is Isa 26:19, a passage already mentioned above for its usage of the term *rĕphā'îm*. Like Daniel, Isaiah is prophesying of Israel's eschatological destiny in light of her history of waffling between stiff-necked rebellion and chastening-induced repentance, yet God's ever enduring faithfulness. Isaiah recognizes that, apart from the power of the living God, "the dead will not live; the departed spirits will not rise" (v. 14). He also recognizes, however, that when God's perfect chastening has completed its sanctifying work, when "indignation runs its course" (v. 20), "Your dead will live; their corpses will rise;" those who lie in the dust (again, cf. Gen 3:19) will awake "and the earth will give birth to departed spirits." Though Isaiah's address is located in a context of national restoration, his particular reference to *mētîm* (individual dead), *rĕphā'îm* (departed spirits), and *nebēlâh* (corpses) indicates more than a corporate implication for the nation; the idea of individual personal resurrection is also indicated. Here again the hope of Israel in her living God anticipates the blessing of

---

meaningless." Continuing the same line of reasoning, he further asserts, "Personality and identity are terms which attach not to the person but to the People; thus, when one dies, personality and identity are not disrupted, for the People continues." See Gatch, *Death*, 36, 39; cf. 45, 48–49.

While solidarity with the covenant community was certainly more meaningful to the ancient Israelite than for the contemporary westerner, Gatch goes too far in virtually ignoring any implications for individual or personal eschatology. Ancient Israel certainly understood both the intrinsic value of each individual (cf. Gen 9:5–6) as well as the truth that each individual would give an accounting to God for his or her own faithfulness to the covenant or lack thereof (cf. Ezek 18:1–13).

120. Cf. Matt 22:32/Exod 3:6, 15–16; Mark 12:27; Luke 20:38. See also Johnston, *Shades of Sheol*, 218–39. Further, Adolph von Harnack observes the uniquely derived Iraelite notion of the living God's power to sustain life beyond death for those in communion with him, as articulated in Ps 73:26. Commenting on von Harnack's observation, Joseph Ratzinger remarks, "Without any borrowing from external sources, without the assistance of any philosophical or mythological structure, the certitude arose quite simply from the psalmist's deeply experienced communion with God that such communion is more potent than the decay of the flesh. Communion with God is true reality, and by comparison with it everything, no matter how massively it asserts itself, is a phantom, a nothing"; see Ratzinger, *Eschatology*, 89; and von Harnack, *Das Wesen des Christentums*, 28.

121. For further discussion see Martin-Achard, *From Death to Life*, 138–46.

(embodied) life and shalom forever. Isaiah is obliged to provide God's inspired answer to Israel's questions about her living fate.[122]

Israel's notion of a bodily resurrection—undeveloped as it was—also distinguished her view of the afterlife from that of her ANE neighbors. Many ANE cultures conceived of some sort of existence after death. This concept is very different, however, from any Old Testament notion of resurrection. For the Old Testament Israelite, the blessing of God could not be forever lost at death; the soul of the faithful would not be abandoned to a sub-living existence in Sheol for eternity.[123] Not only is a postmortem existence in view by ancient Israel, but also a renewed existence at the conclusion of that postmortem existence. N. T. Wright correctly notes, then, a necessary distinction between life after death and "life after life after death"—awkwardly worded as the phrase may be—because the Israelite (and the New Testament Christian) anticipated some form of bodily resurrected life *after* whatever form of existence or "life" the soul experiences after the moment of death.[124] Such an expectation is entirely consistent with Israel's belief in the living God as God of the living. As Aimo Nikolainen affirms, "belonging to God is the motive for the conquest of death."[125]

Life After Death

The language used by Yahweh's old covenant people articulates an undeveloped but clearly present expectation of communion with the living God for the faithful in not only the here and now, but also posthumously. The incursion of death upon Adam's offspring is indeed a serious matter; but it cannot be viewed as ultimate, considering the context of covenant relationship with the living God. Israel possessed an understanding of the blessing of God as life and the curse of God as death. The glory and promise of the living God

---

122. Ibid., 130–38. Additionally, while not as perspicuous an articulation of bodily resurrection, Hos 13:14 firmly predates Isa 26:19 and Dan 12:1–3. John Day's deft argument that Isa 26:19—and by extension, therefore, Dan 12:1–3—is dependent on Hos 13:14 is instructive here. See Day, "A Case of Inner Scriptural Interpretation," 31:309–19; Day, "Development of Belief," 244–45. Moreover, while the text seems to indicate that Yahweh *will not* "redeem them from death," both Isaiah and Daniel (if they have, in fact, been influenced by this text) and later inspired writers take Hosea's oracle in a positive sense. Clearly the apostle Paul takes the passage positively when he references it in context of "the dead [who] will be raised imperishable" and "changed" having obtained "victory through our Lord Jesus Christ" (cf. 1 Cor 15:54–55).

123. Cf. Pss 16:8–11; 17:15b; 49:15; 73:24b; 139:18b; Hos 13:14; Acts 2:24–36.

124. Wright, *Resurrection*, 30–31.

125. Nikolainen, *Der Auferstehungsglaube*, 125, cited in Martin-Achard, *From Death to Life*, 218.

to provide life, however, would prevail over the creature's faithless rebellion and marring of the image of God. As Neal Pryor convincingly concludes, "Israel's faith in her God as the God of history and as a perfectly just God led to the development of an eschatology. If God is a God of righteousness, then right *must* triumph. If not in the present, then in the future, the will of God will be done."[126]

Because the testimony of every offspring of Adam was that "he died," Israel also understood that life does not belong to the creature to *worship* it—for all intents and purposes—as he sees fit.[127] Not only the near extermination of the entire human species (as well as every other species) in the Flood, but also the ongoing reality of death, incontrovertibly make that point.[128] Israel, in distinction from her ANE neighbors, understood that death was not a natural constituent of the created order, but was instituted by her covenant God as penalty against the cosmos' rebellion against his holiness. Rather than unwittingly idolizing life as more valuable than anything, then, Israel was aware that the creature should acknowledge the reality that he is dust (Ps 103:14; Isa 40:17). They were aware that the Lord of the cosmos revealed in the Old Testament both gives and dismisses created human life in accord with his good pleasure and purposes (Ps 90:3–10).[129]

Israel, as the family that this Lord elected as his "kingdom of priests" to which to impart his oracles (Rom 3:1–2) for the benefit of every family of Adam,[130] believed that those oracles contained the promise of eternal life in a state of shalom with her covenant God. As image bearers of the living God, Israel understood that without life—the quality that her Creator inherently possessed—that image could not fully be borne. Death, then, pointedly expressed the disfavor, even curse of God against a creation that rebelled against his infinitely gracious chief end to reflect his splendor to that created order for its own greatest benefit. Along with Israel, the entire created order

---

126. Pryor, "Eschatological Expectations," 34, 36.

127. As Karl Barth rightly avers, "Man's creaturely existence as such is not his property; it is a loan. As such it must be held in trust. It is not, therefore, under the control of man. But in the broadest sense it is meant for the service of God. 'Know that our God indeed is Lord, And for His glory hath us made, T'is wholly on His gracious Word, The life of every man is stayed.' This is the simplest information that can be given concerning the fact and meaning of life." Barth, *Doctrine of Creation*, 327.

128. Indeed, the glory of the God who created human life is an infinitely higher ethic than preservation of human life (cf. Gen 2:17; 6:5–7; Exod 32:32 [even Moses acknowledges the truth that even his *eternal* life is not as valuable as the glory of God revealed in mercy]; Deut 32:50–51; Josh 7:10–12, 15; Judg 13:22, etc.).

129. To be sure, death is not meted capriciously, but only in direct relation to judgment against unholiness.

130. Cf. Gen 5:1–2; 12:3; 28:14.

may acknowledge that for the grace of life and the unambiguously clear disclosure of its relative value by death, God is not to be held in contempt, but rather to be lauded without reservation by all his originally very good created order (Ps 150).

CHAPTER 4

Death in the New Testament

Introduction

THE OLD TESTAMENT CLOSES leaving the human family anticipating a resolution to decadent creation's quintessential problem—death. The God who created all things "very good" "blessed"—i.e., furnished—his new pristine masterpiece with everything required for it to flourish in the *life* that God himself both possessed and wished to give to his beloved creation as a gift of and from himself. The presence of God reigned in life in the midst of his newly created order until the living God was compelled by his holy justice against the corruption of sin to curse the splendor of his masterpiece with death. The Old Testament thus closes with the now undone created order under a curse.

Just as God disclosed himself in the beginning to the creature made in his own image, so also has he progressed purposefully in the New Testament that self-disclosure to his beloved creature.[1] The Ancient of Days, disclosing himself in the flesh of Israel's Messiah, fulfills his promise not only to Abraham, but also to Adam and Eve, thereby securing the rescue of "all the families of the earth" from the otherwise insurmountable threat of death. The New Testament advent of the Messiah evidences God's intention from the beginning that salvation from the curse of death was not merely for the Jews—i.e., the biological offspring of Abraham—but for "the whole world."[2]

---

1. John 1:14–18; Heb 1:1–3; Phil 2:5–11.
2. John 3:16; Rom 3:29; 9:24; 1 Tim 2:4; Titus 2:11; 1 John 2:2; cf. 2 Pet 3:9.

The very purpose for which God has "descended into the lower parts of the earth" is thus to put an end to death, himself overturning the curse and restoring his creation from its just curse to its pristine resplendence. Just as the Old Testament provides revelation of the origin and intent of death, so the New Testament provides revelation concerning the death of death. The disclosure of God's plan for his image bearers was intentionally introductory in the Old Testament. Resolution of the enigma of death for Adam's (and Abraham's) posterity was not intended to be revealed until the inauguration of the kingdom of God by the Lord of life (Heb 11:39–40). Now in this New Testament age, "[God's] own purpose and grace which was granted us in Christ Jesus from all eternity . . . has been revealed by the appearing of our Savior Christ Jesus, who abolished death and brought life and immortality to light through the gospel" (2 Tim 1:9–10). From within this context of fuller revelation of the nature of death may one glean from the divine mind not only an understanding of the meaning of life, but also a proper perspective of the ethic and value of human life.

Portrait of the Ethic of Human Life

Human life is valuable, no doubt, as evidenced by God's action to preserve its perpetuity; however, one may not assert that such divine preservation necessitates human life's rank as ultimate in value. In this light, Karl Barth keenly assesses Albert Schweitzer's ethic of respect for human life. Barth reads Schweitzer as asserting that this precept is the "'fundamental principle of ethics' and therefore the basis and the measure of all ethics. . . . life is for him, in its totality as our own life and that of others, 'the supreme good,' and therefore it is the highest and properly the only lawgiver, and therefore the criterion of all virtue. According to him the first and last word of all ethics is that life must be respected. Its sum is that to preserve and assist life is good, and to destroy and harm it evil." Barth rightly counters, however, "It [Schweitzer's ethic] cannot be accepted here in this broad sense. . . . Where Schweitzer places life we see the command of God. Life cannot be for us a supreme principle at all, though it can be a sphere in relation to which ethics has to investigate the content and consequences of God's command."[3] Indeed—divine revelation being the basic epistemological axiom—as discussed in chapter 2, the ethic has been revealed to humanity that the glory of God and obedience to his command is of infinitely higher value than that of human life. The glory and command of God the Creator alone then, and

---

3. Schweitzer, *Kultur und Ethik*, 239, cited in Barth, *Doctrine of Creation*, 324.

not human life, may be seen rightly as the "'fundamental principle of ethics' and therefore the basis and the measure of all ethics."

Surveying a host of philosophical ethicists, Barth opines, "Everywhere life itself and as such is regarded as the actual ethical lord, teacher and master of man. As we have just remarked concerning Albert Schweitzer, we can only 'encounter' the representatives of this view. In theological ethics the concept of life cannot be given this tyrannical, totalitarian function. But that does not mean that we should avoid it altogether."[4] The ethic of human life may indeed be evaluated as a means of comprehending the infinitely higher ethic of the glory and command of God. Death, as God's definitive boundary delimiter of the ethic of human life, undermines any possible illusion that life is the "ethical lord, teacher and master of man."

Of the direction and purpose of human life as penultimate in value, Barth writes,

> If God speaks in accordance with His creative will, addressing man concerning that for which He has determined human existence, this means that this existence as such is ordained by its Creator to give Him a hearing and obedience. It is thus from the very outset an existence oriented on His service and praise, on the search for Him and the doing of His will. Life as such thus means to live for the One to whom it belongs and from whom it has been received as a loan. Life, human life, thus hastens as such towards freedom before God, and only *per nefas*, as never according to its own nature, can it depart from this direction or take the opposite one. We must accept the fact that, in respect of this natural direction of his life towards God, man is not its owner and lord. Together with everything else which determines and characterises his life, the fact that it is oriented on God is also and particularly God's creation and loan. But we can understand even human life as such only if we gather, not from speculation but from the event of its confrontation by the Word of God, that it too, without any cooperation of its own but by nature and from the very first, has this vertical direction.[5]

Because human life belongs to another and is on loan—as it were—to the creature, it may not be elevated as the supreme good and, for all intents and purposes, worshipped as some mystical apex of all reality, under the power of no one—or again, as Barth renders it, the "ethical lord, teacher and master of man."

---

4. Barth, *Doctrine of Creation*, 326.
5. Ibid., 330–31.

The Word of God, to which Barth refers[6] (the New Testament illuminating the Old), has given the creature a guide for valuing human life no more nor any less than God does. The New Testament is replete with depictions and doctrines that qualify for us God's assessment of the ethic and value of human life—from the gift of childbirth appointed to certain barren mothers, to the deaths of the humbled faithful and damnable unfaithful alike, to the resurrection from the dead (only to die again) of those whom the Son of God willed to restore to life, to the birth, life, death, and resurrection to life again of the consummate human, Jesus Christ himself, as the firstborn from the dead of all the sons of Adam. Just as the Old Testament closes with the puzzle of death yet unresolved, so the New Testament advent of the Messiah to Adam's offspring inaugurates the conclusion of the matter. Accordingly, the New Testament depicts, time and again, the dominion over the curse of death by the Son of Man who, like his Father, has life in himself (John 5:26–27).

The New Testament not only introduces Immanuel—the God-man—but it reveals why God has come to be with the sons of Adam: precisely because he is *for* us, *against* the curse of death.[7] Still, such a magnanimous exhibition of succoring tends to precipitate in tainted creatures a haughty self-esteem. As admonished in chapter 1, a healthy balance is needed between a right embrace of the sanctity of life as an invaluable gift from its gracious Giver yet simultaneously its genuine dispensability as nonessential being. In this regard, contemplating the nature of death as the delimiter of the value of human life, Don Carson offers thoughtful counsel for holding in proper tension both the nonessential nature of human life and its simultaneous immeasurable value.

> Death is God's limit on creatures whose sin is that they want to be gods (Gen 3:4–5; Rom 1:18–23). . . . We are not gods; and by death we learn that we are only human. Our pretensions are

---

6. One must differentiate what Barth may mean by "the *event* of [human life's] *confrontation* by the Word of God" (emphasis added) from an evangelical understanding of the doctrine of verbal plenary inspiration of the Word of God, where the canon of revelation itself is divinely inspired, rather than the divine inspiration being characterized only by the "event" of the matter's "confrontation" by the Word of God. Nevertheless, the revelation of God serves to communicate definitively the divine standard for the valuation of human life.

7. God's being "for us" (Rom 8:31) is penultimate in his divine purpose and plan; ultimate is his own splendor as Creator and Redeemer—the One who alone is able to create (Gen 1), turn his creation back to dust (Gen 3:19; Ps 90:2–3), and then restore to glory his image in that creation even more excellently than originally manifested (2 Cor 3:7–11; Rev 21:1–5).

destroyed. We are cut off, and all our yesterdays "are one with Nineveh and Tyre."

At the same time, we cry out against this limitation, not only because in our rebellion we still want to become gods, but because we have been made in the image of God. We are not mere mammals. We are persons. If we really believed that we are nothing more than accidental collections of atoms, moral outrage over anything would be irrational. But we want to live, even while our hubris means we have been cut off from him who alone gives life. That we are mammals means that our death has a physical side; that we are not merely mammals means that our death is God's determination to limit our arrogance.[8]

Divine revelation holds in undisturbed equilibrium these two poles of human being's nonessential nature and immeasurable value. Human life is certainly *not* that "from whom every family in heaven and earth derives its name" (Eph 3:15). At the same time, however, precisely because human life uniquely images that One, any justifiable "crying out" against the limitation of death must be aimed not at its supposed affront to the creature, but at the desecration of the image of the God who purposed human life to reflect his own splendor.

The Value of Human Life as Illustrated by Christ's Incarnation

The assumption of a human nature by the second person of the Trinity is no small notion. This cosmic reality has vast implications for the valuation of human life. Although the incarnation occurred in time after the procreation of Adam and Eve to fill the earth with the *imago Dei* as commanded, one may legitimately argue that Jesus did not assume human nature because of its great significance, but rather that Adam and Eve and their posterity were so formed by the divine mind as that which Christ would take to himself for eternity. Adam and Eve—although temporally *a priori* to the incarnation—are atemporally *a posteriori* to the divine plan.

Human life, then, is not even first ours; it is derived from another and "on loan" to Adam and all his posterity. Karl Barth again muses accordingly, "Those who handle life as a divine loan will above all treat it with respect."[9] He further elaborates concerning Christianity's attempt to dignify respect for human life upon occasionally deficient means, particularly when the

---

8. Carson, *How Long*, 111.
9. Barth, *Doctrine of Creation*, 338.

incarnation "unmistakeably [*sic*] differentiates human life from everything that is and is done in heaven and earth."

> It is really surprising that the Christian Church and Christian theology have not long ago urged more energetically the importance for ethics of so constituent a part of the New Testament message as the fact of the incarnation, instead of resorting, in the vital question why man and human life are to be respected, to all kinds of general religious expressions and to the assertions of non-Christian humanism. . . . In contrast to every other, the respect of life which becomes a command in the recognition of the union of God with humanity in Jesus Christ has an incomparable power and width. For in this recognition it is really commanded with the authority of God Himself and therefore in such a way that there can be no question whatever of disregard as an alternative. Intellectualistic and materialistic onesidedness in answer to the question what human existence is all about is thus excluded by the grounding of the command in this recognition because the human life in question, the life of the man Jesus, cannot be divided into a psychical or physical but compels us to offer the respect demanded by God to the whole man in his ordered unity of soul and body.[10]

Herein is the clarion proclamation of God concerning his valuation of human life; not that human life is itself intrinsically valuable, but because its Creator has so valued it as his self-identifying imprint of ownership on his entire creation. Any attempt by the creature to remove that imprint, then, is the height of disrespect not only for human life, but also for the Creator whom human life images. No other valuation can compare with the power and width of such a dignifying of the value of human life as the eternal assumption of human nature by God himself.

The Death of the Son of Man

What Does the Human Nature of Jesus Christ Portend?

What is the humanity that the Son assumed? Human nature consists of a body and a soul (yet not necessarily inclusive of a human *person*).[11] Properly

---

10. Ibid., 338–40.

11. See for example Tertullian, *De Carne Christi*, 49. Gen 2:7 reveals that "the Lord God formed man of dust from the ground, and breathed into his nostrils the breath of life; and man became a living being." The Hebrew term translated "living being" is *nephesh*—meaning *soul, life,* or *self* (see chap. 3). Scripture further discloses that this

speaking, Christ's incarnation was *enhypostatic* rather than *anhypostatic*; that is, no human nature existed separate from the person or *hypostasis*, which the divine Son gave to that nature. No self-existent human nature—or any nature, for that matter—possesses a *person* intrinsically; the *nature* subsists *in person*—i.e., *enhypostatic*. In human beings, a single human nature subsists in one human person. In Christ, two natures—one human and one divine—subsist *in* one *hypostasis* or person. So, Christ could not assume a human nature with its own extant person; this would amount to the heresy of Nestorianism (where the Son is said to consist of two natures *and* two persons).[12]

Hylomorphic dualism. Defining human nature on a hylomorphic theory posits an intrinsic unicity of body and soul as mandatory for the "kind of thing" a human being is. The following, therefore, may be predicated of human nature as it relates to human beings, and only in relation to Christ's human nature, but not in relation to his divine person.

> Human persons [i.e., *individuals* as distinguished here from *hypostases*] just are embodied creatures, and thus not only must their souls be attached to their bodies—at least at *some* time in their history—for them to exist, but also their souls, in order to be *souls of persons*, that is, in order to be what they are, must be at some time the forms of bodies. This means that the idea of a human person disembodied throughout its history is incoherent [contra Platonism]. Such a being might be a disembodied person, but it would not be a disembodied *human* person because human persons are just not that kind of thing. In which case, if the human soul has a disembodied existence, that existence can only be made possible by its once having been the form of a body. Further, it is also *identity-dependent* on its once having been the form of a body. In other words, to be the particular soul that it is, it must once have been the form of a particular body making a particular individual substance of a rational nature; just as, in its embodied state, the soul's identity depends on whose, that is, which person's, soul it is. In short, the principle of individuation for persons must be *cross-temporal*.[13]

---

human nature is comprised of both material and immaterial elements. The unique one person/two nature constitution of Jesus Christ, who possesses no *human* person, is treated in what follows.

12. For a detailed discussion of the concepts *anhypostatic* and *enhypostatic*, see Crisp, *Divinity and Humanity*, 72–89.

13. Oderberg, "Hylemorphic [sic] Dualism," 95–96.

So, while the essentially immaterial aspect of human nature can persist independent of the nature's material aspect, an organic and substance-defining link exists between the form and the matter of the human nature that is dissolved only at peril of the *full* human nature. The temporal nature of the body and soul's perichoresis,[14] however, is evidenced by the death of the body and the persistence of the soul until it is reunited with a body at the resurrection. This reunion again completes the human nature, suiting it for its eternal intended embodied existence.[15] The subject or *prosopon* that both constitutes and perpetuates personal identity at the transition of death remains constant throughout the transition. That is, the identity of the individual who dies is contiguous with the identity that exists in the intermediate state and in the resurrection.[16] Since the nature manifestly is not merely a body, the first transition occurs at death. Again, the human nature is not complete however; a final transition of re-embodiment must occur. For Christ, this final transition of *re*-incarnation[17] in a body suited for eternity occurred at his resurrection—as "the first fruits of those who are asleep" (1 Cor 15:20). The human nature that Christ assumed, therefore, in order to be a complete human nature, would necessarily resume its embodiment. The implications of this proposition will surface in what follows.

What Does the Death of Jesus Christ Portend?

One of the very first Christian creeds, the Apostles' Creed, succinctly states the universal Christian tenet, "I believe . . . in Jesus Christ . . . who . . . was crucified, dead, and buried . . . ." The early church acknowledged that "the Lord of glory" literally died and was buried (1 Cor 2:8). The church affirmed

---

14. *Perichoresis* typically refers to the doctrine of the mutual co-inherence of the distinct members of the godhead. Defining the doctrine Gerald Bray writes, "In physical terms, one might say that all three persons occupy the same divine 'space'; to see God is to see all three at once, not one after the other in an ascending order of succession." The term is used here in reference to the similar co-inherence of the human soul and body. Bray, *Doctrine of God*, 158; see also Oliver Crisp's excellent discussion of *nature-perichoresis* in Crisp, *Divinity and Humanity*, 3–27.

15. In 2 Cor 5:1–8 the apostle Paul indicates that the very purpose for which God created humanity is to be clothed with an eternal body suited for eternal worship of the God who created it; yet without a body, we are "found naked"—i.e., incomplete. See also Cooper, *Body, Soul, and Life Everlasting*, 72.

16. Cooper, *Body, Soul, and Life Everlasting*, 160–64, 170–76.

17. The metaphysical notion of the soul's return from a previous life to a new physical form—even species—is not in view here. Rather, simply that Christ, having put-off his corporeal body of his human nature—which he maintained throughout his encounter with death—now re-assumes it in its glorified condition.

that the Son of God assumed humanity for the express purpose of dying on its behalf.[18] The man who was God "tasted" death (Heb 2:9). Death could not hold him, however (Acts 2:24); yet the experience of death may now be predicated of "the Lord of glory." Because deity cannot die, what does the death of the God-man entail?

Patripassianism. The incarnation of Christ presents one of the cosmos' greatest paradoxes. Of this paradox Charles Wesley would write in 1738 the lyrics, "Amazing love! How can it be that thou my God shouldst die for me?" The obvious question raised by Wesley's somewhat cloaked lyric is "How can *God* suffer and die?" This question's tangency to the discussion of the incarnation and death of Jesus Christ warrants only an overview of the doctrine here.[19]

The New Testament clearly affirms the deity of Jesus Christ and the simultaneous oneness of the godhead. This unity of the godhead has led many to question how the person of the Son could suffer and die while the Father—fully one with the Son (and Spirit)—is exempt from that suffering and death. This notion of the suffering of God the Father—*patripassianism*—derives from this questioning and is regarded as heretical.[20]

---

18. See Isa 53:12b; Matt 20:28, Mark 10:45; Rom 8:3–4; 2 Cor 5:21; Phil 2:5–8; Heb 2:9; 10:5, Ps 40:6.

19. For a fuller treatment of the doctrine of *patripassianism*, see Kelly, *Early Christian Doctrines*, 119–23; Erickson, *Christian Theology*, 335–36, 359–60; Tertullian, *Adversus Praxean*; and Leo, *Tome*, 21–25. For an articulation of how the perichoretic union of the godhead may conceive of God as "experiencing" pain distinctly through the agency of the Son, see Macleod, *Person of Christ*, 140–42; cf. 124–26.

20. Not only did Tertullian and later Leo reject *patripassianism*, but Cyril of Alexandria (c. 378–444) also contributed to the debate, articulating the suffering of death by the Son in his own human nature as distinguished from his divine nature. "And since on this account [as a matter of the salvation of the whole world] he wished to suffer, even though he was beyond the power of suffering in his nature as God, then he wrapped himself in flesh that was capable of suffering, and revealed it as his very own, so that even the suffering might be said to be his because it was his own body which suffered and not one else's. Since the manner of the economy allows him blamelessly to chose both to suffer in the flesh, and not to suffer in the Godhead (for the selfsame was at once God and man) then our opponents surely argue in vain, and foolishly debase the power of the mystery, when they think they have made a worthy synthesis." Concerning the clear distinction of natures and the suffering of Christ's human nature only, Cyril further writes, "He suffers in his own flesh, and not in the nature of the Godhead. The method of these things is altogether ineffable, and there is no mind that can attain to such subtle and transcendent ideas. Yet, following these most correct deductions, and carefully considering the most reasonable explanations, we do not deny that he can be said to suffer (in case we thereby imply that the birth in the flesh was not his but someone else's), but this does not mean that we say that the things pertaining to the flesh transpired in his divine and transcendent nature." To illustrate the distinction of

That theological doctrines are deeply connected with one another is evidenced in the unpacking of the notion of *patripassianism*; understanding the doctrine of Christ's hypostatic union is crucial for answering why God the Father may not suffer death although God the Son does. Rightly did Pope Leo I of Rome iterate in the fifth century concerning Christ's hypostatic union, "the property or distinctive character then of each nature and substance [divine and human] remaining entire and coalescing into one person . . . in order to pay the debt of our condition, an impassible [divine] nature was united to a passible [human] one, that . . . the man Jesus Christ, might be capable of death from the one and incapable from the other."[21] In this way could the second person of the divine Trinity experience death as a man while at the same time the impassible divine nature shared by the Father and the Son may never die.

The rending of the godhead. Though no ontological breach could ever assail the unified Godhead, the relational unity of the Godhead was interrupted by the Son's experiencing of the agony of death. The divine Son tasted death—the genuine forsakenness and wrath of the Father in penalty against humanity's infinite guilt of sin.[22] The perfect relational unity of the Godhead was rent for the first and only time in eternity in order that God might reconcile his own image in his creation. The death, "even death on a cross" (Phil 2:8), that the Son experienced was not merely the righteous penalty of physical death (Gen 2:17), but the death that signifies the particular curse of God against deliberate rebellion (Deut 21:22–23; Gal 3:13)—rebellion that was not the Son's own.

No, deity did not suffer death but the one divine Son experienced death in full measure in a nature that was his very own—and no one else's. The Son was truly "made like His brethren in all things, so that He might become a merciful and faithful high priest in things pertaining to God, to make propitiation for the sins of the people. For since He was tempted in that which He has suffered, He is able to come to the aid of those who are tempted" (Heb 2:17–18). The words of Gregory here ring true: "The unassumed is the unhealed, but what is united with God is also being saved."[23]

---

natures, Cyril uses an analogy of iron that may be shaped when fired, but "the nature of the fire is in no way injured by the one who strikes." See Cyril, *Unity of Christ*, 118, 130–31.

21. Leo, *Tome*, 21.

22. See Ps 22:1, Matt 27:46, Mark 15:34; Isa 53:12b, Mark 10:45; Rom 5:12; 6:23.

23. Gregory of Nazianzus, "Letter 101," 158. Grillmeier translates the phrase, "That which is not taken is not healed, but whatever is united to God is saved"; see Grillmeier, *Christian Tradition*, 321; see also 115, 321, 351.

Chalcedonian orthodoxy. The Chalcedonian Definition is as helpful for ruminating the death of Christ as it is for understanding his incarnation. "Following, then, the holy Fathers,"[24] one must speak of the death of Christ in terms that do justice to the unity of his person. Christ's human nature did not die in isolation from his divine nature—the two are ever hypostatically joined in one person.

> [Had there been, in fact, some *tertium quid*], either the Word would have died or the flesh would not have died, if the Word had been converted into flesh for either the flesh would have been immortal or the Word mortal. But because both substances acted distinctively each in its own quality, therefore to them accrued both their own activities and their own destinies.[25]

So, while the perfect human nature of the Son of Man died—including separation from his body and fully experiencing the "agony of death" (Acts 2:24) in his human *nephesh*—the unified person of the divine Son bore the infinite wrath of God as righteous judgment against the sins of all those he would pardon.

The Church Fathers. Chief of the Cappadocian Fathers,[26] Gregory of Nazianzus (c. 330-390) advocated the full humanity of Jesus, arguing that, "The unassumed is the unhealed, but what is united with God is also being saved."[27] As Gregory understood it, Christ had to assume the full reality of humanity; otherwise any unassumed human reality could not be atoned for. Tertullian and Origen, too, had taken this line of argumentation.[28] Arguably, the writer of Hebrews communicates the same idea when he intimates that Christ "tasted death for every man" (Heb 2:9). The *hyper* ("for" or "in behalf of") could signify that Christ tasted death of an identical kind and to the fullest degree that any man could ever possibly experience.[29] Such

---

24. Sellers, *Council of Chalcedon*, 210–11.

25. Tertullian, *Adversus Praxean*, 174.

26. The Cappadocian Fathers consisted of Gregory of Nanzianzus—"the Theologian" (c. 330-390), and brothers Basil ("the Great") c. 330-379), bishop of Caesarea, and another Gregory (c. 335/340–c. 390), bishop of Nyssa. Along with contemporaries Athanasius (c. 295-373) and Cyril of Alexandria (c. 375-444), the Cappadocian Fathers are considered "yardsticks of patristic theology." Concerning the degree of self-disclosure found among the great patristic writers, the Theologian Gregory is second only to Augustine (354-430). See Gregory of Nazianzus, *On God and Christ*, 9.

27. Gregory of Nazianzus, "Letter 101."

28. Tertullian, *De Carne Christi*, 39–41; Origen, *Dialektos pros Hērakleidan*, 136, cited in Grillmeier, *Christian Tradition*, 115, 321.

29. Wayne Grudem rightly argues that the use in Heb 6:4–5 of the term *geusamenous*

a universal notion of death—both physical and spiritual—would be applicable "*for* every man," (while at the same time not signifying a universal atonement). Christ's tasting of the full breadth of death for humanity would leave no depth of sin unatoned for any offspring of Adam.

Concerning the real human body of Jesus, Athanasius queried, "How could the destruction of death have been manifested at all, had not the Lord's body been raised?"[30]

Importantly, as Athanasius further argued about the real physicality of Jesus, Christ's death had to be both public and not as a result of sickness or "natural" causes. In dying a human death, Christ's full humanity would be established as *bona fide* so as to dispel all notions of Docetism. Only the very human incarnate Son of God could provide a satisfactory propitiation on behalf of humanity. Only the *volitional* laying down of his life and subsequent resurrection of the divine Son of God could evidence that he is Lord over both life and death.[31]

The Post-Crucifixion Humanity of Christ

Chalcedon again helps us in reflecting on the humanity of Christ even after his death. While the Chalcedonian Definition does not speak explicitly to the *permanence* of Christ's incarnation (barring either the formidable phrase "without separation," or the statement's parlance concerning the unity of the Son), the council's determination would seem to have only temporal significance if the *homo assumptus* were not permanent. Just as the divine Son cannot properly be said to have laid-aside his divine attributes at his incarnation,[32] neither can the laying-aside of the God-man's post-mortem human nature be affirmed; for only that which is human (in reference to the divine Son) can die. If the Son merely abandoned his human nature at death, the atonement is a sham; for no Savior exists who "might taste death for every man" (Heb 2:9); the Scriptures are then in error; Christ did not rise from the dead (for the divine Son did not actually *die*; he merely abandoned the corporeal shell he previously inhabited—*a la* Apollinarianism); "and if Christ has not been raised, your faith is worthless; you are still in your sins" (1 Cor 15:12-20).

(having tasted) connotes not a sampling but full consumption. Grudem, "Perseverance of the Saints," 145. See also Kistemaker, "Atonement in Hebrews," 170–75.

30. Athanasius, *De Incarnatione Verbi Dei*, 60.

31. Ibid., 50–54. See John 5:21; 10:18; Acts 2:22–36; Rom 14:7–9.

32. For convincing arguments against kenotic Christology, see Crisp, *Divinity and Humanity*, 118–53; and van Driel, "Logic of Assumption," 264–90.

Denial of the continuing humanity of the Son as that *ousious* that tasted death, therefore, necessarily denies the saving work of Christ. We could then mourn with Cleopas, "But we were hoping that it was he who was going to redeem Israel" (Luke 24:21). To the contrary, however, "[God] has fixed a day in which he will judge the world in righteousness through *a Man* whom he has appointed, having furnished proof to all men by raising him from the dead" (Acts 17:31; emphasis added). The perfect image of God in his creation is forever sealed in an embodied human—the *eternal* God-man. The human nature that the second person of the Trinity took to himself is permanent.[33] Again, this truth places immeasurable value on our significance as human beings; for we are by nature what God ordained from eternity he would add to his own person (John 1:1, 14; Phil 2:6–8).

The soteriological significance of the post-crucifixion humanity of Christ. That the Son of Man must maintain his humanity in his death is necessary for the atonement. The Son could no more have atoned for humanity as a dead *phantom* as he could have lived a perfectly obedient life in that same form and have it be worthy of vicarious justification from the Father. The Church Fathers recognized this fact and thus declared the Christology of Docetists and Gnostics *no* Christology at all! Christ, by living and dying as a *man*, fulfilled the righteous requirement of the Law of God against sin (Rom 6:23; 8:3–4). In his triumph over death, in the union of immortal Logos and human nature, the divine Son clothed in incorruption all who by faith acknowledge his death on their behalf.[34] In the sense that the divine person of the Son took-on and maintained human nature throughout his encounter with death, *only* a *dead man* can save us from the wrath to come.[35]

The dashed hopes of the disillusioned Cleopas are indeed resurrected in the truth that the divine Son of Man tasted the full measure of death so that no one who believes in him will have to. The consummate revelation of the mystery for which the whole universe anxiously awaits is this: the very nature that the Creator of all things himself would assume for all eternity was the nature he created as an icon (Gen 1:26; Heb 1:3) for the radiance of his glory throughout the expanse of his created order. That nature *did not* surrender to the corruption of death![36]

---

33. Crisp, *Divinity and Humanity*, 133–36. Crisp forthrightly states, "On a credally orthodox Christology, there is nothing temporary about the assumption of human flesh by the Word."

34. Athanasius, *De Incarnatione*, 34–35.

35. Rom 5:12–19; 1 Cor 15:21–22; 1 Thess 1:10.

36. Deut 32:39; John 10:17–18; Acts 2:22–32; Heb 2:14; 1 John 3:8; 1 Cor 15:55/ Hos 13:14.

Too often, one tends to think that the significance of the humanity of Christ concluded at the cross, and that the "passive obedience" of his earthly passion merely concluded his "active obedience."[37] Well, just as Christ's redemption is not vindicated before his resurrection, so also is redemption not accomplished apart from "the anguish of his soul" (Isa 53:11). The death of Christ's body alone could not propitiate the wrath of God. The Son of Man had to expiate the penalty on behalf of those he came to save. The finite, physical blood of the Son of Man could not provide infinite atonement in isolation from either Christ's human soul or his divine nature. The *person* of the divine Son had to "taste death for every man" in order to accomplish redemption for humanity; for "The unassumed is the unhealed, but what is united with God is also being saved."[38]

Anthropological Solidarity: The Church

The God who assumed human nature purposed from the beginning that the procreation of Adam and Eve would proliferate his image throughout the earth "as the waters cover the sea." Adam and Eve and their posterity reflect the image of God not only individually, but also collectively.[39] The church

---

37. Theologians speak of the *active* and *passive* obedience of Christ as necessary for satisfaction of the requirement of God's law. Some prefer rather to use the terminology *perceptive* and *penal* obedience because of the imprecision of the terms *active* and *passive*. See Reymond, *New Systematic Theology*, 631.

38. Gregory, "Letter 101," 158.

39. Wayne Grudem, while advocating the federal headship of Adam and Christ, also affirms the "organic whole" of the race. Concerning this unity of the church, he writes, "Christ, the representative of all who believe in him, obeyed God perfectly—and God counted us righteous. That is simply the way in which God set up the human race to work. God regards the human race as an organic whole, a unity, represented by Adam as its head. And God also thinks of the new race of Christians, those who are redeemed by Christ, as an organic whole, a unity represented by Christ as head of his people." Grudem, *Systematic Theology*, 495–96.

Further, although divergent from the present work's view on the nature of Christ's atonement, Xavier Léon-Dufour analogizes concerning humanity's solidarity, "Let us be more specific about this revelation by Paul [in Rom 5:12–21]. In Adam all were sinners; in Jesus Christ all are sharers in grace. Humanity is likened unto a sphere that Adam smashed by separating it from God; within this broken sphere, all are born into death. Jesus entered into this sphere; being without sin, he himself became the principle for a new sphere. Jesus is the head of a new humanity.

This is only intelligible in all its depth if one grasps the notion of *corporate personality*. . . . Neither Adam nor Jesus are simply heads of a race; they actually constitute a single body with those who are their descendants either through the flesh or through faith. This depiction is founded not on the concepts of cause and effect but rather on the concepts of one's condition and one's solidarity. Adam is neither the cause nor the

also, the "body of Christ," the new faith humanity seeded by Abraham, reflects the image and glory of God in many regards as a unitary whole. The fellowship of believers in Jesus Christ is not merely a social compact; it is a metaphysical solidarity with the second person of the Trinity that will consummate for participants in Christ in the partaking of God's nature at beatification.[40] For this reason the apostle John can speak categorically of the *koinonia* that believers have with one another and more importantly, with the Father and with his Son, Jesus Christ (1 John 1:3; cf. John 14:23; 1 Cor 10:16).

The impact upon the "body" of the death (or neglect) of one of its members extends to the entire community of the called, whether or not that community acknowledges the impact (1 Cor 11:29-30). When one of the body's members is severed from temporal communion with it, it nevertheless remains in ultimate communal solidarity with the body because of its *koinonia* with Christ. For this reason the writer to the Hebrews may make reference to "the city of the living God . . . to the general assembly and church of the firstborn who are enrolled in heaven . . . and to the spirits of the righteous made perfect" (Heb 12:22-23). The "spirits of the righteous made perfect" almost certainly refers to the dead in Christ, even those pre-Christian saints.[41] Whether those "who are enrolled in heaven" refers only to the dead in Christ or to all members of the church throughout all ages[42] is inconsequential to the reality that all members of the body of Christ—*ecclesia militans* and *ecclesia triumphans*—participate in a single communion of saints. For this reason Christ himself can express fury at the assault of death upon his body.[43]

---

source of my sin, he is merely the one who introduced sin into the world. Through Adam's deed, I am born into a relationship with the power of sin; this is what is called 'original sin.' In passing into the new sphere, bound up through Jesus Christ to God, the human person rediscovers life, that is to say, grace.

Since Christ is the New Adam, he exhausts the significance of the first Adam, 'the type of the one who is to come.' He is the antitype, the very reality awaited. Also I must understand my relationship to Adam, my state as a human being and sinner, not by beginning with my relationship to Adam but by laying hold of my state in Jesus Christ." See Léon-Dufour, *Life and Death in the New Testament*, 213-14. See also Gen 1:27.

40. See 2 Pet 1:4. More on this notion will appear in chap. 7; see also Augustine, *City of God*, 12:2-5; 22:1, 30.

41. Bruce, *Hebrews*, 378.

42. Cf. Luke 10:20; Phil 4:3; Rev 21:27. That the phrase refers to "the whole communion of saints, including those who, while 'militant here in earth,' are enrolled as citizens of heaven" is argued by Bruce, *Hebrews*, 376-77.

43. See John 11:33, 38; cf. also 1 Cor 3:17 where the second person plural indicates the body of believers rather than the individual member.

This solidarity notwithstanding, the New Testament records no deaths of a group in association with the lawlessness of an individual, as does the Old Testament. Sin leading to death (1 John 5:16; cf. Jas 1:15) results in the death of the individual only. The New Testament consigns the group to death only in the sense of death being each individual's due as a result of being offspring of Adam (Rom 5). Perhaps this new economy of death accords with the new covenant about which both Jeremiah and Ezekiel had prophesied: "In those days they will not say again, 'The fathers have eaten sour grapes, and the children's teeth are set on edge.' But everyone will die for his own iniquity; each man who eats the sour grapes, his teeth will be set on edge" (Jer 31:29–30; Ezek 18:2–4). Nevertheless, diverse instances of death—whether individual or *en masse* (cf. Luke 13:1–5)—represent a unitary judgment against violation of the law of the living God. Thus, as in the Old Testament, so also in the New Testament, no death—however or whenever it occurs—may result in charging God with injustice.

Doctrines and Depictions of Death in the New Testament

The Old Testament's deliberately leaving in "mystery" the enigma of death sets the stage for the New Testament's resolution of the enigma. The depictions of encounters with death and the interwoven teachings about the nature of its vanquishing fill the New Testament. Several primary questions arise for which the New Testament grounds reasoned responses: If death is vanquished, why then do people still die? Why do Christians die? What happens after death; or is death final?

Already—Not Yet

Adam was duly warned that death would consume him and his posterity upon his unholy disregarding of the command of his gracious Creator Sustainer. The entirety of human history has evidenced that God's promise to the first man was not an idle threat; as promised and proven, "in Adam all die" (1 Cor 15:22; cf. Rom 5:12, 14, 18–19). Salubriously fortunately, however, that is not the end of the story. The Old Testament foretold of a new covenant that God would establish with Abraham's progeny that would incorporate the full breadth of Adam's progeny. By this new covenant would all of Adam's families be "blessed" and not "cursed."[44] The New Testament,

---

44. Adam and Eve knew both their guilt and the consequent cursing. They knew that death now both infected them and would eventually consume them, putting an end to the "living being" into which God had breathed his breath of life. Much like

quoting God's promise of Isaiah 61 (cf. Luke 4:17–21), reveals that Jesus Christ is the One anointed by God "to proclaim the favorable year of the Lord," "to set free those who are oppressed" through fear of death (Heb 2:14–15). The inauguration of the curse-reversing New Testament reign of the living God was declared by Jesus Christ when he heralded, "Today this Scripture has been fulfilled in your hearing" (Luke 4:21). If death thus has been vanquished, why, then, do offspring of Adam still die? The New Testament's response to that query is twofold.

First, the same reply may be offered here as to the oft posed haughty interrogative, "If God is omnipotent, why does he not put an end to death?" The New Testament's response to this insolence is, "Wait for it." The Son of Man's temporal yet definitive (re)inauguration of the reign of Life may not be conflated with its consummation. In this current New Testament "time between the times," the Son of God works—as he has already informed the sons of Adam—as does his Father (John 5:17), preparing a place of eternal life (John 14:2–3) and assembling from among all the sons and daughters of Adam (Acts 17:26–27, 30–31; Rev 5:9; 14:6) subjects who adhere to his new covenant (Matt 16:18). The Son of Man, who alone has the capacity to give life to any offspring of Adam (John 1:9; 5:25–27), will consummate his work with the final undoing of the last enemy—death (1 Cor 15:25–26). Until the Son's reigning work of kingdom building is complete, death will continue its numbered days among the offspring of Adam. The reality of this death, however, may be divided into different senses—which brings us to the second facet of the New Testament's response to the question of continuing death.

Second, a sense exists in which adherents to God's new covenant do *not* die. Chapters 1 and 2 of this work delineate the weight of death as not only physical/ corporeal, but also as spiritual/eternal. The reality of death as the curse of God that merits his just and eternal wrath, with not even a hint of any parole of grace, will never be the lot of the offspring of Adam who by faith embrace the Son of Man's novation of that penalty on their behalf. Immanuel himself so declares, "I am the resurrection and the life; he who believes in me will live even if he dies, and everyone who lives and believes in me *will never die*. Do you believe this?" (John 11:25–26; emphasis added).

Eve must have contemplated, however, when she bore humanity's first child (Gen 4:1), every human birth heralds the truth that the curse of death did not put and end to mankind's hope for life with the first generation, or with the next, or the next, or the next. Rather, with each birth of a God-image-bearer, the God who granted life from himself (John 5:26) in the first place, reiterates, in a sense, not the curse, but "the blessing—life forever" (Ps 133:3). Each newborn son of Adam, then, represents the divine promise expressed.

Why Do Christians Die?

If death is a product of the curse, and Christ has abrogated the curse for the Christian, one might legitimately inquire, "Why do Christians die?" In reply, Louis Berkhof rather confidently asserts, "It is quite evident that the death of believers must be regarded as the culmination of the chastisements which God has ordained for the sanctification of His people.... In the mystical union with their Lord believers are made to share the experiences of Christ. Just as He entered upon His glory by the pathway of sufferings and death, they too can enter upon their eternal reward only through sanctification."[45] Scripture assures us concerning "the exhortation which is addressed to you as sons, 'My son, do not regard lightly the discipline of the Lord, nor faint when you are reproved by him; for those whom the Lord loves he disciplines, and he scourges every son whom he receives'" (Heb 12:5-6). In faithfully submitting to God's discipline—of which all have become partakers (v. 8)—Christians only further evidence that they are indeed children of God. To be sure, "All discipline for the moment seems not to be joyful, but sorrowful [particularly the scourging of death]; yet to those who have been trained by it, afterwards it yields the peaceful fruit of righteousness" (v. 11). Death is certainly not essential for sharing in God's holiness (v. 10), for the translations of Enoch and Elijah seem to vitiate that proposal.[46] However, God certainly uses death as one means of accomplishing the constitutional transformation necessary for mankind to partake of God's divine nature and righteousness in a beatific manner. The transition of death, for the believer, is merely one final test of his unshakeable faith that God will keep his promise to that believer that Jesus Christ is the resurrection and the life.[47]

---

45. Berkhof, *Systematic Theology*, 670-71. Paul Helm argues similarly; see Helm, *Last Things*, 45-50. See also Strong, *Systematic Theology*, 983. Karl Rahner also argues that death for the Christian, as communal with Christ's death, is man's natural transition from earth to glory; and that death should be regarded by the believer with "the abandonment of the last surrender"; see Rahner, *Theology of Death*, 64-80, 94.

46. Berkhof, *Systematic Theology*, 670.

47. Augustine elaborates, "If anyone is troubled by the question why those whose guilt is removed through grace should suffer the death which is the penalty of sin, this problem has been treated, and its solution given, in another book of mine, *On the Baptism of Infants*. There it is suggested that the experience of the separation of soul from body remains, although its connection with guilt is removed, because if the immortality of the body followed immediately upon the sacrament of regeneration, faith itself would be weakened, since faith is only faith when what is not yet seen in reality is awaited in hope.

Furthermore, it was by the strength of faith and in the conflict of faith that even the fear of death admitted of being conquered, at any rate in the earlier ages; and this was seen pre-eminently in the holy martyrs. This conflict would have had no victory, no

The faithfully dying Christian acknowledges that his life, which is inseparably united with Christ, is not terminating, only transitioning. In his precious death (Ps 116:15), no punishment is even remotely involved; for humanity's only savior, Jesus Christ, being pierced for our transgressions and crushed for our iniquities, bore the penalty for our sins on his cross, having been made sin for us that we might become the righteousness of God in him, the Lord laying on him the iniquity of us all so that he might cancel the certificate of debt consisting of decrees against us, which was hostile to us, having nailed it to his death stake (Isa 53:5–6; Col 2:14; 2 Cor 5:21; 1 Pet 2:24). In this final test of faith working through love, the degree of the Christian's fear is indistinguishable from the degree of his lack of faith. The apostle John encapsulates this truth in his statement, "There is no fear in love; but perfect love casts out fear, because fear involves punishment, and the one who fears is not perfected in love" (1 John 4:18). The Christian is the only human being that is justified to die perfectly without fear.[48]

Millard Erickson. Millard Erickson opposes Berkhof here, asserting that, "A better approach is simply to consider death one of the conditions of humanity as now constituted; in this respect, death is like birth."[49] Isolating Berkhof's conception of sanctification and faith from the benefit of the saint's identification with the Lord in his death, Erickson contends, "That

---

glory, since there could have been no conflict at all, if after the 'washing of regeneration' the saints were straightway exempt from bodily death. If this were so, surely everyone would rush to the grace of Christ, with the children to be baptized, just to avoid being released from the body. And faith would not be tested by the fact that its reward was unseen; indeed, it would not be faith any longer, since the reward of the act of faith would be demanded and taken immediately.

But as it is, the punishment of sin has been turned by the great and wonderful grace of our Saviour to a good use, to the promotion of righteousness. It was then said to man, 'You will die if you sin.' Now it is said to the martyr, 'Die, rather than sin.' It was then said, 'If you break the commandment you will certainly die.' Now it is said, 'If you shrink from death, you will break the commandment.' What was then an object of fear, to prevent man from sinning, is now something to be chosen, to avoid sinning." Augustine, *City of God*, 13:4.

48. Multiple entendres intended. Joseph Ratzinger concurs, "The Christian is the one who knows that he can unite the constantly experienced dispossession of self with the fundamental attitude of a being created for love, a being that knows itself to be safe precisely when it trusts in the unexacted gift of love. Man's enemy, death, that would waylay him to steal his life, is conquered at the point where one meets the thievery of death with the attitude of trusting love, and so transforms the theft into increase of life. The sting of death is extinguished in Christ in whom the victory was gained through the plenary power of love unlimited. Death is vanquished where people die with Christ and into him." Ratzinger, *Eschatology*, 97.

49. Erickson, *Christian Theology*, 1179.

greater degrees of sanctification and faith are realized by some Christians at the time of death is hardly sufficient ground to justify the physical death of all believers." Erickson's argument fails on several fronts.

First, the argument does not comprehend human constitution on a biblical theological anthropology. The image of God in man, upon the fall, is not *reconstituted* into an ontological something else; it is merely grossly disfigured. God possesses life in himself (John 5:26). The *constitution* of God's image bearer, then—particularly his consummate image bearer—the *man* Christ Jesus—must never be said inherently to possess something that is the antithesis of the very nature of that which it was constituted to reflect (as the resurrection of all redeemed image bearers in John 5:29a will evince). The unnaturalness of death—which Erickson himself affirms—cannot, therefore, be considered a "condition of humanity as now constituted." Death remains an unnatural curse and enemy of life, yet an unapologetic, righteous ordinance and instrument of a sovereign God against his self-interested—rather than God's-supremacy-honoring—image bearer.

Second, the equation of birth and death as possessing mutual anthropological value is not only repugnant, it is an affront to the God who is "not the God of the dead, but of the living" (Matt 22:32; Mark 12:27; Luke 20:38), and appeared for the express purpose to "destroy the works of him who had the power of death" (Heb 2:14 with 1 John 3:8) and "abolish death" and bring "life and immortality to light" (2 Tim 2:10) precisely by means of *birth* (John 3:3–8). Birth and death are nowhere in Scripture held in such parity as Erickson cavalierly depicts. Birth is always characterized as a good to be celebrated; death, on the other hand, is always a curse to be greeted with at least mourning and sorrow—even in the case of the Christian (1 Thess 4:13–18).

Third, one can hardly consider such a view of death "a better approach" than the God-exalting hypothesis of Berkhof that renders death not some accidental[50] byproduct of sin that must now be reckoned essentially no differently than understood by Pelagians, Socinians, Rationalists, and Liberals, but as a majestic sword of holy justice in the hand of the Almighty *good* God who chastens whom he loves and scourges every son he receives (Heb 12:6). As Wayne Grudem rightly contends, "Even the death of some Corinthian Christians who had been abusing the Lord's Supper (1 Cor 11:30) is viewed by Paul as a disciplining or chastening process, not as a result of condemnation: he says, 'When we are judged by the Lord, we are being disciplined so that we will not be condemned with the world' (v. 32 NIV)."[51] Indeed, the

---

50. The word is used here in the sense of accompaniment, not unintentionality.
51. Grudem, *Systematic Theology*, 810n1; cf. 810–27.

thanatology exposited by Erickson evinces something of the thesis of the present work: even our contemporary theology has been tainted by the idolization of life to the degree that we unconsciously attempt to redefine death in terms more palatable to our self-interested human sensibilities. Here is further evidence of how radically the curse of the enemy death has dimmed the vision of the living.

A perpetual reminder of the seriousness of sin.[52] An intrinsic link between sin and death exists throughout both testaments of Scripture.[53] Because the penalty of sin is death (Gen 2:17; Rom 6:23), and because "according to the Law, almost all things are cleansed with blood" (Heb 9:22a)—"for the life of the flesh is in the blood, and I have given it to you on the altar to make atonement for your souls; for it is the blood by reason of the life that makes atonement" (Lev 17:11)—then "without the shedding of blood (i.e., death) there is no forgiveness" of sins (Heb 9:22b). Thus death, as a "permanent statute throughout . . . generations" (Lev 16:29–34; Heb 7:27; cf. Exod 12), is a God-designed constant reminder of the seriousness of sin (Heb 10:3).

The covenant people of God—both old and new covenants—must be reminded perpetually of the seriousness of sin. Death effectively accomplishes that goal generation after generation, as a "permanent statute." For New Testament covenant people of God, the Lord's Supper is the Law's parallel reminder of the seriousness of sin, "for as often as [we] eat this bread and drink the cup, [we] proclaim *the Lord's death* until He comes" (Luke 22:19; 1 Cor 11:23–26; emphasis added).[54]

---

52. This utility of death (discussed in chap. 2) bears reiteration here as an additional fitting response to the question "Why do Christians die?"

53. See for example Gen 2:17; 3:17–19; Rom 1:32; 5:12–21; 8:3; 1 Cor 5:22; 2 Cor 5:21; Gal 3:13.

54. Not only is *our* death a perpetual reminder of the seriousness of sin, but even more importantly does the death of Jesus Christ punctuate this truth. Paradox of paradoxes: the greatest news published to humanity is depicted in the perpetual remembrance of this *crudelissimum taeterrimumque supplicium*, "most cruel and disgusting punishment," the crucifixion death of God incarnate! See Stott, *Cross of Christ*, 30; the phrase is taken from Cicero "Against Verres," 2:5.64.

In light of the seriousness and just consequence of sin, this remembrance of God's grace to humanity that grants a stay of our own eternal execution should evoke awe striking gratitude and worship as often as we Christians "proclaim the Lord's death." We would do well to "pay much closer attention" (Heb 2:1) in our commemoration via the Lord's Supper of our Lord's vicarious death so that the sacrament may never become "common" to us with the result that the Lord regards our observance not as worship but as vanity. Israel had grown apathetic in regard to their remembrance of the seriousness of sin and of the amazing covering grace of God, for which reason God regarded their sacrifices as "worthless" (Isa 1:10–15) and without favor (Mal 2:13). In this light of the seriousness of sin and death may the Lord's Supper be observed biblically.

Creator-creature distinction. Another reason that Christians die might well be God's underscoring of the distinction between Creator and creature. Adam and Eve sought to blur this distinction by partaking of the fruit of the tree of the knowledge of good and evil, which the serpent deceptively had indicated would render them like God (Gen 3:5)—i.e., beyond the creaturely limitation with which they were already well constituted by the perfect design of their Creator. This idolatrous coveting[55] to be something more than creature was immediately met with the hard boundary of truth to the contrary. Death, now as much as then, remains *the* indicator that the creature's life is bounded by his finite creation and also wholly dependent upon the only Being in the universe who *inherently* possesses life. This truth remains as veridical for the Christian as it is for the damned; redemption by Jesus Christ does not remove this Creator-creature distinction. When God rescinds the breath of life from the body of dust that he originally constituted as a living being in exchange for the substance of his very own Being to sustain eternally the beatified Christian, then this necessary transition of the Christian will be sated.

Further, rather than being a source of grief for the Christian, as the apostle Paul avers in Phil 1:21–23, death, quite to the contrary, precipitates a confident source of hope as it coveys us to Christ. Karl Barth elaborates.

> As the command *Memento mori!* or *Memento Domini!* is unambiguously and immutably issued to man, it is already there as the hope of mortal and perishing man, and just as clear and reliable as the Word of God, as the promise given to man in Jesus Christ: "I am the resurrection and the life" (Jn 1125). . . . That is why the command to consider that we must die means that we are forbidden to fear death. In place of this fear we do not put a substitute faith which postulates a false beyond or a false present, or which effaces the distinction between them. We put hope in God as He has revealed Himself in Jesus Christ to be the hope of man. From the standpoint of this hope, the fear of death is shown to be perverted. . . . The man who grasps his unique opportunity [i.e., embraces by faith in Jesus Christ his "singular, unique, unrepeatable and irreplaceable" stature as the image of God], who occupies his place, may be known by his constant readiness and joyfulness in face of the fact which unambiguously characterises his being in time as a limited being, namely, that he will one day die.[56]

---

55. See 1 Sam 15:23 and Eph 5:5 for the equation of insubordination and covetousness with idolatry.

56. Barth, *Doctrine of Creation*, 339, 593–94.

The death of the redeemed, then, is indeed "precious" (Ps 116:15) and to be received genuinely joyfully and faithfully by the saint as the actuation of God's promise that Jesus Christ is the resurrection and the life.

Depictions of Death in the New Testament

Human life and death are not ineluctable realities under the power of no one such that life and death continue as though they were necessary constituents of an unguided cycle of nature (2 Pet 3:4). In the New Testament, the living God further reveals himself as the God of the living (Matt 22:31–32), the One who manifestly Lords the blessing of life and the curse of death in accord with his good pleasure and purposes. Immanuel—God with us—has condescended to the depths of the earth not only to reiterate his mark of ownership on his creation, but also to put to rest any doubt that death is *his* instrument. Moreover, the New Testament fully discloses God's intent to abolish it. Each encounter with death recorded in the New Testament, therefore, ought to be viewed in light of these truths.

John the Baptist. John the Baptist is an icon of the Old Testament (Matt 11:11), being the prophet who would announce the end of his own era in which death reigned and the inauguration of the new era in which the Lord of life would make that lordship known. John inquires of Jesus, "Are you the Expected One, or shall we look for someone else?" (Matt 11:3). John's very question indicates that not only he, but also all those Old Testament offspring of Adam, "who through fear of death were subject to slavery all their lives" (Heb 2:15) had long expected One who would "render powerless him who had the power of death" (Heb 2:14). That is, John awaited, if unwittingly, an end to the long reigning enigma of death. Jesus' reply could not have heralded more truthfully that "today . . . Scripture has been fulfilled" (Luke 4:21) and the curse of death was being terminated. He recited a litany of *blessings*, including resurrection from the dead, commensurate with the flourishing of life that only the living God could provide and with which he had furnished his originally very good creation: "the blind receive sight and the lame walk, the lepers are cleansed and the deaf hear, the dead are raised up, and the poor have the gospel preached to them"; and as if to punctuate his self-identification as the curse-reversing living God, Jesus concludes this litany with the provision, "*blessed* is he who does not take offense at me [i.e., as did Adam and Eve in the Garden]" (Matt 11:4–6; emphasis added).

Despite Jesus' assurance to John that he was the Expected One, however, Jesus would still mourn the death of his forerunner, cousin, and good friend. John nevertheless exceeded this present evil age knowing that death no longer reigned over him because the long Expected One had come.

Lazarus. One of the most stunning accounts of Christ's lordship over death is found in John 11. Having lost to death their brother, Lazarus, whom Jesus also loved (v. 3), both Martha and Mary bemoan, "Lord if you had been here, my brother would not have died" (vv. 21, 32). The Lord of life and death responds, likely with the same power that thrust to the ground a contingent of soldiers and dignitaries (John 18:6), "I am the resurrection and the life; he who believes in me will live even if he dies, and everyone who lives and believes in me will never die. Do you believe this?" (John 11:25–26). Beholding the wreckage that death had dealt to his "body"—those he loved (cf. Eph 5:28–30)—Jesus was "deeply moved."[57] Commanding that the stone, which covered the opening of the tomb, be removed, Christ—desiring freedom from the oppression of death for all those who had gathered—prayed to his Father that he might, by what Christ was about to do, cause saving faith to be birthed in them, very much like the earth was about to "give birth" to Lazarus' departed spirit (cf. Isa 26:19). The brief prayer being concluded, in order that he might show himself the *God* of life and death, Jesus "cried out with a loud voice, 'Lazarus, come forth!'" On the same order that "it was impossible for [Jesus] to be held in [death's] power" (Acts 2:24)—because he is Lord over death—neither could death hold Lazarus, or anyone, for that matter, whom the Son of Man commands to be freed from death's power (John 5:21, 26–27). This is good news.

Ananias and Sapphira. The Son of Man, who possesses life to give to whom he wishes (John 5:21, 26–27), also executes his lordship over life and death through the ministry of his word of truth by the apostles endued with his authority. At the inception of the New Testament church, the integrity of the message that heralded the inauguration of the messianic age was vested

---

57. The verb used in John 11:33, 38 to describe Jesus' contempt of death is ἐςμβριμάō μαι (*embrimaomai*). That Christ was "deeply moved" does not portend sympathy here. According to John Stott, the term is used of the snorting of horses, and was transferred to the strong human emotions of displeasure and indignation. See Stott, *Cross of Christ*, 68 n. 4; see also Jeffery, *Pierced for Our Transgressions*, 121–22; and Carson, *How Long*, 266, chap. 7 n. 2.

Another New Testament account depicts Jesus' "deeply moved" compassion for his Father's image bearers under the assault of death—particularly on this occasion, a widow who had lost her only son and would likely, therefore, become destitute at the hand of the enemy death. Luke 7:11–17 tells this story of how the Lord of life and death bid the bereaved mother, "Do not weep," raised her son from the dead in the middle of the funeral procession, and "gave him back to his mother."

with life and death significance precisely because disclosure of the glory of the living God is of greater value than human life. Acts 5 describes God's sovereign revocation of the breath of life from a husband and wife—Ananias and Sapphira—for their self-aggrandizing rebellion of lying to Christ's appointed delegates and therefore to God the Holy Spirit (vv. 3-4). So that the holy glory of the living God might be disclosed and revered by "all who heard of these things" (v. 11) and were joining themselves to the Way, the gift of life was revoked from both Ananias and Sapphira, within the space of three hours of one another, for their Adamic treachery. Here, death is decreed by God and the judgment is announced by Christ's apostle as a depiction of death's clear indication of the seriousness of sin. The advent of the Lord of life, thus, is to negate neither the seriousness of sin nor the necessity of the shedding of blood for remission of it.

The apostle Paul. Although his death is not recorded in the New Testament, the apostle Paul's valuation of his own life is illustrative of what every Christian's should be; it should appear to the unregenerate as though the Christian hates his life (Matt 10:38-39; John 12:25). Paul's vita includes:

> imprisonments, beat[ings] times without number; often in danger of death; . . . five times from the Jews . . . thirty-nine lashes; three times . . . beaten with rods, once . . . stoned, three times . . . shipwrecked, a night and a day . . . spent in the deep; . . . on frequent journeys, in dangers from rivers, dangers from robbers, dangers from my countrymen, dangers from the Gentiles, dangers in the city, dangers in the wilderness, dangers on the sea, dangers among false brethren; . . . labor and hardship, through many sleepless nights, in hunger and thirst, often without food, in cold and exposure; . . . the daily pressure . . . of concern for all the churches; [and being] let down in a basket through a window in the wall [to escape government seizure and likely death].
> 2 Cor 11:23-33

Such a life lived sacrificially for the glory of the God who gave it, rather than for itself, evidences no doubt when its steward avows, "But I do not consider my life of any account as dear to myself, so that I may finish my course and the ministry which I received from the Lord Jesus, to testify solemnly of the gospel of the grace of God" and "I am ready not only to be bound, but even to die . . . for the name of the Lord Jesus" (Acts 20:24; 21:13). The charge of biolatry in heaven's court may lay nothing to the account of such an offspring of the second Adam, one worthy of imitation.

As these few representative depictions exhibit, the incarnation of the living God inaugurates the reversal of his curse upon his rebellious creation—a feat accomplishable only by the curse-instituting Judge himself. The rebellious creation's "warfare has ended . . . iniquity has been removed"; God's offspring have "received of the Lord's hand double for all her sins"; the New Testament now declares a new covenant of comfort and peace and the abolition of the curse.[58] The faithfulness of the living God to keep his curse reversing promise to Adam, Abraham, Noah, David, and his consummate Son (Ps 2:8) is in the New Testament *tetelestai*.

The Resurrection

On a biblical scheme of anthropology, bodily resurrection must occur or death—the sentry guarding the way to life—would have victory over the finally redemptive purpose of God, at least as pertaining to the body. Paul Helm reasons,

> But, Paul says, even if we were to suppose that believers survive the death of the body in some disembodied form, death would still have gained the victory, for death would still reign over their bodies, and this cannot be. Death occurs because of sin, and so if death is not reversed in resurrection it will follow that sin has triumphed. But sin cannot triumph if Christ has conquered sin, as indeed he has (1 Tim 1:10). So it follows then that there must be a resurrection of the body. And only when this takes place will it become apparent in the most public and visible way possible that Christ has redeemed his people by triumphing over death.[59]

In the mean time, creation has witnessed, concerning Christ's death knell to death, vindication by his Father, the Lord of life and death, who himself initiated the curse of death upon the first "living being." This vindication was publicly proclaimed by the Father's resurrecting his Son to life—as it was intended to be—after his death by crucifixion. The life that the resurrected Son of Man now possesses is not merely physical animation, but the quality of life inherently possessed by the God who created human life from the beginning to image his very own. Death can now no more assault the Son of Man than it can the God who himself intrinsically possesses life.

---

58. See Isa 40:1–2; 61; Luke 2:14; John 20:26; 1 Cor 15:23–26; Eph 2:17; Rev 21:3–4.

59. Helm, *Last Things*, 51–52. See also Helm, "Theory of Disembodied Survival," 19; cf. Penelhum, *Survival and Disembodied Existence*, 68–78; and Purtill, "Intelligibility of Disembodied Survival," 16.

Moreover, as the last Adam, Jesus Christ is the *prototokos* of the new humanity. All who are Christ's at his coming, then, will follow in his pattern of resurrection, receiving an imperishable *nephesh* fashioned like "the *soma* of his glory."[60] "We will be like him, because we will see him just as he is" (1 John 3:2). Death will be wholly incapacitated. Of this "participation in [God's] changeless immortality,"[61] Augustine illumines,

> And that Mediator in whom we can participate, and by participation reach our felicity, is the uncreated Word of God, by whom all things were created. And yet he is not the Mediator in that he is the Word; for the Word, being pre-eminently immortal and blessed, is far removed from wretched mortals. He is the Mediator in that he is man, by his very manhood making it plain that for the attainment of that good, which is not only blessed but beatific also, we have not to look for other mediators, through whom, as we may think, we can achieve the approach to happiness [i.e., the Supreme Good]. God himself, the blessed God who is the giver of blessedness, became partaker of our human nature and thus offered us a short cut to participation in his own divine nature.[62]

God's redeeming counter to the holy necessity of death is its destruction by means of resurrection. The testaments of God's self-disclosure narrate his unfathomably wise plan to redeem his creation—a tactical operation that causes "morning stars to sing together and all the sons of God to shout for joy" (Job 38:7), to trumpet, "glory to God in the highest" (Luke 2:13–14), and captivates these angelic hosts with astonishment as they look into these things (1 Pet 1:12)! The entrance of death in the Old Testament curses the "living being" into which God himself had breathed his breath of life and begins the decreation of God's very good creation. Death meant the defacing of God's emblem of ownership upon his creation and the thwarting of participation in the life of God by his *magnum opus*. For the entire—now groaning—creation, it meant cancelation of unhindered enjoyment of the *blessings* provided for the flourishing of God-intended life.

The entrance of Immanuel in the New Testament was as "foreknown before the foundation of the world" (1 Pet 1:20–21) as was the entrance of death in the Old

Testament. "God with us" now overturns ordained decreation and sings the "swan song" of death, as it were (Zeph 3:17). The Son of Man and

---

60. See 1 Cor 15:20–23, 35–57; Phil 3:21.

61. Augustine, *City of God*, 12:21.

62. Ibid., 9:15.

Lord of Life now heralds triumph over the enigma of death. He has inaugurated the kingdom of God where Life will reign again consummately and the last enemy will be abolished. The New Testament confirms that Christ has come to make his blessing flow far as the curse is found, bringing joy to the world.

CHAPTER 5

Death and the Church Triumphant

A View from the Early Church Militant

MANY OF THE "GREAT cloud of witnesses [now] surrounding us" once "resisted to the point of shedding [their own] blood in striving against sin" (Heb 12:1, 4). That is, they did not "consider [their lives] of any account as dear to [themselves]," but rather embraced confidently a disposition that declared with open face, "What are you doing, weeping and breaking my heart? For I am ready not only to be bound, but even to die at Jerusalem for the name of the Lord Jesus" (Acts 20:24; 21:13). This faithful witness to the immutability[1] of the living God was borne by old covenant and new covenant saints alike, all of whom acknowledged tacitly that their earthly life was merely a loan.

> All these died in faith, without receiving the promises, but having seen them and having welcomed them from a distance, and having confessed that they were strangers and exiles on the earth. For those who say such things make it clear that they are seeking a country of their own. And indeed if they had been thinking of that country from which they went out, they would have had opportunity to return. But as it is, they desire a better country, that is, a heavenly one. Therefore God is not ashamed to be called their God; for he has prepared a city for them. (Heb 11:13–16)

---

1. The term is used here in reference to the inability to silence God—i.e., not mutable—rather than the doctrine of his unchanging nature.

The legacy left by the Old Testament witnesses to the faithfulness of the living God encouraged the witnesses of first, second, and third century Rome. These witnesses, under the rule of emperors like Caligula, Claudius, Nero, Domitian, Trajan, and Decius, were not graced with the opportunity to clutch (temporal) life with the frankly idolatrous devotion with which so many twenty-first century moderns covet it.[2] They were compelled, rather, by their providentially ordained circumstance to heed God's self-disclosure and trust Christ as savior from the curse of death. In doing so, they were genuinely liberated to abandon this life, gratefully and often proactively

---

2. Process theist, David Ray Griffin, anthropocentrically understands God's immanence and relationality in such a way that rejects God's authority to do what he will with what belongs to him (yet see Job 9:12; Ps 24:1; Eccl 8:4; Isa 45:9; Rom 9:20–21). On this view of relationality, human life appears to be valued more than God's freedom to ordain suffering for his good and holy ends (see 1 Pet 3:17; 4:19; 5:10). Griffin appeals *ad hominem* to the notion of children burning at the tortuous hands of Hitler's Auschwitz to deny that God stands sovereignly behind suffering. Such a philosophical argument from a standpoint of human sensibilities rather than from divine revelation can neither define nor engender hope in the God who is there and is not silent. See Griffin, "Process Theology," 15–16.

Others so value human life that they challenge God's authority to foreordain the course of his creation as he sees fit, even if that means—as difficult as the concept is to bear—that a vast number of humans will spend eternity glorifying God as instruments of his wrath. Arguing against such foreordination, John Sanders quotes James Mill, who cannot imagine such a God, despite passages like Matt 7:13–14 and Rom 9:22–23. Mill inveighs snidely, "Think of a being who would make a hell, who would create the race with the infallible foreknowledge that the majority of them were to be consigned to horrible and everlasting torment," cited in Sanders, *God Who Risks*, 214. Cf. also, however, Luke 16:26–31; Jude 1:4.

See also Hughes, "Lament, Death, Providence." Hughes epitomizes the view of death as an injustice and divine providence in death as fictional. Mischaracterizing a reformed understanding of providence in death, Hughes writes, "In view of the ancient tradition of lament, a passive submission to the necessity of death is not the only appropriate response. Defying death is consistent with biblical faith.... Pastors who follow the doctrine of providence are inclined to speak with the metaphors of fate and necessity. 'It's God's will,' or 'It's for the best' are pastoral phrases frequently heard by the dying and bereaved. The effect of such phrases is to minimize death as an assault phenomenon and, indirectly, to discourage the need to grieve. Making dying a natural necessity takes the urgency out of mourning. In the spirit of lament, *every* death deserves an intense display of grief, both in personal and ritual form, regardless of the cause of death or age of the deceased." Contrary to "a passive submission," a properly biblical perspective of death regards it as an enemy and a curse, but also as the *necessary* exhibition of the righteous integrity of the God who warned of death as the just penalty against faithless treason. A proper balance is maintained, then, of both mourning the application of the curse in the loss of an irreplaceable image bearer of God and lauding the justice of God in his holy execution of the curse.

surrendering it in clarion witness to the One who gave it in the first place for precisely that purpose.³

> And so Paul, in the name of all Christians, taunts and challenges death and the grave. He mocks them, indicating that through Christ their force has been spent. The remarkable thing about Paul here is that, through faith in what Christ has done, he adopts an attitude which outflanks death. He is not saying that Christians will not die, nor that death is not a reality from which we all shrink. What he is saying is that though, in death, men and women seem to be dealt a final, dreadful blow, this is not so. For the man or woman in Christ there is the prospect of glorious, incorruptible life beyond the grave.⁴

The Christian μάρτυς, *martus*⁵—faithful witness—who is confident that his *life* is immutable,⁶ shares identity with the *peregrinus* depicted in Augustine's *City of God*.⁷ This reborn offspring of Adam holds no idolatrous clutch on the present life. He confesses that he is a stranger and exile on the earth, that his earthly life is on loan from the living God, the Lord of life and death, who has hidden the pilgrim's life with Christ's own indestructible life. He believes the Savior's promise that he, too, will live, even if he dies; so, no fear of death can hinder him because he knows that death possesses no sting whatsoever. He makes clear that he does not value this present life above either the life to come or the ordinance of God, which

---

3. See Acts 20:24; 21:13; Rom 11:35-36; Phil 2:25-30; 2 Tim 4:6-7.

4. Helm, *Last Things*, 131; see also Sproul, *Surprised by Suffering*, 137-40.

5. The term was used of one who testifies in legal matters as a witness. It later became identified with one who witnesses at cost of life; i.e., *martyr*. Bauer, BAGD, 619-20.

6. Again, the term is used here in reference to the inability to silence the life of the one who is hidden with Christ in God (Col 3:3)—i.e., not mutable—rather than the doctrine of God's unchanging nature.

7. Cf. Phil 1:23; Heb 11:13-16. The disposition of the *peregrinus*—(alien) sojourner—is characterized by a yearning for departure (both physically by death and figuratively through ascetic practices) from this present world of sin, temptations, corruption, and depravity, so that one might better glorify God unhindered. The *peregrinus*, or sojourning citizen of the City of God, possesses a strong sense of longing for his heavenly home. He longs for that consummate blissful state of being that will transcend the knowledge of God he now possesses through a host of duly ordained yet nonetheless mediatory instruments, including his own mind. He longs to experience the full felicity of his citizenship, receiving "the impossibility of sinning as a gift from God" by becoming a "partaker of God's nature" to which belongs the inability to sin. This glorious partaking of God, for Augustine, consummates the sojourner's Beatific Vision of the God (see chap. 7) in whose presence he earnestly longs to be. See Augustine, *City of God*, xlix, 1089.

may include his suffering death for the sake of the Name. He has no such longing to "return" to "that country from which [he] went out"; as it is, he desires a better repose, that is, a heavenly one. He thus lives as an alien in the land of temporal promise, as in a foreign land. He is "looking for the city which has foundations, whose architect and builder is God."[8] He is a *peregrinus*, a *martyr*.

No Fear in Death

For the Christian witness, knowledge of and meditating on Christ's wholly vicarious and perfectly sufficient atonement for sin can free the believer from any unwarranted fear of death because he recognizes that the Old Testament's enigma has been solved and he is no longer enslaved to death's penalty (Heb 2:15). That liberty to possess confidence in the day of judgment results from the perfect love that dispels fear, the fear that, according to the apostle John, has to do with punishment, which the believer is assured he will now never have to experience.[9] The faithful witness need not fear death because there is therefore now no condemnation for the one who has faith in the Christ who appeared to destroy the works of him who had power of death.[10]

In Christ, fear of solitude is also abolished. The triune God who created human life in his own image purposed that his image bearer would participate in communion not only with other persons who share the same essence, but also chiefly with his Creator.[11] The curse of death for the one, who in this present life is isolated from gracious fellowship with the living God by virtue of his solidarity with Adam (both ontological and volitional), entails not only the termination of his life under the sun, but also an absence from participation in any of the graces provided by God for the flourishing of life, including the goodness of not being alone.[12]

---

8. 1 Pet 1:23; 4:19; Acts 20:24; 21:13; Gal 2:20; Col 3:2–3; Phil 3:20–21; 1 John 4:18; 1 Cor 15:50–58; 3 John 1:7; Heb 7:16, 24–25; 11:9–10, 13–16; 12:1–4.

9. 1 John 4:17–18.

10. 1 John 3:8; Rom 8:1–2; Heb 2:14.

11. Gen 2:18; 3:8; Exod 33:14–15; Deut 7:21; 12:5–7, 11–12; Ps 41:12; Matt 1:23; 11:28; John 6:37, 44–45, 65–68; 1 John 1:3–4; Rev 3:20–21.

12. This evacuation of the *blessing* of life yields absence from the privileges of vocation and procreation, from God's good creation in nature, from communion with either present or future humanity, from the grace of anything that could be considered pleasure, from every facet of the *blessing* of life. In recognition of this abject absence in (temporal) death, Qohelet would write in Eccl 9:5, "For the living know they will die; but the dead do not know anything, nor have they any longer a reward, for their memory is forgotten."

The individual's integral relationship with his community as it pertains to his death possesses a divinely ordered goodness. Helmut Thielicke ponders, "Evidently I am something more and something other than just a specimen that can perish while the species itself survives."[13] The one who dies in communion with Christ's indestructible life, then, possesses more ontological and relational significance than being merely a generic *one* of many. Consequently, as a member of the community—particularly, the church—the believer's death is of greater significance by virtue of his relationship to the whole body of faithful image bearers of the God who sustains the blessing of life. The believer's death, in some sense, participates in a "filling up what is lacking in Christ's afflictions" (Col 1:24; cf. 1 Pet 4).

Contrasting this communal understanding of the significance of the Christian witness' death with Bernhard Groethuysen's study of French secularism and its more vacuous concept of death, Thielicke further elaborates that, on this individualistic view, "death receives its significance from 'the value that is ascribed to life.' On such grounds one could say that anxiety about death is actually rooted in a man's consciousness of value, in that his life as person (the I) ceases to exist; the unique fades away."[14] Such a valuing of human life is fathoms beneath that which divine revelation ascribes to it, for it limits the value of life merely to its unique biological and social contribution. On a Christian model, however, the value of the life of the dying is not so rooted in the secular reputation of the individual. Rather, it is doubly priceless. First, the value of the individual is incalculable by virtue of his being a creature made in the image of the infinite God.[15] Second, the life of the Christian is of priceless value because he is a member of the body that God purchased with his own invaluable blood (Acts 20:28). The faithful witness who dies surrounded by and aware of his communion with the cloud of witnesses of this priceless fellowship may die well and without fear of solitude. No doubt, such an awareness secured the early Church Militant's witnesses to bear their witness faithfully unto death.

Martyrdom

Before one can rightly grasp the significance of martyrdom, one must consider the distinction of a legitimate yielding of one's life as a witness to Truth in contrast with what could be considered an illegitimate surrender of life.

---

13. Thielicke, *Death and Life*, 14.
14. Ibid., 65.
15. See Gen 1:27; 9:6; Jas 3:9–10.

Pseudomartyrdom

No one can even grasp the concept of martyrdom who cannot consider his life of less value than something else. That being said, the altruistic sacrificing one's life is not always commendable, however. The *so-called* martyr that revels in dying for his cause is no less an idolater than the one who fears death. One who fears death has not been perfected in love (1 John 4:17–18); he has neither arrived at a proper recognition that life is a grant from the only Being in the universe who possesses life intrinsically, nor has he come to rest his confidence fully in the discriminating infinite wisdom of a good and faithful Creator to do with that one's life what He deems right.[16] A terrorist zealot, for example, can never rightly be considered a martyr in any honorable sense, for he takes his own life rather than laying it in the hands of self-willed murderers like himself. The one who thus entertains anything resembling a perverse *will* to die is greatly "mistaken, not understanding the Scriptures nor the power of God" (Matt 22:29). Such a one disdains the image of God in creation and welcomes a curse upon that over which he possesses no authority.[17] This one elevates his "cause" above the ordinance

---

16. Gen 18:25; 1 Pet 4:19; cf. Ps 119:68a. Karl Rahner charges, "Whoever fears death as an animal, with only dumb life-instinct and tries to hide from it, or whoever connects the immediate meaning of death only with the biological anguish of the suffering and has not the heart to practise the abandonment of the last surrender, is in fact not the man he ought to be. His attitude suppresses that which primarily makes him different from animals, that is, the knowledge of the transcendent; a knowledge, that is genuine, not as an abstraction but also as something actually realized in this mortal creature, whom we call man, in the form of a free consciousness of his dedication to death." Rahner, *Theology of Death*, 94–95.

17. For this reason is the one who commits suicide automatically disqualified from the category of martyr. On the disqualification of suicide, Rahner, too, asserts that, "If someone through his free act can avoid death, then what emerges as really achieved is what must be present in each Christian death, veiled and difficult to judge though it may be: the free acceptance of death. Thus is revealed the presence of that love of death which a Christian should have, and which cannot be realized by suicide." Rahner, *Theology of Death*, 105.

One must be careful, however, not to ascribe necessarily to martyrdom the salvific quality that Rahner does (and perhaps others in church history; cf. Tertullian, *On Baptism*, 16; Cyprian, *Letters*, 73:22; Cyril, *Catecheses*, 3:10; Gregory, *Orations*, 39:17; Augustine, *City of God*, 13:7; in Willis, *Teachings of the Church Fathers*, 434–36). Rahner enigmatically writes concerning the "death of the fanatic, of the hero, of the sectarian and also of those many others who may die courageously and freely," that "we must acknowledge that in individual cases the value of such deaths, revealed only before God, may reach even into eternal life" (107). From a Catholic perspective Rahner holds "the crucified character of the Church [that] has to be continuously and repeatedly revealed in her historical life" as the ground for understanding "why tradition, from the earliest times has attributed to martyrdom the same power of justification as Baptism" (110). He further argues that, "One could almost say that martyrdom is the only

of God who alone retains authority to declare his blessing—life forever (Ps 133:3)—or his curse, "you shall surely die" (Gen 2:17).

The martyr lives in a different sphere than does the biolater. The faithful witness of the Lord of life certainly does not commend death, because he recognizes that it represents God's curse on his own very good creation; he knows that it is a decreative enemy of all that is created good. Neither does he fear death, however, because he recognizes that his earthly life is but a loan and that his *life* is hidden in God with Christ's indestructible life; therefore, it cannot possibly be terminated. The true martyr knows that whoever or whatever might assail him to compel him—upon penalty of death—to bear false witness against the Truth can do nothing to threaten his most precious possession—Christ, who *is* his *life*. Joseph Ratzinger affirms as much, categorizing Daniel 12:2, Isaiah 53, Psalm 73, as well as the apocryphal books of Wisdom and Second Maccabees as "martyr literature."

> Confronted with persecution, the believer faces the question as to which he prefers, the righteousness of Yahweh or his own life, his *bios*. Placed before this option between righteousness and life, no presumed connection between action and destiny can avail. It is faith itself, a righteousness mirroring that of God, which brings about the cruelly premature loss of life. The problematic of the seventy-third psalm takes on its sharpest intensity. In this situation, the believer comes to recognize that Yahweh's righteousness is greater than his own biologically conditioned presence to life. He who dies into the righteousness

---

'suprasacrament' which does not admit of an obstacle in the receiver, and which the valid sacrament always and infallibly brings forth its fruit of eternal life.

If it is asked where is the point in human life where the sign will be absolutely true and the truth absolutely signified, where is the point at which both become one, action and suffering, the commonplace and the incomprehensible, death and life, freedom and violence, the most human and the most divine, the dark sinfulness of this world and the grace of God embracing it in mercy, cult and reality—then there is but one answer: in martyrdom.

In martyrdom we have an indissoluble unity of the testimony and the thing witnessed, which is guaranteed by God's most gracious dispensation. . . . The testimony makes present what is testified and what is testified creates for itself its justification, which is indubitable" (111–12).

Despite Rahner's subsequent cursory acknowledgement that such a voluntary death could possibly be "just an empty show," he fails to acknowledge first that the grace of God through faith alone redeems, not any sacrament. (One certainly acknowledges, here, the vast separation of understanding between Catholic and Protestant soteriology.) Secondly, he fails to acknowledge that one who dies even professing faith in Christ may in fact be professing a false Christ (see Gal 1:6–9; Matt 24:23–26); that is, his profession may well be no more than an anthropocentric devotion to his cause no different from the terrorist zealot's.

of God does not die into nothingness, but enters upon authentic reality, life itself.[18]

Ratzinger continues, elaborating on the principle of submission to the greater value of truth than the self, which submission, itself, yields *life*, even in the death of the witness.

> Martyrdom with Christ, the repeated act of granting truth more importance than self, is nothing other than the movement of love itself. If death be essentially the closing-off of the possibility of communication, then the movement which leads to communion is at the same time the inner movement of life. The process of dispossession of self uncovers the abyss of Sheol, the depth of nothingness and abandonment to nothingness which is present in our self-glorying, our desire to survive at the cost of what is right. Consequently, this process which seems death-dealing is really life-giving in the fullest sense.[19]

In such a death is a clear distinction made between one who does not fear death precisely because he knows Truth and one who wills to die precisely because he knows not truth.[20] One is honoring life as the gift of God

---

18. Ratzinger, *Eschatology*, 90–91.

19. Ibid., 98.

20. Tertullian, "Crown of Martyrdom," 48–51. When queried concerning why Christians complain when persecuted, "if you wish to suffer," Tertullian wisely makes a clear distinction between a martyr and a pseudomartyr: "Certainly we wish to suffer, but in the way in which a soldier suffers war. Nobody indeed willingly suffers war, since both panic and danger there must inevitably be faced; but yet the man who just now was complaining about battle fights with all his strength and rejoices when he wins a victory in battle, because he gains both glory and spoil. Our battle is to be summoned before tribunals, where we fight for the truth at the risk of our lives. And our victory is to obtain that for which you strive, a victory which brings with it both the glory of pleasing God and the spoil of eternal life. But, you may say, we are convicted; yes, when we have won the day; we conquer when we are killed, and we escape when we are convicted. You may call us 'faggoted' and 'axle-men,' because bound to a stake half an axle's length we are burned amid heaps of faggots; but that is our garb of victory, our chariot of triumph, our garment decked with palm-leaves. Naturally therefore we do not please those whom we have conquered, and so we are regarded as desperate and reckless men.
Among you, however, such desperation and recklessness raises the standard of virtue in the cause of glory and renown. . . . In these [pagan or secular] cases glory was lawful, because it was human, and no imputation of reckless prejudice or desperate conviction was cast upon them when they despised death and every sort of cruelty. They were allowed for country, for empire, and for friendship to suffer what we are not allowed to suffer for God. For all these you cast statues and write inscriptions on their portraits, and engrave them epitaphs to last for ever. Certainly, as far as records can do it, you yourselves confer a kind of resurrection on the dead. But the man who hopes for a real resurrection from God, if he should suffer for God, you deem to be mad. . . .

in proper relation to the infinitely higher ethic of the glory of God; while the other evidences a callous disregard for the *blessing* of life—both his own and that of others. The latter ignores the fact that "Yahweh's righteousness is greater than his own biologically conditioned presence to life," or the biologically conditioned presence to life of other false witnesses committed to his cause. The dying "witness" of such a one is to the "glory" of no god who could even be said to have regard for the sanctity of life.[21] No such deluded person can be said to bear witness to either the Truth or the living God, who alone possesses life intrinsically and distributes and sustains this gift of himself in accord with his good pleasure, and who also—by the way—providentially ordains even the genuinely tragic (yet still just) death of the false witness.

Martyrdom in the Early Church

Vision is often sharpened by aid of contrast. The twinkling light of a distant star, for example, is completely imperceptible until it appears on the boundless, dark indigo canvas of the evening sky. So too, our contemporary culture's countenance for resisting "to the point of shedding blood in striving against sin" is nearly imperceptible when contrasted with the radiance of the

---

[The words of many men like Cicero, Seneca, Diogenes, Pyrrho, and Callinicus] do not find as many disciples as the Christians make by their deeds. The very obstinacy, with which you reproach us, is our best teacher. Who is there that is not roused by the sight of it to ask what there is really within it? Who does not join us when once he has asked? Who does not long to suffer, when once he has joined, that he may buy back the whole grace of God and procure all indulgence from Him by the payment of his own blood? To this action all sins are forgiven. Hence it is that even in court we thank you for your verdict. There is an enmity between what is of God and what is of man; and when we are condemned by you we are acquitted by God."

21. Life is a priceless gift from God; it is to be neither valued nor devalued to a greater degree than its Creator sets for it. Herein lies a vast difference between the way religious terrorists (of *any* stripe) view death in contrast to those who are committed to the value of human life as articulated to mankind by the God who created it in his own image. For the divine prohibition of the devaluing of human life to the extent of destroying or defaming it, see Gen 9:5; Jas 3:9.

Further, noting the pseudotheological spirituality of *apatheia*, which seeks avoidance of suffering either on a Stoic or Hedonistic paradigm, Ratzinger debunks the presumed nobility of yielding oneself to death absent Truth. From the vantage point of grasping the fallacy of such spirituality "we can understand why the death of Christ is so different from the death of Socrates. Christ does not die in the noble detachment of the philosopher. He dies in tears. On his lips was the bitter taste of abandonment and isolation in all its horror. Here the hubris that would be the equal of God is contrasted with an acceptance of the cup of being human, down to its last dregs [Phil 2:6–11]." See Ratzinger, *Eschatology*, 102.

virtually foreign and manifestly otherworldly *memento mori* of our venerable and exemplary elder siblings of the early Church Militant. Meditation on the genuinely valiant deaths of some of our elder siblings will do well to tune our gazes to a biblical valuation of life under the sun and simultaneously replenish our own *contemptu mundi*.

John Foxe's *Book of Martyrs* is merely one record of the myriads of faithful witnesses of the living God who shed their own blood in striving against sin.[22] As Tertullian remarked, "As often as you mow us down, the more numerous do we become; the blood of the Christians is the seed."[23] In fact, the sheer volume of lives sacrificed during the church's infancy would prompt Jerome to write in the fourth century, "There is no day in the whole year unto which the number of five thousand martyrs cannot be ascribed, except only the first day of January."[24] Why were so many willing to surrender their lives for the sake of the Name? Because this "seed" was so richly fertilized by an unshakable confidence that "all these died in faith . . . having confessed that they were strangers and exiles on the earth" (Heb 11:13). Their common refrain was that they might imitate the sufferings of their God.[25] Herein resides the categorical distinction between the Christian martyr's anticipation of suffering death and the pseudomartyr's false hope in death (Prov 10:28). The Christian martyr is emulating the exemplary vicarious sacrifice of the Lord of life, who both yielded his own innocent life in obedience to his Father, acknowledging the rebellious creature's cursed due, and created human beings to image himself in a multiplicity of ways, which conceivably includes the yielding one's life in acknowledgment of God's authority and justice to put to death. The pseudomartyr, on the other hand, exults in the self-induced sacrifice of his own life (and often the lives of others)—over which he possesses no authority—acknowledging no value whatsoever of the theological significance or necessity of death. Vacuously, rather, his most weighty concern is—at best—his anthropocentric cause. In contrast, enter: the true martyr.

---

22. Foxe, *Book of Martyrs*. Apart from a brief but poignant introductory section on martyrs of the early church, this classic work primarily provides accounts of martyrs of the Protestant Reformation. One must be careful to note that Foxe's accounting of early martyrdom cannot be equated with the historical rectitude of Eusebius, for example.

23. The phrase is popularly extrapolated as "The blood of the martyrs is the seed of the church." See Tertullian, *Apology*, 227. See also Bettenson, *Early Christian Fathers*, 166; Willis, *Teachings of the Church Fathers*, 65; Migne, *PL*, 1:534.

24. Jerome, *Epistle to Cromatius and Heliodorus*, cited in Bettenson, *Early Christian Fathers*, 12.

25. So Perpetua, Ignatius, and Polycarp. See Tertullian, *Passion of Perpetua and Felicity* 6:1; Whitacre, "Ignatius of Antioch," 209; Tertullian, "Martyrdom of Polycarp," 215. Of the apostle Andrew's unshrinking martyrdom, see Foxe, *Book of Martyrs*, 9.

Ignatius. Ignatius[26] was appointed Bishop of Antioch (in Syria) next in succession after the apostle Peter. He was martyred in a third wave of Christian persecution under the reign of Emperor Trajan (AD 98–117). In his *Letter to the Romans*, written while on his way there to be executed for his faith in Jesus Christ, Ignatius presents his most developed discussion of martyrdom. He encourages the Roman Christians not to attempt to prevent his martyrdom because he has long both wanted to see the "god-worthy faces" of the Roman believers and sacrifice his life for Christ as an attestation of the genuineness of his own profession of faith. Importantly here, Ignatius insists that this martyrdom is his heavenly Father's specific "speaking in [him]," bidding him to "come to the Father" (7:2); that is, he is not insinuating that martyrdom ought to be paradigmatic for all believers. He asks the Roman believers to pray for him that he might stand firm in his confession. He invites "fire and cross and encounters with wild beasts, mutilations, tearings apart, scatterings of bones, manglings of limbs, grindings of my whole body, evil tortures of the devil . . . only that [he] may attain Jesus Christ."[27] He annunciates a desire for Jesus Christ that outweighs desire for any earthly thing. His own words express his valuation of the glory of Christ as incomparable with that of his own life.

> For I do not want you to please people, but to please God, as indeed you are pleasing [him]. For I will never [again] have such an opportunity to attain God; nor can you, if you keep silent, be recorded with a better deed. For if you are silent and leave me alone, I [will be] a word of God. But if you desire my flesh, I will again be a [mere] voice. But grant me nothing more than to be poured out as an offering to God while there is still an altar ready, so that, becoming a chorus in love, you may sing to the Father in Jesus Christ, because God has considered the bishop of Syria worthy to be found at the setting, having summoned him from the rising.[28] It is good to "set" from the world to God, that I may "rise" to him.[29]
>
> Only pray for power for me, both inward and outward, that I may not only speak, but also may will, so that I not only be

---

26. Foxe, *Book of Martyrs*, 18–19.

27. Ignatius, *Romans*, 209.

28. Whitacre, *Reader*, 208 n. 3. Whitacre includes a helpful translation note here. "The double meaning of the words used (δύσις, setting/West and ἀνατολή, rising/East) enable Ignatius' play on words in speaking of his journey from Syria in the East to Rome in the West. He also uses the double meaning of δύσις in the next sentence to allude to the completion of his life."

29. Whitacre, *Reader*, 207–08.

called a Christian, but also be found [such]. For if I be found [to be a Christian], I am able also to be called [one], and then [I am able] to be faithful, when I am not visible to the world. Nothing that is visible is good. For our God Jesus Christ, being in the Father, is visible now more than ever. The Work [i.e., Christianity] is not [a matter] of persuasion, but Christianity is [a matter] of greatness when it is hated by the world.[30]

I am writing to all the churches and am commanding them all, because I am dying willingly for God, if indeed you do not hinder [me]. I implore you that you not be an unreasonable kindness[31] to me. Permit me to be possessed by wild beasts, through whom I can attain God. I am God's wheat, and I am ground by the beasts' teeth that I may be found Christ's pure bread. Rather [than hinder me], entice the wild beasts that they may become a tomb for me and leave absolutely nothing of my body, so that when I fall asleep I do not become a burden to anyone. Then I truly will be a disciple of Jesus Christ, when the world will not even see my body. Petition the Lord for me, that through these instruments I be found a sacrifice to God.[32]

May I have the benefit of the wild beasts that have been prepared for me, which [beasts] I also pray be found ready for me, which [beasts], indeed, I will entice to devour me promptly, not as, indeed, with some whom they [the beasts] do not touch, being fearful. And if, in fact, they do not want [to do so] willingly, I will use force.[33]

The ends of the earth profit me in no way, the kingdoms of this age [profit me] in no way. It is better for me to die because of Jesus Christ than to reign over the ends of the earth. I am seeking that one, the one who died on our behalf; I want that one, the one who rose on account of us. The [birth pangs are] upon me. Agree with me, brothers. Do not hinder me from living. Do not want me to die. Do not give to the world the one who wants to be God's, nor entice [him] with material stuff. Permit me to receive pure light; arriving there I will be a human being. Allow me to be an imitator of the sufferings of my God. If anyone has

---

30. Ibid., 208.

31. See also Bettenson, "Ignatius: To the Romans," 45 n. 1, where Bettenson translates the phrase "inopportune kindness" and notes that "a Greek proverb says, 'Inopportune kindness is as bad as enmity.'"

32. Whitacre, *Reader*, 207–08.

33. Ibid., 209.

> him [God] in himself, let that person understand what I want and sympathize with me, knowing the things that are impelling me. . . . Do not talk about Jesus Christ and at the same time desire the world.[34]
>
> I no longer want to live in conformity with humans. And this will take place if you want [it]. Want [it], that you yourselves also may be wanted. . . . Pray for me that I may attain [God] by the Holy Spirit. I do not write to you according to the flesh, but according to the intention of God. If I suffer, you wanted it; if I am rejected, you hated [me].[35]

The passion of this *peregrinus* is clear. Ignatius faithfully witnesses to the truth that he has been transferred from this present domain of darkness into the kingdom of God's dear Son, that his earthly life is a loan, and that his *life* is hid with Christ in God. This martyr's otherworldly life—and death—attests resoundingly that Jesus Christ is Lord to the glory of God the Father.

Polycarp. Polycarp, appointed bishop of the church in Smyrna by apostles in Asia,[36] was martyred ca. AD 155–180[37] in a fourth wave of persecution under Marcus Aurelius. The genteel demeanor of the saintly eighty-six-year-old makes his martyrdom all the more legendary.[38] As he had been persuaded by the church to seek seclusion at a farm not far from the city in order to escape capture and execution, the Roman soldiers who sought

---

34. Ibid.
35. Ibid.
36. Irenaeus, *Against Heresies*, 3:3.4, cited in Whitacre, *Reader*, 55. Irenaeus accounts that Polycarp "was not only instructed by apostles, and conversed with many who had seen Christ, but was also, by apostles in Asia, appointed bishop of the Church in Smyrna, who I also saw in my early youth, for he tarried [on earth] a very long time, and, when a very old man, gloriously and most nobly suffering martyrdom, departed this life, having always taught the things which he had learned from the apostles, and which the Church has handed down, and which alone are true."
37. Whitacre, *Reader*, 55. Whitacre advises, "The text says the martyrdom took place on February 23 at 2 p.m., but the year is not given (*Mart. Pol.* 21). The traditional date for Polycarp's death is February 23, 155, though some scholars suggest February 22, 156, as the actual date. Eusebius, however, places his death a decade later, in 166 or 167, during the widespread persecution of Christians under Marcus Aurelius, who ruled from 161 to 180 (Eusebius, *Hist. eccl.* 4:14:10–15:1). The account was written by an eyewitness and therefore was probably written not long after Polycarp's death, either 155-160 or 170-180."
38. In fact, precisely because of the account's often fantastic imagery, some contend that *The Martyrdom of Polycarp* may be somewhat embellished by Christian lore. See, for example, Musurillo, *Acts of the Christian Martyrs*, liv–lv.

him found two boys of Polycarp's household. Having whipped them, one of them surrendered Polycarp's location.[39] When confronted, Polycarp did not resist; rather, he bid that a meal be prepared for the soldiers while he would resign to pray for them. His hour of prayer being concluded, he was taken to the city where, after interrogation, he was brought to the public stadium where he would be executed. Upon the proconsul's adjuring Polycarp a final time to swear by Caesar and renounce Christ, Polycarp replied, "For eighty-six years I have been his servant, and he did me no wrong. And how am I able to blaspheme my king who saved me?"[40]

Following more threats of torture, an execution by fire was determined. When the executioners intended to nail Polycarp to the stake, he persuaded them that there was no need for that. "For he who grants to endure the fire will also grant to remain in the fire unmoved, without your security from the nails."[41] Looking up to heaven, Polycarp then prayed.

> And after he sent up the 'Amen' and completed his prayer, the men in charge of the fire kindled the fire. And a great flame blazed up, and we saw a wonder, [we] to whom it was given to see, we who also were kept that we might report to the rest the things that happened. For the fire, making the form of a vaulted room, just like a boat's sail filled by wind, surrounded with a wall around the body of the martyr. And he was in the middle, not like burning flesh, but like baking bread, or like gold and silver being burned in a furnace. For indeed we noticed such a strong aroma, like blowing incense or some other precious spice.[42]

When the proconsul observed that Polycarp was not consumed by the flames, he ordered him pierced with a sword. "And having done this, a dove and a large amount of blood came out, so that it put out the fire..."[43]

Spectacular as is the tale, the fact remains that this earliest extant account of a Christian martyr—excepting the Acts 7 account of the martyrdom of Stephen[44]—seeded the church and encouraged the faith of scores

39. Foxe, *Book of Martyrs*, 20–21. Lightfoot, "Martyrdom of Polycarp," 354.
40. Whitacre, "Martyrdom of Polycarp," 213.
41. Ibid., 13:3; 214.
42. Ibid., 215.

43. Ibid., 16:1; 215. Whitacre notes that "Eusebius does not include the reference to a dove in his account (*Hist. eccl.* 4:15:39), and most scholars believe it was added later, perhaps as an expression of, 'the connection in Greece and elsewhere between bird and soul' (Schoedel: 73)."

44. Whitacre, *Reader*, 55. Ignatius' letter to the Romans may not be considered a martyrdom account because it merely provides Ignatius' *perspective* on martyrdom, not the actual *account* of his martyrdom.

of other Christians who, too, would yield their lives in imitation of the sufferings of their God.[45]

Blandina. The same wave of Christian persecution that consummated Polycarp's witness also spread to consume its first saints in Lyons and Vienne, France in AD 177.[46] Among those martyred in this onslaught by the pagan Roman government and its intolerant mobs were Maturus, Sanctus,[47] Attalus, and lastly, Blandina, "through whom Christ showed that things which appear mean and unsightly and despicable in the eyes of men are accounted worthy of great glory in the sight of God, through love towards Him, a love that showed itself in power and did not boast itself in appearance."[48] The unassailable faith in Christ of this "combatant in the ranks of the martyrs" seemed to be granted a supernatural superintendence such that she was sustained to endure more tortures than did her peers.

> Blandina was filled with such power that those who by turns kept torturing her in every way from dawn till evening were worn out and exhausted, and themselves confessed defeat from lack of aught else to do to her; they marveled that the breath still remained in a body all mangled and covered with gaping wounds, and they testified that a single form of torture was sufficient to render life extinct, let alone such and so many. But the blessed woman, like a noble champion, in confession regained her strength; and for her, to say "I am a Christian, and with us no evil finds a place" was refreshment and rest and insensibility to her lot.[49]

Still, these inconceivable tortures did not suffice her possessed captors. Blandina and the others "were led to contend with wild beasts to the amphitheatre, and to the public spectacle of heathen inhumanity" where Blandina was suspended on a stake as food for the beasts.

---

45. Whitacre, *Reader*, 209, 215; Tertullian, *Perpetua*, 6:1.

46. Eusebius, *New Eusebius*, 31–41. Foxe, *Book of Martyrs*, 25–28.

47. Noble Sanctus, when threatened with more and more tortures, confessed in Latin no other words but "I am a Christian." When no other tortures seemed to move him from his confession, "they applied red-hot brazen plates to the most tender parts of his body. And though these were burning, Sanctus himself remained unbending and unyielding, and firm in his confession; for he was bedewed and strengthened by the heavenly *fountain of the water of life* which issues from the bowels of Christ." Eusebius, *New Eusebius*, 33–34. See also, Musurillo, *Acts*, xx–xxi.

48. Eusebius, *New Eusebius*, 33.

49. Ibid., 37.

> Even to look on her, as she hung cross-wise in earnest prayer, wrought great eagerness in those who were contending, for in their conflict they beheld with their outward eyes in the form of their sister Him who was crucified for them, that He might persuade those who believe in Him that all who suffer for the glory of Christ have unbroken fellowship with the living God.[50]

Again, the supernatural superintendence prevented the animals from even touching her in this contest. As a result, she was removed from the stake and returned to prison for later continued passion.

On the last day of the combats, Blandina was returned to the amphitheatre along with a fifteen year old Christian boy, Ponticus, who had been compelled to view the sufferings of the others as they were tortured day after day. Then Ponticus, being tortured for failure to swear by the Roman gods, "encouraged by his sister (so that the heathen themselves saw that it was she who was urging him on and strengthening him), having nobly endured every kind of torture *gave up his spirit*."[51]

> But the blessed Blandina last of all, having, like a high-born mother, exhorted her children and sent them forth victorious to the King, travelled herself along the same path of conflicts as they did, and hastened to them, rejoicing and exulting at her departure, like one *bidden to* a marriage *supper*, rather than cast to the wild beasts. And after the scourging, after the wild beasts, after the frying-pan, she was at last thrown into a basket and presented to a bull. For a time the animal tossed her, but she had now lost all perception of what was happening, thanks to the hope she cherished, her grasp of the objects of her faith, and her intercourse with Christ. Then she too was sacrificed, and even the heathen themselves acknowledge that never in their experience had a woman endured so many terrible sufferings.[52]

"And what more shall I say?" (Heb 11:32)

Perpetua. Martyred on March 7, 202 at Carthage, Tertullian would refer to Perpetua as "the most valiant martyr."[53] This martyrdom account is sig-

---

50. Ibid. Herein resides a key rationale for the circulation of the account of Blandina's martyrdom. In contrast to those who tended venerate the martyr herself—as was often the case concerning the martyrdom of Perpetua (see below)—the account of Blandina's martyrdom specifically directs the reader, rather, to the Christ for whose sake the martyrs were surrendering their lives in the first place.

51. Ibid., 39.

52. Ibid.

53. Tertullian, *De Anima*, 55; see Bettenson, *Fathers*, 161.

nificant because it is the only one substantially narrated from the diary of the martyr, herself, and because, like the account of Blandina, it, too, is the martyrdom of a woman rather than of a man.[54] Moreover, the account is the earliest Christian document known to have been written by a woman.[55] Significant portions of the narrative are dreams given to Perpetua and her predictive interpretations and enacted illustrations of them throughout her final days.

Other portions are the diary entries of Perpetua's catechist, Saturus. This twenty-two-year-old new mother, Vivia Perpetua, was a wellborn and nobly married educated sister of two brothers, one of whom, Dinocrates, had already predeceased her at the age of seven, the other of whom was a catechumen like herself. Perpetua was one of five catechumens[56] who were arrested and imprisoned for their confession of Christ.

When the day of their interrogation came, Hilarianus, the new procurator, playing to Perpetua's sympathies toward her unbelieving, grey haired father and her own newborn son, adjured her to offer sacrifices to the honor of the emperors, to which the young matron replied firmly, "I will not do so." Hilarianus then queried, "Are you a Christian?," to which Perpetua replied unashamedly, "I am a Christian." Upon her response Hilarianus commanded Perpetua's pleading father to be thrown to the ground and beaten with rods. Though seeing her elderly father cruelly punished deeply grieved her, she still recanted not.[57] The judgment against the catechumens was then rendered: condemnation to death by "the wild beasts," whereupon hearing, they "went down cheerfully to the dungeon" to await their execution.

In this same dungeon, Felicitas—one of the detained catechumens—would give premature birth to a healthy girl, which a certain sister subsequently raised as her own daughter. God's grant of an early delivery was a grace to Felicitas, for "she was in great grief lest on account of her pregnancy she should be delayed—because pregnant women are not allowed to be

---

54. Tertullian, *Passion of Perpetua and Felicity*; see also Musurillo, *Acts*; and Butler, *New Prophecy*, 3, 57, where Butler asserts, "Overall, arguments for Tertullian's editorship [of the *Passion*] outweigh but do not overwhelm arguments to the contrary."

55. Butler, *New Prophecy*, 1.

56. Saturus would join the five soon after their imprisonment. He is perhaps their catechist who chose to share their punishment. Only Secundulus is not named here in this chapter.

57. The motivation for Hilarianus' action is not articulated by the author. At least one or a combination of two options exists: first, that Perpetua's father was likely a Roman dignitary, which would render culturally deplorable his undignified public display of pleading with his daughter; second, that Hilarianus was attempting further to induce Perpetua's compliance by injuring her honored father.

publicly punished—and lest she should shed her sacred and guiltless blood among some who had been wicked subsequently."[58]

On the day of their "fight," the birthday of Geta Caesar,[59]

> The day of their victory shone forth, and they proceeded from the prison into the amphitheatre, as if to an assembly, joyous and of brilliant countenances; if perchance shrinking, it was with joy, and not with fear. Perpetua followed with placid look, and with step and gait as a matron of Christ, beloved of God; casting down the luster of her eyes from the gaze of all. Moreover, Felicitas, rejoicing that she had safely brought forth, so that she might fight with the wild beasts; from the blood and from the midwife to the gladiator, to wash after childbirth with a second baptism.[60]

When they arrived at the gate, they were constrained to don sporting garb honoring the pagan deities Saturn (for the men) and Ceres (for the women); but they all refused and were permitted to remain adorned as they were. They entered the stadium.

> Perpetua sang psalms, already treading under foot the head of the Egyptian [a metaphor from one of Perpetua's dreams]; Revocatus, and Saturninus, and Saturus uttered threatenings against the gazing people about this martyrdom. When they came within sight of Hilarianus, by gesture and nod, they began to say to Hilarianus, "You judge us," say they, "but God will judge you." At this the people, exasperated, demanded that they should be tormented with scourges as they passed along the rank of the venatores.[61] And they indeed rejoiced that they should have incurred any one of their Lord's passions.[62]

Saturninus and Revocatus first battled a leopard and a bear. Saturus "held nothing in greater abomination than a bear; but he imagined that he would be put an end to with one bite of a leopard."[63] In the course of fighting, Saturus would escape twice unhurt, even though one of his trials would

---

58. Tertullian, *Perpetua*, 5:2.

59. Ibid., 2:3, 5:3.

60. Ibid., 6:1.

61. *Venatores* was the contemporary term for the rank of stadium combatants who battled beasts. The *ancient* Roman term was *bestiarii* (singular: *bestiarius*). *Venatores* are sometimes erroneously called *gladiators*—the combatants who fought specifically other men.

62. Tertullian, *Perpetua*, 6:1.

63. Ibid., 6:2.

entail his being bound on the floor near a bear, which did not so much as come out of his den.

> Moreover, for the young women the devil prepared a very fierce cow, provided especially for that purpose contrary to custom, rivalling their sex also in that of the beasts. And so, stripped and clothed with nets, they were led forth. The populace shuddered as they saw one young woman of delicate frame, and another with breasts still dropping from her recent childbirth. So, being recalled, they are unbound. Perpetua is first led in. She was tossed, and fell on her loins; and when she saw her tunic torn from her side, she drew it over her as a veil for her middle, rather mindful of her modesty than her suffering. Then she was called for again, and bound up her dishevelled hair; for it was not becoming for a martyr to suffer with disheveled hair, lest she should appear to be mourning in her glory. So she rose up; and when she saw Felicitas crushed, she approached and gave her her hand, and lifted her up. And both of them stood together; and the brutality of the populace being appeased, they were recalled to the Sanavivarian gate. Then Perpetua was received by a certain one who was still a catechumen, Rusticus by name, who kept close to her; and she, as if aroused from sleep, so deeply had she been in the Spirit and in an ecstasy, began to look round her, and to say to the amazement of all, I cannot tell when we are to be led out to that cow. And when she had heard what had already happened, she did not believe it until she had perceived certain signs of injury in her body and in her dress, and had recognized the catechumen. Afterwards causing that catechumen and the brother to approach, she addressed them, saying, "Stand fast in the faith, and love one another, all of you, and be not offended at my sufferings."[64]

The battle again turned to Saturus, who exhorted Pudens—a soldier and assistant overseer of the prison who, beholding the power of God among these martyrs, had begun to favor them—to "believe with your whole heart!"

> And immediately at the conclusion of the exhibition he was thrown to the leopard; and with one bite of his he was bathed with such a quantity of blood, that the people shouted out to him as he was returning, the testimony of his second baptism, "Saved and washed, saved and washed." Manifestly he was assuredly saved who had been glorified in such a spectacle. Then

---

64. Ibid., 6:3.

to the soldier Pudens he said, "Farewell, and be mindful of my faith; and let not these things disturb, but confirm you." And at the same time he asked for a little ring from his finger, and returned it to him bathed in his wound, leaving to him an inherited token and the memory of his blood. And then lifeless he is cast down with the rest, to be slaughtered in the usual place.[65]

The spectacle would conclude before the watching populace—"that they might make their eyes partners in the murder"—as a sword would be plunged into the bodies of the survivors. Being summoned, the catechumens rose of their own accord and proceeded to their queues.

But they first kissed one another, that they might consummate their martyrdom with the kiss of peace. The rest indeed, immoveable and in silence, received the sword-thrust; much more Saturus, who also had first ascended the ladder, and first gave up his spirit, for he also was waiting for Perpetua. But Perpetua, that she might taste some pain, being pierced between the ribs, cried out loudly, and she herself placed the wavering right hand of the youthful gladiator to her throat. Possibly such a woman could not have been slain unless she herself had willed it, because she was feared by the impure spirit.[66]

So concludes the passion of "the most valiant martyr," Perpetua.[67] This first hand account would come to inspire so many and would acquire such veneration in the early church that Augustine would have to warn the faithful not to elevate the record to the level of canonical Scripture.[68]

We Are Not Our Own

Through the contrasting lens of these early accounts of faithful witnesses—our dear elder brothers and sisters—who resisted to the point of shedding blood in striving against sin, we may amend our own view of the value of

65. Ibid., 6:4.
66. Ibid.
67. The author closes his account with this benediction: "O most brave and blessed martyrs! O truly called and chosen unto the glory of our Lord Jesus Christ! Whom whoever magnifies, and honours, and adores, assuredly ought to read these examples for the edification of the Church, not less than the ancient ones, so that new virtues also may testify that one and the same Holy Spirit is always operating even until now, and God the Father Omnipotent, and His Son Jesus Christ our Lord, whose is the glory and infinite power for ever and ever. Amen."
68. Augustine, *De Anima et Eius Origine*, 1:12. See also Musurillo, *Acts*, xxv–xxvii, for commentary on the Christian lore of the account.

our lives in relation to the command of God who granted us life for the glory of *his* Name. We may weigh the legitimacy of our own confession of Christ against that of the *peregrinus* who lives as an alien in a foreign land; who does not fear death, but prefers, rather—if God so wills—to sacrifice his life for Christ as an attestation of the genuineness of his own profession of faith. His vision of life is so piercingly otherworldly that he appears to the citizens of the "city of man" to hate his life (John 12:25; Luke 17:32–33).

In view of our twenty-first century, Western, feebly comparable, "momentary, light affliction" (2 Cor 4:17), can we fathom a release of our idolatrous clutch on our precious lives in such a way that we can affirm without equivocation, "I do not consider my life of any account as dear to myself," and, rather, invite "fire and cross and encounters with wild beasts, mutilations, tearings apart, scatterings of bones, manglings of limbs, grindings of my whole body, evil tortures of the devil" only that *we* may attain Jesus Christ? Are we to be considered biolatrous pseudomartyrs; or are we *peregrinoi*, faithful witnesses to the truth that our lives are not our own?

CHAPTER 6

Excursus: The Frowning Providence of Infant Death

Hard Sayings about Death

IN LUKE 13 JESUS uses the unfortunate occasions of a political mass murder and a building collapse resulting in a death toll of eighteen to teach that the death of any image bearer of God inherently exhibits the patient grace of God toward surviving image bearers and communicates to them that they are commanded to value God and his holy ordinances above all else, including their own lives. In his admonition, Jesus surely neither dismissed the grief of the bereaved nor did he regard flippantly the reality that unique and irreplaceable individual image bearers of his Father had been robbed of the gift of life by the horror and absence of death. "Nevertheless, the firm foundation of God stands" (2 Tim 2:19a). That is, the holy integrity of the living God renders Gen 2:17 irrevocable; every offspring of Adam *will* die.[1]

In chapter 8 of the same Gospel, Jesus not only rebukes the tumult of a gale force storm that threatened the lives of his disciples, he also rebukes those same disciples for their fear of death, which they had allowed to displace their trust of the Christ who was present with them.[2] Here again the

---

1. In light of this hard yet inescapable truth, Lev 10:3 and Job 40:4 come to mind.

2. Compare the faith of the eighteenth-century German Moravians who, also on board a ship threatened with capsizing by a gale force storm, exhibited, rather, the peaceful and fearless disposition of the slumbering Jesus in Luke 8:23. These disciples of Christ sang hymns of praise to God in the face of their imminent deaths. On Sunday, January 25, 1736, John Wesley would record in his journal concerning the episode:

"At noon our third storm began. At four it was more violent than before. At seven I went to the Germans. I had long before observed the great seriousness of their

proper perspective of both the value of human life "on loan" from the God who possesses life intrinsically and the ethic of valuing that human life in relation to yielding it, rather, to the ordinance of God equips Jesus with an unassailable imperturbability[3]—an imperturbability that he rebukes his disciples for lacking.

Part of our own culture's multifaceted aversion to the judgment of death has to do not only with the disappearance of a unique and irreplaceable individual, but also with our inability to cope with the thought that someone respected, revered, honored, or loved by virtually everyone will be consigned ultimately to the due penalty that is the unending wrath of almighty God. One way we attempt to suppress this truth is by recasting God in our own image or any image other than the one of himself he has revealed to us. We make him more merciful and, frankly, less holy than we are. "God is love" is the mantra chanted by many who cannot bear the thought of the execution of any subsequent penal justice after this already often difficult life has finally ended.[4] Jesus Christ himself taught that countless "good" people will spend eternity bereft of any of God's grace.[5] As hard as this saying is to hear, because of their rejection of the disclosure of God in the person of Jesus Christ, some of those who have already been consigned to this eternal fate, according to their own attestations in contrast with bibli-

---

behaviour. Of their humility they had given a continual proof by performing those servile offices for the other passengers which none of the English would undertake; for which they desired and would receive no pay, saying, 'It was good for their proud hearts,' and 'their loving Saviour had done more for them.' And every day had given them occasion of showing a meekness, which no injury could move. If they were pushed, struck or thrown down, they rose again and went away; but no complaint was found in their mouth. There was now an opportunity of trying whether they were delivered from the spirit of fear, as well as from that of pride, anger and revenge.

In the midst of the Psalm wherewith their service began, the sea broke over, split the mainsail in pieces, covered the ship and poured in between the decks, as if the great deep had already swallowed us up. A terrible screaming began among the English. The Germans calmly sang on. I asked one of them afterward, "Were you not afraid?" He answered, 'I thank God, no.' I asked, 'But were not your women and children afraid?' He replied mildly, 'No; our women and children are not afraid to die.'" See Wesley, *Heart of John Wesley's Journal*, 28–29.

3. One must be careful, however, not to misconstrue imperturbability (e.g., the 1 Tim 6:13–16 "blessed" state of "God, who gives life to all things") with a notion of impassibility that connotes apathetic emotionlessness.

4. See for example, Pinnock, "Finality of Jesus Christ," 166; Pinnock, *Wideness*; Sanders, "Is Belief in Christ Necessary for Salvation?," 249–252; Sanders, *No Other Name*; Fackre, "Divine Perseverance"; Leckie, *World to Come*; Lindbeck, *Nature of Doctrine*; Clark-Soles, *Death and the Afterlife*, 102–04, 184–85; Bell, *Love Wins*. For a strong rejoinder to this novel doctrine, see Nash, "Is There Salvation after Death?"

5. Matt 7:13; 22–23; 25:41–46; Mark 9:42–48.

cal Scripture, are Socrates, Plato, and Aristotle, Ghandi, Golda Meir, and Albert Einstein, Joseph Smith, Malcolm X, and Steve Jobs, specifically to name a few; also included among these lost are sweet old grandmothers and "innocent" islanders. In considering the final state of these and other dear ones, one must not ask questions like, "Why do people who have never heard the gospel go to hell?" but, "Why do people go to hell?" The answer to that question, which humbles each of us literally to the dust, is: in Adam all die (Rom 5:12, 14, 18a; 1 Cor 15:22). The hard saying of divine revelation is that there are no exceptions.

Aaron Kept Silent

The preceding chapters of this work have attempted to articulate the importance of several foundational principles that are necessary for grounding the assertions of this very difficult chapter; principles like human life as nonessential being, yet its simultaneous immeasurable value; the reason for the origin and necessity of death; and the incontrovertible lordship of God in Jesus Christ over both life and death.[6] Grasping these principles—these divinely revelatory truths—before the face of the God, in whose image we have been created such that we possess life "on loan," equips us creatures to countenance rightly the very difficult reality of both the temporal and eternal deaths of precious creatures cut from the same cloth—as it were—from which we ourselves have been cut. It equips us to resist our fallen and self-aggrandizing tendency to overestimate the value of human life to the degree that we worship it—albeit unwittingly—and rather to laud the living God, the Lord of life and death, for his resistance to become like us and forsake his holy ordinance in exchange for pacified sensibilities.[7]

---

6. The phrase "Aaron kept silent" is taken from Lev 10:3 where Aaron's two unholy sons, Nadab and Abihu, have just been put to death by the Lord, who will be honored as holy by all who come near him. Moses—the man who was more humble than any man on the face of the earth (Num 12:3)—rather than focusing on the deaths of Aaron's children, immediately admonishes his mourning friend concerning God's holiness. "So Aaron, therefore, kept silent" in recognition of the primacy of holy Yahweh's ordinance over the preservation of the lives of his own sons.

7. Although conditions, gratefully, are not the same, we would do well to cultivate a sovereignty-honoring, self-deprecating pathos characteristic of our sixteenth-century forbears, when the likelihood of death was not an expectation reserved only for the elderly. Then, the discipline of philosophy offered wisdom to assuage an improper regard for life. Jean-Jacques Rousseau cautioned,

"Although we know approximately the limits of human life and our chance of attaining those limits, nothing is more uncertain than the length of the life of any of us. Very few reach old age. The chief risks occur at the beginning of life; the shorter our past life,

Karl Barth has given much thought to the ethic of valuing human life as penultimate. Accordingly, he poses a deeply probing query.

> Is it really true that the command of God in all cases and circumstances contains the imperative that man should will to live? Must not this imperative in some cases at least be formulated in what is from the literal standpoint a very paradoxical sense if it is really to be understood as the command of God? Understood in its most literal sense, it is hardly an unconditional and absolutely valid imperative which as such has necessarily to be included in every form of the divine command. Precisely as the command of God, does it not have a restricted validity, since the God who commands is not only the Lord of life but also the Lord of death? Is it really so unthinkable that, when his command summons man to freedom before Him and fellowship with his fellow-men, it might include a very different imperative that man should not will to live unconditionally, to spare his life, to preserve it from death, but that he should rather will to stake and surrender it, and perhaps be prepared to die? According to Mk. 8:35 he may save it in so doing, whereas he would lose it if he tried to save it. Is not the peculiarity of the freedom for existence to which man is summoned by God discernible in the fact it might also mean freedom from existence, a superior

---

the less we must hope to live. Of all the children who are born scarcely one half reach adolescence, and it is very likely your pupil will not live to be a man." See Rousseau, *Emile*, 44, cited in Hick, *Death and Eternal Life*, 83.

Similarly, Michel de Montaigne would intimate personally, "I myself have lost two or three children, not without grief, but without brooding over it; but they were still only infants." See Screech, *Michel de Montaigne*, 64, cited in Ariès, *Centuries of Childhood*, 39; and Hick, *Death and Eternal Life*, 83.

Cold as it sounds to the modern ear, Montaigne voiced a deeper grasp of the significance of life as a loan rather than as a personal possession. These philosophers' pathos clearly contrasts with our own medically advanced culture's often idolatrous perspective of the value of human life. Their probably representative commentary evidences that frequent confrontation with death enabled—even propelled—many of our predecessors to sustain a proper and often transformative contemplation of the value of life and of their own end. This view of life and death, more than our own contemporary mindset, postures against the sin of biolatry.

Of the sober pathos of that past era, Ariès opines, "It is recorded that the people of the Basque country retained for a very long time the custom of burying children that had died without baptism in the house, on the threshold, or in the garden. Here we may perhaps see a survival of ancient rites, of sacrificial offerings, or rather it may be that the child that had died too soon in life was buried almost anywhere, much as today we bury a domestic pet, a cat or a dog. He was such an unimportant little thing, so inadequately involved in life, that nobody had any fears that he might return after death to pester the living." Ariès concludes, "There is nothing about this callousness which should surprise us: it was only natural in the community conditions of the time." Ariès, *Centuries*, 39.

freedom as opposed to the necessity of having to live and to will to live, the superior freedom of man to be able also to surrender his life, and give it back to God, for the sake of his orientation on God and solidarity with his fellow-men? . . . [The ethic of respect for human life] is not an absolutely valid demand for the affirmation of life, for the "will to live," but one that exists for the time being, until abrogated, and within the framework of the presuppositions and intentions with which God causes it to be issued.[8]

Human life, then, cannot be, as Albert Schweitzer asserted, "the highest and properly the only lawgiver, and therefore the criterion of all virtue."[9] As creature, it can be only of penultimate value at best. Further, the creature is obliged to yield his loaned life—or the loaned lives of any of his "fellow-men," for that matter—to this command of God, whether or not one is assured that such yielding will result in a Mark 8:35 saving of that life. The good command of good God[10] in accord with his own holy integrity and glory is obliged to be lauded by the creature above the preservation of human life, even when that command is death for the creature.[11]

God-ordained Frowning Providence of Death

No direct indication of God's specific appointment of death appears in Luke 13; yet the parable that Christ teaches in reply to the crowd's query indicates that God is in sovereign control of "cutting down" any "tree" he sees fit, when he sees fit, whether or not it exhibits fruit-bearing capacity. Again, as hard as this saying is to hear, we must be reminded that while death may come as unexpected by the finite creature or occur under observably tragic circumstances, no death nor circumstance precipitating such death occurs apart from the sovereign appointment of the Lord of life and death.[12] Any

---

8. Barth, *Doctrine of Creation*, 334–35.
9. Schweitzer, *Kultur und Ethik*, 239.
10. The modified proper noun "God" here is intentionally non-articular in attempt to dissuade comparison with any alternative. Ps 119:68 declares of the incomparable Being that is God, "You are good and do good."
11. So commands Gen 3:19 (cf. Isa 13:3–19; Jer 13:8–14; Hos 13:16 with Amos 1:13). We must be very careful, here also, not to construe that this command entails any form whatsoever of either vigilantism, personal vendetta, or terrorism; for God's command of death is never executed apart from either his own immediate intervention or at the hand of the ordained municipal authority (Rom 13:1–7).
12. Sherlock agrees, "No man can go out of this world, no more than he can come

so-called "untimely death," then, from the perspective of the God who ordains the landing of a sparrow and numbers the hairs of heads (Luke 12:7), is a misnomer. Even deaths that appear accidental to the creature are not gratuitous[13] but purposed by God, at the very least as a summons to sobriety for the living.[14] Too often in the face of death, we self-adulating creatures are so captivated by the personal affront to our hallowed contentment by death that we disregard the irremovable exhibition of the holiness of God in *each* death. Ironically, many Christians regularly celebrate the death of the impeccably innocent Jesus Christ with little or no appetite for lauding the justice of God in the damnation of sinners.[15]

Many of the deaths recorded in Scripture appear to occur simply as a matter of the natural course of events. People are fatally bitten by snakes; a child dies from an apparent sun-stroke; houses and gaming arenas and towers collapse, killing the occupants; an old man falls out of a chair and breaks his neck; children are mauled by wild animals; a ruler is mortally struck by a stray projectile; people die from illness; infants die. Are these incidents indications that God does not providentially preside over these kinds of death? Or can these incidents be categorized in accord with God's meticulous providential control of all things? The biblical text itself, in fact, delineates God's meticulous providence—albeit frowning—over each of the aforementioned examples.[16]

---

into it, but by a special Providence; no man can destroy himself, but by God's leave; no disease can kill, but when God pleases; no mortal accident can befal [sic] us, but by God's appointment; who is therefore said to deliver the man into the hand of his neighbour, who is killed by an evil accident, Deut. xix. 4, 5"; see Sherlock, *Practical Discourse*, 180–81. Calvin also affirms, "we must know that God's providence, as it is taught in Scripture, is opposed to fortune and fortuitous happenings"; see Calvin, *Institutes*, 1:197–98.

13. In the conversation of the problem(s) of evil, the phrase "gratuitous evil" is sometimes used to describe evils in the created order that are considered excessive. However, one may argue legitimately that no such thing as "gratuitous evil" exists, at least not so far as any creature can judge. Certainly no finite creature—and that includes everything in existence except God—possesses the capacity to determine just how much wrath from an infinitely holy Sovereign can be equitable penalty against a creation in rebellious confederation with its premier. For a thoughtful treatment of the problem(s) of evil, see Feinberg, *Many Faces of Evil*.

14. See Lewis, *Problem of Pain*, 93; and Thielicke, *Living with Death*, 125.

15. Edwards, "Justice of God," 1:669–70. No finite creature should hypocritically rejoice in the eternal destruction of another image bearer of God, who deserves judgment no more nor less than himself. The holiness of Yahweh will be displayed and lauded for eternity, nevertheless, in his execution of wrath against all that is unholy.

16. See Num 11:33–34; 16:46–50; 21:6–9; 25:7–13; 1 Sam 2:27–36; 3:12–14; 4:18; 1 Kgs 22; 2 Kgs 2:23–24; 2 Kgs 4:8–37; Jdgs 16:28–30; Job 1:8, 12, 18–19; Ezek 9; Luke 13:1–9.

Rather than losing hope, therefore, presuming that death has run amok under the sovereign God's watch,[17] the creature may be assured all the more that the living God remains Lord of life and death, meticulously ordering both in accord with his good purposes. He is the God who has revealed himself perspicuously to his creatures as the God "who keeps lovingkindness for thousands [to those who love me and keep my commandments (Exod 20:6)], who forgives iniquity, transgression and sin; yet he will by no means leave the guilty unpunished, visiting the iniquity of fathers on the children and on the grandchildren to the third and fourth generations [of those who hate me (Exod 20:5)]" (Exod 34:7). Reinforcing that gracious self-disclosure, he warns sternly—yeah, even commands—against recasting him in any other image, namely one that acquits the guilty.[18]

Framing the Issue

The Greek word κανών is translated into English as "reed." Because this instrument was a straight reed used for measuring, the nomenclature came to be interpreted "rule" or "standard." The word is commonly used in reference to the Christian *canon* of Scripture—"the supreme standard by which all human conduct, creeds, and religious opinions should be tried."[19]

Before any discussion can be engaged regarding the extremely sensitive subject of the death and eternal condition of deceased infants, we must first establish that that which is measured must never impose its standard on the Measurer (Rom 9:14–24). "The everlasting God, the LORD, the Creator of the ends of the earth" (Isa 40:28) retains sole authority to determine what is right or just, and what is unjust.[20] The creature certainly may not exercise this privilege. *De facto*: Adam and Eve, in their *libertas*, representatively incurred for humanity its current radically corrupted and God-condemned state by means of their attempt to exercise this privilege, which was not only a capacity beyond their finite creaturely constitution, but was (particularly in Adam's case) in direct violation to the immediate revelation they had received from their Sovereign Creator.[21]

---

17. For arguments that suggest such is the case—albeit perhaps without the same directness of language—see Pinnock, *Openness of God*; Boyd, *God of the Possible*; Sanders, *God Who Risks*. For counterarguments, see Ware, *God's Lesser Glory*; Ware, *God's Greater Glory*; Ware, *Their God is Too Small*; Frame, *No Other God*; Piper, *Beyond the Bounds*.

18. Exod 20:4–7; 32:1–10; Deut 5:8–11.

19. SBC, *Baptist Faith and Message*, 7.

20. Cf. n. 81 above.

21. Cf. Gen 2:17; 3:6–7, 23–24.

Secondly, the issue of human sensibilities must be duly acknowledged. *To be sure*, no sentient, empathetic image bearer of God would take comfort in contemplating the death of an infant or a cognitively impaired person or their being consigned to the very real and eternal fires of hell.[22] Candidly, if we consider the genuineness of our profession—and our Lord's teaching—of the reality of the wrath of God, we must similarly query ourselves concerning our contemplation of the final state of *any* living being cut from the same sinful cloth from which we ourselves have been cut. As with every area of theological construct, however, we must endeavor with every ounce of sincerity we can muster to allow neither our purely creaturely pathos nor our sin-infected, self-honoring noetic structure to taint the *knowable* revelation disclosed to us from our Sovereign Creator.

Thirdly, the question must be asked (and answered), "Why even raise such a question?" Several answers may be tendered. (1) As noted in chapter 1, no biblical treatment of the topic of death should avoid this necessary conversation. (2) Real people are confronted daily with very real circumstances that make this question inescapable. (3) The question is answered dogmatically and variously both by respected authorities and those of somewhat less theological repute.[23] (4) Because God has "granted to us [who have a faith in Christ in accord with his apostles' teachings] everything pertaining to life and godliness, through knowledge of him" (2 Pet 1:3), we can be assured that there is an answer at least commensurate with the promised grace and peace inherent in God's so granting. The following, therefore, will attempt to provide a fair and biblical assessment of the matter.

Augustine on Original Sin and Its Implications for the Destiny of Deceased Infants

No doctrine develops outside of a context.[24] The matter of the eternal state of deceased infants is no different; the issue certainly has hosted its

---

22. In this sense does Ezek 18:23 and 33:11 address God's pathos toward the death of his image bearers.

23. See for example Calvin, *Institutes*, 2:1332, 1338–59; Hodge, *Systematic Theology*, 1:25–27; Stagg, *Calvin, Twisse and Edwards*; Warfield, *Studies in Theology*, 389–410 and 411–46; Grudem, *Systematic Theology*, 499–500; Erickson, *Christian Theology*, 654–55; 1101–02; MacArthur, *Safe*; Nash, *When a Baby Dies*; Webb, *Infant Salvation*; Mohler and Akin, *Salvation of the 'Little Ones'*; Piper, *Why Do You Believe*; Lightner, *Safe in the Arms of Jesus*; Harwood and Patterson, *Spiritual Condition of Infants*. For treatment from less theologically developed viewpoints, see Hayford, *I'll Hold You In Heaven*; McDavid, *Infant Salvation & The Age of Accountability*; Bell, *Love Wins*.

24. Augustine, citing 1 Cor 11:19, is not deterred by heresies; he argues that "the

share of debate throughout church history. The church's understanding of paedosoterism[25] has been influenced by the doctrine of original sin, more than any other doctrine; and the church's understanding of the doctrine of original sin has been influenced by Augustine, more than any other teacher. What prompted Augustine's passion for clear articulation of this doctrine was his conflict with Pelagius over the answer to the question, why does the church baptize infants? In fact, Augustine's development of his understanding of the doctrine of original sin would prove so irremovably intertwined with the question that his treatise *On Original Sin* opens not with a working definition of the depravity of man, but instead with the subject of infant baptism.[26] Because the doctrine of original sin as understood from Romans 5 is so closely intertwined with the notion of paedosoterism, because the corpus of Augustine's treatment of the issue is so substantive, and because his articulation of the matter has influenced the discussion more than any other,[27] Augustine's thoughts on the subject will serve as basis for further discussion.

Church may be benefited by that which the enemy devised for her destruction"; see his *On Original Sin*, 2:25. Additionally, of the development of the doctrine of original sin prior to Augustine, Stéphane Harent writes, "It is not true that the doctrine of original sin does not appear in the works of the pre-Augustinian Fathers. On the contrary, their testimony is found in special works on the subject. Nor can it be said, as Harnack maintains, that St. Augustine himself acknowledges the absence of this doctrine in the writings of the Fathers. St. Augustine invokes the testimony of eleven Fathers, Greek as well as Latin (*Contra Julian*, II, x, 33). Baseless also is the assertion that before St. Augustine this doctrine was unknown to the Jews and to the Christians; as we have already shown, it was taught by St. Paul. It is found in the fourth Book of Esdras. . . It is therefore impossible to make St. Augustine, who is of a much later date, the inventor of original sin." Harent, "Original Sin," 11:313.

25. This term is derived from combining the Greek terms *paidos* and *soterios* to connote "child salvation." This term will hereafter refer to the doctrine of the salvation of infants or otherwise cognitively incompetent persons dying in such a state.

26. The opening line of *On Original Sin* is, "Now pay careful attention. You must listen to these people with caution on the subject of the baptism of little ones"; see Augustine, *On Original Sin*, 2:1.

27. Not only did Augustine's argumentation influence the direction of the church regarding paedosoterism post-Augustine, but Augustine's theology took into consideration the discussion to date. Some of the particular figures who contributed to Augustine's development of the doctrine of original sin and its implications for paedosoterism are as follows:

Tertullian: Tertullian argued that the stage of infancy is the *innocens aetas*, "age of innocence." This designation is not intended to deny inherited sin; rather, Tertullian is asserting that because baptism is for the remission of sins, it is basically a needless ritual for innocent infants. Because Tertullian believed that baptism only washed away sins committed up to that point, he counseled that baptism should be deferred until the candidate was prepared for a life of holiness in devotion to Christ. The connection between original sin and baptism is not made by Tertullian. See Tertullian, *De Baptismo*, 18;

and Tertullian, *De Testimonio Animae*, 40–41, 56–58, 447–59; see also Wright, *Infant Baptism*, 25–26, 28. For a survey of ascriptions to infants of innocence or sinlessness, see Aland, *Neutestamentliche Entwrufe*, 17–21, cited in Wright, *Infant Baptism*, 28n19.

Cyprian: Cyprian believed in the impunity of original sin and therefore staunchly advocated infant baptism chiefly due to his polemic against African bishop Fidus in 253. Fidus argued for a direct correlation between New Testament baptism and Old Testament circumcision, and that infants should therefore be baptized "on the eighth day after birth and not before it." (See Wright, *Infant Baptism*, 29. On similar grounds Augustine argued for the lost condition of infants both Old Testament and New Testament due to original sin. He writes, "Consider also that, even when those patriarchs had children, the soul of the little one would be lost from its people, if it were not circumcised on the eighth day, and answer me: On what grounds would it be lost, since you [Julian] deny that it was subject to original sin?"; see Augustine, *Against Julian*, 5:45). Agreeing with Tertullian both that the infant need not be baptized for committed sins and that the infant "has contracted the contagion of the ancient death at his earliest birth," Cyprian develops the exact opposite argument of Tertullian. Because infants have no lifestyle of sin to which they have grown accustomed to prevent them from surrendering to baptism, Cyprian all the more heartily encouraged the baptism of newborn innocents (Gregory of Nanzianzen agrees. "Do you have an infant child? Do not allow sin any opportunity. Let him be sanctified from babyhood, and consecrated by the Spirit from his tenderest days"; see Wright, *Infant Baptism*, 34n34). Augustine cites Cyprian's letter to Fidus in one of his treatises against the Pelagians. He writes of Cyprian, "Do you see how he thinks that to depart from this life without that saving sacrament is deadly and lethal, not merely to the flesh, but also to the soul of the infant?" Cyprian's reason for this lethal sentence against infants is their "contagion of the ancient death" (i.e., original sin), not personal sins, which Cyprian asserted they had none. He encouraged the baptism of infants because "The infant comes to receive the forgiveness of sins with greater ease [than adults] by reason of the fact that it receives forgiveness, not for its own sins, but for those of another [i.e., original sin inherited from Adam]"; see Augustine, *Punishment and Forgiveness*, 3:10.

Origen: Cyprian's older contemporary in the East, Origen of Alexandria, also strongly advocated infant baptism. His rationale, however, was a bit unorthodox. Origen asserted not only the immortality of the soul but also a pre-cosmic fall of these *pre-existent* souls. So, he insisted upon infant baptism not because of humanity's solidarity with fallen Adam, but in order to remit the soul's *pre-incarnate* transgressions. Because of this awareness of the soul's inborn impurity, Origen argued that the apostles, too, mandated infant baptism. Origen, writing in c. 240, is thus the first Christian writer to connect the practice of infant baptism to the apostles; see Origen, *Romans*, cited in Wright, *Infant Baptism*, 32. Augustine would later argue that the church's custom of baptizing infants is not to be scorned because of its apostolic tradition; see Augustine, *Literal Meaning of Genesis*, 10:23:39. Also, in a letter to Jerome, Augustine writes, "Anyone who would say that even infants who pass from this life without participation in the sacrament of baptism shall be made alive in Christ goes counter to the preaching of the Apostle and condemns the whole church, because it is believed without doubt that there is no other way at all in which they can be made alive in Christ"; see Augustine, *Letter 166*, 7:21.

Ambrose: The keen mind of Ambrose possessed a view of original sin that was "Augustinian before Augustine" (Williams, *Ideas of the Fall*, 300). He does not articulate his understanding, however, with either the volume or the clarity of Augustine's anti-Pelagian treatises. Of the eternally lost condition of the unbaptized deceased Ambrose

The Early Church on Original Sin

The doctrine of original sin in the post-apostolic period did not inherently entail original *guilt* also;[28] yet evidences of infant baptism are certainly found by the time of Augustine—even possibly routinely in some regions.[29]

---

would write, "No one is excepted: not the infant, nor the one prevented by any necessity" (Ambrose, *Abraham* [Migne, *PL*, 14:500]); and in his *Against the Novatians*, "All of us human beings are born under the power of sin, and our very origin lies in guilt . . ." (Ambrose, *Penance*, 1:3, 13, cited in Augustine, *Grace of Christ*, 1:47; and Augustine, *Against Julian*, 2:5). Augustine held in deep admiration Ambrose and his wisdom; see Augustine, *Confessions*, 5:13–14. One could only reasonably assume, therefore, that the instruction of Ambrose, at least to some degree, contributed to Augustine's own thinking in his wrestling with this theological dilemma.

28. Augustine opposed the creationist teaching asserted by Pelagius and Caelestius. In his *The Literal Meaning of Genesis*, Augustine queries, if the soul of the infant has *not* descended from Adam—and is therefore innocent of inherited sin, and has done neither good nor evil, on what ground would one have for any fear of *just* condemnation of this innocent one if it dies unbaptized? Here Augustine uses the creationists' logically necessary conclusion of the infant's innocence in order to charge that, if a creationist understanding were true, then the church's practice of infant baptism has been completely superfluous. Further, against Julian, Augustine writes, "Whoever wants to undermine in the Christian faith the words of scripture, *Death comes through a man, and the resurrection of the dead comes through a man, for just as in Adam all die, so too in Christ all will be brought to life* (1 Cor 15:21–22), tries to destroy our whole faith in Christ." See Augustine, *Literal Meaning of Genesis*, 10:11:19; and Augustine, *Against Julian*, 1:22; see also Wright, *Infant Baptism*, 74–75.

Jerome, too, held a creationist anthropology; see Augustine, *Letter 166*, 4:8. Robert. O'Connell suggests that while Augustine argued convincingly against the Pelagians for a traducianist view of the origin of the soul, he maintained some uncertainties about which model best accounted for the biblical articulation of the generation of each new soul at birth with the inherent guilt of sin; see O'Connell, *Origin of the Soul*, 201–45.

For definitions of creationism and traducianism, see Denzinger, *Catholic Dogma*, 44–45. Creationism is the first of three positions held by the Pelagians that was also condemned at Carthage; against this fundamental error Catholics cited especially Rom 5:12, where Adam is depicted as transmitting not only sin but also the correlative penalty of death. The second point, that the "sin" Adam transmitted entailed "death" and not corruption, was condemned at the Second Council of Orange in France, 529, and again at Trent, 1545–63; see Denzinger, *Catholic Dogma*, 75–76. A third point was that Adam's sin is transmitted only by way of example, not heredity. This point was condemned at Carthage and again at Trent; see Denzinger, *Catholic Dogma*, 247; 45; see also Augustine, *Nature and Origin of the Soul*, 1:16.

29. Hippolytus, *Apostolic Tradition*, 45; Wright, *Infant Baptism*, 8, 20, 28; Wright suggests that while infant baptism may have become routine before 200 in Rome (though the accounts of Irenaeus and Justin conflict), Southern Gaul, Asia Minor, and possibly North Africa, it took the form of service devised for professing believers, with the infant's parent or sponsor responding to the interrogative, "Does he/she believe?" with an affirmative, "He/she believes"; see Wright, *Infant Baptism*, 7, 40, 79–80. In a response to a question from Boniface (possibly bishop of Cataquas) regarding how a parent or sponsor could possibly answer so confidently concerning the faith of a candidate

Because original guilt was not the primary concern of many practitioners of infant baptism, however, the practice was not performed either with an eye toward making the infant a member of the covenant community or necessarily for the cleansing of the stain of *original* sin, but "for the remission of [personal] sins."[30] Yes, a considerable number of the Church Fathers were convinced that salvation could not be secured apart from baptism ("or its higher surrogate, martyrdom"[31]). Because of their yet undeveloped understanding of the relationship between original sin and baptism, however, emergency or necessary baptism (of infants or children) was often administered.[32] John 3:5 would indeed become "the favourite baptismal

---

who "does not so much as know that there is a God," Augustine, rather weakly, replies, "Just as, then, in a certain way the sacrament of the body of Christ is the body of Christ and the sacrament of the blood of Christ is the blood of Christ, so the sacrament of faith is the faith. . . . And for this reason when the answer is given that the little one believes, though he does not yet have the disposition of faith, the answer is given that he has faith on account of the sacrament of the faith and that he is converted to the Lord on account of the sacrament of conversion, because the response itself also pertains to the celebration of the sacrament"; Augustine, *Letter 98*, 9. For further discussion of the presence (or absence) of the practice of infant baptism in the early church, see Ferguson, *Baptism in the Early Church*.

30. See Acts 2:38; cf. also Mark 1:4; Luke 3:3; 24:47; Acts 10:43; 13:38; 26:18; Col 1:14; Wright, *Infant Baptism*, 25-27, 34-36; Ferguson, "Inscriptions," 45-46. Though original sin was certainly not denied, personal sin rather than inherited Adamic sin was the concern in baptism. The connection between original sin and baptism simply had not yet been developed. In fact, Tertullian, while not invalidating infant baptism, sanctioned a subsequent *proper* baptism. Siricius, bishop of Rome in 385, issued a decretal statement that infants who could not speak for themselves should be baptized lest, dying unbaptized, they should forfeit both eternal life and the kingdom of heaven—anticipating the error of Pelagius and Caelestius; see Siricius, *Epistle*, 1:3, cited in Wright, *Infant Baptism*, 36 n. 42; see also Augustine, *Against Julian*, 3:52.

31. Wright, *Infant Baptism*, 27. See also Tertullian, *On Baptism*, 16; Cyprian, *Letters*, 73:22; Cyril, *Catecheses*, 3:10; Gregory, *Orations*, 39:17; Augustine, *City of God*, 13:7; in Willis, *Teachings of the Church Fathers*, 434-36. Regarding this martyr's "baptism of blood," Tertullian would even assert, "The sole key to unlock Paradise is your own life's blood" in Tertullian, *De Anima*, 55:5, cited in Butler, *New Prophecy*, 42.

32. Augustine was disappointed that his mother refused to baptize him during a serious childhood illness, despite his pleas. Here is an indication of Augustine's conviction both of the contemporary preference to defer baptism until the last possible season of life and of the necessity of baptism for salvation. Significantly, however, Augustine nowhere mentions infant baptism in his *Confessions*. Probably his first mention of infant baptism would come in *On The Size of the Soul*, written in Rome in 388. In that work he wonders about the benefit of infant baptism, but defers further inquiry until "it falls to be investigated"; see Augustine, *Confessions*, 1:11, 21; and Augustine, *De Quantitate Animae*, 36:80, cited in Wright, *Infant Baptism*, 72.

EXCURSUS: THE FROWNING PROVIDENCE OF INFANT DEATH   173

text of the second century."[33] The "rule of the Church universal"[34]—East and West—including Fathers such as Chrysostom, Tertullian, Origen, Cyprian, Ambrose, Augustine, Jerome, Innocent of Rome, Hilary of Gaul, Basil the Great, Gregory Nazianzen, Gregory of Nyssa, and even Pelagius, was that John 3:5 was to be interpreted to mean that without being "born again of water"—i.e., baptism—one could not enter the kingdom of heaven. In fact, in light of this understanding of water baptism did the phrase "one baptism for the remission of sins" find its way into the 381 Nicene Creed.[35]

So then, if these same Fathers either baptized infants for the remission of *original* sin—for which the infants presumably may not be held guilty anyway—or for the remission of *actualized* sins—which they have yet to commit—of what benefit, then, was infant baptism?[36] This dilemma surfaced the question of the eternal destiny of all the unbaptized deceased, specifically, whether a distinction existed between the significance of adult baptism and infant baptism. A second class of baptism would thus necessarily be implied—in overt contradiction to the determination of Nicaea.

33. Wright, *Infant Baptism*, 12.
34. Augustine, *On Original Sin*, 2:5.
35. Wright, *Infant Baptism*, 25–27, 34–36; Williams, *Ideas of the Fall*, 553–54; Ferguson, "Inscriptions," 45, 46; Tertullian, *On Baptism*, 12:1; Augustine, *On Original Sin*, 2:5, 19, 21; Augustine, *Against Julian*, 1:22. In fact, the 1545–63 Council of Trent still affirms this understanding; see Denzinger, *Catholic Dogma*, 247; cf. 36.

36. Wright, *Infant Baptism*, 81. For some, infant baptism was for the reception of the gifts of sanctification, adoption, strengthening against future sin, etc. For others, infant baptism was only to ensure entrance into the kingdom of heaven—an argument whose nuances will be addressed below. Quoting Chrysostom, Augustine writes that some of the "ten benefits" of baptism are "holiness, righteousness, and adoption, that they may be heirs, brothers and sisters of Christ, and his members"; see Augustine, *Against Julian*, 1:21. Additionally, during the third and fourth centuries, reasoned arguments for the deferment of baptism arose. "Because baptism's capacity to deal with sin was limited to the burden of sin already accumulated by the candidate, it must be sought only with the utmost caution and sense of responsibility [because of the possibility of post-baptism moral lapses], and hence would normally never be granted to, because never requested by, infants"; see Wright, *Infant Baptism*, 28. Wright cites Chrysostom concerning the gravity of baptism: "The sins committed before baptism are all cancelled by the grace and kindness of the strength of Christ crucified. The sins committed after baptism require great earnestness, that they may again be cancelled. Since there is no second baptism, there is need of our tears, repentance, confession, almsgiving, prayer, and every other kind of devotion"; Chrysostom, *De Sancta Pentecoste, Homilies*, 1:6 (Migne, *PG*, 50,463), cited in Wright, 28 n. 18. Noteworthy also is the notion that because baptism was effective only in the remission of sins committed up to that point, the die was now cast for the development of what would become the intricate Roman Catholic penitential system (and later, the doctrine of purgatory) to remit sins committed after baptism.

This very division of baptism is what Augustine would so strongly inveigh against the Pelagians because of its implication on original sin.

Augustine's Development of the Doctrine of Original Sin

David Wright, critiquing Karl Barth's assertion that "infant baptism had long since become the rule in Christendom" by the time of the Reformation, notes that the "rule" did not come about as a result of "'the greatest historical transformation which Christianity had thus far undergone'—namely, the Constantinian revolution,"[37] but because of "the epochal influence of Augustine of Hippo's development of the doctrine of original sin and the necessity of baptism *quam primum* (at the first opportunity) to deliver the otherwise hell-bound newborn from its guilt."[38] Wright continues, singling Augustine as the catalyst for the practice's longevity.

> More than any other factor, Augustine's anti-Pelagian theology universalized infant baptism in the West. Although the full severity of this Augustinian teaching was never wholly canonized in medieval Catholicism, the Council of Trent [1545–63] found it imperative to reaffirm in its decrees on original sin and on baptism, against the Reformers' denial that infants dying unbaptized were condemned eternally . . .[39]

Augustine became convinced theologically that baptism was the sole remedy for the guilt of original sin in infants.[40] His advocating of universal infant baptism would thus naturally follow. While Augustine's polemic against Pelagius over the doctrine of original sin would prove immensely

37. Wright, *Infant Baptism*, xxvi; see also Barth, *CD*, 4:3, 167.

38. Wright, *Infant Baptism*, xxvii; 68, 82.

39. Wright, *Infant Baptism*, xxvii. The Council of Trent republished in full the critical canon of the decisive anti-Pelagian Council of Carthage of AD 418; see Council of Trent, "Decree Concerning Original Sin," esp. 4–5, *Trent*, 22–23; see also Augustine, *Carthage*, in *WSA*, I/23, 389–91.

40. Augustine would write, "Now, to what sin do infants die in their regeneration [i.e., baptism] but that sin which they bring with them at birth? And therefore to these also applies what follows: 'Therefore we are buried with Him by baptism into death; that, like as Christ was raised up from the dead by the glory of the Father, even so we also should walk in newness of life.'" Of his certainty that no one is made alive in Christ apart from baptism, Augustine writes, "there is no one born of Adam but is subject to condemnation, and that no one, unless he be new born in Christ, is freed from condemnation"; see Augustine, *Enchiridion*, 51–52; see also Augustine, *On Original Sin*, 2:21–22; Augustine, *Punishment and Forgiveness*, 1:41; 3:10; Augustine, *Letter 98*, 9–10; Augustine, *Letter 166*, 7:21; Augustine, *Retractions*, 2:71. See also Ratzinger, *Catechism*, 102.

helpful to the church in its articulation of the gospel, his corresponding development of the doctrine of infant baptism, which divorced the ordinance from the biblical depiction of attendant repentance and conversion,[41] would greatly devalue baptism.[42] Nevertheless, "[f]or Augustine, the answer to the question 'why?'[43] emerged with crystal clarity from a consideration of basic Christian beliefs."[44]

The Condition of Deceased Infants

Against the Pelagians, Augustine's *causa gratiae*, "case for grace,"[45] along with a series of providential circumstances—including the death of Innocent, bishop of Rome, and his succession by Zosimus, a "weak . . . conservative politician"[46]—would culminate in the empire-wide official condemnation of Pelagianism by Emperor Honorius on April 30, 418.[47] At the Council of Carthage in the same year, Zosimus would write the decision of the Apostolic See concerning original sin and its direct implication for the condition of deceased unbaptized infants, and the church's corollary teaching of the necessity of baptism.

> If anyone says that, because the Lord said "In My Father's house are many mansions," it might be understood that in the Kingdom of Heaven there will be some middle place, or some place anywhere, where the blessed infants live who departed from this life without Baptism, without which they cannot enter into the Kingdom of Heaven which is life eternal: Let him be anathema. For when the Lord says "Unless one be born again of water and the Holy Ghost, he shall not enter into the Kingdom of God," what Catholic will doubt that one who has not deserved to be a co-heir with Christ will be a partner of the Devil? For one who does not stand on the right will surely be assigned to the left side.[48]

---

41. For an excellent argument for the biblical portrayal of a model of believers baptism, see Schreiner and Wright, *Believer's Baptism*. Stephen Wellum's chapter, "Baptism and the Relationship between the Covenants," keenly frames the discussion.

42. Wright, *What Has Infant Baptism Done*; Wright, *Infant Baptism*, 68, 88.

43. Augustine's examination of God's self-revelation was ever "punctuated by '*Quare . . . quare . . . quare*,' 'Why? . . . why? . . . why?'" That is, he was the consummate apologist, his faith continually seeking understanding. Brown, *Augustine*, 250.

44. Wright, *Infant Baptism*, 38–39.

45. Brown, *Augustine*, 355–56

46. Ibid., 360–61.

47. Ibid., 363.

48. The epistle *Tractatoria ad Orientales ecclesias, Aegypti diocesim, Constantinopolim,*

In *The Nature and Origin of the Soul* Augustine echoes the decision. He charges that no one should promise "to unbaptized little ones some sort of middle place of rest or happiness of any sort or in any place between damnation and the kingdom of heaven. The Pelagian heresy, after all, promised them this."[49] Later, the 1274 Second Council of Lyon[50] would reaffirm the decision. The 1439 Council of Florence would follow suit stating, "The souls of those who die in actual mortal sin, or only in original sin, immediately descend into Hell";[51] as would the 1563 counter-Reformation Council of Trent.[52]

Augustine does not have in view merely temporal death for the unbaptized. Citing Gen 17:14 of God's warning that the uncircumcised will be "cut off from his people," Augustine argues that the text implies more than temporal death.

> For, pray tell me, what evil has an infant committed of his own will, that for the negligence of another in not circumcising him, he himself must be condemned, and with so severe a condemnation, that the soul must be cut off from his people? It was not of any temporal death that this fear was inflicted, since of righteous persons, when they died, it used rather to be said, "And he was gathered unto his people;" or, "He was gathered to his fathers:" for no attempt to separate a man from his people is long formidable to him, when his own people is itself the people of God.[53]

Taking a queue from physical or other adversities that infants incur, Augustine deduces their guilt. Citing John 9:3, Augustine argues that these evils that infants incur sometimes from birth—and beyond—ought not to

---

Thessalonicam, Hierosolymam was Zosimus' famous condemnation. Zosimus would further write, "By His death that bond of death introduced into all of us by Adam and transmitted to every soul, that bond contracted by propagation is broken, in which no one of our children is held not guilty until he is free through baptism"; see Denzinger, *Catholic Dogma*, 45n2; 47–48; see also Augustine, *Carthage*, in *WSA*, I/23, 389; Brown, *Augustine*, 363.

49. Augustine, *Nature and Origin of the Soul*, 1:11.
50. Denzinger, *Catholic Dogma*, §464, 184.
51. Ibid., §693, 220.
52. Session 5:4, *Decree On Original Sin*, of the 1563 Council of Trent states, "If anyone denies that infants newly born from their mothers' wombs are to be baptized, . . . let him be anathema"; see Denzinger, *Catholic Dogma*, §791, 247; Council of Trent, "Decree Concerning Original Sin," esp. 4–5, *Trent*, 22–23.
53. Augustine, *On Original Sin*, 2:35. Augustine does argue that "unbaptized little ones who have only original sin and are not burdened by any personal sins will suffer the lightest punishment of all" (Augustine, *Against Julian*, 5:44).

be regarded by us as unjust, but rather, as was the case with the man born blind, "so that the works of God might be revealed in him."

> Many, of course, are not healed at all, but die with the same defects either at a later age or in infancy itself. In the case of some little ones who have already been reborn [i.e., baptized], the evils with which they were born remain, or such evils befall them, and *heaven forbid that we should say that these evils are not deserved*. We should, rather, understand that the fact that they are reborn is of benefit to them for the other world. But on account of the vice of pride by which human beings abandoned God, life in this world is lived amid various human evils under the heavy yoke *upon the children of Adam from the day they leave the womb of their mother until the day of their burial in the mother of all* (Sir 40:1).[54]

Augustine's burden is evidently not to soothe the conscience of the creature captivated by "the vice of pride," but rather to exalt the righteousness of the unimpeachable living God of grace who is also the holy God of justice against a diverse creation and humanity unified in sinful confederation against his holiness.

The Consequence of Original Sin/The Meaning of θάνατο'

When God warned Adam that he would surely die in the day that he ate of the tree of the knowledge of good and evil (Gen 2:17), what did that signify? Was only physical death in view? Only spiritual? Or did death signify every consequent entailment of transgressing the Law of God? When Heb 2:9 says of Christ that he tasted death (θάνατου) for all, what did he taste?[55]

---

54. Augustine, *Against Julian*, 3:13; first emphasis added. Of the justice of God in the damnation of sinners Augustine writes further, "For then he [any inquirer of the justice of God] perceives that the whole human race was condemned in its rebellious head by a divine judgment so just, that if not a single member of the race had been redeemed, no one could justly have questioned the justice of God; and that it was right that those who are redeemed should be redeemed in such a way as to show, by the greater number who are unredeemed and left in their just condemnation, what the whole race deserved..."; see Augustine, *Enchiridion*, 99; see also Edwards, "Original Sin Defended," 1:175–77, 226–27; Edwards, "Justice of God," 1:669–70.

55. See also chap. 4 of this work, the sections entitled "What Does the Death of Christ Portend?" and "The Post-Crucifixion Humanity of Christ"; and chap. 2, the section entitled, "Inexorable Law of Nature or Catastrophic Disorder?"

The Wages of Original Sin

In agreement with some in the early church, who did not equate original guilt with original sin,[56] some contemporary thinkers have argued that the consequence of original sin is not eternal condemnation; rather, eternal condemnation is only a consequence of actualized sin, tenable only from a state of "moral culpability."[57] Adam's transgression only commuted to human nature depravity but not condemnation.[58] As we have seen, however,

---

56. See the section above entitled "The Early Church and Original Sin."

57. MacArthur, *Safe*, 39; Erickson, *Christian Theology*, 654–55; Nash, *When a Baby Dies*, 59–64; Mohler and Akin, "Salvation of the 'Little Ones'"; Cragoe, "Examination of the Issues," 77.

Erickson asserts that, because of humanity's germinal presence in Adam at the Fall, "There is no injustice, then, to our condemnation and death as a result of original sin," and "We were involved, although not personally, and are responsible for [Adam's] sin." Erickson concludes, however, that "the *biblical* teaching is that children are not under God's condemnation for this sin, at least not until attaining an age of responsibility in moral and spiritual matters"; Erickson, *Christian Theology*, 654–55; emphasis added. The texts Erickson cites as "biblical teaching" for such presumed grace are Matt 18:3; 19:14 (which Augustine himself refutes, noting that humility, not conditional innocence, is the character of the little ones to whom Christ compares the inheritors of the kingdom of heaven; see Augustine, *Punishment and Forgiveness*, 47; cf. Isa 7:15–16; and Jonah 4:11). Erickson conjectures that, in the case of the morally incompetent, "there is only a conditional imputation of guilt" until the individual commits personal sin, thus "ratifying Adam's sin"; Erickson, *Christian Theology*, 656. He presumes upon a general grace acquired through Christ's atonement for a *conditioned* mercy upon morally incompetent sinners. Augustine argued, however, against a similar assertion made by Pelagius. Pelagius' interpretation of Rom 5:15–19—like some inclusivists of our own day—argues that "If Adam's sin injured those who have not sinned, then also Christ's righteousness profits those who do not believe." Augustine sharply retorts that he has already refuted such "so-called exposition" in his *On the Baptism of Infants*; see Augustine, *On Original Sin*, 2:24, 446.

Harwood, in *Spiritual Condition of Infants*, 153–55, agrees with Erickson and argues for the salvation of all morally incompetent offspring of Adam. He affirms original sin but denies the corollary original guilt. The commutation of Adam's sin nature, then, only corrupts his posterity; it does not condemn them because the guilt is only actualized upon the sinner's initial sin.

58. Some of the early Church Fathers, because of their biblical and historical (to date) understanding of the significance of original sin, yet undeveloped and arguably counter-biblical understanding of the significance of baptism, veered into the error of baptismal regeneration. See Warfield, *Studies in Theology*, 402. Warfield cites Justin Martyr, Iraeneus, Origen, and Cyprian as proponents of baptismal regeneration. He follows with the logic: "The early Church did come to believe that baptism was necessary to salvation; this doctrine forms a natural reason for the extension of baptism to infants, lest dying unbaptized they should fail of salvation." Even Augustine would assert, "Now infants are strangers to this salvation and light, and will remain in perdition and darkness, unless they are joined [through baptism] to the people of God by adoption, holding to Christ who suffered the just for the unjust, to bring them unto God"; Augustine, *Punishment and Forgiveness*, 1:41.

this understanding does not accord with the more convincing arguments for the equation of original guilt with original sin as articulated by Augustine and others who would follow his thinking. Let us survey a sampling of recent opinions.

While biblically unfounded, Rome's *response* to this "certainty of faith"—the equation of original guilt with original sin—is at least consistent with its grasp of the seriousness of original sin and the meaning of "death."

> [Adam] has transmitted to us a sin with which we are all born afflicted, a sin which is the "death of the soul." Because of this certainty of faith, the Church baptizes for the remission of sins even tiny infants who have not committed personal sin.[59]

The reason for the practice of infant baptism, which continues to this day in Catholicism, is remission of the guilt of sin that mandates eternal condemnation.[60]

Regarding this equation of original guilt with original sin and the consequent condemnation even of infants, Jonathan Edwards—customarily quite thoroughly—affirmed,

> *One* of them supposes, that this sin, though truly *imputed* to INFANTS, so that thereby they are exposed to a proper *punishment*, yet is not imputed to them in such a *degree*, as that upon this account they should be liable to *eternal* punishment, as Adam himself was, but only to *temporal death*, or *annihilation;* Adam himself, the immediate actor, being made infinitely *more guilty* by it, than his posterity. On which I would observe; that to suppose, God imputes not *all* the guilt of Adam's sin, but only some *little part* of it, relieves nothing but one's *imagination*. To think of poor little *infants* bearing such torments for Adam's sin, as they sometimes do in this world, and these torments ending in death and annihilation, may sit easier on the imagination, than to conceive of their suffering eternal misery for it. But it does not at all relieve one's *reason*. There is no rule of reason, that can be supposed to lie against imputing a sin in the *whole* of it, which was committed by one, to another who did not personally commit it, but what will also lie against its being

---

59. Ratzinger, *Catechism*, 102.

60. Seemingly equivocating, however, on the Catechism's affirmation concerning the final state of deceased infants, Rome has recently stated its opinion dismissing the doctrine of limbo, qualifying, however, that the "ordinary teaching" of this "possible theological hypothesis" "never entered into the dogmatic definitions of the Magisterium." See the 2007 report published by Rome's International Theological Commission entitled *The Hope of Salvation for Infants Who Die without Being Baptized*.

so imputed and punished in *part*. For all the reasons (if there be any) lie against the *imputation;* not the *quantity* or *degree of what is* imputed . . . . It seems to me pretty manifest, that none can, in good consistence with themselves, own a real *imputation* of the guilt of Adam's first sin to his posterity, without owning that they are *justly* treated as *sinners,* truly guilty, and *children of wrath,* on that account; nor unless they allow a just imputation of the *whole* of the *evil* of that transgression; at least, all that pertains to the essence of that act, as a full and complete violation of the *covenant,* which God had established; even as much as if each one of mankind had the like covenant established with him singly, and had by the like direct and full act of rebellion, violated it for himself.[61]

Here, "one of the most brilliant theological minds ever produced in North America"[62] renders inescapable the logic of the imputation, as biblically articulated, of Adam's guilt and consequent penalty to all of his posterity. Any attempt to alter the biblical disclosure of either that condemnation or the articulated prescription for rescue from that condemnation, says Edwards, "relieves nothing but one's *imagination* . . . [b]ut it does not at all relieve one's *reason*."[63] Moreover, one ought to give great care before

---

61. Edwards, "Original Sin Defended," 1:226-27. Edwards' argument formidably anticipates the existentialist reasoning of thinkers like Paul Tillich, whose presentation of immortality "rejects the notion of the continued life of the individual beyond the grave"; so assesses Hick, *Death and Eternal Life,* 216-17. Tillich asserts, rather, that all that is good in the created order will find its consummation in the divine "eternal memory." He resolves the problem of infant death, therefore, by dismissing individual destinies entirely. He excuses from any form of judgment at all those who, through no fault of their own, "are unable to reach a fulfillment of their essential *telos* even to a small degree, as in the case of premature destruction, the death of infants, biological and psychological disease . . ." Tillich concludes, "From the point of view which assumes separate individual destinies, . . . there is no answer at all. The question and the answer are possible only if one understands essentialization or elevation of the positive into Eternal Life as a matter of universal participation"; see Tillich, *Systematic Theology,* 3:409, cited in Hick, *Death and Eternal Life,* 217.

62. Hoiberg, *New Encyclopædia Britannica,* s.v. Edwards, Jonathan.

63. Edwards, "Original Sin Defended," 1:226. Furthermore, elevating the imperfect ethic of valuing human life above or even equal to the ethic of honoring the ordinance of God inevitably perverts truth and razes the glory of God. Case in point: the conception and development of the doctrine of limbo derived from just such a tension felt between what Catholic theologian and historian Michael Simpson notes as "the eschatological tradition of the Church and *a common sense of humanity and justice."* Simpson continues, "Christians could not tolerate the thought that those good people who through no fault of their own were born outside the Christian community should be destined to the eternal torment of hell." See Simpson, *Death and Eternal Life,* 26-27; emphasis added. If that creaturely determination of what is *just* is deemed insufficient

promulgating any such conjecture in light of the injunction of the apostle John that such promulgation may constitute adding to "the words of the prophecy of this book"—i.e., the canon of God's revelation in Scripture (Rev 22:18).

Surely giving great care, but nonetheless positing necessarily an alternative mode—or at least an alternative interpretation of that mode—of salvation than perspicuously presented in Scripture, pastor-teacher John Piper argues for paedosoterism from a premise interpreted from Rom 1:19–20 that pre-cognitives are excluded from accountability for guilt. In addition to voicing his opinion that, "in the case of infants, who don't have the mental wherewithal to process the information, their accountability before God is not the same as those who do," Piper supposes,

> The "therefore" at the end [of verse 20] says that mankind would seem to have an excuse if they had not seen clearly in nature what God is like. And so, because I don't think little babies can process nature and make conclusions about God's grace, glory or justice, it seems they would fall into the category of still having an excuse. . . . The way I see it is that God ordains, for his own wise purposes, that at the judgment day all the children who died in infancy will be covered by the blood of Jesus. And they will come to faith, either in heaven immediately or later in the resurrection. And God will not condemn them because he wants to manifest openly and publicly that he does not condemn those who did not have the mental capacities to put their faith in him.

---

pride, hear the further biolatrous hubris of such thinking, particularly regarding the notion of the damnation of infant sinners: "While several early theologians, and notably St Augustine, found no alternative than to consign such infants to the eternal torments of hell, even if of the least painful (*mitissimi*) kind, *a more humane solution* was later found by postulating a Limbo specially provided for such children. In Limbo there would be no enjoyment of the Beatific Vision, but neither would there be any suffering. This conception found firm acceptance in the Middle Ages"; see Simpson, *Death and Eternal Life*, 27; emphasis added.

That "a more humane solution" would find "firm acceptance in the Middle Ages"—not to mention in the equally anthropocentric proposals of our own day—is indicative of precisely the human aggrandizing, glory evaporating biolatry that is at the heart of the present work. To imagine that "a more humane solution" in some way entails a higher or more commendable moral ethic than that ordained by God is, needless to say, the height of creaturely arrogance, indeed, indistinguishable from the pride of Lucifer (Isa 14:12–14). Rather than contriving options against the justice of God in the damnation of sinners, why is the creature not more poised, like Aaron at God's slaying of his two sinner sons (Lev 10:3c), to place his hand over his mouth and submissively bless the righteous exhibition of holy, promise keeping integrity by the God who created and sustains *every* soul in accord with *his* own good purposes?

I don't think imbeciles have that capacity, and I don't think babies do. Therefore I hold out hope to parents that the loss of an infant is not their eternal loss.[64]

To the sin-infected modern ear attuned to "a more humane solution,"[65] this proposal certainly rings persuasive and pacifies creaturely sensibilities.[66] However, in exegeting the matter of paedosoterism, one must neglect neither the justice of God in the damnation of sinners nor the context and subject of Romans 1 any more so than in exegeting any part of divine revelation.

The apostle Paul, under the inspiration of the Holy Spirit, has as his subject in Romans 1 the range of human beings who are cognitive of "that which is known about God . . . for God made it evident to them" (Rom 1:18). Those subjects to whom God has made nothing cognitively evident are not even in consideration in the text.[67] So, Piper is correct when he asserts that only these cognitive and God-ignoring ones are the ones without excuse; for these ones—whether Jew or Gentile (3:9)—are the ones being considered in Paul's address. The entirety of the race is not Paul's specific concern here. Not until Romans 5 does both age and pre-cognition come into view. Then, *all* are judged condemned, regardless of age (5:12–14, 18). The condemnation here of the "all" incorrigibly includes infant offspring of Adam. If ever an opportunity—even clamoring—for an articulation of an exception for infants was warranted, no better occasion than this portion of Romans 5 could prove more availing and clarifying; yet the inspired apostle presents no such case.[68] Beyond Romans 5, the Scriptures' entire message

---

64. Piper, *Why Do You Believe*. Piper's argument for what he posits as God's public justice fails to account for the violent deaths of "children" and "little ones" in passages like Deut 2:34; 3:6; Hos 13:16; Ezek 9:5–6; cf. Amos 1:13; Ps 137:9; for no "public justice" appears in the judgment of these texts beyond that which is satisfactorily injunctioned by a holy God in Gen 2:17 and 1 Cor 15:22.

65. Simpson, *Death and Eternal Life*, 27. See also n. 63 above.

66. One should note that Piper does not deny original sin and its corollary original guilt. He affirms, "I believe [that infants dying in infancy go to heaven] not because of a sentimental notion that babies aren't participants in the Fall. They are. Babies are participants in original sin. The question is whether God has a way to cover their sin even before they have a chance to believe." Piper, *Why Do You Believe*.

67. The same objection may apply to John 9:41.

68. One might contest that this premise represents an argument from silence. Nonetheless, Scripture nowhere presents an argument for salvation from the curse of death by any means other than repentance of sin and faith in Jesus Christ. Any alternative proposal, then, would represent a non-revelatory hypothetical presumption (see 186 and 193 below). This presumption is made by Charles Hodge, based on his understanding of Rom 5:18–19—Christ's making many righteous. Hodge argues, "The Scriptures nowhere exclude any class of infants, baptized or unbaptized, born in Christian or in

of glad tidings—the *blessing* of life by Jesus Christ—can be genuinely and encompassingly "good," in the sense in which the New Testament depicts it, only against the backdrop of the universal *curse* of death—which is precisely the message that the Old Testament delineates. The apostle could articulate faithfully nothing more than the Scriptures articulate; that is, in Adam all die, and only by novation[69] into Christ can any be made alive (1 Cor 15:22).

Contemporary expositor John MacArthur affirms *traducianism* (the doctrine of the propagation—*traducem*—of Adam's sin to all his posterity), and also agrees that this propagation of Adam's sin is one of the book of Romans' most hotly debated doctrines, yet he denies that the doctrine necessitates eternal condemnation as a result.[70] MacArthur comments,

> Paul's discussion of the perpetuation of Adam's sin (5:12–21) is one of the deepest, most profound theological passages in all of Scripture. The nature of mankind's union with Adam, and how his sin was transferred to the human race has always been the subject of intense debate.[71]

Citing Jer 19:4–7, MacArthur elsewhere states:

> Some apparently imagine that infants whose parents are believers are safe because of the parents' faith, but infants from heathen cultures are condemned for their parents' sins. On the contrary, Scripture clearly teaches that the children of idolatrous parents are also considered "innocent" in God's eyes until they reach a state of moral culpability.

---

heathen lands, of believing or unbelieving parents, from the benefits of the redemption of Christ. All the descendants of Adam, except Christ, are under condemnation; all the descendants of Adam, except those of whom it is expressly revealed that they cannot inherit the kingdom of God, are saved . . . that the number of the saved far exceeds the number of the lost"; see Hodge, *Systematic Theology*, 1:26.

69. Proverbs 17:15 and Rom 4:5 are not in contradiction. In contract law, *novation* involves "the substitution of a new debtor, creditor, contract, etc., in place of an old one" (*The Oxford English Dictionary*, 1989). Justification, therefore, executes a novation of the sinner's metaphysical solidarity with Adam with metaphysical solidarity with Christ. All that is Christ's, therefore, is the believer's by virtue of real union with Him, i.e., being *in* Christ (1 Cor 3:21–23; Rom 8:16–17; Heb 1:2). See also, Murray, *Imputation of Adam's Sin*, 33–34; 87; cf. 40–41; and 85–95, where Murray states the reality of the believer's union with Christ in terms of his being "given property in the obedience of Christ with the result that his judicial status is that belonging to the obedience in which he has come to have property; this is the act of grace involved in being 'constituted righteous' [Rom 5:19]."

70. Cf. Augustine's counter argument in n. 28, as well as Edwards' at n. 61 above.

71. MacArthur, *MacArthur Study Bible*, 1689.

> In the days of the prophet Jeremiah, those who followed false gods in the land of Israel were guilty of offering their children as burnt sacrifices. God spoke of His judgment on those who followed this horrific practice, at the same time calling the sacrificed children "innocent."[72]

This exposition of Jeremiah rendered by MacArthur fails, however, on at least two counts. First, Jeremiah's reference to the sacrificed children's innocence is not of original sin; that sin is certainly not in view in the passage. Secondly, the sin that is in view is the idolatrous practices of their guilty parents—for which sin those same parents will be judged,[73] *in addition to* their extant condemnation for being offspring of the justly cursed Adam and Eve.[74] The term "innocent," then, in Jer 19:4 refers not to image bearers of God who are not culpable for the guilt of original sin, but to those children being sacrificed to idols—murdered—who are "innocent" of the capital crime committed against them by their parents.[75]

R. A. Webb also affirms traducianism *and* the correlate condemnation of the soul. He affirms, however, that by the sovereign grace of God, "all infants dying in infancy are elect, redeemed, regenerated and glorified. . . . The death of an infant, therefore, is the [irrefutable] *proof* of its salvation."[76] Following this line of thinking, Ronald Nash refers to Jeremiah (Jer 1:5) and John the Baptist (Luke 1:15, 44), suggesting that they "were regenerated and sanctified by God's grace before birth."[77] Nash continues, "If this sort of

---

72. MacArthur, *Safe*, 38–39; see also Nash, *When a Baby Dies*, 60.

73. See Jer 17:10; 32:18–19; Matt 16:24–27; Rom 2:5–11; 2 Cor 5:10; 2 Tim 4:14.

74. See Pss 51:5; 58:3; John 3:17–18; Rom 5:18; 1 Cor 15:22; Eph 2:1–3.

75. As a social commentary on our own culture, frankly, one is at a complete loss to explain how the sin of these "innocent" ones' parents can be reckoned as any different from the sacrificing, in our own day and nation, of approximately four thousand image bearers of God per day to abortion.

76. Webb, *Infant Salvation*, 4, quoted in Nash, *When a Baby Dies*, 64; brackets and italics, original. See also Westminster Confession of Faith, Chapter X, Section III, and 1689 London Baptist Confession of Faith, Chapter X, Section III, where the confessions presume that "elect infants dying in infancy are regenerated and saved by Christ through the Spirit," but that "others not elected . . . may have some common operations of the Word, yet not being effectually drawn by the Father, they never [LBC reads "they neither will nor can"] truly come to Christ, and therefore cannot be saved."

77. Nash, *When a Baby Dies*, 64–65; see also MacArthur, *Safe*, 20–21. Wayne Grudem makes the same argument, asserting that "John the Baptist was 'born again' before he was born" and "it is possible, therefore, that God is able to save infants in an unusual way, apart from the hearing and understanding them gospel, by bringing regeneration to them very early, sometimes even before birth." Grudem further lists several passages of Scripture that note either rescue from temporal judgment or household conversions, but do nothing to guarantee equation with salvific rescue of particular individuals of any age. Grudem, *Systematic Theology*, 500.

thing happens even once, it can certainly happen in other cases."[78] Yet Nash defines regeneration this way, "When we are regenerated, it is because God convicts us of sin, enables us to understand the gospel, and produces the repentance and faith that leads us to Christ."[79] On this assessment by both Webb and Nash, not only does consideration of proleptic language[80] and non-salvific anointings of the Holy Spirit[81] fail here, but these qualifications for regeneration—contrary to Nash's previously asserted "sort of thing"—are limited to the cognitive.

Presbyterian theologian B. B. Warfield, in arguing for his communion's view of paedobaptism, iterates the qualifications for regeneration delineated by Nash while fairly articulating his Baptist opponents' requisites for baptism.

> It is on the basis of the Puritan conception of the Church that the Baptists are led to exclude infants from baptism. For, if we are to demand anything like demonstrative evidence of actual participation in Christ before we baptize, no infant, who by reason of years is incapable of affording signs of his union with Christ, can be thought a proper subject of the rite.[82]

Warfield observes correctly the Baptist assertion of the biblical connection between "demonstrative evidence of actual participation in Christ" and the subsequent administration of the ordinance of baptism. For this very reason—lack of evidence of participation in Christ—do Baptists prohibit the administration of the ordinance of baptism to infants. In deference to paedosoterists, however, the peril of infants is not necessitated by this argument.[83]

Second Samuel 12:23 is often cited as a definitive case for infant salvation.[84] In light of Old Testament believers' limited conception of death, Sheol, and any possible afterlife, however, one must be careful not to overstate the implications of David's affirmation. Commenting on the appeal to

---

78. Nash, *When a Baby Dies*, 65.
79. Ibid., 75.
80. See Pss 58:3; 139:3–4, 16.
81. See Num 24:2 with 2 Pet 2:15, Jude 11, and Rev 2:14; 1 Sam 10:10; 19:23–24.
82. Warfield, *Studies in Theology*, 389–90.
83. To be sure, because Baptists do not deem baptism as salvific, presumption of an infant's regeneration does not necessitate baptism, nor does restriction from baptism necessarily signify an infant's unregenerate state; for the destiny of the infant is not determined by baptism.
84. MacArthur, *Safe*, 91–95.

the notion of elect infants rendered by the *1689 Baptist Confession of Faith*, Samuel Waldron cautions against such overstatement.

> The assumption in this appeal is that David's reference is to heaven. The parallel passages in the Old Testament convincingly suggest that David's reference is to Sheol or the grave (Job 7:8–10; Eccles. 3:20). David will go to the grave, Sheol, but the baby will not return from the grave to David. No certain support for the doctrine here asserted in the Confession may be gleaned from a passage which has another and much more likely interpretation.[85]

The arguments for cognitive embrace of Jesus Christ by faith as the Bible's lone revelation of the means of salvation from the curse of death appear to be insurmountable. In order for salvation to be relegated to any deceased pre-cognitive, then, it must be done so by means alternative to those unambiguously revealed in Scripture, namely by grace alone, through faith alone, in Christ alone. To be sure, God is sovereign in the salvation of whom he deigns to save; yet because Scripture does not reveal a means of salvation apart from the aforementioned, the argument that God saves "by an unconditional application of the grace of Christ to [infants'] souls, through the immediate and irresistible operation of the Holy Spirit prior to and apart from any action of their own proper wills"[86] can be inescapably no more than a non-revelatory hypothetical presumption.

The Justice of God in the Damnation of Sinners

Physical death as a judgment against sin ought not to be so cavalierly *dis*integrated from eternal death—the culmination of that for which physical death is an indicator, apart from contrariwise rescuing grace. That infants are subject to physical death is an irrefutable indicator that sin has affected

---

85. Waldron, *Modern Exposition*, 150. Philip Johnston also interprets the passage as a reference to the irreversibility of death, rather than as David's indication of his belief that the child was in heaven; see Johnston, *Shades of Sheol*, 32. See also Anthony Hoekema's excellent discussion of "The Intermediate State" in his *The Bible and the Future*, 92–108.

86. Boettner, *Reformed Doctrine of Predestination*, 142, quoted in MacArthur, *Safe*, 78. See also Warfield, *Studies in Theology*, 429–44, where Warfield presents a case for the salvation of covenant community infants and elect infants. For discussions of "dispositional faith" and "Augustinian universalism," see Owen, *WJO*, 10:249–53; Edwards, "Miscellany 393"; Shedd, "Westminster Standards," 134; and Crisp, "Is Universalism a Problem for Particularists?" 1–23.

them.[87] Why do infants die at all if no sin exists whereby they may be judged, since death can never be defined in terms less than a judgment against sin?[88] Is physical death, then, the extent of the judgment against original sin for infants? Again, Edwards argues to the contrary.

> We may well argue from these things, that infants are not sinless, but are by nature children of wrath, seeing this terrible evil [death] comes so heavily on mankind at this early period. But, besides the mortality of infants in general, there are some *particular cases* of their death attended with circumstances, which, in a peculiar manner, give evidence of their sinfulness, and of their just exposedness to divine wrath. Particularly, [Edwards goes on to cite, at length, cases involving the judgment of infants by death in Sodom and Gomorrah, the Flood, in Canaan, Egypt, Midian, Amalek, Edom, and at length about the "just recompense" against Jerusalem, including infants, in Ezek 9].[89]

The justice of God in the damnation of sinners knows of no distinction between adult "children of wrath" and those who have not yet progressed to maturity in their capacity to sin. The creature, who has received life as a loan from the Lord—who himself both possesses life intrinsically and dispenses judgment of life and death as he deems *right*—is obliged to render praise to whom praise is due for the exhibition of his holy splendor, no matter how "hard" the unfolded scenario.[90]

In What Way Does God Pass Over Sin?

Paedosoterists might argue also from passages such as Acts 17:30, Rom 3:25, 4:15, and 5:13 that eternal condemnation is not imputed for non-actualized

---

87. Charles Hodge agrees, "the death of infants is a Scriptural and decisive proof of their being born destitute of original righteousness and infected with a sinful corruption of nature. Their physical death is proof that they are involved in the penalty the principal element of which is the spiritual death of the soul." Hodge resolves his dilemma, however, by arguing that Rom 5:18–19 articulates Christ's provision of redemption for all infants. See Hodge, *Systematic Theology*, 1:26. See also Augustine, *Against Julian*, 3:13.

88. See Gen 2:17; Rom 5:12–14; 8:20; and chap. 2 herein.

89. Edwards, "Original Sin Defended," 1:175–77.

90. Cold and apathetic detachment is not intended here, as much as such statements might sound so to the modern ear. Rather, a creaturely deprecation, selfless humility, and God-exalting imperturbability is being encouraged in light of both the hard truths of divine revelation and the reality of living in a justly cursed universe. Cf. nn. 70, 71, 74, and 75 above. A more empathetic and nouthetic demeanor will accompany the closing chapter of this work.

sin. Let us examine the contexts and authorial intent of Paul's assertions in these passages.

"The overarching theme of Romans is the righteousness that comes from God: the glorious truth that God justifies guilty, condemned sinners by grace alone through faith [alone] in Christ alone"[91]—indeed, the cardinal doctrine and material cause of the sixteenth-century Reformation—*articulus stantis et cadentis ecclesiae*—and locus for any genuine revival.[92] Contextually, Paul is addressing the age-old question, "How then can a man be just with God? Or how can he be clean who is born of woman?" (Job 25:4).

That "all have sinned and fall short of the glory of God" (Rom 3:23) is scripturally irrefutable. Paul follows this premise with the contemplation in 3:25 that God, in his forbearance under the Old Covenant "had passed over the sins that were previously committed." Acts 17:30 reiterates this contemplation. Paul cannot mean that God, being full of grace, indiscriminately acquitted all the guilty in Adam. Nor can he mean that unexercised faith (even though James 2:14–26 tells us there is no such thing) will not eventually be met with justice. He denies any veracity of these propositions in Romans 5:14.[93] Neither does Paul suggest by Rom 4:15 or 5:13 that original sin has no consequence (beyond the corruption of the human will), assuming that sin actualized *before* institution of the Mosaic Law may not be considered transgression against God, nor that adhering to the Mosaic Law, of itself, remits consequence of original sin. In 4:13 Paul charges that that would make faith "void and the promise of no effect," thus eliminating *any* significance of the gospel. The good news is precisely that, because the

judgment of damnation is remitted and peace is declared; not simply because the bondage of the will can now be ended. Paul's meaning, therefore, is that judgment against the believing—both Old Covenant and New Covenant—is deferred to the Christ at his advent.[94] *This* judgment is what Christ "tastes" for every man.[95]

The Judgment Seat

In the discussion of paedosoterism, Mohler, Akin, Nash, and MacArthur neglect the distinction between eternal judgment and assessment for *degree*

---

91. MacArthur, *MacArthur Study Bible*, 1689.

92. Murray, *Revival and Revivalism*, 24–5, 199, 219; Edwards, *Religious Affections*, 308.

93. See also Exod 20:5; 23:7; Num 14:18; Deut 5:9; Hab 1:13a.

94. See John 3:16–18.

95. Cf. Ps 22:1/Matt 27:46; Isa 53; Rom 6:10; 2 Cor 5:21; Heb 2:9; 9:12b.

of reward or punishment. This distinction is a biblical and germane one, however. Concerning the nature of original sin and guilt and its consequence, Mohler and Akin aver,

> The imputation of Adam's sin and guilt explains our inability to respond to God without regeneration, but the Bible does not teach that we will answer for Adam's sin.[96]

Given the authors' context, this statement stands somewhat at odds with biblical and historical parsing of the relationship between Adam's sin and that of his posterity as articulated above, as well as the gospel's message of "peace to mankind" (Luke 2:14) otherwise under a curse. All of Adam's posterity die not merely by virtue of their own actualized sins, but by virtue of their having sinned *in* Adam.

Mohler and Akin further argue that Israel's "little ones . . . who this day have no knowledge of good or evil" (Deut 1:39) were "exempted from the judgment . . . because of their age."[97] In actuality, the only judgment from which they were exempted was that they did not get their parents' "[wish] that we had died in this wilderness" (Num 14:2). This exemption did *not* signify that they were no longer subject to sin or damnation, as Deut 4:25–31, Josh 24:19, Judges 2, and Jer 32:21–23 evince. Neither entrance into nor failure to enter the Promised Land can be singularly an indication of final judgment, for that would mean that Moses himself is lost (Deut 1:37). So, this "judgment" cannot refer to final judgment any more than "innocent" can refer to innocence of original sin in Jer 19:4.

Judgment for "deeds in the body, according to what [one] has done, whether good or bad" (2 Cor 5:10) has a two-tiered explication. First, deeds done in the body simply evidence *to whom* one truly belongs.[98] Therefore, determination of whether one inherits the kingdom is rightly based on the evidenced reality (or lack thereof) of one's faith in the saving Christ (Jas 2:14–26). Secondly, that *measures* exist of both reward and punishment for deeds done in the body, whether by a child of God or a child of the devil, is biblical.[99] That there is also a separate, final judgment either unto eternal life or eternal condemnation is equally—and incontestably—biblical.[100]

96. Mohler and Akin, "Salvation of the 'Little Ones.'"
97. Ibid.
98. See Gen 22:15–18; Ezek 21:24; Matt 12:33–37; John 5:42; 8:42–44; 14:15; 1 John 3:6–10.
99. See 1 Sam 26:23 with Titus 3:5–8; Hos 12:2; Luke 6:37–38 with Matt 6:14–15; 11:22, 24; Luke 12:47–48; Rom 2:5–6; 2 Cor 11:13–15; Heb 10:29.
100. See Matt 13:40–43, 49–50; 25:46; John 5:25–29; Rom 3:3–6; 9:21–24; Rev 19:20; 20:12–15.

Argument from Silence

> The "good news" of the New Testament includes not only an announcement of the person of Christ and his work in our behalf, but a declaration of *how the benefits of Christ's work are appropriated* by, in, and for the *believer*.[101]

The New Testament heralds the good news of the vanquishing of death by Jesus Christ. Some of those not willing to embrace paedosoterism wholesale, take comfort by asserting that the grace and mercy of salvation obtained by Jesus Christ is sufficient to redeem the cognitively incompetent and even the "irresistibly" or "inculpably ignorant,"[102] or that the Bible is silent on the issue.[103] However, the Bible can be said, rightly, only to be *asymmetrically* silent on the issue. That is, it contains no unambiguous *pre*scriptive indications of condemned deceased pre-cognitives (barring Jonathan Edwards' formidable assertions above); but *de*scriptive indications of the state of humanity apart from the grace of God appropriated by faith is the Bible's core message.

Surely, one enters dangerous territory when one posits a means of appropriation of the accomplished work of Christ about which the Bible is purportedly "silent." Inclusivists and purveyors of the *pneumatological proposal*[104] and "wider mercy" make such a foray on similar grounds, through a

---

101. Sproul, *Faith Alone*, 18; emphasis added.

102. On inculpable ignorance, see Abbott, "Church's Missionary Activity," 593, where the dogma states, "Therefore though *God in ways known to Himself can lead those inculpably ignorant of the Gospel to find that faith without which it is impossible to please Him* (Heb 11:6), yet a necessity lies upon the Church (1 Cor 9:16), and at the same time a sacred duty, to preach the Gospel. And hence missionary activity today as always retains its power and necessity" (emphasis added). See also Pinnock, *Wideness*, 158, 179; and Shedd, "Westminster Standards," 121–36, where Shedd argues that "the great majority of mankind, not the small minority of it, will be the subjects of redeeming grace" based on principles such as: covenantal family relationships of believers, "regenerate infants" (123, 129–30), the "disposition" to believe of "elect persons who are incapable of being outwardly called by the ministry of the word" (134), and the presumption that "it is utterly improbable that such a stupendous miracle as the incarnation, humiliation, passion, and crucifixion of one of the Persons of the Godhead . . . should have a lame and impotent conclusion" (131).

103. Grudem, *Systematic Theology*, 500; Waldron, *1689 Baptist Confession*, 150; and Hubmaier, "Baptism of Believers," 140, where Hubmaier concedes, "I confess here publicly my ignorance. I am not ashamed not to know what God did not want to reveal to us with a clear and plain word."

104. Pinnock, *Flame of Love*, 192. This proposal suggests, "Christ represents particularity by being the only mediator between God and humanity (1 Tim 2:5–6), while Spirit upholds universality because no soul is beyond the sphere of the Spirit's operations. . . . Spirit is not confined to the church but is present everywhere, giving life and creating community." See also Pinnock, *Wideness*, 149–50, 153–55.

logical extrapolation of the interpretation of John 3:8 rendered by both the Westminster and Baptist Confessions of Faith.[105] Because the Spirit of God is sovereign, so is his grace—the argument goes. That is, the saving grace of the sovereign God cannot be constrained by any criteria, not even by the revealed "word of faith which we preach," "the word [that] is near you, in your mouth and in your heart," the word that one cannot hear unless one is sent; the word that one cannot believe unless he hears; the word that proclaims the name upon which one cannot call unless he believes (Rom 10:8–15). Again, because divine revelation is the basic epistemological axiom, positing a means of appropriation of the finished work of Christ alternative to that which has been disclosed by divine revelation is surely a dangerous employment of creaturely hubris.

Imagination Yields to Revelation

The concept is inconceivable that all that the Scriptures have to say about the fall and sinfulness of humanity and cosmic rebellion by the creation against the perfect Creator applies only to those who can understand it.[106] Only if humanity were *neutral* in this scheme, would the opposite be inconceivable; that is, to think that all that the Scriptures have to say about condemnation could apply to those who cannot understand why they are condemned. This inconceivability is the assertion of the paedosoterist. The premise fails, however, because (1) humanity is *not* neutral, and (2) justice from a holy God is against that which is unholy (Hab 1:13a), not primarily for the sake of the awareness of the vessel of wrath (Rom 9:22). Paedosoterist Webb argues,

> [If a deceased infant] were sent to hell on no other account than that of original sin, *there would be a good reason to the divine mind for the judgment*, but the child's mind would be a perfect blank as to the reason of its suffering. Under such circumstances, it would know suffering, but it would have no understanding of the reason for its suffering. It could not tell its neighbor—it could not tell itself—why it was so awfully smitten; and consequently the whole meaning and significance of its sufferings, being to it a

---

105. Westminster Confession of Faith, Chapter X, Section III; 1689 London Baptist Confession, Chapter X, Section III. John 3:8 is cited as a reference text for the Spirit of God moving salvificly *without* the use of means.

106. Ps 90:2; Prov 8:22–31; Jer 1:5; John 8:58 all communicate that unalterable truth pre-exists the circumstance and cognition of any creature.

conscious enigma, the very essence of penalty would be absent, and justice would be disappointed of its vindication.[107]

No wonder Charles Spurgeon considers a "miscreant" anyone "who would dare say that there were infants in hell."[108] The language used by both Webb and Spurgeon, however, must be evaluated not only in light of the genuinely sympathetic pathos of said miscreants, but also the man-honoring, revelation-ignoring human sensibilities mentioned in the above section entitled "Framing the Issue."[109] Additionally, the converse of Webb's argument could be posited with equal validity. Apart from a divine disclosure of such things to the creature, on what grounds would a child's mind be any less "a perfect blank as to the reason" of its gracious habitations, and thereby unprepared to glorify that Being which is not only infinitely worthy of such worship, but is also responsible for that deceased one's gracious state? Again, *divine revelation* must reign; not the most desirable *imagination* of the one making an argument.

The energy expended by divine revelation, Christ, his apostles, and church history on requisites for rescue from the curse cannot be dismissed for an entire class of fallen humans with the stroke of the simple phrase "unless they are cognitively incompetent." For then, a second class of humanity must, of necessity, be posited. If those who die prior to cognitive culpability are saved, they manifestly are granted separate status in the sovereign God's reckoning. Such reckoning represents a firm contradiction of Acts 10:34, Rom 2:11, Gal 2:6, and James 2:1, 4, 9.[110] Otherwise, some sort of *fides late dicta* or *fides virtualis* must be granted.[111] At best, what can be argued is that God graciously, sovereignly, somehow elects *some* of that group, or even that he elects *all* of that group—but not on the grounds that they are cognitively incompetent, nor that they are saved by grace through faith as

---

107. Webb, *Infant Salvation*, 288–89, quoted in Nash, *When a Baby Dies*, 64; and in MacArthur, *Safe*, 86; emphasis added.

108. Spurgeon, "Expositions of the Doctrines of Grace," 300, cited in MacArthur, *Safe*, 75.

109. See 167–68 above.

110. To be sure, the contexts of these passages regard hypocritical discrimination; however, the principle remains that God does not discriminate based upon respect for any characteristic of the creature. Paedosoterists must substantiate biblically, then, cognitive incompetence as a characteristic of the cursed creature that merits the divine discrimination of a differentiated grace.

111. *Fides late dicta* refers to faith in some broader sense than divinely revealed. *Fides virtualis* refers to a moral disposition virtually equivalent to the saving faith generated by the Holy Spirit in response to the special revelation of the gospel message.

conventionally understood[112] (which is a more challenging dilemma—indeed, possibly insurmountable).

If made, the hypothetical presumption[113] that deceased pre-cognitives are saved must be based not on any extant revelation—for none exists—but only on hope in the merciful, gracious, and compassionate character of the living God of life and death who created all things for his glory—the criteria for which is determined alone by the Judge of all the earth who will do right (Gen 18:25). Any creature beautified with salvation by God (Ps 149:4)—despite his just damnation of *any* other soul—will be compelled awfully to proclaim, "Blessed be the name of the Lord."

---

112. Here is where Piper's argument fails to be ultimately convincing. Although the compassion of God (upon those who lack the cognitive competence to exercise faith in Christ) is surely an attribute to which to look for just such a circumstance, apart from justification by faith alone in Jesus Christ, such compassion could not truthfully be considered an attribute of God, for it would contradict his holiness. An indeterminate or even posthumous appropriation of faith, then, would need to be presumed, which Piper affirms. Piper's non-revelatory hypothetical presumption (which he proffers in terms of more than a "guess") is that, "God in his justice will find a way to absolve infants who die of their depravity. It will surely be through Christ. But beyond that we would be guessing. It seems to me that the most natural guess would be that babies will grow up in the kingdom (either immediately, or over time) and will by God's grace come to faith so that their justification is by faith alone just like ours." See Perman, *What Happens to Infants Who Die?*

113. Cf. 186 and 182 n. 68 above.

CHAPTER 7

The Laud of God for His Ordinance of Death

Wise king Solomon asserted, "love is as strong as death" (Song 8:6). This wisest of all Israel's kings recognized that while every human would eventually succumb to death—because human *being* is neither necessary nor of ultimate value—death, too, possesses only *consequent* necessity, and is not ultimate in power. The God whose essence is love[1] designed and created both human life and the phenomenon of death (not to mention everything else that exists) as instruments for the display of his multifaceted glory and *necessary* Being. Neither human life nor death, then, can be construed as phenomena beyond the boundary of the sovereign living God's ordinance and purposes. Such construction would constitute an inaccurate understanding of reality for both immediate and any subsequent discussions tendered from such a false premise.

Further, because God is good and does (only) good (Ps 119:68), and he—as Sovereign Lord of the cosmos—does only as he pleases (Ps 115:3; Isa 46:9–11), and because he is incontestably worthy of the laud of his entire creation for all that he does (Ps 148), we human creatures, created in his image as his *magnum opus* for the express purpose of reflecting back to him (and to all of creation) the glory of his *life*, are obliged to herald his praise for *everything* he does, including death.[2]

---

1. One must be careful here not to assume that because love is constituent to God's nature—as are light and spirit (1 John 4:8, 16; 1:5; John 4:24)—that this quality precludes possession or exhibition of any or all of his concurrent "divine perfections."

2. For biblical examples of just such imperturbable laud of the God of life and death, see 2 Kgs 4:18–26; 2 Sam 12:15b–23; Job 1:21; 13:15; 42:1–6; cf. Lev 10:1–3; Ezek 24:15–27.

Summary and Concluding Theological Reflections

The preceding chapters have attempted to portray the contrast between the creature's extant antipathy toward death as an unfit and cosmically unjust phenomenon and the biblical articulation of the righteous exhibition of the glory of the holy and living God in his instrumental institution and ordering of death among a faithlessly treasonous creation. The divine fiat of death to decreate an originally "very good" creation is equal in irresistible authority and force to the fiat of creation *ex nihilo*. Indeed, the same Sovereign voice decreed and orders both. The scheme of the deceiver, who is the father of lies (John 8:44), is to disguise this truth at every turn, challenging, rather, whether God has indeed said so (Gen 3:1). The deceived, too, will suppress this truth in any number of ways, ultimately reimaging the God who has disclosed himself as one who will not acquit the guilty. Acknowledging the truth about the holy origin of death equips the creature with the imperturbable peace of Christ in the face of this last enemy.

The rebellion against the authority of God and the force of his command to his *magnum opus* to trust him alone as creation's Supreme Sustainer Provider is met in the Old Testament with the repeated refrain, "and he died" (Genesis 5). Herein is the promise of God established as sure among the creatures created in his image. God's promise to curse his pristine creation upon its rebellion is proven no idle threat. God's provision of *blessing* is clearly contrasted with the *curse* of his disfavor. Adam and even the very first generation of his offspring would come to understand clearly that the *blessing* of the living God entailed the provision of everything needed for the procreation and flourishing of life, while his disfavor was evidenced by the *curse* of death against all that is unholy. This contrast set the paradigm for the unfolding of God's self-disclosure in the Old Testament not only as Creator, but also as Judge and later, Redeemer.

The value of human life relative to the command of God was revealed from the very beginning of creation. The blessing of life for faithful obedience to God's ordinance was established in juxtaposition with the curse of death as exchange for indulging any ethic to the contrary. Because the living God possesses life intrinsically and because death conflicts with his intent to be *with* his magnum opus *in life*, the living God promised that his own faithfulness will extend to every generation of Adam's offspring (Ps 119:90). That is, despite the necessity of the curse of death, the only wise God has made provision for "the blessing—life forever" (Ps 133:3). The offspring of Adam in the Old Testament era, although captured by the enigma of death, were not abandoned by their Creator to exit "life under the sun" without a hope beyond death of some fortune with the living God. The covenant that this same God voluntarily established with the elect family of Abraham would assure, by sovereign grant, the living God's *blessing* for families from all of Adam's offspring (Gen 22:18; Rev 5:9). The Sovereign's original intent to be *with* his creature in the life he himself possessed could not be thwarted by the institution of the curse of death.

No offspring of Adam is exempt from the just curse of death adjudicated against him and all his posterity in solidarity with him. This judgment of death for all offspring of unholy Adam is just; the judgment of life is granted to those whom the last Adam judges, in accord with his good pleasure, in solidarity with himself.[3] The second person of the Trinity was "made like his brethren in all things" (Heb 2:17) for this express purpose of reversing the curse of death. This addition of human nature to the eternally divine person, Immanuel—God with us—marks the judgment-worthy dispensability of human nature as *nonessential* being and simultaneously dignifies its immeasurable value as the brand upon creation of the Creator's own identity as necessary Being. The execution of each and every death, then, is an exhibition of the holiness of the righteous Judge who both promised and forewarned such judgment. Failure to execute that judgment would render unholy the holy God who can judge in no manner other than righteously.[4] To expect such dereliction of justice is to humanize the Creator and deify the creature (Rom 1:18–23). The creature is obliged, rather, in each such exhibition to laud the good and holy God for the righteous execution of his glorious good pleasure, despite any difficulty the myopic creature may have in reconciling either the goodness or the justice of such an act, which ought to be rather unsurprising.

The New Testament reveals that the self-disclosure of the living God and his purposes for the created order was, in the Old Testament, "little by little."[5] The Old Testament's "ministry of death, in letters engraved on stones, came with glory." "The ministry of the Spirit" of life, however, comes with "even more with glory. For if the ministry of condemnation has glory, much more does the ministry of righteousness abound in glory" (2 Cor 3:7–9). The Old Testament revelation of God and his purposes—glorious as it was—left the enigma of death unresolved. The closing of this chapter of the human saga was intentionally incomplete (Heb 4:8; 11:39–40), however, so that the progressed revelation of the living God in the New Testament could inaugurate the spectacle of the kingdom of God by means of the van-

---

3. John 5:21–29; 1 John 5:11–13, 20; cf. Rom 9:14–18.

4. Gen 18:25; Pss 7:11; 9:8; 45:6; 96:13; 98:9; Jer 11:20; 1 Pet 2:23; Rev 19:2, 11.

5. The Greek word in Heb 1:1, πολυμερως, may be translated "*little by little.*" See Nestle, *Novum Testamentum Graece*, 146–7; Bauer, BAGD, s. v. "πολυμερως."

quishing of death and the reversal of the curse by the conquering Lord of Life, Immanuel, Jesus Christ. Indeed, the entrance of Immanuel in the New Testament was as "foreknown before the foundation of the world" (1 Pet 1:20–21) as was the entrance of death in the Old Testament. "Oh, the depth of the riches both of the wisdom and knowledge of God! How unsearchable are his judgments and unfathomable his ways!" (Rom 11:33)

The depth of riches and unfathomable ways of the living God that prompted the apostle Paul to interject such doxology in his prose epistle to the Romans is the same otherworldly origin that sustained the early Church Militant's faithful witnesses as they faced tortuous deaths by the hand of Romans. These martyrs are exemplars of affirming the ordinance of God above the value of their own lives. The apostle Peter had warned, "For you have been called for this purpose, since Christ also suffered for you, leaving you an example for you to follow in His steps" (1 Pet 2:21). These faithful witnesses to Truth attested with their own blood their devotion to the ordinance of God above the value of their own lives. Being grounded in the unfathomable riches of God's divine revelation, they joyfully surrendered their loaned lives in imitation of the sufferings of their God. The contemporary church would do well to glean wisdom, strength, and encouragement from these exemplars whose testimonies were recorded "for our instruction, upon whom the ends of the ages have come" (1 Cor 10:11).

The record of death's reign among Adam's offspring was generated, in part, so that the glory of the living God might radiate to the creature for his own good, "though he slay me" (Job 13:15). Adam, on his own behalf and that of all his posterity, was duly forewarned concerning the curse of death (Gen 2:17). This warning bore irrevocable and universal significance. The providence of death occurs nowhere beyond the divine appointment of the sovereign God of the Bible. At this juncture of the holy God's sovereignty and the reality of indiscriminate death, one encounters some of divine revelation's most difficult sayings. No matter how difficult the scenario, however, in light of the forewarned expectation, the creation is obliged to render praise to whom praise is due for the exhibition of his integrity and holy splendor. The utterances of the creature, in the presence of the God whose holy "eyes are too pure to approve evil" and "cannot look upon wickedness" (Hab 1:13) and will not acquit the guilty (Exod 23:7; 34:7; Nah 1:3), ought rather to resonate with Aaron as he "kept silent" in the face of the deaths of his two unholy sons (Lev 10:3), with Job as he heralded the blessedness of the Lord who both gives and takes away life as he deems right (Job 1:21), with Abraham as he acknowledges that the Judge of all the earth will deal justly (Gen 18:25), and with the Shunammite woman as she confidently asserts "it is well," despite her only son's having died on her lap only hours before (2 Kgs 4:26).[6] Life does not belong to the creature essentially to worship as he sees fit; it is the grant of the God who possesses life in himself and who graciously gives and rescinds the gift as he deems right. No creature may deign to challenge his divine decree against that which is unholy by saying to him, "What are you doing?"[7] Rather, any creature beautified with God's gracious salvation will for all eternity proclaim, "Blessed be the name of the LORD from this time forth and forever" (Ps 113:2)!

The Justice of God in His Ordinance of Death

"The soul that on Jesus doth lean for repose"[8] views death not with a haughty contempt, but as a just ordinance of God for which he is to be lauded. To be sure, death is both unnatural and an enemy by virtue of its being in diametric opposition to the living God's original design for (living) man to be near him.[9] However, that designed opposition is equally ordained by the very same God. Death is the prescribed contagion of any creature that rejects its only source of life; what else would one expect? Adam certainly could not have expected otherwise, for he was duly forewarned (Gen 2:17). So, he had no reason to hold in contempt anyone or anything, except himself, for the consequence of his self-centered distrust of his perfect Provider who had given him no reason whatsoever to distrust him. (Mind you, lest we go too far in our indictment of Adam, we may contemplate the implications of the identical assertion for ourselves![10])

---

6. The account recorded in 2 Kings 4 depicts a variety of the woman's emotions as well as her immediate pursuit of Yahweh's prophet and his subsequent resurrection of her son; nevertheless, her faith in the God who provided her unrequested son equipped her to affirm "it is well," even before she had any awareness that her son would be restored to her.

7. Job 9:12; Eccl 8:4; Isa 45:9; Rom 9:20.

8. The opening line of the sixth and final stanza of the hymn "How Firm a Foundation."

9. Thielicke, *Death and Life*, 105–14. Death is not a natural part of the human experience. Rather, it is an actuality only in a post-Genesis 3:6 world. Thielicke convincingly argues, "In biblical thought human death is simply unnatural. At no time and in no place is it the expression of any sort of normality of nature, as if it signified the necessary ebb in the rhythm of life. Death is rather the expression of a catastrophe which runs on a collision course with man's original destination or, in other words, directly opposite to his intrinsic nature." Thielicke concludes accurately, therefore, "Death is unnatural since it most assuredly conflicts with man's original destiny to be near God; for wherever God is, there life reigns, not death." See also chap. 2 of the current work.

10. See Prov 19:3 for the Bible's affirmation of this truth applicable to all sinners.

Helmut Thielicke describes the unnaturalness of death—the inexorable repercussion of sin.

> Death really is unnatural. Death ought not to be. But insofar as it nevertheless is, it constitutes only the symptom of a much deeper unnaturalness, namely, that we have torn ourselves loose from God, that we are no longer in the Father's house (Luke 15:11 ff.), and that we have thus alienated ourselves from our intrinsic nature of being God's children.[11]

Thielicke then notes that the biblical articulation of death is not limited to the *fact* of man's death. It also addresses the *why*. Only death[12] can sufficiently evidence the gravity of the disorder between holy God and unholy man.[13] The creature's biolatrous disdain for his just punishment, then, only further evidences the depth of his rebellion and sin's disorder (cf. Gen 4:6-7, 13). In this vein Thielicke continues, "For it is impossible to hold anything in contempt unless I can degrade that thing and elevate myself above it. And this is precisely what happens in contempt for death, which is blasphemy and hubris."[14] On the other hand, the humble, yielding creature will trust the good will of the righteous Lord, "though he slay me" (Job 13:15).

Thielicke further elaborates how this submissive disposition both honors the justice of God in the ordinance of death and serves to order godly the life of the one who has faith in Jesus (cf. Pss 39:4; 90:12; 1 John 3:2-3).

> Since death is a verdict of God upon our life, it then also qualifies the entire course of this life. Death is not the terminal point of life, but a qualifying characteristic of life. Consequently I am not living in the truth unless in my awareness of death I relate my entire life to the action of God manifest in my dying.
>
> On this basis contempt for death is forbidden whether it arises from defiance or ignorant security. I am not to elevate myself contemptuously above death and its author; I am attentively to acknowledge it and submit myself to it. Only in this way do I allow for the fact that there is nothing (myself included) that is greater than God, on the basis of which I might nourish the hope of overcoming his blow and his punishment. Only God himself can heal the wounds which he has inflicted; only God's love is greater than his wrath.[15]

---

11. Thielicke, *Death and Life*, 113.
12. See 57 n. 57 above.
13. Thielicke, *Death and Life*, 131–32.
14. Ibid., 157–58.
15. Thielicke, *Death and Life*, 161. Cf. also Song 8:6.

In unison with Thielicke, the psalmist Moses faithfully prophesied the mind of God concerning the wisdom of regularly contemplating one's own finitude and ineluctable death as a gracious effectual means of sanctification of the life one lives *coram Deo*. Moses prayed, "So teach us to number our days, that we may present to you a heart of wisdom" (Ps 90:12).

Martin Luther's grasp on the nature of death well informs Thielicke's articulation. Luther comments on the misstep of leaders as they have instructed contempt for death—a misstep that, unfortunately, many a leader in our own day unwittingly repeats.

> Both Gentiles and monks have indeed said a great deal about the need of scorning death. But what they said was wrong. As a result of such prattle men become either hardened sinners or blasphemers, since they discard all reverence for God, become angry with Him, and regard Him to be a tyrant, who for no reason whatever abandons man, this poor creature, to death.[16]

Sagely, Luther here corrects and dismisses the charge of the one who, in unrighteous indignation, impugns the goodness or justice of God in ordaining the death of anyone at any age.

Admonition Concerning a Proper Disposition toward Death

Two thousand years removed from the incarnation and earthly sojourn of the Lord of life and death—the One who displayed his unassailable lordship by healing the infirmed, raising the dead, and presenting himself as the firstborn from the dead—contemporary culture has departed from some of the more valiant attitudes toward death exhibited by our early siblings.[17]

---

16. Luther, *LW*, 13:98, cited in Thielicke, *Death and Life*, 158.

17. See chap. 5. Beyond the attitudes toward death precipitated by the persecution in the early Church Militant, contemplation of death and dying was compelled by the most significant loss of life of the medieval period, which has come to be known as the Black Death (ca. 1348–1400)—a milestone that some suggest is the dividing marker between the Middle Ages and the Renaissance. See Cohn, "Place of the Dead," 21.

Because the Black Death decimated regions of what is now Europe—in some cases claiming half of cities' populations—the post-plague population came to identify with death in multifaceted ways—some constructive, some *macabre* (a word which itself first appeared in France ca. 1376; see Boase, *Death in the Middle Ages*, 104). Commenting on the permeating effect of the Black Death on medieval culture, historian Johan Huizinga asserts, "No other epoch has laid so much stress as the expiring Middle Ages on the thought of death. An everlasting call of *memento mori* resounds through life . . . The medieval soul demands the concrete embodiment of the perishable: that of the putrefying corpse." Huizinga, *Waning of the Middle Ages*, 124, cited in Binski, *Medieval Death*, 130.

Paul Helm assesses candidly the contemporary pathos concerning death and dying.

> The modern western attitude to dying and death is all too obvious. It is to avoid it, to avoid mentioning it, and where mention of it is unavoidable, to use euphemisms and circumlocutions . . .[18]

By so regarding this defeated enemy, we follow our unholy father, Adam, and believe the lie of bondage to fear of death, while suppressing the truth that God has proclaimed irrevocably *in Son* (Heb 1:2; 2:15)—namely, that perfect love has appeared to destroy the works of the devil and cast out fear (1 John 3:8; 4:18). The gracious self-disclosure of God's divine power has granted to us "every spiritual blessing in the heavenlies in Christ" (Eph 1:3), including "everything pertaining to life and godliness, through the true knowledge of him who called us by his own glory and excellence" (2 Pet 1:3). The revealed knowledge of the resident enemy, death, included in the divine self-disclosure, enables sons and daughters of Adam and Eve to subdue death's debilitating power and know it as the now disempowered

---

The impact on the culture's social, religious, economic, and political structures was immeasurable. As a result of the mass population drop, feudal structures and oligarchies were realigned and/or abrogated, agriculture prices dropped, wages rapidly increased, and the period unavoidably experienced an unprecedented redistribution of wealth (Binski, 127–29). Social upheaval, the brevity of life, and the realization of a very real possibility of sudden death precipitated an inescapable contemplative sobriety. Not only was the sanctity of life elevated by those who did manage to survive another day, but an acceptance of the temporal nature of that which was abundantly clearly subjected to futility (cf. Rom 8:20–21; 2 Cor 3:10–11) now permeated every thought and prayer. From the presence of the body of a recently expired loved one in the home, to the frequency of funeral processions, living with death became a common experience for all; see Daniell, *Death and Burial*, 2. Concerning the deceased, St. Bernard of Clairvaux (d. 1153) was among the first to promulgate the theme, "What I am, they were, and what they are, I will be," which became a common burial epitaph during the plague era (Binski, 132). Such clichés of death, no doubt, caused many to contemplate the brevity of their own lives, and thus, the manner of their own dying and what would come after.

18. Helm, *Last Things*, 35–36; see also Carson, *How Long*, 116–20; and Anderson, *Theology, Death and Dying*, 116–25. Helm continues his keen assessment of our culture's dismissal of *memento mori*: "An emphasis upon such aspects of the biblical teaching [about death; e.g., living daily in light of the very real potential of one's own sudden entrance into eternity] will be thought by many to be macabre, but only by those who have been inoculated by modern culture into postponing the thought of one's death. Yet such an attitude is not a distinctively twentieth-century one but is characteristic of anyone who is preoccupied with this life to the virtual exclusion of what may follow" (Helm, 40). That preoccupation with this life is precisely the biolatry asserted in the thesis of this work.

prisoner of war that the Savior of the world died to make it so. The consequence of adopting such a transformed pathos is the provision of liberty to release a covetous hold of the present life in exchange for an unimpeded life of conscious glad anticipation that death can bring only gain. Such a pathos of *memento mori* and *contemptu mundi*, contrary to "the modern western attitude," has the ability to equip the families of Adam for warlike engagement of gospel proclamation without idolatrous concern for self. Such an army of faithful witnesses can—as it has done in ages past—transform this world by emanating the splendor of the holy and living God throughout his dominion.

Fear not! For the one who possesses confidence in the reality that the sovereign God who created all things from nothing has an equally firm command—just as effortlessly—over every occurrence of death, enslavement to the fear of death no longer has any force. Christ has "rendered powerless him who had the power of death, that is, the devil" (Heb 2:14–15). Death no longer possesses a sting (1 Cor 15:55–56).[19] Further, a biblical (i.e., "God's-eye") view of human death rests the problem of evil because the view does not idolize human life as something more than a creation of God designed, generated, and sustained by him for his good purposes, and not primarily for the benefit (in *any* particular sense) of the human creature. The grievous sadness, then, that frequently accompanies death, that supposes that a monstrous injustice is done, can be ingratiatingly superseded by a peace that surpasses all mournful woe. Life does not have to be clutched with such idolatrous devotion.

As with any battle, the best strategy for engaging an enemy is not to wait until one is attacked, but rather to be in perpetual readiness for inevitable confrontation with a known and advancing enemy. The candidate for death (or bereavement), having been furnished with "everything pertaining to life and godliness" (2 Pet 1:3), ought to be in perpetual preparation "to encounter the one coming against him" (Luke 14:28–33). The optimal time to theologize about death is not at the gravesite; for that is the time and place to console. As C. S. Lewis compassionately counsels, "When pain is to be borne, a little courage helps more than much knowledge, a little human sympathy more than courage, and the least tincture of the love of God more than all."[20] The recipient of such consolation, if also established with

---

19. Thielicke, *Living with Death*, 165. Of Christ's death—rather than the death of the first Adam—being prototypical for the believer, and of the loss of the sting of death, Thielicke writes, "To be sure, death is still there, as the sinner in fact is still there, but only as a mask with no authority or power, like a snake that has lost its fangs, so that it is still a snake but has no power as such."

20. Lewis, *Problem of Pain*, xi.

a proper *memento mori*, will be well equipped to bless the Lord for the full counsel of his divine ordinance.

Even though death is an unwelcome intrusion into the created order, because it remains under the dominion of God (Deut 32:39; 2 Kgs 5:7; Rev 1:18), facets of it exist that even God deems valuable. Although God "takes no pleasure in the death of the wicked" (Ezek 18:23; 33:11), and a sense exists in which he has "no pleasure in the death of anyone who dies" (Ezek 18:32), he declares, "precious in the sight of the Lord is the death of his saints" (Ps 116:15). That is, for the one who consummates his judgment of death *in Christ*, not only is a crown of righteousness and life laid-up for him (2 Tim 4:8; Jas 1:12; Rev 2:10), but also a mutually joyous reconciliation with his God (John 17:20–24; Luke 15:20–24; Zeph 3:17) where pleasures forevermore await him (Ps 16:11). Additionally, for the one who delights in bearing the image of God in truth, not only does the "preciousness" of death conclude the pains and evils of this life (Isa 57:1–2), but it also makes and end of sins and vices as the saint's sanctification is consummated in glorification (Phil 3:21). In this freeing regard to death, Martin Luther poignantly comments:

> And this renders death far more desirable to believing souls . . . than the former blessing [i.e., escape from the tragedy of this world's ills]; . . . This alone, did we but know it, should make death most desirable. But if it does not, it is a sign that we neither feel nor hate our sin as we should. For this our life is so full of perils—sin, like a serpent, besetting us on every side—and it is impossible for us to live without sinning; but fairest death delivers us from these perils, and cuts our sin clean away from us.[21]

Oh glorious redemptive day! (Eccl 7:1b)

Ars Moriendi

One who possesses a balanced view of both the sanctity of human life as an invaluable gift from its gracious Giver and simultaneously its genuine dispensability as nonessential being may both live and die well. The tenor of Holy Scripture concerning "how should we then live" is that all of temporal life should be oriented in light of its end. Regular, godward contemplation of one's death is invaluably instructive for how one is to live in this present age and how one may die well.

---

21. Luther, "Fourteen of Consolation," 1:149, cited in Kerr, *Compend of Luther's Theology*, 241.

Contemplation of One's Own End

Gregory the Great wrote, "He will greatly rouse himself to doing good works who always bears in mind his end."[22] The ninth resolution of Jonathan Edwards reads, "Resolved, to think much on all occasions of my own dying, and of the common circumstances which attend death."[23] The psalmist Moses prayed, "So teach us to number our days that we may present to you a heart of wisdom" (Ps 90:12). For millennia the thoughtful, wise, and inspired have admonished the living to contemplate the ineluctable reality of death. None of these sages, however, had in mind a morbid, vitality-sapping, and neurotic obsession with the darkness of death. No, each of them counseled that in order to live fully and intentionally the existence one was created to live—as the image of the living God—one must learn how to die well; for death, as part and parcel of the (fallen) human experience, is variously and immeasurably instructive of life—designedly so.

Because each of us, without exception, will eventually succumb to death, and because the life we have been granted so graciously is not our own, we ought to "lift up the cup of salvation and call upon the name of the Lord" and pour-out our invested lives "as a drink offering."[24] The life consumed upon the self is one most miserable and vacuous. The life returned to its Giver, however, receives a hundred fold the riches it has yielded.[25]

Familiarity with the biblical articulation of the God-ordained origin, justice, and purpose of death is the only means of equipping one to countenance well this ordinance. Only in biblical Scripture is the enigma of death truthfully exposed and vanquished by the living God of life and death, himself, in his incarnate Son. One may die well only in the knowledge that the very cause of death—sin—has been expiated by God the Father's unleashing of his holy and infinite wrath against the sin of the world upon his unique Son, who singularly is qualified to propitiate such wrath, and who, on the cross, "tasted death" (Heb 2:9) on behalf of those whom the Father had given to him, such that he faithfully "guarded them and not one of them perished" (John 17:6–12). No death outside of this divinely revelatory construct can truthfully be considered "dying well."

The reality of being present with and aware of Christ after death is good news for all those "who through fear of death were subject to slavery all their lives" (Heb 2:15). The sufferings of the curse of death in this

---

22. Shinners, "Art of Dying Well," 525.
23. Edwards, "Resolutions," 1.lxii.
24. Ps 116:12–19; Matt 25:19–23, 29; 2 Tim 4:6–8.
25. Mark 10:37–39; 16:24–27; 19:27–29; Luke 12:16–34; Phil 2:17; Jas 4:3–10.

present time will be proven unworthy to be compared with the benefits of "the blessing—life forever" (Ps 133:3): absence of conflict, pride, injury, and grief; eternal and unwaning vitality; warranted and unguarded perfect transparency; perpetually satiating sustenance; fathomless universal and mutual uninterrupted love unending; "the impossibility of sinning as a gift from God" as the immediate product of becoming a "partaker of God's nature"—to which belongs the inability to sin;[26] all *coram Deo*. Indeed, "this alone, did we but know it, should make [fairest] death most desirable."[27]

Sixteenth-century Protestant *ars moriendi* were apt to recognize this stark contrast between the sufferings of the present time and the glories to be revealed in us. These handbooks on dying well provided pastoral instruction concerning the assurance of salvation and confidence in the forgiveness of sins based on one's hope in the atoning death of Christ alone. Martin Luther, for example, in his *Eyn Sermon von der bereytung zum sterben* [A sermon on preparing to die][28]—this was the first Reformation *ars moriendi*—encouraged the dying Christian to receive joyfully and by faith three deathbed sacraments—confession, the body of Christ, and unction. Such joyful reception of the sacraments was intended to signify that Christ's victory of the power of death, sin, and hell is also the Christian's victory. Luther further sought to encourage the believer's confidence that through Christ's passion, the salvation and life of the former would be eternally secured.[29] The joyful image bearer of God, who would thus "thynke on the passion of Cryste,"[30] when meeting his temporal end, was assured that his sins were forgiven and that he could now die, literally, in peace. He could now die well.

---

26. Augustine, *City of God*, 22:30.

27. Luther, "Fourteen of Consolation," 6:150.

28. Luther, "Preparing to Die," 42:95–115. The term "sermon" refers to various genres of work, not merely a preached sermon manuscript. Here, it is more akin to a position paper. Citing Susanne Dähn, Austra Reinis writes, "for Luther 'Sermon' was a term encompassing, but not limited to, 'Predigt.' While 'Predigt' was the term for a sermon delivered orally, 'Sermon' could be either a 'Predigt' or the thematic exposition of a particular theological problem. According to Dähn, for Luther a 'Sermon' is in most cases a written form of instruction. It is characterized by a clear structure, understandable language and logical argument. It does not use the scholarly argumentation of a treatise, since the addressees are laypeople, both educated and uneducated." See Reinis, *Reforming*, 13.

29. Reinis, *Reforming*, 47–49.

30. Atkinson, "Crafte and Knowledge For To Dye Well," 5:11. See also Shinners, "Art of Dying Well," 526; Reinis, *Reforming*, 35–40; Comper, *Craft of Dying*, 23, 93–94.

Puritan Theology

As the Middle Ages gave way to the Renaissance and the Protestant Reformation, many of the more macabre obsessions with death and dying were exchanged for less fanciful notions of the afterlife and a more gospel-centered preparation for the life to come by means of a godly life in the present age. To be sure, contemplation of death remained common because its occurrence remained common. Rather than the anguish of deathbed torments[31] and fears of judgment depicted in the *Ars moriendi*, more complex perspectives of death and dying began to appear. Puritan theology embraced "three patently true and quite rational beliefs": the omnipotence, justice, and inscrutability of God; the radical and unalterable depravity of man; and the unspeakable terrors of Hell.[32] Consequently, a self-effacing humility—even doubt—concerning individuals' salvation accompanied their contemplations of their own deaths. If a dying one evidenced no "woeful apprehensions of death" but rather appeared to be "indulging [himself] in a stupid secure frame [i.e., confidence or security of one's own redemption],"[33] one's salvation was believed to be less secure than one who did so wrestle. Moreover, whereas the *Ars moriendi*, in its focus on the manner of dying, facilitated the possibility of a disparate detachment of one's death from the character of one's life, the constant tension between security and doubt of one's salvation—on the Puritan scheme—provided little or no such hope of deathbed conversions. Cotton Mather would write concerning such deathbed pursuits of repentance (cf. Heb 12:17), "There is no Real Conversion in it. . . . Men are then only like Iron softened in the Fire; they soon Return to their former Hardness if God spare them from going down into the *Unquenchable* Fire."[34]

This trepidation concerning one's preparedness to die was paradoxically mingled with a *contemptu mundi*.[35] Ecclesiastes 7:1 would characterize

---

31. The *Ars moriendi* instructed the dying (and those ministering to him) concerning a variety of demons that would engage the dying in the *agonies of death* on his deathbed. The demons would press the person with the "greatest and most grievous temptations, and such as they have never had before in all their life." The areas in which the dying would be tempted were faith, despair, impatience, complacence/ vainglory, and avarice. See Comper, *Craft of Dying*, 9–21; and Stannard, *Puritan Way*, 84.

32. Stannard, *Puritan Way*, 89.

33. Hoar, *Sting of Death*, 3–4, cited in Stannard, *Puritan Way*, 81.

34. Mather, *Thoughts of a Dying Man*, 40–41, cited in Stannard, *Puritan Way*, 87–88.

35. Ralph Waldo Emerson writes, however, concerning his aunt Mary Moody Emerson's rather strange obsession with death: "For years she had her bed made in the form of a coffin . . ." Further, "She made up her [burial] shroud, and death still refusing

the era's pathos, asserting, "The day of one's death is better than the day of one's birth."[36] Similarly, John Collins would console, "Death is only sweetened to us as we can look upon it our priviledge; as an out-let from sin and misery, and an in-let to *Glory* both in Holiness and Happiness."[37]

The Puritan community esteemed the group higher than the individual.[38] Communities were commonly so intimately interwoven that the entire community viewed itself as having "contracted a 'social covenant' with God by which they promised strict obedience to his laws. Failure to obey on the part of any individuals within the community—even children[39]—could

---

to come, and she thinking it a pity to let it lie idle, wore it as a night-gown, or a day-gown, nay, went out to ride in it, on horseback, in her mountain roads, until it was worn out. Then she had another made up, and as she never traveled without being provided for this dear and indispensable contingency, I believe she wore out a great many." See Emerson, "Mary Moody Emerson," 544, 563, cited in Stannard, *Puritan Way*, 167.

36. Stannard, *Puritan Way*, 80, 88; see also Comper, *Craft of Dying*, 6.

37. Collins, "To the Reader," 4–5, cited in Stannard, *Puritan Way*, 76.

38. Roger Bastide has well noted that characteristic pathos of the colonists was to "think in terms of 'We' rather than 'I.'" This sense of community among the early American Puritan community tended to represent more closely the biblical articulation of fellowship. See Bastide, "Messianism and Social Economic Development," 470, cited in Stannard, *Puritan Way*, 170.

39. While the mortality rates of seventeenth- and eighteenth-century New England were not as catastrophic as the late medieval period, death remained a common—albeit unwelcomed—guest. Sadly, the mortality rate of children and infants was even higher than that of adults. During the period of 1640–1759, more than one child in four failed to see his tenth birthday in a community with an average births-per-family rate of 8:8. The statistical low for that generation has been figured at a 63 percent rate of survival to age ten. A young couple embarking upon marriage at that time, then, would do so with the grim anticipation that, in all probability, two or three of their children would die before reaching the age of ten. See Stannard, *Puritan Way*, 55–56.

The families of Puritan figures Samuel Sewall and Cotton Mather serve as examples. Both men fathered fourteen children. "One of Sewall's was stillborn, several died as infants, several more as young adults. Seven Mather babies died shortly after delivery, one died at two years and six survived to adulthood, five of whom died in their twenties. Only two Sewall children outlived their father, while Samuel Mather was the only child to survive [his father] Cotton." See Thomas, *Diary of Samuel Sewall*, 1:592; Thomas, *Diary of Cotton Mather*, 380–82, cited in Stannard, *Puritan Way*, 56.

Stannard therefore counsels us, "When the Puritan parent urged on his children what we would consider a painfully early awareness of sin and death, it was because the well-being of the child and the community *required* such an early recognition of these matters" (Stannard, 60). Indeed, not only adults, but also children were continually warned to escape the present evil age by fleeing to their only source of hope, a life of faith in Jesus Christ. Because child mortality rates were so high, children were not shielded from the realities of their own mortality; they, too, were exhorted to "remember Death; think much of death; think how it will be on a death bed;" or instructed by their pastor, in an address particularly to them, to "Go into *Burying*-Place, CHILDREN; you will there see *Graves* as short as your selves. Yea, you may be at *Play* one Hour;

result in the venting of God's wrath on the entire community" with any number of consequences, natural or personal—death included.⁴⁰

Signals from *Ars Moriendi* for Today's Living

Just as *ars moriendi* evolved from the thirteenth to the eighteenth centuries, so may the *art of dying* in our own day equip the saints both to live and die to the greater glory of the Lord of life and death (Deut 32:39).

The communion of the saints. The unity of the community is paramount for any godly exercise of dying well. While personal faith in Christ certainly was exercised by each individual believer, the believers in the early church were not merely members of a voluntary society;⁴¹ they were in *fellowship* with one another as the Holy Spirit constituted church of Jesus Christ. N. T. Wright captures well the sense of the biblical term "fellowship" in his commentary on the apostle Paul's use of the term in his letter to the Philippian church.

> As with some of Paul's other key terms, this word has often been allowed, in the history of interpretation, to slide into referring simply to the way in which Christians feel toward and with one another; but for Paul it was severely practical. It meant a sharing in common life that resulted directly in mutual support; and also

---

Dead, Dead the next." Even Jonathan Edwards candidly instructed a group of children, "I know you will die in a little time, some sooner than others. 'Tis not likely you will all live to grow up." Further, James Janeway's children's instructional book *A Token for Children* was intended for the very purpose of reminding children "of the ever-nearness of death and its possible consequences. It may have been exceeded in popularity only by the *New England Primer*" from which many early American children learned the alphabet. See Morison, "Book of Joseph Green," 204; Mather, *Perswasions from the Terror of the Lord*, 35; Fleming, *Children and Puritanism*, 100; all cited in Stannard, *Puritan Way*, 65–66, 68.

40. Stannard, *Puritan Way*, 69.

41. Michael Jinkins chastens the free church notion of the church as a voluntary society. He writes, "This description of the church stands in profound contrast to the biblical description of the church. The New Testament does not describe a church as a voluntary society. It certainly does not assume the kind of 'like-mindedness' necessary for the banding together of a voluntary society. Instead, in the New Testament, one finds very contrary people summoned together by the Word who overrides, but ultimately does not minimize, their differences. Indeed, the New Testament glories in the plurality and diversity of gifts and perspectives that the Spirit gives to the various 'members' of the 'Body.'" See Jinkins, *Church Faces Death*, 97, cited in Allison, *Sojourners and Strangers*, 131.

it meant that Paul and his supporters belonged to one another with a family identity. What happens to one, happens to all.[42]

This familial intimacy among the household of faith was part and parcel of the biblical family identity. Because of the close community relationships of each member of the "tribe," as it were, what happened to one—e.g., death—happened to all. That is, the death of one member of the faith community was not an isolated event that garnered the attention of only the immediate family of the deceased (if such a family had even survived), and only for the moment of the announcement, only then to be promptly filed away as history in order to make room for more relevant current events. No, the community gathered around the dying in full acknowledgement of his human personhood in solidarity with the rest of the community.

Such communion naturally aids in providing what Ray Anderson calls a human ecology of death and dying.[43] Instead of a transition from this life to the next characterized by reflection on what it means to be a human being created in the image of and for the purposes of God, our contemporary setting resembles more of a "technological womb" where there is even "an umbilical cord which connects both patient and healer to a 'third force' which powers up the life-preserving apparatus."[44] The ecology of human death and dying is a theological concern "because it is fundamentally a human concern and a concern for the dignity of human personhood through the experience of death."[45] More precisely, a human ecology of death and dying means that "human life is a co-responsibility which includes the death of one another as part of that mutuality of concern."[46]

The cohesiveness of the community provides for the esteeming of the death of one as an impact and responsibility of all. Such *community* has significantly dissipated in our contemporary setting, significantly leaving individuals isolated.[47]—which itself is a product of the decreation of death.

---

42. Wright, "Philippians," 135, cited in Allison, *Sojourners and Strangers*, 444.
43. Anderson, *Theology, Death and Dying*, 143–45.
44. Ibid., 144.
45. Ibid.
46. Ibid., 148.
47. See Allison, *Sojourners and Strangers*, 304, where he writes of the "exaggerated autonomy promoted by rugged American individualism"; and Horton, *People and Place*, 170–171, where Horton writes of the "contractual ecclesiology" of the twenty-first century West; Harper and Metzger, *Exploring Ecclesiology*, 39–45, where the authors write of the West's "contractual model of human identity"; and Hellerman, *When the Church Was a Family*, 206, where Hellerman writes, "Social anthropologists refer to modern America as a weak-group society where the needs, goals, and desires of the individual come first. Personal allegiance to the group—whether that group is my

David Stannard correctly assesses the ill effects of this isolation, asserting that we currently live in a culture "in which virtually every individual can be replaced with such facility that his absence deeply affects at best only his most intimate relations. In a world bereft of ultimate meaning either in life or in death—in which neither the community of the living nor the vision of a mystical but literal afterlife any longer provides solace—modern man, in the face of death, has been forced to choose between the alternatives of outright avoidance or a secularized masquerade."[48] Fortunately, however, divine revelation debriefs intelligence regarding the enemy death such that, beyond these limited two options, offspring of Adam may heed the revealed truth of a biblical portrait of death and practice rightly and faithfully an ethic of valuing the dignity of human life and death in community.

Confident that the penalty of death had been vanquished by Christ, Luther recognized that, in one sense, each believer must face death alone; yet in another sense the dying believer, all the while, is never separated from the communion of the saints—the church. He wrote, "The summons of death comes to us all, and no one can die for another. Everyone must fight his own battle with death by himself alone. . . . I will not be with you then, nor you with me."[49] On the other hand, Luther acknowledged, "If I die, then I am not alone in death; if I suffer they [the fellowship] suffer with me."[50] In accord with N. T. Wright's assessment of fellowship, noted above, "what happens to one happens to all." Luther further admonished that "all the members of the communion of the saints get involved not only in offering advice, but also in actively helping the dying person: 'There is no doubt, as the sacrament of the altar indicates, that all of these in a body

---

family, my church, my co-workers, or a civic organization of some sort—is a secondary consideration. We tend to view the groups in our lives in a rather utilitarian way. These broader social entities serve as resources that we as individuals draw on in order to realize our own goals and to navigate our personal pathways through life."

48. Stannard, *Puritan Way*, 194. Stannard pointedly observes, "One of the most deeply disturbing facts of modern life—one that poets and novelists and philosophers and theologians never tire of discussing—is the apparent anonymity and simple unimportance of the individual; except in the most intimate of relationships, few men or women can ever regard themselves or anyone else as truly unique and irreplaceable"; see 189–90. See also Thielicke, *Death and Life*, 111, where he writes concerning the irreplaceableness of the individual, "The more intimately I am bound to another human being, the more icily and disruptively his death touches me. The well-known psychological effect on me when a close friend dies is but a testimony and reflection of a much more profound reality, namely, the fact that something unique and irreplaceable—or more precisely, something for which there is no substitute—has been destroyed."

49. Luther, *LW*, 51:70, cited in Bonhoeffer, *Life Together*, 77; and Thielicke, *Death and Life*, 158.

50. Luther, *LW*, 51:70, cited in Bonhoeffer, *Life Together*, 77.

run to him as one of their own, help him overcome sin, death and hell, and bear all things with him.'"[51] In Luther's mind, death was not to be an event experienced by the dying person alone in a medical facility unbeknownst to his church family.[52]

The communion of the saints renders the ecology of human death and dying both meaningful and faithful for the dying. Secured *in Christ*, the dying is a member of the church, which God purchased with his own blood (Acts 20:28). In that regard, the dying can never die alone. Any fear of death that engenders isolation is illusory. As Thielicke ponders, "Evidently I am something more and something other than just a specimen that can perish while the species itself survives."[53] The individual believer, then, possesses more ontological and relational significance than being merely a generic *one* of many. Consequently, as a member of the community—particularly, the church—the believer's death possesses equal significance. The value of the life of the dying Christian is incalculable; first, by virtue of his being a creature made in the image of the infinite God (see Gen 1:27; 9:6; Jas 3:9–10). Further, the life of the Christian is of priceless value because he is a member of the body, which God purchased with his own invaluable blood. The Christian who dies surrounded by and aware of his communion with this cloud of witnesses may die well and without fear.

"Commendacion" of death.[54] Death is not merely the cessation of the biological corpus of the human person. As Thielicke notes, human death must also take into account man's personhood—that is, the dimension of his history with the God in whose image he is made.

> Human death transcends biological death, therefore, to the same degree that man as a creature of personhood transcends his own quality as a biological being, as a mammal. Death viewed in the biblical sense consequently takes place in a different dimension from the biological, namely, in the dimension of man's history with God, which means in the dimension of personhood. Only

---

51. Luther, *LW*, 42:112, cited in Reinis, *Reforming*, 70.

52. For an excellent treatment of the inception and deleterious effects of "medicalized dying" by the Baconian project, see Verhey, *Christian Art of Dying*, 1–75, 300–85.

53. Thielicke, *Death and Life*, 14.

54. The phrase is used often as a section or chapter title in *ars moriendi*. It is not to be construed as advocating *celebration* of God's curse. Rather, read in the context of Moriendi's departure from an originally very good—but now decaying—world to the consummate and blessed state of his *nephesh* (i.e., "living being" or "self"), the "commendacion of death" simply refers to the presentation of information regarding dying—i.e., "a handbook on dying well." See, for example, Atkinson, "Crafte and Knowledge For To Dye Well," 1.

if we begin here is it possible to comprehend in depth the notion that the wages of sin is death. We dare not twist this thought to mean that the cause is man's sin and the effect is his biological death. Such a misunderstanding would inevitably lead to the elimination of the personhood which underlies it. It would thus lead to a completely erroneous analogy with biological causality in nature. No, it is only that God uses the medium of the biological to give his answer to man's rebellious urge. By this means God places boundaries on the one out of bounds.[55]

Joseph Ratzinger recognizes the ecology of death and dying reflected by the Catholic prayer, the Litany of the Saints. That ecology shunned the desire for a sudden and unacknowledged death—a desire characteristic of our own culture. The saints' plea was "*A subitanea morte, libera nos, Domine*" [From a death that is sudden and unprepared for, deliver us, O Lord].[56] That is, for the one who knows God and is known by him, death is the paramount catalyst compelling him to contemplate his own finitude, brevity and significance of (earthly) life, inability to secure or sustain himself, and utter dependence on God for his very being. The Christian ought not to disregard these verities either during his life or at its conclusion. Further elaborating on the meaning of death, Ratzinger thus proscribes this spiritually anemic desire for instantaneous death.

> The uncontrollable Power that everywhere sets limits to life is not a blind law of nature. It is a love that puts itself at our disposal by dying for us and with us. The Christian is the one who knows that he can unite the constantly experienced dispossession of self with the fundamental attitude of being created for love, a being that knows itself to be safe precisely when it trusts in the unexacted gift of love. Man's enemy, death, that would waylay him to steal his life, is conquered at the point where one meets the thievery of death with the attitude of trusting love, and so transforms the theft into increase of life. The sting of death is extinguished in Christ in whom the victory was gained through the plenary power of love unlimited. Death is vanquished where people die with Christ and into him. This is why the Christian attitude must be opposed to the modern wish for instantaneous death, a wish that would turn death into an extensionless moment and banish from life the claims of the metaphysical. Yet it is

---

55. Thielicke, *Death and Life*, 186.
56. Ratzinger, *Eschatology*, 71.

in the transforming acceptance of death, present time and again to us in this life, that we mature for the real, the eternal life.[57]

Such a cruciform life culminating in death with Christ and into him, writes the apostle Peter throughout his first general epistle, is the path to life. Any death divorced from its significance as ordered by the living God, in accord with his purposes, misses also the significance of life as rendered by God.

Counselors like Moses, Gregory, and Edwards are right, then. Regular, godward contemplation of one's death is invaluably instructive for how one is to live in this present age and how he may die well. Only the believer in Jesus Christ, nurtured by the communion of saints—the church—can confidently affirm already that he has died and his life is hidden with Christ in God (Col 3:3). In light of this truth, Thielicke affirms, "Faith lives from the resources of its object."[58] From the infinite resources of the ever living object of our faith that is Christ, the believer is sustained uninterrupted throughout this present life, through death, and into the new age. Only Spirit-filled members of the church of Jesus Christ can instruct and nurture candidates for death in this universal and insuppressible reality.[59]

The Beatific Vision

Our elder brothers Peter, James, and John had probably the closest relationship of all the disciples with their Master as he ministered during his earthly sojourn. These three communicate perspectives of an often indescribable living hope concerning what will happen after the death of those of us "who have received a faith of the same kind as ours, by the righteousness of our

57. Ibid., 97–98.
58. Thielicke, *Death and Life*, 216.
59. Concerning the grace and responsibility of the missional church to nurture its members and bear witness to the world in the art of dying, Gregg Allison remarks in an unpublished draft of his *Sojourners and Strangers*, "One final stage in the application of salvation also intersects with the church's missional endeavor. Though glorification—the reception of resurrection bodies at the return of Christ—is still in the future, at the death of its faithful members, the church announces the hope of their ultimate resurrection at their funerals (or memorial celebrations). While it grieves at the loss of its loved ones, the church also preaches the blessed hope of the Lord's return and the resurrection of all Christ followers that will accompany this future event. Death, though very real and deeply sensed at funerals, is not the last word, and the missional church verbally carries its deceased members beyond the grave to their ultimate, glorious destiny still to come. Funerals, standing as a strong counter-cultural witness against the surrounding culture of death and hopelessness, are an important element of the missional church."

God and Savior, Jesus Christ" (2 Pet 1:1). These three were convinced of the greater value of the ordinance of their God and Savior than that of their own lives. They were unwavering witnesses to the revealed truth that the God who instituted his just curse of death against his rebellious creature—whom he had designed for eternal communion with himself—had now incontrovertibly provided for the reversal of that curse, thereby demonstrating his holy integrity in promising "the blessing—life forever" (Ps 133:3), which would include eternal communion, as originally purposed, with the God who possesses life intrinsically. Peter himself affirms that God's "precious and magnificent promises" are the means by which the faithful "become partakers of the divine nature" (2 Pet 1:4).[60] James paradoxically assures those who persevere in faith that they will be crowned with life upon death (Jas 1:12). The beloved disciple, John, articulates the reversal of the curse and readmission of access to both the tree of life and the presence of God by offspring of Adam (Rev 22:2–3). This renewed access to the presence of God will transcend the communion with God that the *first* Adam was granted; for offspring of the *last* Adam will be secured in communion with their Creator in a manner beyond that of the first Adam.[61] Such an eternally secured communion is facilitated by what the church has come to articulate as the Beatific Vision.

---

60. For additional commentary on the meaning of "partaking of the divine nature" (2 Pet 1:4), see Bauckham, *Jude, 2 Peter*, 179–82; Schreiner, *1, 2 Peter, Jude*, 290–95; Kelly, *Peter and Jude*, 301–3; Davids, *2 Peter and Jude*, 167–76.

61. While parallels exist between the (pre-Fall) Garden of Eden and the eschatological "Heavenly City," contrasts also exist. The key distinction, Augustine argues, between the paradise Adam enjoyed and the bliss of the citizen of the City of God is certainty about the future. Because he was created *posse non peccare et posse peccare*, and because he was created in the *imago Dei*, yet not as a *partaker* of the divine nature, Adam's future depended on his purely creaturely ability to maintain obedience to the command of God. Because the citizen of the City of God, however, will have been made partaker of the divine nature (2 Pet 1:4)—which cannot sin—and because his new body will be fashioned like Christ's glorious resurrection body (Phil 3:21), he will enjoy a "serene avoidance of sin," like Adam in the Garden, yet without any fear of expulsion from the Garden, because by grace he has been eternally secured against any warrant for expulsion (Augustine, *City of God*, 14:10). The soul will be freer than it has ever been, being "immovably fixed in a delight in not sinning" (22:30). Thus, the citizen of that City will possess assurance of the eternal uninterrupted enjoyment of the bliss of the Beatific Vision (11:12; 12:21). In concluding his response to the many who were inquiring, "Where was God when Rome collapsed," Augustine pastorally echoes this assurance to the citizens of the City of God. For them, enjoyment of the Beatific Vision of the God who sovereignly ordained the fall of Rome will be "deathless" (10:32; 12:21).

The Beatific Vision in Augustine

Augustine would describe the Beatific Vision[62] as the experiencing of the full felicity of heavenly citizenship which entails receiving "the impossibility of sinning as a gift from God" by becoming a "partaker of God's nature"—to which belongs the inability to sin.[63] This consummate blissful state of being will transcend the knowledge of God that offspring of the first Adam now possess through a host of duly ordained yet nonetheless mediatory instruments, including their own minds. Additionally, this state will entail enjoyment of the eternal and ever-increasing bliss of *immediate* knowledge of God.[64]

God has constituted man "capable of contemplating him, able to apprehend him." To be sure, although God is apprehendable—and *immediately* so in beatification—he remains inexhaustible (i.e., *finitum non capax infinitum*). In partaking of God's nature, then, offspring of the last Adam are not in some sense deified. Rather, God himself is the means of their life

---

62. Augustine's *City of God* serves as the source of his understanding of the Beatific Vision. Because the work is arguably Augustine's *magnum opus*, as well as the source of his most prolific articulation of the doctrine, readers are encouraged to consult the treatise for fuller context and detail.

63. Augustine, *City of God*, 22:30. Augustine further argues, "The first freedom of will, given to man when he was created upright at the beginning, was an ability not to sin, combined with the possibility of sinning. But this last freedom will be more potent, for it will bring the impossibility of sinning; yet this also will be the result of God's gift, not of some inherent quality of nature. For to be a partaker of God is not the same thing as to be God; the inability to sin belongs to God's nature, while he who partakes of God's nature receives the impossibility of sinning as a gift from God."

64. Against any possible prospect of "heavenly boredom," John Hick quotes the studied response of Aquinas: "Nothing that is contemplated with wonder can be tiresome, since as long as the thing remains in wonder it continues to stimulate desire. But the divine substance is always viewed with wonder by any created intellect, since no created intellect comprehends [i.e., exhausts] it. So, it is impossible for an intellectual substance to become tired of this vision. And thus, it cannot, of its own will, desist from this vision." See Aquinas, *On the Truth of the Catholic Faith*, 205, cited in Hick, *Death and Eternal Life*, 206. Hick further suggests that the idea of the Beatific Vision "reached its full doctrinal development in the medieval period," though the notion preceded that period and indeed Christianity (Hick, 204).

In contemplating the bliss of the Heavenly City, Augustine does not shy away from some of the Bible's more "hard sayings" concerning these things. He suggests that, via communion with the Lord, the citizens in the Heavenly City will have full knowledge of the sufferings of those who are excluded because they are citizens of the other city. The felicity of the heavenly citizens will be magnified because of their recognition of their Lord's righteous judgment concerning the situation of the wicked—those "outside . . . in outer darkness"—in contrast to their own having entered "inside" the joy of their Lord (Augustine, lii; cf. 20:22).

and felicity.[65] Only in beholding God face to face does created intelligence find this consummate felicity—which Augustine asserts is "man's Supreme Good."[66] The vision is "beatific," then, because the vision of God *beatifies* the recipient of this transforming, gracious gift.

One might imagine that the doctrine of finite creatures coming to partake of the divine nature might impinge upon the doctrine of the immutability of God. In evaluating some of the similarities between Christianity and paganism, Augustine takes note of one very important feature of the nature of God that handily refutes any notion of change in the nature of God upon the beatification of his saints. The idea of *undiminished giving* is one similarity between Neoplatonic philosophy and Christianity. The notion asserts that "the divine cause of all things, as it overflows into the gift of being to creatures, is itself unchanged and not in any way lessened."[67] Because "God is existence in supreme degree," that is, he "supremely *is*,"[68] the dissemination of his nature in no way diminishes or changes his essence. Rather, in this way, the eternally emanating and sanctifying "vision of the unchanging truth"[69] and "changeless immortality"[70] reconciles God's saints to himself in perfect and living unity, just as originally divinely designed and purposed.

---

65. Augustine, *City of God*, 22:1; cf. Ps 73:28.

66. Augustine, *City of God*, 19:4, 11. Augustine ponders, "The end [i.e., consummation] of this City, whereby it [the soul] will possess its Supreme Good may be called either 'peace in life everlasting' or 'life in everlasting peace' . . . in fact, nothing better can be found." Augustine further argues that, "no god is to be worshipped by men except the God who can make men happy" (preface; 5:1–5; see also 10:1). Felicity, then, i.e., "peace in life everlasting" or better put, "life in everlasting peace," is man's Supreme Good. This Supreme Good can only be found in fullest extent in the beatific vision of God at the culmination of that City. Eternal death, by the way, is the Supreme Evil (9:4, 11). Here, using what he believes to be humanity's clear consensus of the *summum bonum*—the highest good—Augustine argues against the purveyors of the worship of any number of pagan gods. None of those gods has ever evidenced—nor ever could—an ability to bring about consummate felicity for mankind. Notable, too, is the fact that Augustine wrestles with how to designate this state; for he understands the biblical concept of "life everlasting" to mean much more than "life forever." He prefers, then, and intentionally uses the alternative term "life in everlasting peace" to indicate the perfect and perpetually ameliorating quality of that felicity, not merely its eternal endurance. This bliss is not only blessed (i.e., merely a state of personal consummate happiness); it is indeed *beatific*. That is, it is transformational; it is "participation in [God's] own divine nature" (9:16).

67. Augustine, *City of God*, xxiii.

68. Ibid., 12:2.

69. Ibid., 10:23.

70. Ibid., 12:21.

Because God is incorporeal, upon beatification, citizens of the "city of God" will perceive God with "spiritual bodies." That is, unlike with the warfare between the flesh and the spirit in this present evil age, the flesh will live in blissful accord with the spirit in joyful obedience to God. The body will derive perfect delight from the soul's peace with God. While offspring of the last Adam will possess bodies and will see God *in* the body, whether we will see the immaterial God who is spirit *through* the eyes of that body is no easy question for Augustine. Augustine understands seeing God "face to face" and the "face" of God as referring to his revelation or self-disclosure— which we perceive with the intellect and/or heart of faith. Therefore, "the saints will certainly need no bodily eyes to see what is there to be seen."[71]

The Eschaton: *Sabbatum Christianum*

In conjunction with the saint's beatification, Augustine considers that the eternal Heavenly City will consummate the Christian's rest.[72] This eternal rest *coram Deo* will entail: eternal life, which Augustine describes as the peace of intense communication (i.e., communion) with God; rest in God and all that that divine rest entails; illumination and eternal "knowing" of God equal to the capacity of our finite creaturely being—a knowing that will constitute an "unimaginable heightening" of the creature's being[73]; no evil, and no good withheld; and eternal leisure (i.e., opportunity) for the praises of God. This Christian rest will consummate, for all offspring of the last Adam, God's reversal of the curse of death and establish for eternity his designed purpose of being *with* his image bearing *magnum opus* and filling his earth with the knowledge of the glory of the Lord, as the waters cover the sea (Isa 11:9; Hab 2:14). "Then will come about the saying that is written, 'Death is swallowed up in victory. O death, where is your victory? O death, where is your sting?' The sting of death is sin, and the power of sin is the law; but thanks be to God, who gives us the victory through our Lord Jesus Christ" (1 Cor 15:54–57).

---

71. Ibid., 22:29.
72. Ibid., lii–liii; cf. 22:30.
73. Ibid., 20:21.

Bibliography

Aalders, Gerhard C. *Genesis*. Translated by William Heynen. Grand Rapids: Zondervan, 1981.
Abbott, Walter M., ed. "Decree: On the Church's Missionary Activity: *Ad Gentes*." In *The Documents of Vatican II*, 584–630. New York: Herder & Herder, 1966.
Aland, Kurt. *Neutestamentliche Entwrufe*. Theologische Bucherei Neues Testament 63. Munich: Christian Kaiser, 1979.
Alberione, James. *The Last Things*. Boston: Pauline, 1964.
Alcorn, Randy. *Heaven*. Carol Stream, IL: Tyndale, 2004.
Allison, Gregg R. Classroom Lecture Notes. The Southern Baptist Theological Seminary, 27077—*The Doctrine of Humanity and Sin*, Fall 2007. Internet.
———. Classroom Lecture Notes. The Southern Baptist Theological Seminary, 84920—*Theological Anthropology*, Fall 2008. Internet.
———. *Sojourners and Strangers: The Doctrine of the Church*. Foundations of Evangelical Theology. Wheaton, IL: Crossway, 2012.
Althaus, Paul. *Die letzten Dinge: Lehrbuch der Eschatologie*. 6th ed. Gütersloh: Carl Bertelsmann, 1956.
Althaus, Paul. "Retraktionen zur Eschatologie." *Theologische Literatur Zeitung* 75 (1950) 256.
Ambrose. *Abraham*. In *Patrologia Latina*, edited by Jacques-Paul Migne, 478–524. Cambridge: Chadwyck-Healey, 1996.
Anderson, Gary. *Sin: A History*. New Haven, CT: Yale University Press, 2009.
Anderson, Ray S. *Theology, Death and Dying*. New York: Basil Blackwell, 1986.
Anselm. *Cur Deus Homo?* The Ancient and Modern Library of Theological Literature. London: Griffifth Farran Okeden & Welsh, 2010.
Aquinas, Thomas. *On the Truth of the Catholic Faith, Summa contra Gentiles*, Book III: Providence. Translated by Vernon J. Bourke. New York: Image, 1956.
———. *Summa Theologica*. Vol. 1. Edited by Robert Maynard Hutchins. Great Books of the Western World. 19 vols. Chicago: Encyclopedia Britannica, 1952.
Ariès, Philippe. *Centuries of Childhood: A Social History of Family Life*. Translated by Robert Baldick. London: Jonathan Cape; New York: Alfred Knopf, 1962.
———. *The Hour of Our Death*. Translated by Helen Weaver. 2nd ed. London: Vintage, 2008.

———. *Western Attitudes toward Death: From the Middle Ages to the Present.* Baltimore: Johns Hopkins University Press, 1974.

Athanasius. *On the Incarnation: De Incarnatione Verbi Dei.* Translated by A Religious of C.S.M.V. S.Th. New York: Macmillan, 1946.

———. *On the Incarnation: De Incarnatione Verbi Dei.* Popular Patristics Series. Translated by Penelope Lawson. New York: St. Vladimir's Seminary Press, 1996.

Atkinson, David William, ed. *The English 'ars moriendi.'* New York: Peter Lang, 1992.

Attridge, Harold W. *Hebrews: A Commentary on the Epistle to the Hebrews.* Hermeneia 72. Philadelphia: Fortress, 1989.

Augustine. *Admonition and Grace.* In *Selections.* Translated by J. C. Murray. Writings of Saint Augustine. Vol. 4. Fathers of the Church 2. Washington, DC: Catholic University of America Press, 1968.

———. *Against Julian.* In *The Works of Saint Augustine.* Edited by John E. Rotelle. Translated by Roland J. Teske, I/24. New York: New City, 1998.

———. *Against Julian.* In *Writings of Saint Augustine.* Vol. 16. Fathers of the Church 35. Translated by M. A. Schumacher. Washington, DC: Catholic University of America Press, 1984.

———. *Answer to the Pelagians, III: Unfinished Work in Answer to Julian.* In *The Works of Saint Augustine.* Edited by John E. Rotelle. Translated by Roland J. Teske, I/25. New York: New City, 1999.

———. *The Canons of the Council of Carthage.* In *The Works of Saint Augustine.* Edited by John E. Rotelle. Translated by Roland J. Teske, I/23. New York: New City, 1997.

———. *City of God.* Translated by Henry Bettenson. London: Penguin, 1972.

———. *Confessions.* Translated by R. S. Pine-Coffin. London: Penguin, 1961.

———. *The Confessions of Saint Augustine.* Translated and edited by Edward B. Pusey. New Kensington, PA: Whitaker, 1996.

———. *De Quantitate Animae* [On the Measure of the Soul]. Translated by Francis Edward Tourscher. Philadelphia: Peter Reilly, 1933.

———. *Enchiridion.* In *Basic Writings of Saint Augustine.* Vol. 1. Edited by Whitney J. Oates. New York: Random, 1948.

———. *Enchiridion.* In *A Select Library of Nicene and Post-Nicene Fathers of the Christian Church.* Edited by Philip Schaff. 1st series. 14 vols. 3.229–76. New York: Christian Literature, 1887–1900. Reprint, Grand Rapids: Eerdmans, 1956.

———. *Enchiridion.* In *The Works of Saint Augustine.* Edited by John E. Rotelle. Translated by Roland J. Teske, II/8. New York: New City, 1997.

———. *The Grace of Christ and On Original Sin.* Vol. 2. In *The Works of Saint Augustine.* Edited by John E. Rotelle. Translated by Roland J. Teske, I/23. New York: New City, 1997.

———. *Letter 98.* In *The Works of Saint Augustine.* Edited by John E. Rotelle. Translated by Roland J. Teske, II/1. New York: New City, 1997.

———. *Letter 166.* In *The Works of Saint Augustine.* Edited by John E. Rotelle. Translated by Roland J. Teske, II/3. New York: New City, 1997.

———. *The Literal Meaning of Genesis.* Ancient Christian Writers. Vol. 42.2. Edited by Johannes Quasten, Walter J. Burghardt, and Thomas Comerford Lawler. Translated by John Hammond Taylor, Ramsey, NJ: Paulist, 1982.

———. *The Nature and Origin of the Soul.* In *The Works of Saint Augustine.* Edited by John E. Rotelle. Translated by Roland J. Teske, I/23. New York: New City, 1997.

———. *On Faith and Works*. Ancient Christian Writers. Vol. 48. Edited by Walter J. Burghardt, and Thomas Comerford Lawler. Translated by Gregory J. Lombardo. New York: Newman, 1988.
———. *On the Merits and Forgiveness of Sins and on the Baptism of Infants*. New Advent. Online: www.newadvent.org/fathers/15011.htm.
———. *On Order*. Translated by Silvano Borruso. South Bend: St. Augustine's, 2007.
———. *The Punishment and Forgiveness of Sins and the Baptism of Little Ones*. In *The Works of Saint Augustine*. Edited by John E. Rotelle. Translated by Roland J. Teske, I/23. New York: New City, 1997.
———. "Retractions." In *The Fathers of the Church*. Translated by Mary Inez Bogan. Washington, DC: Catholic University of America Press, 1968.
Badham, Paul. *Christian Beliefs about Life after Death*. London: SPCK, 1978.
Bailey, Lloyd R. *Biblical Perspectives on Death*. Philadelphia: Fortress, 1979.
Bailey, Lloyd R., and Karl-Johan Illman. "Review of Old Testament Formulas about Death." *Journal of Biblical Literature* 100.2 (1981) 257.
Baker, Larry N. "A Semantic Study of 'Soul' in the Hebrew Old Testament." *Evangelical Theological Society Papers*. Dallas: Evangelical Theological Society, 2003.
Balke, Willem. *Calvin and the Anabaptist Radicals*. Grand Rapids: Eerdmans, 1981.
Balthasar, Hans Urs von. "Eschatology." In *Theology Today: Renewal in Dogma I*, edited by J. Feiner, 222–24. Milwaukee: Bruce, 1965.
Balthasar, Hans Urs von. *A Theology of History*. New York: Sheed and Ward, 1963. Reprint, San Francisco: Ignatius, 1994.
Barbarin, Georges. *Der Tod als Freund*. Stuttgart: n.p., 1938.
Barclay, William. *By What Authority?* Bungay, Suffolk: Darton, Longman and Todd, 1974.
Barker, Kenneth, ed. "The Conquest and the Ethical Question of War." In *NASB Study Bible*, edited by Authur Lewis, 271. Grand Rapids: Zondervan, 1999.
Barr, James. *The Bible in the Modern World*. New York: Harper & Row, 1973.
Barth, Karl. *Church Dogmatics*. Edited by G. W. Bromiley, and T. F. Torrance. Vol. 1. *The Doctrine of the Word of God*. Pt. 1. Translated by G. W. Bromiley. New York: T. & T. Clark, 2010.
———. *Church Dogmatics*. Edited by G. W. Bromiley, and T. F. Torrance. Vol. 3. *The Doctrine of Creation*. Pt. 4. Translated by A. T. Mackey. Edinburgh: T. & T. Clark, 1961.
———. *Church Dogmatics*. Edited by G. W. Bromiley, and T. F. Torrance. Vol. 4. *The Doctrine of Reconciliation*. Pt. 1. Translated by G. W. Bromiley. Edinburgh: T. & T. Clark, 1968.
———. *Credo*. Translated by J. Strathearn McNab. Eugene, OR: Wipf & Stock, 2005.
———. *The Epistle to the Romans*. Translated by Edwyn C. Hoskyns. New York: Oxford University Press, 1968.
———. *The Resurrection of the Dead*. Translated by H. J. Stenning. Eugene, OR: Wipf & Stock, 2003.
Bastide, Roger. "Messianism and Social Economic Development." In *Social Change: The Colonial Situation*, edited by Immanuel Wallerstein, 3–14. New York: Wiley, 1966.
Bauckham, Richard. *The Fate of the Dead: Studies on the Jewish and Christian Apocalypse*. Supplements to Novum Testamentum 93. Leiden: Brill, 1998.
———. *Jude, 2 Peter*. Word Biblical Commentary, vol. 50. Columbia, GA: Word, 1983.

Bauer, Walter. *A Greek-English Lexicon of the New Testament and Other Early Christian Literature*. Edited and translated by William F. Arndt, Felix Wilbur Gingrich, and Frederick William Danker. Chicago: University of Chicago Press, 2000.

Bavinck, Herman. *Reformed Dogmatics*. Vol. 1, *Prolegomena*. Edited by John Bolt. Translated by John Vriend. Grand Rapids: Baker, 2003.

———. *Reformed Dogmatics*. Vol. 2, *God and Creation*. Edited by John Bolt. Translated by John Vriend. Grand Rapids: Baker, 2004.

———. *Reformed Dogmatics*. Vol. 3, *Sin and Salvation in Christ*. Edited by John Bolt. Translated by John Vriend. Grand Rapids: Baker, 2006.

———. *Reformed Dogmatics*. Vol. 4, *Holy Spirit, Church, and New Creation*. Edited by John Bolt. Translated by John Vriend. Grand Rapids: Baker, 2008.

Baxter, Richard. *Rich. Baxter's Review of the State of Christian Infants: Whether They Should Be Entered in Covenant with God by Baptism, and Be Visible Members of His Church, and Have Any Covenant-Right to Pardon and Salvation? (1700)*. Early History of Religion. Ann Arbor, MI: Proquest, 2011.

Bealer, George. "On the Possibility of Philosophical Knowledge." In *Metaphysics*, vol. 10, *Philosophical Perspectives*, edited by James E. Tomberlin, 1–34. Cambridge: Blackwell, 1996.

Beare, Francis Wright. *The First Epistle of Peter*. Oxford: Basil Blackwell, 1970.

Beaty, Nancy Lee. *The Craft of Dying: A Study in the Literary Tradition of the Ars Moriendi in England*. New Haven, CT: Yale University Press, 1970.

Bell, Rob. *Love Wins: A Book about Heaven, Hell, and the Fate of Every Person Who Ever Lived*. New York: HarperOne, 2011.

Bernstein, Alan. *The Formation of Hell: Death and Retribution in the Ancient and Early Christian Worlds*. Ithaca, NY: Cornell University Press, 1993.

Berkhof, Louis. *The History of Christian Doctrines*. Carlisle, PA: The Banner of Truth Trust, 1996.

———. *Systematic Theology*. Grand Rapids: Eerdmans, 1996.

Berkouwer, G. C. *Man: The Image of God*. Grand Rapids: Eerdmans, 1962.

Best, Ernest. *I Peter*. London: Oliphants-Blundell, 1971.

Beth, K. "Über Ursache und Zweck des Todes." *Glauben und Wissen* (1909) 285–304 and 335–48.

Bettenson, Henry. *The Early Christian Fathers*. Oxford: Oxford University Press, 1969.

Binski, Paul. *Medieval Death: Ritual and Representation*. Ithaca, NY: Cornell University Press, 1996.

Blackburn, Simon. *The Oxford Dictionary of Philosophy*. New York: Oxford University Press, 2008.

Blackburne, Francis. *A Short Historical View of the Controversy concerning an Intermediate State and the Separate Existence of the Soul between Death and the Resurrection*. London: T. Field, 1765. Reprint, Farmington Hills, MI: Gale ECCO, 2010.

Blackwell, Ben. "Immortal Glory and the Problem of Death in Romans 3.23." *Journal for the Study of the New Testament* 32.3 (2010) 285–308.

Boase, T. S. R. *Death in the Middle Ages: Mortality, Judgment and Remembrance*. New York: McGraw-Hill, 1972.

Boettner, Loraine. *The Reformed Doctrine of Predestination*. Phillipsburg, NJ: P&R, 1992.

Bonhoeffer, Dietrich. *Ethics*. New York: Macmillan, 1955; London: Collins, 1963.

———. *Life Together*. Translated by John W. Doberstein. San Francisco: Harper & Row, 1954.
Bonjour, Laurence. *In Defense of Pure Reason*. Cambridge: Cambridge University Press, 1998.
Boros, Ladislaus. "Death: A Theological Reflection." In *The Mystery of Suffering and Death*, edited by Michael Taylor, 141–42. New York: Image, 1973.
———. *The Moment of Truth: Mysterium Mortis*. London: Burns & Oats, 1965.
———. *The Mystery of Death*. New York: Seabury, 1973.
———. *Pain and Providence*. New York: Seabury, 1972.
Boyd, Gregory A. *God of the Possible: A Biblical Introduction to the Open View of God*. Grand Rapids: Baker, 2000.
Bray, Gerald. *The Doctrine of God*. Contours of Christian Theology. Downers Grove, IL: InterVarsity, 1993.
Brown, C., ed. *New International Dictionary of New Testament Theology*. Exeter: Paternoster, 1975–78.
Brown, Peter. *Augustine of Hippo: A Biography*. Berkeley, CA: University of California Press, 2000.
Bruce, F. F. *The Canon of Scripture*. Downers Grove, IL: InterVarsity, 1988.
———. *The Epistle to the Hebrews*. Grand Rapids: Eerdmans, 1964.
Brueggemann, Walter. *Isaiah 40–66*. Westminster Bible Companion. Louisville: Westminster John Knox, 1998.
Budge, E. A. Wallis. *Egyptian Religion: Egyptian Ideas of the Future Life*. New York: Penguin, 1987.
Bultmann, Rudolph. *Die zweite Brief an die Korinther*. Göttingen: Vanderhoek & Ruprecht, 1976.
———. *History and Eschatology: The Presence of Eternity*. New York: Harper, 1962.
Burpo, Todd. *Heaven Is for Real: A Little Boy's Astounding Story of His Trip to Heaven and Back*. Nashville: Thomas Nelson, 2010.
Butler, Rex. *The New Prophecy and "New Visions": Evidence of Montanism in the Passion of Saint Perpetua and Felicitas*. Washington, DC: Catholic University of America Press, 2006.
Calvin, John. *Commentary on Genesis*. Translated by John King. Grand Rapids: Eerdmans, 1948.
———. *Institutes of the Christian Religion*. Edited by John T. McNeill. Translated by Ford Lewis Battles. Library of Christian Classics. Philadelphia: Westminster, 1960.
Carson, Donald A. *Becoming Conversant with the Emerging Church: Understanding A Movement and Its Implications*. Grand Rapids: Zondervan, 2005.
———. *The Difficult Doctrine of the Love of God*. Wheaton, IL: Crossway, 2000.
———. *The Gagging of God: Christianity Confronts Pluralism*. Grand Rapids: Zondervan, 1996.
———. *How Long, O Lord? Reflections on Suffering and Evil*. Grand Rapids: Baker, 1999.
———. *Love in Hard Places*. Wheaton, IL: Crossway, 2002.
———. *Scripture and Truth*. Grand Rapids: Baker, 1992.
Carson, D. A., and John D. Woodbridge, eds. *Hermeneutics, Authority, and Canon*. Grand Rapids: Baker, 2005.

Cavallin, Hans Clemens Casesarius. *Life and Death: Paul's Argument for the Resurrection of the Dead in 1 Corinthians 15*. Pt. 1. *An Enquiry into the Jewish Background*. Lund, Sweden: Gleerup, 1974.

Cerny, Ladislav. *The Day of Yahweh and Some Relevant Problems*. Prague: Nakladem Filosoficke Fakulty University Karlovy, 1948.

Chalmers, David J. *The Conscious Mind: In Search of a Fundamental Theory*. Oxford: Oxford University Press, 1996.

Charles, Robert H. *Eschatology*. London: A. and C. Black, 1889.

Charlesworth, James H. "Where Does the Concept of Resurrection Appear and How Do We Know That?" In *Resurrection: The Origin and Future of a Biblical Doctrine*, ed. James H. Charlesworth, 1–21. New York: T. & T. Clark, 2006.

Childs, Brevard S. *Isaiah: A Commentary*. Old Testament Library. Louisville: Westminster John Knox, 2001.

Clark, David K. "Narrative Theology and Apologetics." *Journal of the Evangelical Theological Society*, 36.4 (1993) 499–515.

Clark, Neville. *Interpreting the Resurrection*. London: SCM, 1967.

Clark-Soles, Jaime. *Death and the Afterlife in the New Testament*. New York: T. & T. Clark, 2006.

Clayton, Philip. "Neuroscience, the Person, and God: An Emergentist Account." In *Neuroscience and the Person*. Scientific Perspectives on Divine Action Series, ed. Robert John Russell, Nancey Murphy, Theo C. Meyering, and Michael A. Arbib, 181–214. Berkeley, CA: Center for Theology and the Natural Sciences, 1999.

Coakley, Sarah. "What Does Chalcedon Solve and What Does It Not?" In *The Incarnation: An Interdisciplinary Symposium on the Incarnation of the Son of God*, ed. Stephen T. Davis, Daniel Kendall, and Gerald O'Collins, 143–63. New York: Oxford University Press, 2004.

Corcoran, Kevin. "Physical Persons and Postmortem Survival without Temporal Gaps." In *Soul, Body, and Survival: Essays on the Metaphysics of Human Persons*, edited by Kevin Corcoran, 201–17. Ithaca, NY: Cornell University Press, 2001.

Collins, John. *Daniel: A Commentary on the Book of Daniel*. Hermeneia. Minneapolis: Fortress, 1993.

Comper, Frances M. M. *The Book of the Craft of Dying, and Other Early English Tracts Concerning Death*. London: Longmans, Green, and Co., 1917.

Cooper, John W. *Body, Soul, and Life Everlasting: Biblical Anthropology and the Monism-Dualism Debate*. 2nd ed. Grand Rapids: Eerdmans, 2000.

Cote, Maureen. *Death and The Meaning of Life: Selected Writings of Leo Tolstoy*. Huntington, NY: Troitsa, 1999.

Cottrell, Jack. *What the Bible Says about God the Ruler*. Eugene, OR: Wipf & Stock, 1984.

Cragoe, Thomas. "An Examination of the Issues of Infant Salvation." PhD diss., Dallas Theological Seminary, 1987.

Cranfield, C. E. B. *1 & II Peter and Jude*. London: SCM, 1960.

Cribb, Bryan Howard. "Speaking on the Brink of Sheol: Form and Theology of Old Testament Death Stories." PhD diss., The Southern Baptist Theological Seminary, 2007.

Crick, Francis. *The Astonishing Hypothesis: The Scientific Search for the Soul*. New York: Simon & Schuster, 1994.

Crisp, Oliver D. *Divinity and Humanity*. Cambridge: Cambridge University Press, 2007.

Cullmann, Oscar. *Christ and Time: The Primitive Christian Conception of Time and History*. London: SCM, 1952.

———. *Immortality of the Soul or Resurrection of the Dead? The Witness of the New Testament*. London: Macmillan, 1955. Reprint, Eugene, OR: Wipf & Stock, 2000.

Cyril. *On the Unity of Christ*. Translated by John Anthony McGuckin. Crestwood, NY: St. Vladimir's Seminary Press, 1995.

Dalton, William Joseph. *Christ's Proclamation to the Spirits: A Study of 1 Peter 3:18—4:6*. Analecta Biblica 23. Rome: Pontifical Biblical Institute, 1965.

Daniell, Christopher. *Death and Burial in Medieval England 1066-1550*. New York: Routledge, 1997.

Davids, Peter H. "Death." *Evangelical Dictionary of Theology*. Grand Rapids: Baker, 1984.

———. *The Letters of 2 Peter and Jude*. The Pillar New Testament Commentary. Grand Rapids: Eerdmans, 2006.

Davis, Stephen T. *Death and Afterlife*. New York: St. Martin's, 1989.

Day, John. "A Case of Inner Scriptural Interpretation: The Dependence of Isaiah xxvi.13—xxvii.11 on Hosea xiii.4—xiv.10 (Eng. 9) and Its Relevance to Some Theories of the Redaction of the 'Isaiah Apocalypse.'" *Journal of Theological Studies* 31 (1980) 309-19.

———. "The Development of Belief in Life after Death in Ancient Israel." In *After the Exile*, ed. John Barton and David Reimer, 231-58. Macon: Mercer University Press, 1996.

———. "Resurrection Imagery from Baal to the Book of Daniel." In *Congress Volume: Cambridge 1995*, edited by John Adney Emerton, 125-33. Leiden: Brill, 1997.

Dembski, William A. *The End of Christianity: Finding a Good God in an Evil World*. Nashville: B & H Academic, 2009.

Denzinger, Henry. *Enchiridion Symbolorum Definitionum et Declarationum de Rebus Fidei et Morum*. 24th ed. Barcelona: Herder & Herder, 1946.

———. *The Sources of Catholic Dogma*. Translated by Roy J. Deferrari. London: Herder, 1955.

Descartes, René. *The Passions of the Soul*. Edited by Stephen H. Vos. Indianapolis, IN: Hackett, 1989.

Dewart, Jaonne E. McWilliam. *Death and Resurrection*. The Fathers of the Church, 22. Wilmington, DE: Michael Glazier, 1986.

Dodd, C. H. *The Authority of the Bible*. Rev. ed. New York: Harper Torchbook, 1962.

Doka, Kenneth J., and John D. Morgan, eds. *Death and Spirituality*. Amityville, NY: Baywood, 1993.

Doss, Richard. *The Last Enemy*. New York: Harper and Row, 1974.

Douie, D. L. "John XXII and the Beatific Vision," *Dominican Studies* 3 (1950): 154-74.

DuBois, Paul M. *The Hospice Way of Death*. New York: Human Sciences, 1980.

Due, Noel. *Created for Worship: From Genesis to Revelation to You*. Fearn, Scotland: Christian Focus, 2005.

Duncan, J. Ligon. *Fear Not: Death and the Afterlife from a Christian Perspective*. Fearn, Scotland: Christian Focus, 2008.

Edwards, Jonathan. "Concerning the Endless Punishment of Those Who Die Impenitent." In *The Works of Jonathan Edwards*, edited by Patrick H. Alexander, 2.515-25. Peabody, MA: Hendrickson, 2003.

———. "Dissertation on the End for which God Created the World." In *The Works of Jonathan Edwards*, edited by Patrick H. Alexander, 1.94–121. Peabody, MA: Hendrickson, 2003.

———. *The Freedom of the Will*. Morgan, PA: Soli Deo Gloria, 1996.

———. "The Great Christian Doctrine of Original Sin Defended." In *The Works of Jonathan Edwards*, edited by Patrick H. Alexander, 1.143–233. Peabody, MA: Hendrickson, 2003.

———. "The Justice of God in the Damnation of Sinner." In *The Works of Jonathan Edwards*, edited by Patrick H. Alexander, 1.668–679. Peabody, MA: Hendrickson, 2003.

———. "Miscellany 393." In *The "Miscellanies" (Entry Nos, a–z, aa–zz, 1–500). The Works of Jonathan Edwards*. Vol. 13. Edited by Thomas A. Schafer. New Haven, CT: Yale University Press, 1994.

———. "The Preciousness of Time and the Importance of Redeeming It." In *The Works of Jonathan Edwards*, edited by Patrick H. Alexander, 2.233–36. Peabody, MA: Hendrickson, 2003.

———. "Procrastination or the Sin and Folly of Depending on Future Time." In *The Works of Jonathan Edwards*, edited by Patrick H. Alexander, 2.237–42. Peabody, MA: Hendrickson, 2003.

———. *The Religious Affections*. Carlisle, PA: The Banner of Truth Trust, 2001.

———. "Resolutions." In *The Works of Jonathan Edwards*, edited by Patrick H. Alexander, 1.lx–lxv. Peabody, MA: Hendrickson, 2003.

Eichrodt, Walter. *Theology of the Old Testament*. 2 vols. Philadelphia: Westminster, 1967.

Elledge, C. D. "Resurrection of the Dead: Exploring Our Earliest Evidence Today." In *Resurrection: The Origin and Future of a Biblical Doctrine*, edited James H. Charlesworth, 22–52. New York: T. & T. Clark, 2006.

Ellingworth, Paul. *The Epistle to the Hebrews: A Commentary on the Greek Text*. New International Greek Testament Commentary. Grand Rapids: Eerdmans, 1993.

Elliott, John H. *1 Peter: A New Translation with Introduction and Commentary*. New York: Doubleday, 2000.

Elwell, Walter A. "Intermediate State." In *Baker Theological Dictionary of the Bible*, edited by Walter A. Elwell. Grand Rapids: Baker, 1996.

Erickson, Millard J. *Christian Theology*. Grand Rapids: Baker, 2003.

Erickson, Millard, Paul Kjoss Helseth, and Justin Taylor, eds. *Reclaiming the Center: Confronting Evangelical Accommodation in Postmodern Times*. Wheaton, IL: Crossway, 2004.

Ernst, C. "The Theology of Death," *Clergy Review* 44 (1959) 588–602.

Eusebius. "The Martyrs of Lyons and Vienne." In *A New Eusebius: Documents illustrative of the History of the Church to A.D. 337*, edited by J. Stevenson, 31–41. London: SPCK, 1957.

Evans, C. Stephen. *Exploring Kenotic Christology: The Self-Emptying of God*. Oxford: Oxford University Press, 2006.

———. *Preserving the Person*. Downers Grove, IL: InterVarsity, 1977.

Evans, Craig A., and Emanuel Tov, eds. *Exploring the Origins of the Bible: Canon Formation in Historical, Literary, and Theological Perspective*. Grand Rapids: Baker, 2008.

Evans, Mary J. "Blessing/curse." In *New Dictionary of Biblical Theology*, edited by T. Desmond Alexander, Brian S. Rosner, D. A. Carson, and Graeme Goldsworthy. Downers Grove, IL: InterVarsity, 2000.
Fackre, Gabriel. "Divine Perseverance." In *What about Those Who Have Never Heard?* edited by John Sanders, 71–95. Downers Grove, IL: InterVarsity, 1995.
Fairweather, Eugene R., ed. *A Scholastic Miscellany: Anselm to Ockham*. New York: Macmillan, 1970.
Feenstra, Ronald J. "A Kenotic Christology of the Divine Attributes." In *Exploring Kenotic Christology: The Self-Emptying of God*, edited by C. Stephen Evans, 139–64. Oxford: Oxford University Press, 2006.
Feifel, Herman. *The Meaning of Death*. New York: McGraw-Hill, 1959.
———. *New Meanings of Death*. New York: McGraw-Hill, 1977.
Feinberg, John. "1 Peter 3.18–20, Ancient Mythology, and the Intermediate State." *Westminster Theological Journal* 48.2 (1986) 303–36.
———. "God Ordains All Things." In *Predestination and Free Will: Four Views of Divine Sovereignty and Human Freedom*, edited by David Basinger, and Randall Basinger, 17–44. Downers Grove, IL: InterVarsity, 1986.
Feinberg, John S. *The Many Faces of Evil: Theological Systems and the Problems of Evil*. Wheaton, IL: Crossway, 2004.
———. *No One Like Him*. Wheaton, IL: Crossway, 2001.
———. *Where Is God? A Personal Story of Finding God in Grief and Suffering*. 2nd rev. ed. Nashville: B & H, 2004.
Fenwick, Peter, and Elizabeth Fenwick. *The Art of Dying*. London and New York: Continuum, 2008.
Ferguson, Everett. *Baptism in the Early Church: History, Theology, and Liturgy in the First Five Centuries*. Grand Rapids: Eerdmans, 2009.
———. "Inscriptions of Infant Baptism." *Journal of Theological Studies* 30.1 (1979) 45–46.
Ferguson, Paul. "Curse, Accursed." In *Baker Theological Dictionary of the Bible*, edited by Walter A. Elwell. Grand Rapids: Baker, 1996.
———. "Death, Mortality." In *Baker Theological Dictionary of the Bible*, edited by Walter A. Elwell. Grand Rapids: Baker, 1996.
Fitzmyer, Joseph A. "The Consecutive Meaning of ejf w|/ in Romans 5.12." *New Testament Studies* 39 (1993) 321–39.
Flavel, John. *The Mystery of Providence*. Carlisle, PA: The Banner of Truth Trust, 1678. Reprint, 1995.
Flew, Anthony. *A New Approach to Psychical Research*. London: Watts, 1955.
Forshaw, Bernard. "Benedictus Deus." In *New Catholic Encyclopedia*. 2.304–05. Washington, DC: Catholic University of America Press, 1967.
Forsyth, P. T. *The Church, The Gospel, and Society*. London: Independent, 1962.
Fortman, Edmund J. *Everlasting Life after Death*. New York: Alba, 1976.
Foster, John. *The Immaterial Self*. London: Routledge, 1991.
Foxe, John. *Foxe's Book of Martyrs*. Edited by William Grinton Berry. New Kensington, PA: Whitaker, 1981.
Frame, John. *The Doctrine of the Knowledge of God*. Phillipsburg, NJ: P & R, 1987.
———. *The Doctrine of the Word of God*. Phillipsburg, NJ: P & R, 2010.
———. *No Other God: A Response to Open Theism*. Phillipsburg, NJ: P & R, 2001.

France, Richard T. "Hebrews." In *Hebrews-Revelation*. Expositor's Bible Commentary, edited by Tremper Longman, III, and David E. Garland, 13.17–196. Grand Rapids: Zondervan, 2006.

Fulton, Robert, ed. *Death and Identity*. New York: John Wiley, 1965.

Gaster, Theodor Herzl. "Resurrection." In *Interpreter's Dictionary of the Bible*. Vol. 1. Nashville: Abingdon, 1962.

Gatch, Milton. *Death: Meaning and Morality in Christian Thought and Contemporary Culture*. New York: Seabury, 1969.

Geary, Patrick J. *Living with the Dead in the Middle Ages*. Ithaca, NY: Cornell University Press, 1994.

George, Timothy. "Calvin's Psychopannychia: Another Look." In *In Honour of John Calvin, 1509-64*, edited by E. J. Furcha, 297–329. Montreal: McGill University Press, 1987.

———. *The Theology of the Reformers*. Nashville: B & H, 1988.

Goethe, J. Wolfgang von. *Faust*. Translated by George Madison Priest. New York: Covici Friede, 1932.

Goetz, Stewart, and Charles Talieferro. *A Brief History of the Soul*. Oxford: Blackwell, 2011.

Goldingay, John. *Isaiah*. New International Biblical Commentary. Peabody, MA: Hendrickson, 2001.

Gordon, Bruce, and Peter Marshall, eds. *The Place of the Dead: Death and Remembrance in Late Medieval and Early Modern Europe*. Cambridge: Cambridge University Press, 1990.

Green, Joel B. *What about the Soul? Neuroscience and Christian Anthropology*. Nashville: Abingdon, 2004.

Green, Joel B., and Stuart L. Palmer, eds. *In Search of the Soul*. Downers Grove, IL: InterVarsity, 2005.

Gregory of Nazianzus. "Letter 101: The First Letter to Cledonius the Presbyter." In *On God and Christ: The Five Theological Orations and Two Letters to Cledonius*, translated by Lionel Wickham, 158–70. Popular Patristics Series. New York: St. Vladimir's Seminary Press, 2002.

Gregory of Nyssa. *On the Soul and the Resurrection*. Popular Patristics Series. Translated by Catharine P. Roth. New York: St. Vladimir's Seminary Press, 2002.

Grenz, Stanley. *The Social God and the Relational Self*. Louisville: Westminster John Knox, 2001.

Gressman, Hugo. *Der Ursprung der israelitisch-judischen Eschatologie*. Göttingen: Vanderhoek & Ruprecht, 1905.

Grillmeier, Aloys. *Christ in Christian Tradition*. Vol. 1. Translated by John Bowden. Atlanta: John Knox, 1975.

Grof, Stanislav, and Christina Grof. *Beyond Death: The Gates of Consciousness*. New York: Thames and Hudson, 1978.

Grof, Stanislav, and Joan Halifax. *The Human Encounter with Death*. New York: E. P. Dutton, 1978.

Grudem, Wayne. "Perseverance of the Saints: A Case Study from the Warning Passages in Hebrews." In *Still Sovereign: Contemporary Perspectives on Election, Foreknowledge, and Grace*, ed. Thomas Schreiner, and Bruce Ware, 133–82. Grand Rapids: Baker, 2000.

———. *Systematic Theology*. Grand Rapids: Zondervan, 2000.

Gunkel, Hermann. *Genesis*. Göttingen: Vanderhoek & Ruprecht, 1910.

———. *Schopfung und Chaos in Urzeit und Endzeit*. Göttingen: Vanderhoek & Ruprecht, 1897.

Gunton, Colin "Trinity, Ontology, and Anthropology." In *Persons: Divine and Human*, ed. Christoph Scwöbel, and Colin Gunton, 47–61. Edinburgh: T. & T. Clark, 1991.

Guthrie, Donald. *The Letter to the Hebrews*. Tyndale New Testament Commentaries. Leicester: InterVarsity, 2009.

Habermas, Gary R., and J. P. Moreland. *Beyond Death: Exploring the Evidence for Immortality*. Eugene, OR: Wipf & Stock, 2004.

———. *Immortality: The Other Side of Death*. Nashville: Thomas Nelson, 1992.

Hallote, Rachel S. *Death, Burial, and Afterlife in the Biblical World*. Chicago: Ivan R. Dee, 2001.

Hamilton, Michael, and Helen Reid, eds. *A Hospice Handbook: A New Way of Caring for the Dying*. Grand Rapids: Eerdmans, 1980.

Harent, Stéphane. "Original Sin." In *The Catholic Encyclopedia*, edited by Charles G. Herbermann, 11.312–15. New York: The Encyclopedia Press, 1913.

Harper, Brad, and Paul Louis Metzger. *Exploring Ecclesiology: An Evangelical and Ecumenical Introduction*. Grand Rapids: Brazos, 2009.

Harris, Harriet A. "Should We Say That Personhood Is Relational?" *Scottish Journal of Theology* 51.2 (1998) 222–23.

Harris, Murray J. "Death." In *New Dictionary of Theology*. Downers Grove, IL: InterVarsity, 1988.

———. "Intermediate State." In *New Dictionary of Theology*. Downers Grove, IL: InterVarsity, 1988.

Harwood, Adam. *The Spiritual Condition of Infants: A Biblical-Historical Survey and Systematic Proposal*. Eugene, OR: Wipf & Stock, 2011.

Heidel, Alexander. *The Epic of Gilgamesh and Old Testament Parallels*. Chicago: University of Chicago Press, 1946.

Heidler, Fritz. *Die biblische Lehre von der Unsterblichkeit der Seele: Sterben, Tod, ewiges Leben im Aspekt lutherischer Anthropologie*. Göttingen: Vanderhoek & Ruprecht, 1978.

Hellerman, Joseph H. *When the Church Was a Family: Recapturing Jesus' Vision for Authentic Christian Community*. Nashville: B & H Academic, 2009.

Helm, Paul. *The Last Things: Death, Judgment, Heaven and Hell*. Carlisle, PA: The Banner of Truth Trust, 1989.

———. *The Providence of God*. Downers Grove, IL: InterVarsity, 1994.

———. "A Theory of Disembodied Survival and Re-embodied Existence." *Religious Studies* 14.1 (1978) 15–26.

Hemingway, Ernest. "A Natural History of the Dead." In *The Complete Short Stories of Ernest Hemingway*, edited by Charles Scribner, Jr., 335–41. New York: Simon & Schuster, 1987.

Hendriksen, William. *The Bible on the Life Hereafter*. Grand Rapids: Baker, 1959.

———. *Romans*. New Testament Commentary. Grand Rapids: Baker, 1981.

Henry, Carl F. H. *God, Revelation and Authority*. 6 vols. Wheaton, IL: Crossway, 1999.

Herbermann, Charles, ed. *Catholic Encyclopedia*. New York: Robert Appleton, 1913.

Herring, George. *Introduction to the History of Christianity*. New York: New York University Press, 2006.

Hick, John. *Death and Eternal Life*. Louisville: Westminster John Knox, 1994.

Hippolytus. *Apostolic Tradition* (ca. 215). Translated by Burton Scott Easton. Cambridge: Cambridge University Press, 1934. Reprint, Hamden, CT: Archon, 1962.

Hobbes, Thomas. *Leviathan*. Oxford World's Classics. Oxford: Oxford University Press, 2008.

Hoche, Alfred E. *Jahresringe: Innenansicht eines Menschenlebens*. Munich: Lehmanns, 1936.

Hodge, Archibald Alexander. *The Confession of Faith*. Carlisle, PA: The Banner of Truth Trust, 1998.

———. *Popular Lectures on Theological Themes*. Philadelphia: Presbyterian Board of Publication, 1887.

Hodge, Charles. *Systematic Theology*. 3 vols. New York: Scribner's, 1872–73. Reprint, Grand Rapids: Eerdmans, 1973.

Hoekema, Anthony. *The Bible and the Future*. Grand Rapids: Eerdmans, 1979.

———. *Created in God's Image*. Grand Rapids: Eerdmans, 1994.

———. *The Four Major Cults*. Grand Rapids: Eerdmans, 1963.

Hoffmann, Paul. *Die Toten in Christus: Eine religionsgeschichtliche und exegetische Untersuchung zur paulinischen Eschatologie*. Munich: Aschendorff, 1966.

Honeycutt, Roy L. Jr. *Exodus. The Broadman Bible Commentary*. Vol. 1 Edited by Clifton J. Allen. Nashville: Broadman, 1969.

Hornung, Erik. *The Secret Lore of Egypt: Its Impact on the West*. Translated by David Lorton. Ithaca, NY: Cornell University Press, 2001.

Horton, Michael S. *The Christian Faith: A Systematic Theology for Pilgrims on the Way*. Grand Rapids: Zondervan, 2011.

———. *Covenant and Eschatology: The Divine Drama*. Louisville: Westminster John Knox, 2002.

———. *Covenant and Salvation: Union with Christ*. Louisville: Westminster John Knox, 2007.

———. *People and Place: A Covenant Ecclesiology*. Louisville: Westminster John Knox, 2008.

Hubmaier, Balthasar. "On the Christian Baptism of Believers." In *Balthasar Hubmaier: Theologian of Anabaptism*. Vol. 5, *Classics of the Radical Reformation*, edited and translated by H. Wayne Pipkin and John H. Yoder, 95–149. Scottdale, PA: Herald, 1989.

Huizinga, Johan. *The Waning of the Middle Ages*. Oxford: Benediction, 2010.

Humbert, Paul. "The Old Testament and the Problem of Suffering." *The Biblical World*. 52.2 (1918) 115–34.

Huyssten, J. Wentzel Vrede van, ed. "Christianity, History of Science and Religion." In *Encyclopedia of Science and Religion*. Vol. 1. Farmington Hills, MI: Gale Cengage, 2003.

International Theological Commission. *The Hope of Salvation for Infants Who Die without Being Baptized*. The Vatican. Online: www.vatican.va/roman_curia/ congregations /cfaith/cti_documents/rc_con_cfaith_doc_20070419_un- baptised-infants_en.html.

Irenaeus. "Against Heresies." In *The Apostolic Fathers with Justin Martyr and Irenaeus*. The Ante-Nicene Fathers. Vol. 1. Edited by Alexander Roberts, James Donaldson, and A. Cleveland Coxe, 309–567. Buffalo: Christian Literature, 1885. Reprint, Grand Rapids: Eerdmans, 1975.

Janeway, James. *A Token for Children: Being an Exact Assessment of the Conversion, Holy and Exemplary Lives, and Joyful Deaths of Several Young Children*. Reprint, Grand Rapids: Soli Deo Gloria, 1997.

Jeeves, Malcom. "Brain, Mind, and Behavior." In *Whatever Happened to the Soul? Scientific and Theological Portraits of Human Nature*, edited by Warren S. Brown, Nancey Murphy, and H. Newton Malony, 73–98. Minneapolis: Fortress, 1998.

Jeeves, Malcolm, ed. *From Cells to Souls—and Beyond: Changing Portraits of Human Nature*. Grand Rapids: Eerdmans, 2004.

Jeffery, Steve, Michael Ovey, and Andrew Sach, eds. *Pierced for Our Transgressions: Rediscovering the Glory of Penal Substitution*. Wheaton, IL: Crossway, 2007.

Jenson, Robert. *Systematic Theology*. New York: Oxford University Press, 1997.

Jeremias, Joachim. *Theological Dictionary of the New Testament*. Vol. 5. Edited by Gerhard Kittel, and Gerhard Friedrich. Translated by Geoffrey W. Bromiley. Grand Rapids: Eerdmans, 1985.

Jinkins, Michael. *The Church Faces Death: Ecclesiology in a Post-Modern Context*. New York: Oxford University Press, 1999.

Jobs, Steve. "Commencement Address—Stanford University 2005." Stanford University. Online: www.news.stanford. edu /news/2005/june15/jobs-061505.html.

John of Damascus. "An Exact Exposition of the Orthodox Faith." In *The Nicene and Post- Nicene Fathers*. 2nd series. Vol. 9. Edited by Philip Schaff. Grand Rapids: Eerdmans. Reprint, 1982.

Johnston, Philip S. "Death and Resurrection." In *New Dictionary of Biblical Theology*, edited by T. Desmond Alexander and Brian S. Rosner, D. A. Carson, and Graeme Goldsworthy. Downers Grove, IL: InterVarsity, 2000.

———. "Heaven: The Intermediate State." In *New Dictionary of Biblical Theology*, edited by T. Desmond Alexander, Brian S. Rosner, D. A. Carson, and Graeme Goldsworthy. Downers Grove, IL: InterVarsity, 2000.

———. *Shades of Sheol: Death and Afterlife in the Old Testament*. Downers Grove, IL: InterVarsity, 2002.

Jones, David Albert. *Approaching the End: A Theological Exploration of Death and Dying*. New York, Oxford University Press: 2007.

Jüngel, Eberhard. *Death: The Riddle and the Mystery*. Philadelphia: Westminster, 1974.

Jupp, Peter C. *Death Our Future: Christian Theology and Pastoral Practice in Funeral Ministry*. London: Epworth, 2008.

Kaiser, Otto, and Eduard Lohse. *Death and Life*. Nashville: Abingdon, 1981.

Kaufmann, Yehezkel. *The Religion of Israel: From Its Beginnings to the Babylonian Exile*. Translated by Moshe Greenberg. Chicago: Schocken, 1972.

Keefer Luke L. "Paradise." In *Baker Theological Dictionary of the Bible*, ed. Walter A. Elwell. Grand Rapids: Baker, 1996.

Kelly, J. N. D. *Early Christian Doctrines*. San Francisco: Harper and Row, 1978.

———. *The Epistles of Peter and of Jude*. Black's New Testament Commentary. Grand Rapids: Baker, 1993.

Kerr, Hugh Thomson, Jr., ed. *A Compend of Luther's Theology*. Philadelphia: Westminster, 1963.

Kettler, Christian D. *The Vicarious Humanity of Christ and the Reality of Salvation*. Lanham, Maryland: University Press of America, 1991.

Key, Andrew F. *The Concept of Death in the Old Testament*. PhD diss., Hebrew Union College, 1961.

Kierkegaard, Søren. *Concluding Unscientific Postscript*. Translated by David F. Swenson, and Walter Lowrie. Princeton, NJ: University Press, 1941.

———. *Fear and Trembling*. London: Penguin, 1986.

Kiernan, Stephen. *Last Rites: Rescuing the End of Life from the Medical System*. New York: St. Martin's, 2006.

Kilner, John F., and Arlene B. Miller, Edmund D. Pellegrino, eds. *Dignity and Dying: A Christian Appraisal*. Grand Rapids: Eerdmans, 1996.

Kirk, J. Andrew. "The Confusion of Epistemology in the West and Christian Mission." *Tyndale Bulletin* 55 (2004) 131–56.

Kirk, Kenneth E. *The Vision of God: The Christian Doctrine of the Summum Bonum*. The Bampton Lectures for 1928. Longmans, Green: London, 1931. Reprint, Harrisburg, PA: Morehouse, 1991.

Kistemaker, Simon J. "Atonement in Hebrews: A Merciful and Faithful High Priest." In *The Glory of the Atonement: Biblical, Historical & Practical Perspectives: Essays in Honor of Roger R. Nicole*, edited by Charles E. Hill, and Frank A. James, III, 163–75. Downers Grove, IL: InterVarsity, 2004.

———. *James, Epistles of John, Peter, and Jude*. New Testament Commentary. Grand Rapids: Baker, 2002.

Kline, Meredith. *The Structure of Biblical Authority*. Eugene, OR: Wipf & Stock, 1997

Köberle, J. *Sünde und Gnade im religiösen Leben des Volkes Israel bis auf Christum: Eine Geschichte des vorchristlichen Heilsbewusstseins*. Munich: Beck, 1905.

Koester, Craig R. *Hebrews*. In *The Anchor Bible Commentary*. New York: Doubleday, 2001.

Koslofsky, Craig M. *The Reformation of the Dead: Death and Ritual in Early Modern Germany, 1450–1700*. London: Palgrave Macmillan, 2000.

Kübler-Ross, Elisabeth. *Death, the Final Stage of Growth*. New York: Macmillan, 1975.

———. *Living with Death and Dying*. New York: Collier, 1981.

———. *On Death and Dying*. New York: Macmillan, 1969.

———. *Questions and Answers on Death and Dying*. New York: Macmillan, 1975.

———. *Tunnel and the Light: Essential Insights on Living and Dying with A Letter to a Child with Cancer*. New York: Marlowe, 1999.

Küng, Hans. *Eternal Life? Life after Death As a Medical, Philosophical, & Theological Problem*. London: Herder & Herder, 1984.

Kunneth, Walter. *The Theology of the Resurrection*. St. Louis, MO: Concordia, 1965.

Kushner, Harold S. *When Bad Things Happen to Good People*. New York: Avon, 1981.

Kuyper, Abraham. *The Death and Resurrection of Christ*. Grand Rapids: Zondervan, 1960.

Lake, Kirsopp, ed. "The Martyrdom of Polycarp." In *The Apostolic Fathers*. 2 vols. Loeb Classical Library. Cambridge, MA: Harvard University Press, 1913.

Landis, Robert Wharton. *The Doctrine of Original Sin as Received and Taught by the Churches of the Reformation Stated and Defended, and the Error of Dr. Hodge in Claiming That This Doctrine Recognizes the Gratuitous Imputation of Sin, Pointed Out and Refuted*. Richmond, VA: Whittet & Shepperson, 1884.

Leadingham, J. "Is Physical Death a Penalty?" *The Old and New Testament Student* 15.6 (1892) 207–34.

Leckie, Joseph. *The World to Come and Final Destiny*. Edinburgh: T. & T. Clark, 1922.

Le Goff, Jacques. *The Birth of Purgatory*. Chicago: University of Chicago Press, 1984.

Leo I. "Pope Leo I's Letter to Flavian of Constantinople." In *The Christological Controversy*, edited and translated by Richard Alfred Norris, 145–54. Minneapolis: Fortress, 1980.

Léon-Dufour, Xavier. *Life and Death in the New Testament: The Teachings of Jesus and Paul*. Translated by Terrence Prendergast. San Francisco: Harper & Row, 1979.

Leontius. *Leontius of Jerusalem: Against the Monophysites: Testimonies of the Saints and Aporiae*. Edited and translated by Patrick T. R. Gray. New York: Oxford University Press, 2006.

Lessing, Gotthold Ephraim *"Über den Beweis des Geistes und der Kraft"* [On the proof of spirit and power]. In *Gotthold Ephraim Lessings sämtlichen Schriften*, edited by Karl Lachmann, 4:11–8.20. Berlin: Goschen'sche Verlagshandlung, 1897.

Leupold, Herbert C. *Exposition of Genesis*. Grand Rapids: Eerdmans, 1941.

Lewis, Charlton T., and Charles Short. "Ars." In *A New Latin Dictionary*. New York: American, 1907.

Lewis, Clive Staples. *A Grief Observed*. New York: Bantam, 1976.

———. *The Problem of Pain*. New York: HarperCollins, 1996.

Lewis, H. D. *The Elusive Mind*. New York: Humanities, 1969.

Lifton, Robert J. *The Broken Connection: On Death and the Continuity of Life*. New York: Simon & Schuster, 1979.

Lifton, Robert, and Eric Olson. *Living and Dying*. New York: Praeger, 1974.

Lightfoot, Joseph B. *The Apostolic Fathers* 1891. Edited by J. R. Harmer. Berkeley, CA: Apocryphile, 2004.

Lightner, Robert P. *Safe in the Arms of Jesus: God's Provision for The Death of Those Who Cannot Believe*. Grand Rapids: Kregel, 2000.

Lindbeck, George. *The Nature of Doctrine: Religion and Theology in a Postliberal Age*. Philadelphia: Westminster, 1984.

Lints, Richard, Michael S. Horton, and Mark R. Talbot, eds. *Personal Identity in Theological Perspective*. Grand Rapids: Eerdmans, 2006.

Litfin, Duane. *Conceiving the Christian College*. Grand Rapids: Eerdmans, 2004.

Lokhorst, Gert-Jan. "Descartes and the Pineal Gland." In *The Stanford Encyclopedia of Philosophy*, edited Edward N. Zalta. Standford, CA: Standford University Press, 2011. Online: https://plato.stanford.eud/archives/sum2016/entires/pineal-gland.

Longenecker, Richard, ed. *Life in the Face of Death: The Resurrection Message of the New Testament*. Grand Rapids: Eerdmans, 2006.

Luther, Martin. *Luther: Lectures on Romans*, Library of Christian Classics. Vol. 15. Edited and translated by Wilhelm Pauck. Philadelphia: Westminster, 1961.

Luther, Martin. "Disputation Against Scholastic Theology." In *Luther's Works*. Vol. 31. *Career of the Reformer* I. Edited by Helmut T. Lehmann. Translated by Harold J. Grimm, 3–16. Philadelphia: Fortress, 1957.

———. "The Fourteen of Consolation for Such as Labor and Are Heavy Laden." In *Luther's Works*. Vol. 42. *Devotional Writings* I. Edited by Helmut T. Lehmann. Translated by Harold J. Grimm, 117–66. Philadelphia: Fortress, 1969.

———. *Lectures on Romans*. In *Luther's Works*. Vol. 25. Edited by Hilton C. Oswald. Translated by Jacob O. Preus. Saint Louis: Concordia, 1972.

———. *Luther's Works*. Edited by Jaroslav J. Pelikan, and Helmut T. Lehmann. 55 vols. Philadelphia: Fortress, 1955–86.

———. "Two Kinds of Righteousness." In *Luther's Works*. Vol. 31. *Career of the Reformer* I. Edited by Helmut T. Lehmann. Translated by Harold J. Grimm, 297–306. Philadelphia: Fortress, 1957.

———. "A Sermon on Preparing to Die." In *Luther's Works*. Vol. 42. *Devotional Writings* I. Edited by Helmut T. Lehmann. Translated by Martin H. Bertram, 95–115. Philadelphia: Fortress, 1969.

MacArthur, John. *Safe in the Arms of God: Truth from Heaven about the Death of a Child*. Nashville: Thomas Nelson, 2003.

MacKay, Donald. *Brains, Machines, and Persons*. Grand Rapids: Eerdmans, 1980.

Mackintosh, H. R. *The Doctrine of the Person of Jesus Christ*. New York: Charles Scribner's Sons, 1942.

MacLeod, David J. "The Resurrection of Jesus Christ: Myth, Hoax, or History." *The Emmaus Journal* 7.2 (1998) 157–99.

Macleod, Donald. *The Person of Christ*. Downers Grove, IL: InterVarsity, 1998.

Marshall, I. Howard. *Biblical Inspiration*. Grand Rapids: Eerdmans, 1982.

Marti, K. *Geschichte der israelitischen Religion*. 3rd ed. Strassburg: F. Bull, 1897.

Martin-Achard, Robert. *From Death to Life: A Study of the Development of the Doctrine of the Resurrection in the Old Testament*. London: Oliver and Boyd, 1960.

Martyr, Justin. *The First and Second Apologies*. Edited by Walter J. Burghardt, John J. Dillon, and Dennis D. McManus. Translated by Leslie William Barnard. New York: Paulist, 1997.

Matthes, J. C. "De Inrichting van den Eeredienst bij Jerobeam, I Kon. 12.26–33," *Theologische Tijdschrift* 24.6 (1890) 239–54.

Mayer, Marvin. *The Ancient Mysteries: A Sourcebook: Sacred Texts of the Mystery Religions of the Ancient Mediterranean World*. Philadelphia: University of Pennsylvania Press, 1999.

McGrath, Alister E. *Iustitia Dei: A History of the Christian Doctrine of Justification*. Cambridge: Cambridge University Press, 2005.

———. *Reformation Thought*. Cambridge: Blackwell, 1993.

———. *A Scientific Theology*. Vol. 1. Grand Rapids: Eerdmans, 2001.

McKelvey, R. J. "Temple." In *New Dictionary of Biblical Theology*, ed. T. Desmond Alexander, Brian S. Rosner, D. A. Carson, and Graeme Goldsworthy. Downers Grove, IL: InterVarsity, 2000.

McLeod, Frederick G. *Theodore of Mopsuestia*. London: Routledge, 2009.

Meilaender, Gilbert. *Neither Beast Nor God: The Dignity of the Human Person*. New York: Encounter, 2009.

Metzger, Bruce Manning. *Chapters in the History of New Testament Textual Criticism*. New Testament Tools and Studies. Boston: Brill, 1960.

Miller, Randolph Crump. *Live Until You Die*. Philadelphia: United Church, 1973.

Moffat, James. *A Critical and Exegetical Commentary on the Epistle to the Hebrews*. International Critical Commentary. New York: Scribner's, 1924. Reprint, Edinburgh: T. & T. Clark, 1948.

Mohler, R. Albert, Jr. "God, the Tsunami and the Death of Children." In *Towers* 3, no. 11. Louisville: The Southern Baptist Theological Seminary, 2005.

Mohler, R. Albert, Jr., and Daniel L. Akin. "The Salvation of the 'Little Ones': Do Infants who Die Go to Heaven?" Albert Mohler. Online: www.albertmohler. com/2009/07/16/the-salvation-of-the-little-ones-do-infants-who-die-go-to-heaven/.

Moll, Rob. *The Art of Dying: Living Fully into the Life to Come*. Downers Grove, IL: InterVarsity, 2010.

Mollat, Guillaume. "Benedict XII." In *New Catholic Encyclopedia*, 2.275–76. Washington, DC: Catholic University of America Press, 1967.

Montaigne, Michel de. "That the Taste of Good and Evil Things Depends in Large Part on the Opinion We Have of Them." In *Michel de Montaigne: The Complete Essays*, edited and translated by Michael A. Screech, 52–72. London: Penguin, 2003.

Moo, Douglas J. *The Epistle to the Romans*. New International Commentary on the New Testament. Grand Rapids: Eerdmans, 1996.

Moore, James R. "The Rise of Modern Science." In *Introduction to the History of Christianity*, edited by Tim Dowley, 48–50. Minneapolis: Fortress, 1995.

More, Henry, ed. *Ars Moriendi* (ca. 1450). Historia Provinciae Anglicanae Societatis Jesu. London: The Holbein Society, 1881.

Moreland, J. P. *Scaling the Secular City*. Grand Rapids: Baker, 1987.

Moreland, J. P., and David M. Cioochi, eds. *Christian Perspectives on Being Human*. Grand Rapids: Baker, 1993.

Moreland, James Porter, and Scott B. Rae. *Body & Soul: Human Nature and the Crisis in Ethics*. Downers Grove, IL: InterVarsity, 2000.

Morgan, Christopher W. and Robert A. Peterson, eds. *Hell Under Fire: Modern Scholarship Reinvents Eternal Punishment*. Grand Rapids: Zondervan, 2004.

Morison, Samuel Eliot, ed. "The Commonplace Book of Joseph Green (1696)." *Colonial Society of Massachusetts Publications* 34 (1942) 191–253.

Morris, Henry M. *The Biblical Basis for Modern Science*. Grand Rapids: Baker, 1984.

Morris, Thomas V., ed. *God and the Philosophers: The Reconciliation of Faith and Reason*. New York: Oxford University Press, 1996.

Motyer, J. Alec. "Judgment." In *New Dictionary of Biblical Theology*, ed. T. Desmond Alexander, Brian S. Rosner, D. A. Carson, and Graeme Goldsworthy. Downers Grove, IL: InterVarsity, 2000.

———. *The Prophecy of Isaiah: An Introduction and Commentary*. Downers Grove, IL: InterVarsity, 1993.

Mounce, Robert H. *Romans*. The New American Commentary, vol. 27. Nashville: B & H, 1995.

Mounce, William D. *A Graded Reader of Biblcal Greek*. Grand Rapids: Zondervan, 1996.

Murphy, Nancey. *Bodies and Souls, or Spirited Bodies*. Cambridge: Cambridge University Press, 2006.

———. "I Cerebrate Myself: Is There a Little Man Inside Your Brain?" *Books and Culture: A Christian Review* 5.1 (1999) 24–26.

———. "Nonreductive Physicalism: Philosophical Issues." In *Whatever Happened to the Soul? Scientific and Theological Portraits of Human Nature*, edited by Warren S. Brown, 127–48. Minneapolis: Fortress, 1998.

———. "Science and Society." In *Systematic Theology*. Vol. 3, *Witness*, ed. James William McClendon, Jr., and Nancey Murphy, 99–131. Nashville: Abingdon, 2000.

Murray, Ian H. *Revival and Revivalism: The Making and Marring of American Evangelicalism 1750–1858*. Edinburgh: The Banner of Truth Trust, 1994.

Murray, John. *The Epistle to the Romans*. Grand Rapids: Eerdmans, 1965.

———. *The Imputation of Adam's Sin*. Phillipsburg, NJ: P & R, 1992.

———. *Redemption—Accomplished and Applied*. Grand Rapids: Eerdmans, 1955.

Musurillo, Herbert Anthony. *The Acts of the Christian Martyrs*. Oxford: Oxford University Press, 1972.

Nash, Ronald. "Is There Salvation after Death? The Answer to Postmortem Evangelism." *Christian Research Journal* 27.4 (2004).

———. *When a Baby Dies*. Grand Rapids: Zondervan, 1999.

Neal, Robert E. *The Art of Dying*. New York: Harper & Row, 1973.

Nestle, Eberhard, Erwin Nestle, and Kurt Aland, eds. *Novum Testamentum Graece*. Stuttgart: Deutsche Bibelgesellschaft, 1993.

Nicol, Andrew. "Why Do Humans Die? An Exploration of the Necessity of Death in the Theology of Robert Jenson with Reference to Karl Barth's Discussion of 'Ending Time.'" In *Trinitarian Theology after Barth*, edited by Myk Habets and Phillip Tolliday, 241–54. Eugene, OR: Pickwick, 2011.

Nikolainen, Aimo T. *Der Auferstehungsglaube in der Bibel und ihrer Umwelt: Die deuteropaulinischen Schriften und die johannäische Literatur des Neuen Testaments*. Annales Academiae Scientiarum Fennicae. Germany: Suomalainen Tiedeakatemia, 1992.

Nowell, Robert. *What a Modern Catholic Believes about Death*. Chicago: Thomas Moore, 1972.

O'Connor, Mary Catherine. *The Art of Dying Well: The Development of the Ars moriendi*. New York: AMS, 1942.

Oderberg, David S. "Hylemorphic Dualism." In *Personal Identity*, edited by Ellen Frankel Paul, Fred Dycus Miller, Jr., and Jeffrey Paul, 70–99. Cambridge: Cambridge University Press, 2005.

O'Donnell, Douglas Sean. *The Beginning and End of Wisdom: Preaching Christ from the First and Last Chapters of Proverbs, Ecclesiastes, and Job*. Wheaton, IL: Crossway, 2011.

O'Connell, Robert J. *The Origin of the Soul in St. Augustine's Later Works*. New York: Fordham University Press, 1987.

Ombres, Robert. *The Theology of Purgatory*. Hales Corner, WI: Clergy Book Service, 1978.

Origen. *Commentary on the Epistle to the Romans*, Books 1–5. Fathers of the Church. Translated by Thomas P. Scheck. Washington, DC: Catholic University of America Press, 2001.

———. *Contra Celsum* [Against Celsus]. Translated by Henry Chadwick. London: Cambridge University Press, 1965.

———. *De Principiis* [On First Principles]. Translated by G. W. Butterworth. London: SPCK, 1936.

Oswalt, John N. *The Book of Isaiah, Chapters 40–66*. New International Commentary on the Old Testament. Grand Rapids: Eerdmans, 1998.

Owen, John. "Causes, Ways, and Means, of Understanding the Mind of God." In *The Works of John Owen*. Edited by William H. Goold. Vol. 4. London: Johnstone & Hunter, 1850–53. Reprint, Carlisle, PA: The Banner of Truth Trust, 1990.

———. *The Death of Death in the Death of Christ*. Edinburgh: The Banner of Truth Trust, 1959. Reprint, 2002.

———. "The Doctrine of Justification by Faith." In *The Works of John Owen*. Edited by William H. Goold. Vol. 5. London: Johnstone & Hunter, 1850–53. Reprint, Carlisle, PA: The Banner of Truth Trust, 1990.

———. "On Communion with God." In *The Works of John Owen*. Edited by William H. Goold. Vol. 2. London: Johnstone & Hunter, 1850–53. Reprint, Carlisle, PA: The Banner of Truth Trust, 1990.

———. *The Works of John Owen*. 16 vols. Edited by William H. Goold. Edinburgh; Carlisle, PA: The Banner of Truth Trust, 1966.

Packer, J. I. *A Grief Sanctified: Passing through Grief to Peace and Joy*. Ann Arbor, MI: Servant, 1997.

———. "Introductory Essay." In *The Death of Death in the Death of Christ*, 1–25. Edinburgh: The Banner of Truth Trust, 1995.

Palmer, Stuart L. "Pastoral Care and Counseling Without the 'Soul': A Consideration of Emergent Monism." In *What about the Soul? Neuroscience and Christian Anthropology*, edited by Joel B. Green, 159–70. Nashville: Abingdon, 2004.

Park, Joseph S. *Conceptions of Afterlife in Jewish Inscriptions: With Special Reference to Pauline Literature*. Tübingen: Mohr Seibeck, 2000.

Pannenberg, Wolfhart. *Anthropology in Theological Perspective*. Translated by Matthew J. O'Connell. Philadelphia: Westminster, 1985.

Paxton, Frederick S. *Christianizing Death: The Creation of a Ritual Process in Early Medieval Europe*. Ithaca, NY: Cornell University Press, 1990.

Pearson, Leonard. *Death and Dying—Current Issues in the Treatment of the Dying Person*. Cleveland: Case Western Reserve University Press, 1969.

Pedersen, Johannes. *Israel: Its Life and Culture*. London: Oxford University Press, 1964.

Pelikan, Jaroslav. *The Shape of Death: Life, Death and Immortality in the Early Fathers*. Nashville: Abingdon, 1961. Reprint, Westport, CT: Greenwood, 1978.

Penelhum, Terence. *Survival and Disembodied Existence*. New York: Humanities, 1970.

Perman, Matthew. *What Happens to Infants Who Die?* Desiring God. Online: www.desiringgod.org/resource library/articles/what-happens-to-infants-who-die.

Peterson, Robert A. *Hell on Trial: The Case for Eternal Punishment*. Phillipsburg, NJ: P & R, 1995.

Phillips, Rachael. *Well with My Soul: Four Dramatic Stories of Great Hymn Writers*. Heroes of the Faith. Uhrichsville, OH: Barbour 2004.

Philo. *De Congressu Eruditionis Gratia*. The Works of Philo of Alexandria 16. Edited by Monique Alexandre. Paris: Éditions du Cerf, 1967.

Pieper, Josef. *Death and Immortality*. Translated by Richard and Clara Winston. South Bend: St. Augustine's, 2000.

Pinnock, Clark. "The Finality of Jesus Christ in a World of Religions." In *Christian Faith and Practice in the Modern World*, edited by Mark Noll, and David Wells, 152–68. Grand Rapids: Eerdmans, 1988.

———. *Flame of Love: A Theology of the Holy Spirit*. Downers Grove, IL: InterVarsity, 1996.

———. *A Wideness in God's Mercy: The Finality of Jesus Christ in a World of Religions*. Grand Rapids: Zondervan, 1992.

Pinnock, Clark H., et al., eds. *The Openness of God: A Biblical Challenge to the Traditional Understanding of God*. Downers Grove, IL: InterVarsity, 1994.

Piper, Don. *90 Minutes in Heaven: A True Story of Death and Life*. Grand Rapids: Baker, 2004.

Piper, John. "Are There Two Wills in God." In *Still Sovereign*, edited by Thomas Schreiner, and Bruce Ware, 107–32. Grand Rapids: Baker, 2000.

———. *God's Passion for His Glory*. Wheaton, IL: Crossway, 1998.

———. *Why Do You Believe That Infants Who Die Go to Heaven?* Desiring God. Online: www.desiringgod.org/resource-library/ask-pastor-john/why-do-you-believe-that-infants-who-die-go-to-heaven.

Piper, John, Justin Taylor, and Paul Kjoss Helseth, eds. *Beyond the Bounds: Open Theism and the Undermining of Biblical Christianity*. Wheaton, IL: Crossway, 2003.

Plantinga, Alvin. *God and Other Minds: A Study of the Rational Justification of Belief in God*. New York: Cornell University Press, 1967.

———. *God, Freedom, and Evil*. Grand Rapids: Eerdmans, 1977.

———. *Warrant and Proper Function*. New York: Oxford University Press, 1993.

———. *Warrant: The Current Debate*. New York: Oxford University Press, 1993.

———. *Warranted Christian Belief*. New York: Oxford University Press, 2000.

Plantinga, Alvin, and Nicholas Wotersdorff, eds. *Faith and Rationality: Reason and Belief in God*. Notre Dame: University of Notre Dame Press, 1999.

———. "On Heresy, Mind, and Truth." *Faith and Philosophy* 16.2 (1999) 182–93.

———. "Reason and Belief in God." In *Faith and Rationality: Reason and Belief in God*, edited by Alvin Plantinga and Nicholas Wolterstorff, 16–93. Notre Dame, IN: University of Notre Dame Press, 1983.

———. "When Faith and Reason Clash: Evolution and the Bible," *Christian Scholar's Review* 21 (1991) 29–31.

Plantinga, Cornelius, Jr. *Not the Way It's Supposed to Be: A Breviary of Sin*. Grand Rapids: Eerdmans, 1995.

Plato. "Theaetetus." In *Plato in Twelve Volumes*. Vol. 12. Translated by Harold N. Fowler. Cambridge: Harvard University Press; London: William Heinemann Ltd., 1921.

Popper, Karl Raimund, and John C. Eccles. *The Self and its Brain: An Argument for Interactionism*. New York: Routledge, 2003.

Pratt, J. B. *Matter and Spirit*. New York: Macmillan, 1926.

Prestige, George Leonard. "Hades in the Greek Fathers," *Journal of Theological Studies* 24 (1923) 476–85.

Prokes, Mary Timothy. *Toward a Theology of the Body*. Grand Rapids: Eerdmans, 1996.

Pryor, Neale. "Eschatological Expectations in The Old Testament Prophets." In *The Last Things*, edited by Jack P. Lewis, 32–59. Austin, TX: Sweet, 1972.

Purtill, Richard L. "The Intelligibility of Disembodied Survival." *Christian Scholar Review* 5.1 (1975) 3–22.

Rad, Gerhard von. *Old Testament Theology*. Vol. 1. Translated by D. M. G. Stalker. Edinburgh: Oliver and Boyd, 1962.

Rahner, Karl. *On the Theology of Death*. Translated by Charles H. Henkey. New York: Herder & Herder, 1961. Reprint, 1967.

———. "Purgatory." *Theological Investigations* 19 (1984) 181–93.

Ratzinger, Joseph, ed. *Catechism of the Catholic Church*. New York: Doubleday, 2003.

———. *Eschatology: Death and Eternal Life*. Translated by Michael Waldstein. Edited by Aidan Nichols. Washington, DC: Catholic University of America Press, 1988.

Reichenbach, Bruce. "Life after Death: Possible or Impossible?" *Christian Scholar Review* 3.3 (1973) 232–44.

———. *Is Man the Phoenix? A Study of Immortality*. Grand Rapids: Eerdmans, 1978.

Reicke, Bo. *The Disobedient Spirits and Christian Baptism: A Study of 1 Peter III.19 and Its Context*. Copenhagen: Hakan Ohlssons Boktryckeri, 1946.

Reinis, Austra. *Reforming the Art of Dying: The* ars moriendi *in the German Reformation*. Hampshire, England: Ashgate, 2007.

Reymond, Robert L. *A New Systematic Theology of the Christian Faith.* Nashville: Thomas Nelson, 1998.

Ridderbos, Herman. "Death Before the Parousia: the Intermediate State." In *Paul,* edited by Herman Ridderbos, 497–508. Grand Rapids: Eerdmans, 1975.

———. "The Resurrection." In *Paul,* edited by Herman Ridderbos, 537–51. Grand Rapids: Eerdmans, 1975.

Riddlebarger, Kim. "Human Sin and God's Purpose: Some Thoughts on the Doctrine of Divine Concurrence." *Modern Reformation* 11.5 (2002) 32–37.

Roberts, A., and J. Donaldson, eds. *The Martyrdom of Polycarp.* In *The Ante-Nicene Fathers.* 10 vols. Grand Rapids: Eerdmans, 1979.

Robinson, John A. T. *The Body.* London: SCM, 1952.

Robinson, Theodore H. *Prophecy and the Prophets in Ancient Israel.* London: Gerald Duckworth, 1953.

Rosen, Jonathan "The Final Stage." *The New York Times Magazine,* December 26, 2004. Online: www.nytimes.com/2004/12/26/magazine/26KUBLER.html.

Rousseau, Jean-Jacques. *Emile: Or Treatise on Education.* Translated by William H. Payne. New York: Prometheus, 2003.

Runia, David T. *Philo of Alexandria and the* Timaeus *of Plato.* Leiden: Brill, 1986.

Rush, A. C. *Death and Burial in Christian Antiquity.* Washington, DC: Catholic University of America Press, 1941.

Sanders, John. *The God Who Risks: A Theology of Divine Providence.* Downers Grove, IL: InterVarsity, 2007.

———. "Is Belief in Christ Necessary for Salvation?" *The Evangelical Quarterly* 60 (1988) 249–52.

———. *No Other Name.* Grand Rapids: Eerdmans, 1992.

Schaeffer, Francis A. "Escape from Reason" In *The Francis A. Schaeffer Trilogy.* Wheaton, IL: Crossway, 1990.

———. "He Is There and He Is Not Silent." In *The Francis A. Schaeffer Trilogy.* Wheaton, IL: Crossway, 1990.

———. *How Should We Then Live? The Rise and Decline of Western Thought and Culture.* Wheaton, IL: Crossway, 2005.

Schmitt, Keith Randall. *Death and After-life in the Theologies of Karl Barth and John Hick: A Comparative Study.* Amsterdam: Rodopi, 1985.

Schreiner, Thomas R. *1, 2 Peter, Jude.* The New American Commentary, vol. 37. Nashville: B & H, 2003.

———. *Romans.* Baker Exegetical Commentary on the New Testament. Grand Rapids: Baker, 1998.

Schopenhauer, Authur. "On Death and Its Relation to the Indestructibility of our Inner Nature." In *The World as Will and Representation* [Die welt als wille und vorstellung, 1844]. 2 Vols. New York: Dover, 1966.

Schreiner, Thomas R., and Shawn Wright. *Believer's Baptism.* Nashville: B & H, 2006.

Schultz, Adolph Hermann. *Die Voraussetzungen der christlichen Lehre von der Unsterblichkeit dargestellt.* Göttingen: Vanderhoek & Ruprecht, 1861.

Schwally, Friedrich *Das Leben nach dem Tod nach den Vorstellungen des Alten Israel und des Judentums einschließlich des Volksglaubens im Zeitalter Christi: eine biblische Untersuchung.* Giessen, Germany: Ricker, 1892.

Schweitzer, Albert. *Kultur und Ethik.* Munich: C. H. Beck, 1923.

Searle, John. *The Rediscovery of the Mind.* Cambridge, MA: MIT Press, 1992.

Segal, Alan. *Life after Death: A History of the Afterlife in Western Religion.* New York: Doubleday, 2004.
Sellers, R. V. *The Council of Chalcedon.* London: SPCK, 1953.
———. *Two Ancient Christologies.* London: SPCK, 1940.
Shedd, William G. T. *Calvinism: Pure and Mixed: A Defence of the Westminster Standards.* New York: Scribner's, 1893. Reprint, 1986.
Sherlock, William. *A Practical Discourse Concerning Death.* London: R. Edwards, 1810.
Shibles, Warren. *Death: An Interdisciplinary Analysis.* Whitewater, WI: Language, 1974.
Shinners, John. "The Art of Dying Well." In *Medieval Popular Religion, 1000–1500, A Reader,* edited by John Shinners, 526–35. Orchard Park, NY: Broadview, 1997.
Shogren, G. S. "Life and Death." In *Dictionary of the Later New Testament and Its Developments,* ed. Ralph P. Martin, and Peter H. Davids. Downers Grove, IL: InterVarsity, 1997.
Shults, F. LeRon. *Reforming Theological Anthropology.* Grand Rapids: Eerdmans, 2003.
Simpson John Andrew, and Edmund S. C. Weiner, eds. *The Oxford English Dictionary.* Vol. 10. Oxford: Clarendon, 1989.
Simpson, Michael. *Dying, Death and Grief: A Critically Annotated Bibliography and Source Book of Thanatology and Terminal Care.* New York: Plenum, 1977.
———. *The Facts of Death.* Englewood Cliffs, NJ: Prentice Hall, 1979.
———. *The Theology of Death and Eternal Life.* Theology Today. Notre Dame, IN: Fides, 1971.
Sire, James W. *The Universe Next Door.* Downers Grove, IL: InterVarsity, 2004.
Smend, R. *Lehrbuch der alttestamentlichen Relgionsgeschichte* Freiburg i.B.: Mohr, 1893.
Smith, David. *With Willful Intent: A Theology of Sin.* Wheaton, IL: BridgePoint, 1994.
Smith, Gary V. *Isaiah 40–66.* The New American Commentary, vol. 15b. Nashville: B&H, 2009.
Smith, S. M. "Intermediate State." In *Evangelical Dictionary of Theology.* Grand Rapids: Baker, 1984.
Southern Baptist Convention. "The Scriptures." In *The Baptist Faith and Message.* Nashville: LifeWay Church Resources, 2000.
Spinoza, Benedict de. *Ethics.* Edited by Edwin Curley. London: Penguin, 1996.
Sproul, R. C. *Faith Alone: The Evangelical Doctrine of Justification.* Grand Rapids: Baker, 1995.
———. *Surprised by Suffering.* Wheaton, IL: Tyndale, 1989.
Spurgeon, Charles. "Expositions of the Doctrines of Grace." In *The Metropolitan Tabernacle Pulpit* 7.297–303. London: Passmore and Alabater, 1862.
Stagg, John W. *Calvin, Twisse and Edwards on The Universal Salvation of Those Dying in Infancy.* Richmond, VA: Whittet & Shepperson, 1902.
Stannard, David E. *The Puritan Way of Death: A Study in Religion, Culture, and Social Change.* New York: Oxford University Press, 1977.
Starenko, Ronald C. *God, Grass, and Grace: A Theology of Death.* St. Louis: Concordia, 1975.
Stendahl, Krister. *Immortality and Resurrection.* London: Macmillan, 1965.
———., ed. *Immortality and Resurrection: Death in the Western World, Two Conflicting Currents of Thought.* London: Macmillan, 1968.
Stoddard, Sandol. *The Hospice Movement: A Better Way of Caring for the Dying.* Briar Cliff Manor, NY: Stein and Day, 1978.
Stott, John. *The Cross of Christ.* Downers Grove, IL: InterVarsity, 2006.

Strong, Augustus H. *Systematic Theology: A Compendium Designed for the Use of Theological Students*. Valley Forge, PA: Judson, 1907.
Sullivan, Francis A. *The Christology of Theodore of Mopsuestia*. Rome: Universitatis Gregorianae, 1956.
Swete, Henry Barclay. "Theodorus of Mopsuestia." In *A Dictionary of Christian Biography, Literature, Sects and Doctrines*, ed. William Smith, and Henry Wace. Boston: Little, Brown, and Company, 1887.
Swinburne, Richard. "Body and Soul." In *The Mind-Body Problem: A Guide to the Current Debate*, edited by R. Warner, and T. Szubka, 311–16. Cambridge: Blackwell, 1994.
―――. *The Evolution of the Soul*. Oxford: Clarendon, 1997.
Swinton, John, and Richard Payne, eds. *Living Well and Dying Faithfully: Christian Practices for End-of-Life Care*. Grand Rapids: Eerdmans, 2009.
Taylor, Michael J. *The Mystery of Suffering and Death*. New York: Image, 1973.
Taylor, Nathaniel W. *Essays, Lectures, Etc. upon Select Topics in Revealed Theology*. New York: n.p., 1859.
Tertullian. *Adversus Marcionem* [Against Marcion]. Edited and translated by Ernest Evans. Oxford: Clarendon, 1972.
―――. *Adversus Praxean* [Against Praxeus]. Edited and translated by Ernest Evans. London: SPCK, 1948.
―――. *Apologeticus* [Apology]. Edited by T. E. Page. Translated by T. R. Glover. Loeb Classical Library. London: William Heinemann, 1931.
―――. *De Baptismo* [On Baptism]. Edited and translated by Ernest Evans. London: SPCK, 1964.
―――. *De Carne Christi* [On the Incarnation of Christ]. Edited and translated by Evans, Ernest. London: SPCK, 1956.
―――. *De Testimonio Animae* [On the Evidences of the Soul]. Edited and translated by J. H. Waszink. Amsterdam: Meulenhoff, 1947.
―――. *The Passion of Perpetua and Felicity*. New Advent. Online: www.newadvent.org/fathers/0324.htm.
Theodore of Mopsuestia. *Catechetical Homilies*. Translated by Alphonse Mingana. Woodbrooke Studies 5. Cambridge: W. Heffer & Sons, 1932.
Thiel, John E. *Nonfoundationalism*. Minneapolis: Fortress, 1994.
Thielicke, Helmut. *Being Human . . . Becoming Human*. Translated by Geoffrey W. Bromiley. New York: Doubleday, 1984.
―――. *Death and Life*. Translated by Edward H. Schroeder. Philadelphia: Fortress, 1946.
―――. *Living With Death*. Translated by Geoffrey W. Bromiley. Grand Rapids: Eerdmans, 1983.
Tillich, Paul. *Systematic Theology*. Vol. 3. London: Nisbet, 1964.
Tolstoy, Leo. *The Death of Ivan Ilych*. Translated by Louise Maude and Aylmer Maude. New York: Health Sciences, 1973.
Torrance, Thomas F. *Atonement: The Person and Work of Christ*. Edited by Robert T. Walker. Downers Grove, IL: InterVarsity, 2009.
Toynbee, Arnold. "The Relation between Life and Death, Living and Dying." In *Man's Concern with Death*, edited by Arnold Toynbee, 259–71. St. Louis: McGraw-Hill, 1969.
Trent, Council of. "Decree Concerning Original Sin." In *Canons and Decrees of the Council of Trent*, translated by H. J. Schroeder, 17–28. Rockford, IL: Tan, 1978.

Tromp, Nicholas J. *Primitive Conceptions of Death and the Nether World in the Old Testament*. Rome: Pontifical Biblical Institute, 1969.

Turner, Max. "Approaching Personhood." *Evangelical Quarterly* 3 (2005) 211–33.

Turretin, Francis. *Institutes of Elenctic Theology*. Edited by James T. Dennison, Jr. Translated by George Musgrave Giger. 3 vols. Phillipsburg, NJ: P & R, 1997.

Unger, Merrill F. "Intermediate State." In *The New Unger's Bible Dictionary*, edited by R. K. Harrison, 623–26. Chicago: Moody, 1988.

Vanauken, Sheldon. *A Severe Mercy*. London: Hodder & Stoughton, 2011.

Van Driel, Edwin Christian. "The Logic of Assumption." In *Exploring Kenotic Christology: The Self-Emptying of God*, edited by C. Stephen Evans, 264–90. Oxford: Oxford University Press, 2006.

VanGemeren, W. A., ed. *New International Dictionary of Old Testament Theology and Exegesis*. Carlisle: Paternoster, 1997.

Vanhoozer, Kevin J. *The Drama of Doctrine: A Canonical-Linguistic Approach to Christian Theology*. Louisville: Westminster John Knox, 2005.

———. *Is There Meaning in This Text?* Grand Rapids: Zondervan, 1998.

Vaux, Kenneth L. *Will to Live/Will to Die: Ethics and the Search for a Good Death*. Minneapolis: Augsburg, 1978.

Waldron, Samuel E. *A Modern Exposition of the 1689 Baptist Confession of Faith*. Durham, England: Evangelical, 1989.

Walton, Douglas N. *On Defining Death: An Analytic Study of the Concept of Death in Philosophy and Medical Ethics*. Montreal: McGill-Queen's University Press, 1979.

Ware, Bruce A. *God's Greater Glory: The Exalted God of Scripture and the Christian Faith*. Wheaton, IL: Crossway, 2004.

———. *God's Lesser Glory: The Diminished God of Open Theism*. Wheaton, IL: Crossway, 2000.

———. *Their God is Too Small: Open Theism and the Undermining of Confidence in God*. Wheaton, IL: Crossway, 2003.

Ware, Kallistos. T. "One Body in Christ: Death and the Communion of Saints," *Sobornost* 3.2 (1981) 179–96.

Warfield, Benjamin Breckenridge. "On the Antiquity and Unity of the Human Race." In *Biblical and Theological Studies*, edited by Samuel G. Craig, 235–60. Phillipsburg, NJ: P&R, 1952.

———. *The Person and Work of Christ*. Philadelphia: P&R, 1950.

———. *Studies in Theology*, Carlisle, PA: The Banner of Truth Trust, 1988.

Weaver, Richard. *Ideas Have Consequences*. Chicago: University of Chicago Press, 1984.

Webb, R. A. *The Theology of Infant Salvation*. Richmond, VA: Presbyterian Committee, 1907.

Wedderburn, A. J. M. *Baptism and Resurrection: Studies in Pauline Theology against Its Graeco-Roman Background*. Eugene, OR: Wipf & Stock, 2011.

Wellum, Stephen J. Classroom Lecture Notes. The Southern Baptist Theological Seminary, 84940—*Christology and Incarnation*, Spring 2009. Internet.

———. Classroom Lecture Notes. The Southern Baptist Theological Seminary, 27425—*The Doctrine of the Work of Christ*, Fall 2007. Internet.

Wesley, John. *The Heart of John Wesley's Journal*. Edited by Percy Livingston Parker. Peabody, MA: Hendrickson, 2008.

Whitehead, Alfred N. *Process and Reality*. New York: Macmillan, 1929.

Whybray, Roger N. *Isaiah 40-66*. New Century Bible Commentary. Grand Rapids: Eerdmans, 1981.
Wiese, Bill. *23 Minutes in Hell*. Lake Mary, FL: Charisma, 2006.
Williams, Jarvis J. "Maccabean Martyr Traditions in Paul's Theology of Atonement." Ph.D. diss., The Southern Baptist Theological Seminary, 2007.
Williams, Norman P. *The Ideas of the Fall and Original Sin*. London: Longmans, Green and Co., 1927.
Willis, John R. *The Teachings of the Church Fathers*. New York: Herder & Herder, 1966.
Wolff, Hans Walter. *Anthropology of the Old Testament*. Philadelphia: Fortress, 1974.
Wolff, Richard. *The Last Enemy*. Washington, DC: Canon, 1974.
Wolfson, H. A. "The Immortality of the Soul and Resurrection in the Philosophy of the Church Fathers," *Harvard Divinity School* 22 (1956-57) 5-40.
Wolterstorff, Nicholas. *Lament for a Son*. Grand Rapids: Eerdmans, 1987.
———. *Reason within the Bounds of Religion*. Grand Rapids: Eerdmans, 1984.
Wood, W. Jay. *Epistemology: Becoming Intellectually Virtuous*. Contours of Christian Philosophy. Downers Grove, IL: InterVarsity, 1998.
Wright, David. *Infant Baptism in Historical Perspective*. London: Paternoster, 2007.
———. *What Has Infant Baptism Done to Baptism?* London: Paternoster, 2005.
Wright, F. A. *Fathers of the Church*. London: Routledge, 1928.
Wright, J. Edward. *The Early History of Heaven*. New York: Oxford University Press, 2000.
Wright, John Hickey. "Death (Theology of)." In *New Catholic Encyclopedia* 4.686-95. Washington, DC: Catholic University of America Press, 1967.
Wright, N. T. "Philippians." In *Theological Interpretation of the New Testament: A Book-by-Book Survey*, edited by Kevin J. Vanhoozer, 134-39. Grand Rapids: Baker Academic, 2008.
———. *The Resurrection of the Son of God*. Fortress: Minneapolis, 2003.
Yandell, Keith. "A Defense of Dualism." *Faith and Philosophy* 12.4 (1995) 48-566.

Subject Index

Ambrose, 170–71n27, 173, 219
angels, 36n2, 51n41, 64n81, 79, 138
Anselm, 38n7, 219, 227
Aquinas, Thomas. *See* Thomas Aquinas.
Ars moriendi, vii, 2, 2n5, 3n5, 28,
    29n103, 203, 205, 206, 206n31,
    208, 211n54, 220, 222, 235, 236,
    238
Athanasius, 122n26, 123, 123n30,
    124n34, 220
Augustine, Saint, viii, xii, 11n31, 16,
    16n50, 21, 23, 23n79, 24n79,
    38n7, 42n16, 44, 44n20, 45,
    45n21, 47, 51n41, 52n42, 53,
    53nn45,47, 83n50, 95n86,
    122n26, 126n40, 129n47,
    130n47, 138, 138n61, 142,
    142n7, 159, 159n68, 168,
    168n24, 169, 169nn23,26,27,
    170–71n27, 171, 171n28
    172nn30–32, 173, 173nn34–
    36, 174, 174nn39–40,
    175, 175nn43,45, 176,
    176nn48,49,53, 177, 177n54,
    178nn57–58, 181n63, 183n70,
    187n87, 205n26, 214n61, 215,
    215nn62–64, 216, 216nn65–67,
    217, 220, 221, 223, 236, 237

beatification, 53, 215–217

beatific vision, 26, 32, 51n41, 142n7,
    181n63, 213, 214, 214n61, 215,
    215nn62,64, 216, 225
biolatry, 4, 8, 17, 18, 26,30, 31n107,
    34, 100, 136, 164n7, 181n63,
    201n18
Blandina, 154, 155, 155n50, 156

Contemptu mundi, 5n12, 6, 6–7n17, 33,
    149, 202, 206
Council of Trent, 171n28, 173n35, 174,
    174n39, 176, 176n52, 241

evil, ix, 7n18, 13, 14, 14n43, 20, 21n65,
    51n40, 54, 54nn48,49, 55,
    55n49, 57n57, 58, 60, 60n66,
    64n81, 66, 67n88, 69, 69n97,
    83n50, 90, 113, 154, 166n13,
    176, 177, 187, 202, 216n66,

Gilgamesh, 5nn13–14, 6n14, 13n41,
    44n18, 46n28, 73nn3,5,6,
    74nn7–8, 76n22, 89, 89nn64–
    65, 90nn66,68,69, 91, 91nn71–
    75, 92, 92nn76–78, 94n85,
    95n87, 96n90, 229

holiness, 8, 55, 55n50, 57, 58n61, 96,
    97n92, 99n97, 101, 110, 129,
    163n6, 166, 169n27, 173n36,
    177, 193n112, 196, 207

SUBJECT INDEX

immortality, 18n57, 21, 26, 37, 43, 44n18, 46, 46n28, 47, 50, 88n63, 113, 131, 138, 170n27, 180n61, 216
International Theological Commission, 13n40, 179n60, 230

limbo, 13n40, 20, 179n60, 180n63, 181n63
Luther, Martin. *See* Martin Luther.

Martin Luther, xi, 47, 49n36, 56n53, 57n57, 58n61, 65, 66n85, 70n98, 200, 200n16, 203, 203n21, 205, 2105nn27,28, 210, 210nn49,50, 211, 211n51, 231, 233, 234
Memento mori, vii, 1, 8, 33, 62, 63, 133, 149, 200n17, 201n18, 202, 203

non-revelatory hypothetical presumption, 182n68, 186, 193, 193n112

Origen, 122, 122n28, 170n27, 173, 178n58, 236
original sin, viii, 12n37, 44, 83n50, 126n39, 168, 169, 169nn24,26,27, 170n27, 171, 172, 172n30, 173, 173nn34,35, 174, 174nn39,40, 175, 176, 176nn52,53, 177, 177n54, 178, 178nn56-58, 179, 180nn61,63, 182n66, 184, 187, 187n89, 188, 189, 191, 220, 226, 229, 232, 241, 243

paedosoterism, 21n65, 169, 169n27, 181, 182, 185, 187, 188, 190, 191, 192n110
Perpetua, 149n25, 154n45, 155, 155n50, 156, 156nn54,57, 157, 157nn58,62, 158, 159, 223, 241

Sheol, 11n33, 12, 70, 73, 74, 75, 75nn18-19, 76, 76n26, 77, 78, 79, 81n44, 82n46, 102, 109, 147, 185, 186

Tertullian, 12n37, 117n11, 120nn19-20, 122, 122nn25,28, 145n17, 147n20, 149, 149nn23,25, 154n45, 155, 155n53, 156n54, 157nn58,62, 169n27, 170n27, 172nn30-31, 173, 173n35, 241
thanatology, 9, 10, 11, 13, 14, 16, 17, 19, 21, 21n65, 22, 27n92, 28, 30, 34, 132, 240
Thomas Aquinas, 38n7, 215n64, 219
Trent, Council. *See* Council of Trent.

Author Index

Barth, Karl, 10n28, 56, 57n56, 93, 93n82, 110n127, 113, 113n3, 114, 114n4, 115, 115n6, 116, 116n9, 133, 133n56, 164, 165n8, 174, 174n37, 221, 236, 239

Bavinck, Herman, 5n12, 10n28, 23, 23nn76–77, 24, 24nn80–84, 25, 26, 26n88, 48, 48nn33–34, 53n48, 80nn38,42, 222

Berkhof, Louis, 9n24, 20, 20n63, 21, 1n65, 22, 22n66, 80n42, 129, 129nn45–46, 130, 131, 222

Carson, Donald, 8n21, 10n28, 16n48, 54n49, 55n49, 58n61, 60n66, 62n70, 68n93, 82n45, 99n97, 115, 116n8, 135n57, 201n18, 223, 227, 231, 234, 235

Edwards, Jonathan, vii, 4n11, 15n47, 58n61, 71n99, 99n97, 166n15, 168n23, 177n54, 179, 180, 180nn61–63, 183n70, 186n86, 187, 187n89, 188n92, 190, 204n23, 208n39, 213, 225, 226

Erickson, Millard, 14n43, 16n48, 21, 21n65, 22, 22n67, 38n7, 46, 46n29, 47, 80n42, 120n19, 130, 130n49, 131, 132, 168n23, 178n57, 226

Feinberg, John, 14n43, 17n54, 41n14, 54n48, 58n61, 60n66, 67n88, 68n92, 69n97, 70n98, 166n13, 227

Grudem, Wayne, 22n66, 23, 23n75, 55, 55n52, 122–23n29, 125n39, 131, 131n51, 168n23, 164n77, 190n103, 228

Helm, Paul, 8n21, 29, 29n100, 61n68, 63n75, 71n99, 80n42, 129n45, 137, 137n59, 142n4, 201, 201n18, 229

Piper, John, 63n79, 68n94, 101n102, 167n17, 168n23, 181, 182, 182nn64,66, 193n112, 237, 238

Rahner, Karl, 9n27, 27, 27nn92,93,95, 28, 28n96, 38n7, 45, 45nn22,23, 47n31, 48, 49, 50, 53, 80n42, 129n45, 145nn16–17, 146n17, 238

Ratzinger, Joseph, 29n104, 45n22, 59n65, 74, 74n11, 77n27, 80n42, 106n111, 107n117, 108n120, 130n48, 146, 147, 147n18, 148n21, 174n40, 179n59, 212, 212n56, 238

Thielicke, Helmut, 4n8, 8n22, 17n54, 19n58, 26, 26n89, 27, 27nn89–91, 34n116, 41n14, 48, 49, 49n36, 57, 57nn57,58, 58n61, 59, 59n65, 60n67, 61n67, 62n72, 70n98, 80n42, 144, 144n13, 166n14, 198n9, 199, 199nn11,13,15, 200, 200n16, 202n19, 210nn48,49, 211, 211n53, 212n55, 213, 213n58, 241

Ware, Bruce, 55n51, 67n88, 69n97, 96n89, 167n17, 228, 237, 242
Wellum, Stephen, x, 175n41, 242
Wright, David, 170n27, 171nn27–29, 172nn30,31, 173nn33,35,36, 174, 174nn37–39, 175nn42,44, 243

Scripture Index

Genesis

1:26	36, 36n2, 41n14, 96, 124
1:27–28	87, 126n39, 144n15, 211
1:31	14, 69, 105
2:7	11, 36, 54n48, 106, 117n11
2:9,	50, 51n41, 52, 52n43
2:17	24, 28, 39, 50, 50n38, 51n41, 53, 54, 57, 68n95, 69, 87, 90, 98, 100, 110n128, 121, 132, 146, 161, 167n21, 177, 182n64, 187n88, 197, 198
2:18	143n11
3:1	64n80, 195
3:3	52
3:4–5	115, 133
3:6	51n41, 56n55, 167n21
3:8	7, 51n41, 86, 143n11
3:17	40, 51n41
3:19	24, 39, 41, 41n14, 46, 51n41, 90, 107, 108, 115n7, 165
3:22–24	17n55, 39, 41, 50, 51n39, 51n41, 52n43, 54, 68n95, 97n92, 167n21
4:1	128n44
4:3–11	68n95
4:6–7	56, 199
5:1–2	110n130
5:5	64n80, 68n95, 90
6:3	63n80
6:5	96n89, 110n128
6:8	86
6:11–13	4n10, 6n15, 54
6:23	5
9:5–6	96, 108n119, 148, 211
11:32	64n80
12:2	85
12:3	110n130
15:15	80
15:16	103, 103n105
17:8	84n55
17:14	83n50, 176
18:19	89
18:25	15, 58, 145n16, 193, 196n4, 197
19:24–25	68n95
22:15–18	189n98, 196
23:1	64n80
25:7	64n80
25:8	80
28:14	110n130
35:18	79
50:19–20	54n49, 67n88

Exodus

3:6	74n9, 80n41, 108n120
4:11	67n88
5:3	17n55
7:13, 22	104n107
8:15, 19	104n107
9:7, 12, 34–35	104n107
10:1–2, 16–17	94, 104n107
11:4–6	4n10, 68n95, 104
11:10	104n107
12:12	104, 132
12:29–30	104
14:8	104n107
14:21	101n100
15:22–27	104
16:4, 35	52n43, 104
17:1–7	104
19:5–6	81n45
20:3	94
20:5	32n110, 104n109, 167, 167n18, 188n93
21:12–17	83n49
22:22–24	17n55
23:7	188n93, 197
23:23–33	103
32:9–10	7n19, 54, 167n18
32:32	5n12, 110n128
33:3, 5	51n41, 65n84
33:11	86
33:14–15	143n11
34:7	32n110, 167, 197
34:9	87
34:14	104n109

Leviticus

10:1–3	4n10, 6n16, 101, 161n1, 163n6, 181n63, 194n2, 197
13	86n58
16:29–34	132
17:11	52n43, 132
20:2–5	83n49, 90n67, 100n99
20:7–8	54n49
20:27	74n9
24:17–21	83n49

Numbers

6:24–26	85
11:31	101n100, 104, 166n16
12:3	163
14:2	189
14:18	32, 188n93
15:32–36	83n49
16:21	4n10, 7n19, 54, 65n84, 68n95
16:30	73nn3–4, 102
16:44–50	102, 166n16
21:6–9	166n16
24:2	185n81
25:1–11	102, 109, 105, 166n16
35:16–21	83n49

Deuteronomy

1:37, 39	189
2:11, 20	78n32
2:24–37	68n95, 182n64
3:13	78n32
4:12	11
4:25–31	189
4:40	70
5	32n110, 84, 98, 104n109, 167n18, 188n93
7:2, 3–14	68n95, 82n45, 84, 85n56, 87, 102–103, 143n11
12:5–7, 11–12	143n11
13:6–11	96n91
8:3	51n41, 52n43
18:11	74n9
19:4–5	68, 83n49, 166n12
21:23	93n81, 121
25:4	50n38
26	75n16
28:20–22	17n55
29:29	39, 68n94, 69n97

30:15–16	49, 85
30:19–20	40, 41n15, 105n110
31:26	32n110
32:22	73nn3,5, 75n17
32:39	39, 55, 65, 67n88, 68n95, 75n17, 81n44, 94, 100, 105n110, 124n36, 203, 208
32:46–47	41n15, 51n41
32:50–51	5n12, 110n128
34:10	86

Joshua

3:10	75n16
6:21	17n55
7	5n12, 110n128
8:24–27	17n55
11:20	68n95
12:4	78n32
23:14	31
24:19	104n109, 189

1 Samuel

2:6–8	67n88, 73n3
2:12–17, 22–25	101
2:27–36	166n16
3:11–14	101, 166n16
4:18	166n16
6:6	104n107
10:10	185n81
13:14	6n15
17:26, 36	75n16
19:23–24	185n81
22:19	17n55
25:37–38	68n95
26:23	189n99
28:11–19	74n9, 79, 95n86

2 Samuel

2:5, 6	68n95, 93
5:18	78n32
8:15	56n61, 99n97
12:10	17n55
28:19	68n95

1 Kings

2:2–9	31, 73n3
8:31–32	40n11
8:46	7n19, 54n49
11:7	90n67
11:11–13	54n49
12:1–15	54n49
14:11–13	93
16:4	93
17:1	101n100
17:21	79, 101
18:1, 41–45	101n100
18:38	104n108
21:24	93
22:34–35	68n95, 166n16

2 Kings

2:23–24	68n95, 166n16, 68n95
4:8–37	166n16, 198
5:7	65, 67n88, 100, 203
16:3	99n98
17:17	99n98
19	68n95, 75n16
23:10,13	90n67

1 Chronicles

10:13	74n9
16:29	58n61, 99n97
21:7–13, 27–30	17n55

2 Chronicles

6:36	7n19
18–23	68n95
20:21	58n61, 99n97
33:6	99n98

SCRIPTURE INDEX

Job

1:12–22	68n95, 93, 101n100, 104n108, 166n16, 194n2
2:10	105n110
3	74n10, 91
7:8–10	186
9:12	96n89, 97n92, 141n2, 198n7
10:1	74n10
10:12	66n87
13:15	194n2, 197, 199
14:1–3	65, 68n95
14:13	74n10, 91
17:13–16	76n21, 91
18:13	34n115
19:7	6n15
25:4	188
26:6	34n115, 75n17, 77n31, 91
28:22	34n115, 91
33:18	73, 74n7
38:7	138
40:4–5	6n16, 161n1
42:2	67n88, 194n2
42:7	6n15

Psalms

1	85
2:8	137
6	82n47, 91
7:11	196n4
8	7n19, 79n34
9:8	196n4
14:3	7n19
16:11	65, 73n3, 84n53, 106n111, 109n123, 203
17:15	109n123
18:4–5	34n115
22	17n55, 121n22, 188n95
23:4	34n115
24:1	102, 141n2
27:1–8	51n41
28:1	74n8
29	58n61, 99n97
30	73n3, 74nn7–8, 91
33:5	58n61, 99n97
34:21	57n57
39	65n84, 82n47, 199
40:6	120n18
41:12	143n11
42:2	75n16
45:6	196n4
49	34n115, 73n3, 84n53, 106n111, 109n123
50	58n61, 67n88, 99n97
51:5	184n74
53:3	7n19
55	73n3, 74n7
58:3	184n74, 185n80
63:9	79
68:18	80
69:28	107n118
71:20	79
73	51n41, 76, 84nn53,55, 108n120, 109n123, 216n65
75:6–7	67n88
76:6–7	91
78:56–62	17n55
79:3	93
82:1,6	79n34
84:2	75n16
86:13	73n3
88	73n6, 77n31, 91
89	58n61, 73n3, 99n97
90	6, 15n47, 24, 34, 62, 63n77, 65n84, 110, 115n7, 191n106, 199, 200, 204
91	70
94:17	91
95:4	79n37
96	58n61, 99n97, 196n4
98:9	196n4
99	58n61, 99n97
103:14	6, 110
104	87

106:37–38	99n98	6:3	9, 93
110	99n97	7:1	66n86, 203, 206–207
113:2	198		
115	11, 67n88, 82n47, 91, 194	7:20	7n19
		7:29	100
116:15	vi, 65, 130, 134, 203, 204n24	8:4	141n2, 95n89, 97n92, 141n2, 198n7
119:68	15, 31, 54, 145n16, 165n10, 194	8:11	98
119:89–91	97n92, 195	9:5–6	82, 91, 143n12
133:3	106, 128n44, 146, 195, 205, 214	9:10	70, 76n26
		12:7	79
135:5–7	67n88	19:5	74
137:9	182n64		
139	68n95, 73n5, 75n17, 79n37, 109n123, 185n80		

Song of Solomon

8:6	73, 106n111, 194, 199n15

141:7	73n3
148	194
149:4	193
150	111

Isaiah

1:10–15	132n54
1:18–21	17n55, 58n61, 99n97
5	58n61, 86n58, 99n97
6:3	54
7:11	73n3
7:15–16	178n57
9:14–17	96n91
10	67n88, 68n95, 69n97
11:9	33n113, 36n1, 217
13:3–19	165n11
14:9–15	34n115, 73n3, 74n9, 77n31, 56n55, 64n81, 73nn3,5, 74n8, 76, 181n63
14:19	93
19	94
26:19–20	74n10, 77n31, 84, 108, 109n122, 135
28:18	34n115
29:16	67n88
38	34n115, 74n7, 76n21, 81, 91

Proverbs

2:18	77n31
3	51n41, 52, 70
4:13	41n15
7:27	82n46
8:22–31	191n106
9	77n31, 82n46, 83n51
10	83n51, 149
11	51n41, 52, 83n51
15	51n41, 73n3, 75n17
16	67n88
18:12	51n41
19	73n3, 198n10
21	67n88, 77n31, 91
23:13–14	73n3
27:20	34n115
28:17	74n8
29:1	73n3
30:16	34, 34n115

Ecclesiastes

4:1–3	65

Isaiah (continued)

40	6, 110, 137n58, 167
45:5–7	54, 55, 67n88, 81n44, 87, 105n110
45:9–10	31, 96n89, 97n92, 141n2, 196n7
46:9–10	67n88, 194
47:8–11	7n18
51:14	74n7
53:5–6	130, 188n95
53:11–12	120n18, 121n22, 125
57	65, 73n3, 91, 203
59:2	51n41
59:21	32n111
61	137n58
64:8	67n88
66:24	41n15, 55, 76n20

Jeremiah

1:5	184, 191n106
3:1–9	83n48
8:1–2	93
9:21	34n115
10:1	75n16
11:20	196n4
13:8–14	165n11
15:3	17n55
16:4	93
17:10	184n73
19:4–7	183, 184, 189
24:7	51n41
31:29–30	127
31:31–34	32n111, 51n41
32:18–23	184n73, 189
32:35	100n99
51:39	91

Lamentations

3:37–38	67n88
3:55	74n8

Ezekiel

5:12	17n55
8:18	96n91
9:5–6	96n91, 166n16, 182n64, 187
16:20–21	99n98, 100n99
16:60–63	32n111
18:4	105n110, 105n110, 108n119, 127
18:23,32	65, 168n22, 203
21:24	189n98
24:25–27	194n2
28:8	74n7
32:2–11	17n55, 73n3
32:21	76
33:11	65, 168n22, 203
36:22–38	32n111
37:24–28	32n111, 51n41

Daniel

4:32–35	67n88
11:32	108
12:2	84, 91, 107, 109n122

Hosea

2:1	75n16
12:2	189n99
13:4–16	4n10, 34n115, 73n3, 105, 106n111, 109nn122–123, 124n36, 165n11, 182n64

Amos

1:13	165n11, 182n64
3:2	82n45
9:2	73nn3,5, 75n17

Nahum

1:3	197

Habakkuk

1:2	6n15
1:13	54, 188n93, 191, 197
2:4–5	34n115, 56
2:14	33n113, 36n1, 217

Zephaniah

3:17	65, 138, 203

Haggai

2:13	79, 93n81

Zechariah

2:10–11	51n41
7:11	4n9

Malachi

2:10–16	83n48, 132n54

Matthew

1:23	143n11
7:13–14	141n2, 162n5
8:23–26	67n88
10:17–39	1n1, 136
11	134, 143n11
12:6	105
12:20	80n38
12:31–32	83n50
12:33–37	189n98
13:40–43	189n100
13:49–50	71, 189n100
16:18	128
16:24–27	184n73
18:3	175n57
20:28	120n18
22:29	145, 162n5
22:31–32	74n9, 108n120, 131, 134
23:16–22	105, 162n5
23:22	51n41
24:23–26	146n17
24:42–44	53
25:19–23	204n24
25:41	71, 162n5
25:46	189n100
26:26–29	52n43
26:37–38	25
27:46	25, 121n22, 188n95
27:50–53	74n9

Mark

1:4	172n30
4:37–41	101n100
8:35	165
9:42–48	41n15, 55, 162n5
10:37–39	204n25
10:45	120n18, 121n22
12:25–27	74n9, 80n41, 108n120, 131
13:9–13	1n1
14:33–35	25, 80n40
15:34	25, 121n22
16:24–27	204n25
19:27–29	204n25

Luke

1:15,44	184, 199
2:14	137n58, 138, 189
3:3	172n30
4:17–21	128, 134
7:11–17	135n57
8:23	161n2
10:20	126n42
12:4–7	56, 63n78, 166
12:14–34	27n90, 68n95, 86, 204n25
13:1–5	127, 161, 165
14:28–33	202
15:11	49
15:20–24	65, 203

Luke (continued)

16:19–31	74n9, 77n27, 141n2
17:26–27	96n89
17:32–33	160
20:34–38	74n9, 80n41, 108n120, 131
22:19	65, 132
22:44	25
23:43	74n9
24:21	124
24:47	172n30

John

1:1	124
1:4	52n43
1:12	51n41
1:14–18	112n1, 128
3:3–8	131, 172, 173, 191
3:17–18	7n19, 184n74, 188n94
4:24	11, 194n1
5:17	128
5:21–26	41n15, 49, 51n41, 52n43, 96, 115, 123n31, 128, 128n44, 131, 135, 189n100, 196n3
5:42	189n98
6	36n3, 51n41, 52–53n43, 69n97, 143n11
8:42–44	4n9, 55n50, 189n98, 195
9:3–4	62n73, 176
9:41	182n67
10:18	123n31
11	51n41, 52n43, 61n70, 69n97, 101, 128, 135, 135n57
12:4	68n95
12:25–27	25, 136, 136, 160
14	41n15, 51n41, 126, 128, 189n98
17:12	51n41, 204
17:20–24	65, 203
18:6	65n84, 135
19:10–11	69n97
20:26	137n58
21:18–19	68n95

Acts

2:11	192
2:22–38	44n18, 67n88, 71, 80n38, 84n53, 106n111, 109n123, 120, 122, 123n31, 135, 172n30
3:25	81n45
4:23–31	54n49, 67n88
5	136
7:51–54	4n9, 153
10:34	192
10:42–43	81n44, 172n30
13:38	172n30
17:6	33n113
17:25–31	68n95, 67n88, 100, 124, 128, 187, 188
20:24	23, 140, 142n3, 143n8
20:28	144, 211
21:13	23, 140, 142n3, 143n8
24:2	66n87
25:11	23
26:18	172n30
27:14–44	101n100

Romans

1:16–23	56, 56n55, 59, 64n82, 115, 181, 182, 196
2:5–11	64n82, 184n73, 189n99, 192
3:1–6	81, 82n45, 107, 110, 189n100
3:23–25	96, 187, 188
3:29	112n2
4:5	183n69
4:11–16	97n93, 188
5:12–21	39, 41, 42n16, 44, 52n43, 53, 90, 96, 121n22, 125n39, 127, 163, 169, 171n28, 178n57,

6:9–10	183n9, 184n74, 187nn87–88, 188
6:23	57n57, 188n95
	7n19, 39, 43, 54, 90, 96, 121n22, 124, 132
7	49, 66n86
8:1–4	120n18, 124, 143n10
8:9	51n41
8:16–23	37, 41n14, 70, 183n69, 187n88, 201n17
8:28–32	42n16, 67n88, 115n7
9:14–18	196n3, 67n88, 104n107, 167
9:20–24	96n89, 97n92, 112n2, 141n2, 167, 189n100, 198n7
10:8–15	191
11:33–36	142n3, 197
13:4	17n55, 165n11
14:7–9	123n31

1 Corinthians

2:8–9	28, 119
5:22	132n53
8:3	51n41
9:9,16	50n38, 190n102
10:11–16	31n107, 33, 126, 197
11:19–25	52n43, 65, 168n24
11:29–30	126, 131, 132
13	86
15:14–29	13, 58, 97, 100, 119, 123, 124n35, 127, 128, 137n58, 138n60, 163, 171n28, 182n64, 183, 184n74, 11, 70
15:32–35	42n16, 52n43, 53
15:45	34n115, 45, 109n122, 124n36, 143n8, 202, 217
15:50–58	

2 Corinthians

2:11	30
3:7–18	86, 115n7, 196, 201n17
4:17	160
5:1–10	83, 119n15, 184n73, 189
5:21	51n41, 120n18, 130, 132n53, 188n95
6:16	51n41, 84n55
11:2	104n109
11:23–32	136

Galatians

1:6–9	146n17
2:6	192
2:20	35, 62n73, 143n8
3:13	121, 132n53

Ephesians

1:3–4	69, 201
1:11	67n88, 68
1:21–23	75n18
2:1–8	49, 51n41, 184n74
2:12	83n50
2:17	137n58
3:8–15	69, 97, 116
4:8–10	75n18, 80
5:28–30	135
6:2–3	70
6:12	64

Philippians

1:3	x
1:6	51n41
1:18–23	33, 74n9, 133, 142n7
2:5–11	4, 6, 97, 112n1, 120n18, 121, 124, 148n21
2:12–13	54n49, 67n88
2:17	204n25
2:25–30	142n3

Philippians (continued)

3:20–21	65, 138n60, 143n8, 203, 214n61
4:3	107n118, 126n42

Colossians

1:14–18	42n16, 172n30
1:24	144
2:10–15	33n112, 51n41, 130
3:1–4	16, 49n37, 52n43, 142n6, 143n8, 213

1 Thessalonians

4:13–18	131
5:2	63
5:10	74n9

2 Thessalonians

1:9	41n15, 64n82
4:13–17	12

1 Timothy

1:10	137
2:4	112n2
2:5–6	190n104
4:16	35, 62n73
5:18	50n38
6:13–16	162n3

2 Timothy

1:9–10	113
2:10	131
2:19	161
3:4	7n18
3:12	1n1
4:1	81n44
4:6–8	65, 142n3, 203, 204n24
4:14	184n73

Titus

2:11–12	15, 112n2
3:5–8	189n99

Hebrews

1:1–3	32n111, 36, 75n18, 112n1, 124, 183, 201
2:9	1n1, 26, 34, 80n38, 120, 122, 123, 177, 188n95, 204
2:14–15	8n23, 30, 32n112, 124n36, 128, 131, 134, 143, 143n10, 201, 202
2:17–18	121, 196
5:7–8	25
6:4–5	122n29
7:16, 24–27	16, 132, 143n8
8:10	51n41
9:12	188n95
9:22	132
9:27	63, 68n95
10:1–3	36n3, 132
10:14	25
10:27–29	71, 189n99
11:6	190n102
11:9–10, 13, 16	140, 142n7, 143n8, 149
11:28–32	42n16, 155
11:37–40	1n1, 32n111, 113
12:1–4	140, 143n8
12:5–6	129, 131
12:17	206
12:22–23	74n9, 126
12:29	65n84
13:17	15

James

1:12	65, 203, 214
1:15	49, 127
2:1,4,9	192
2:12	63, 65n84
2:14–26	188–189

3:9–10	144n15, 148n21, 211	2:2	112n2
4:3–10	83n48, 192, 204n25	2:17–25	51n41
4:12	7n18	3:1–3	63n77, 65n84, 138, 199
4:15	67n88, 70	3:6–10	124n36, 131, 143n10, 189n98, 201
5:11	6n15		
5:17–18	101n100	4:8	194n1
		4:18	9, 130, 143nn8–9, 145, 201

1 Peter

1:10–12	106, 138	5:11–13	41n15, 51n41, 52n43, 196n3
1:20	67n88, 69, 197	5:16	127
1:23	143n8		
2:18–19	80		
2:21	197		

3 John

1:7	143n8

2:23–24	130, 196n4
3:17	1n1, 141n2
4:17	104n109, 144
4:19	15, 141n2, 143n8, 145n16
5:8	8n23
5:10	141n2

Revelation

1:5	42n16
1:18	65, 203
2:7	51n41, 52n43
2:10–11	23, 65, 203
2:14–16	17n55, 185n81

2 Peter

1:1	214
1:3–4	126n40, 168, 201–202, 214, 214nn60–61
2:5	5
2:15	185n81
3:4	38, 134
3:9	112n2
3:10–14	62n71, 63n77, 65n84

3:5	107n118
3:20–21	143n11
5:9	128, 196
6:8–11	4n10, 34n115, 74n9
9:15	4n10
12:9–11	64n81, 107n118
13:8	107n118
14:6–11	41n15, 128
14:20	12n37
17:8	107n118
19:2, 11	196n4
19:20–21	17n55, 189n100
20:12–15	41n15, 107n118, 189n100
21:3–4	51n41, 84n55, 115n7, 137n58
21:10	40n9
21:27	107n118, 126n42
22:2–3	39n9, 51n41, 52, 52n43, 214
22:18	181

Jude

1:4	141n2
1:11	185n81

1 John

1:2–3	52n43, 126, 143n11
1:5	36n1, 54, 194n1

www.ingramcontent.com/pod-product-compliance
Lightning Source LLC
Chambersburg PA
CBHW051517230426
43668CB00012B/1645